TOWARDS NORTH AMERICAN MONETARY UNION?

Towards North American Monetary Union?

The Politics and History of Canada's Exchange Rate Regime

ERIC HELLEINER

McGill-Queen's University Press

Montreal & Kingston · London · Ithaca

© McGill-Queen's University Press 2006
ISBN 13: 978-07735-3056-0
ISBN 10: 0-7735-3056-8

Legal deposit second quarter 2006
Bibliothèque nationale du Québec

Printed in Canada on acid-free paper that is 100% ancient forest free
(100% post-consumer recycled), processed chlorine free.

This book has been published with the help of a grant from the Canadian
Federation for the Humanities and Social Sciences, through the Aid
to Scholarly Publications Programme, using funds provided by
the Social Sciences and Humanities Research Council of Canada.

McGill-Queen's University Press acknowledges the support of the Canada
Council for the Arts for our publishing program. We also acknowledge
the financial support of the Government of Canada through the Book
Publishing Industry Development Program (BPIDP) for our publishing
activities.

Library and Archives Canada Cataloguing in Publication

Helleiner, Eric, 1963–
    Towards North American monetary union?: the politics and history
of Canada's foreign exchange regime / Eric Helleiner.

    Includes bibliographical references and index.
    ISBN-13: 978-0-7735-3056-0
    ISBN-10: 0-7735-3056-8

    1. Foreign exchange rates – Canada. 2. Monetary unions –
North America. 3. Foreign exchange rates – Canada – History.
4. North America – Economic integration. I. Title.

HG3915.H43 2006   332.4'56'097   C2005-907100-1

This book was typeset by Interscript in 10.5/13 Sabon.

To Jennifer, Zoë, and Nels

Contents

List of Figures

Preface

At the 1997 annual meeting of the International Studies Association in Toronto, a number of participants arrived at the conference centre and attempted to pay their conference registration in Canadian dollars. They were refused. The conference organizers would only accept American currency. The decision provoked a storm of controversy among many Canadian scholars who demanded, often in quite passionate terms, to know how this US-headquartered organization devoted to international understanding could display such a thoughtless attitude in infringing on the monetary sovereignty of their country.

I recalled this episode when the debate on North American monetary union (NAMU) broke out within Canada two years later. Supporters of this idea confidently predicted that the days of the Canadian currency were numbered, and that the union might even occur within the next five years. But they clearly underestimated the attachment of many Canadians – even Canadian academics – to their currency. The five-year death sentence for the Canadian dollar has now come and gone, and the loonie seems unlikely to pass away soon.

This book attempts to explain why. It does so by exploring the politics of Canada's exchange rate regime choices from the birth of the Canadian dollar in the 1850s to the recent NAMU debate. Particular attention is devoted to explaining the political foundation of the longstanding Canadian commitment to a floating exchange rate.

It has been said that the owl of Minerva, which brings wisdom, flies only at dusk. If that is true, this study has been written too soon. Neither Canada's currency nor its floating exchange rate appear as yet to be nearing the end of their lives. Still, I hope this study of the politics of the Canadian exchange rate regime helps shed light on an important feature of the Canadian and North American political economy which has hitherto been quite neglected by scholars.

Many people have helped me to research and write this book. I would like to thank a number of librarians and archivists for their assistance and advice: Paul Banfield, Donald Richan, Charles Laroque, Jennifer McNenly, Jane Boyko, and Heather Ryckman. I am also very grateful to the following research assistants: Angela Aranas, Geoff Cameron, Asha Gervan, Masaya Llavaneras-Blanco, Isabel MacDonald, Antulio Rosales Nieves, and Ana Maria Vega Baron. I would like to express my gratitude to a number of colleagues and friends who provided important comments during this project: Michael Artis, Paul Bowles, Duncan Cameron, Stephen Clarkson, Wallace Clement, Jerry Cohen, Andy Cooper, Bill Dobson, Charles Doran, Philippe Faucher, Christina Gabriel, Randy Germain, Herbert Grubel, Derek Hall, Richard Harris, Ken Jameson, Peter Katzenstein, Peter Kenen, Jonathan Kirshner, David Laidler, David Leblang, Peter Leslie, Laura MacDonald, Ian McPherson, Bryan Palmer, Lou Pauly, Larry Schembri, Mario Seccareccia, Jim Stanford, Pamela Starr, Amy Verdun, Leah Vosko, Michael Webb, Tom Willett, Sue Wurtele, and Robert Young. For their reading of the entire manuscript and helpful comments, special thanks go to Bill Hunter, David Schwinghamer, and two anonymous reviewers. I am also very grateful to the Social Sciences and Humanities Research Council of Canada and the Canada Research Chair program for their support of this project and to Philip Cercone for his commitment to it. My greatest thanks go to Jennifer Clapp for her invaluable insights and intellectual contributions to this project as well as her wonderful companionship for which I am forever grateful. Without her, and without Zoë and Nels whose love for life is a constant inspiration, this book could never have been finished.

PERMISSIONS

I am grateful to the Bank of Canada, Queen's University Archives, and Harvard University Archives for their permission to quote and cite passages from documents in their holdings. Portions of chapter 6 were originally published in "The Strange Politics of Canada's NAMU Debate," *Studies in Political Economy* 71–2 (autumn 2003/winter 2004): 67–99. Portions of chapters 7 and 8 were originally published in *Canadian Foreign Policy* 11, no. 2 (winter 2004). Portions of chapter 8 were originally published in "Why Would Nationalists Not Want a National Currency? The Case of Quebec" in E. Helleiner and A. Pickel, eds, *Economic Nationalism in a Globalizing World* (Ithaca: Cornell University Press, 2005). Portions of chapter 9 were originally published in "A Fixation with Floating: The Politics of Canada's Exchange Rate Regime," *Canadian Journal of Political Science* 38, no. 1 (2005): 1–22.

TOWARDS NORTH AMERICAN MONETARY UNION?

Introduction

In 1999, an unusual and high profile debate broke out in Canadian politics. The issue suddenly being discussed was whether the country should join a monetary union with the United States. Although, since Confederation, Canadians had debated many aspects of their country's economic relations with the US, this idea had never received serious attention. Even at the time of the introduction of the 1989 Canada–United States Free Trade Agreement (FTA), few had predicted that a monetary union with the US might soon follow.

In fact, Canadian governments had not even been willing to fix the Canadian dollar to the value of the US currency for most of the twentieth century. Since 1914, Canada's exchange rate floated vis-à-vis the US dollar for all but three brief periods: 1926–31, 1939–50, and 1962–70. So strong was the preference of Canadian policy-makers for floating that Canada was the only major industrial country to demand and receive special exemption from the rules of the Bretton Woods system in the period 1950–62 so that it could pursue a float. It then became the first Western country to embrace a floating exchange rate again in 1970, a regime that has stayed in place to this day.

Given this history, Canada would seem the most unlikely country to join in a monetary union with the US. And yet, in another respect, the country is an obvious candidate. It is commonly assumed that countries with very open economies will prefer a fixed exchange rate or monetary union with their most important economic partners in order to minimize

the impact of exchange rate variability on their extensive trade and investment relations. With one of the most open economies in the industrial
world, Canada has long been an exception to this rule.

Its exceptional status has become even more glaring as the country's
economic integration with the US has accelerated with the introduction
of the FTA. Over 40 per cent of Canada's GNP now consists of exports,
and over 80 per cent of these exports go to the US. Supporters of North
American monetary union (NAMU) argue that a floating exchange rate
is increasingly an anachronism within this integrated North American
economic space.[1] They reinforce this argument by pointing to a larger
and growing worldwide interest in the benefits of regional monetary
unions, an interest that has already led to the creation of the euro in Europe. Given these trends, they argue forcefully that the creation of a
NAMU is a very likely – even "inevitable"[2] – development in the coming
years. As one proponent put it rather melodramatically, "the Canadian
dollar is doomed."[3]

Is the emergence of the NAMU debate a sign that Canada's odd preference for a floating exchange rate is finally coming to an end? Is the Canadian currency really destined to disappear? This book argues that
there is nothing inevitable or even likely about NAMU. The language of
inevitability employed by some NAMU supporters hides the fact that
Canada's exchange rate regime – both in the past and in the future –
rests on political foundations and political choices. And when we examine the *politics* of Canadian policy-making towards exchange rate regimes – the task taken up in this book – NAMU appears a much less
certain prospect.

To date, scholarly literature about NAMU has been dominated by
economists focusing on the economic pros and cons of the proposal.
Their analysis is important, but it does not address the more political issue of whether NAMU is likely to happen. To be sure, exchange rate regime choices are influenced by the ideas of economists – this is certainly
true in the Canadian context, as we shall see. But policy-making in this
area is also subject to a much wider range of political influences. As
John Crow, a former governor of the Bank of Canada, noted recently:
"how to decide what exchange rate set-up works best for a country is
truly a question in the realm of the broadest political economy."[4]

To examine whether Canada is on the cusp of a dramatic monetary
change, we need a better understanding of the politics of Canadian exchange rate regime policy. What have been the political determinants of

Canada's longstanding fixation with floating? What political forces are now supporting the NAMU proposal and who is aligned against them? Unfortunately, existing literature in the field of political science is not very helpful in answering these questions. The study of the politics of exchange rate regimes across the world has blossomed in the last decade, but the Canadian case has been almost entirely ignored in this literature. The rich scholarship on the politics of Canadian foreign economic policy has also not addressed these issues in much depth. This literature has focused much more on Canadian policy towards international trade and foreign investment than exchange rate regimes.[5]

EXPLAINING CANADA'S FIXATION WITH FLOATING

This book fills these gaps in existing literature. Drawing on much previously unpublished archival material, the first half of the book provides a detailed political history of the evolution of the Canadian exchange rate regime from the mid-nineteenth century up until the free trade era. The objective is to develop a better understanding of the politics of Canadian exchange rate policy-making. Special attention is devoted to the question of why Canadian policy-makers have been so attached to a floating exchange rate during the twentieth century. Rather than reflecting some kind of historical fluke, this attachment is shown to have been grounded in some clear political foundations which can be briefly summarized.

To begin with, since the early twentieth century, Canadian policy-makers have not been lobbied in a clear and consistent manner by the Canadian business sector to establish a fixed exchange rate. This finding will surprise many scholars of the politics of exchange rate regimes. In other countries with very open economies, the business sector has often pushed hard for a fixed exchange rate regime in order to reduce uncertainty and transaction costs for their internationally-oriented activities – hence the common assumption that countries with open economies will favour fixed rates. This kind of lobby was certainly present in Canada in the pre-1914 period, but it became increasingly less apparent after this. One reason was that Canada's floating exchange rate generally did not fluctuate in value as much as that of many other countries. Also important was the fact that an increasingly large proportion of Canadian trade took place within large multinational corporations where the impact of exchange rate movements could be offset by adjustments to intra-firm pricing and fund transfers.

This is not to say that Canadian private economic actors – in the business community and beyond – were uninterested in exchange rate issues. On the contrary, they often expressed very strong views about the specific *level* of exchange rate. In such an open economy, the exchange rate was in fact one of the most important prices they faced and it affected them in many ways, ranging from its influence on their international competitiveness to its impact on external debt servicing. But here again, these private views did not encourage Canadian policy-makers to embrace a fixed exchange rate. Because of the diversity of their links to the international economy, Canadian private actors rarely expressed consistent views and the question of the proper value for the Canadian dollar was often the subject of intense domestic political debate. These debates frequently reinforced regional tensions within the country because of the concentration of specific economic sectors in different parts of Canada. In this context, Canadian policy-makers often saw a floating exchange rate as a way to insulate themselves from these tensions and debates. They found it politically expedient simply to allow the market to determine the currency's level. A freely floating rate, in other words, provided a way of "depoliticizing" the exchange rate question.[6]

Strong private sector opposition to controls on cross-border financial movements reinforced the interest of Canadian policy-makers in a floating exchange rate for much of post-1930s period. After the Great Depression, and especially during the postwar years, other countries relied heavily on capital controls to maintain a fixed exchange rate. By contrast, Canada employed such controls for only a brief period between 1939 and 1951. The internationally-oriented Canadian business sector – and many policy-makers themselves – saw capital controls as an unacceptable nuisance which discouraged US investment and interfered with the country's extensive international economic relations. When faced with a choice between controls and a floating exchange rate, they opted for the latter.

Even without capital controls, Canadian policy-makers could have maintained a fixed exchange rate if they had been willing to adjust domestic monetary conditions to keep the country's balance of payments in equilibrium. During the pre-1914 period, they were indeed willing to sacrifice their monetary policy autonomy in this way. But thereafter, and especially after the early 1930s, the maintenance of monetary policy autonomy became a fairly consistent priority for Canadian policy-makers and a floating exchange rate was the logical consequence. The choice of a floating exchange rate regime has thus been linked to a broader set of preferences within the so-called "impossible trinity" of open macroeconomics. Canadian policy-makers recognized they could simultaneously only achieve two of the following three goals: financial openness, monetary policy autonomy, and a fixed exchange rate. For most of the post-1914 period, they prioritized the first two over the third.

As we shall see, the specific rationale for preserving monetary autonomy changed over time. But a relative constant was the belief among Canadian policy-makers that Canadian monetary policy needed to be independent from that of the US. In some eras, a floating rate was seen as a way to avoid importing US inflation. At other times, US monetary policy was seen as too deflationary and restrictive. Sometimes, both of these views were even put forward at the same moment by different Canadian advocates of floating rates. The common thread, however, was a kind of nationalist distrust of US monetary policy-making and an associated confidence in the ability of the Bank of Canada to pursue policies which reflected Canadian preferences in conditions of a floating exchange rate.

Canadian policy-makers also often saw a floating exchange rate as a useful tool for adjusting to balance of payment disequilibria. This preference initially appeared in government circles in the early 1930s when the Great Depression and the growing power of populist groups generated support for currency depreciation as a means of adjusting to external shocks without undergoing further painful domestic deflation. The argument that the exchange rate regime should protect domestic actors from painful adjustments – rather than discipline them, as under the gold standard – was promoted particularly by a new class of professional economists who rose to prominent positions in Canadian exchange rate policy-making in this period. It remained a significant defense – albeit often contested – of the floating exchange rate regime in subsequent decades.

This basis of support for the floating exchange rate was strengthened by the fact that Canada experiences quite distinct external shocks as a result of the country's high dependence on the resource sector, a dependence that is among the highest among industrialized countries. Policy-makers also argued that Canada's prices and wages were less flexible than those in many other countries. While some small European countries were able to adjust domestic wages and prices quickly through nationwide corporatist arrangements in response to changing circumstances, Canadian policy-makers recognized that key features of the Canadian political economy – particularly disorganized wage bargaining – made this difficult. In this context, the floating exchange rate was used not just to buffer external shocks but also to accommodate domestic wage and price trends.

Canadian officials also appreciated how a floating exchange rate helped ease adjustments in the bilateral Canada-US economic relationship. During the periods of a fixed exchange rate, officials from the two countries found themselves engaged in complicated bilateral negotiations that were designed to resolve bilateral payments imbalances. These covered subjects such as the level of Canada's foreign exchange reserves, the use of capital and trade controls, and even the specific level at which Canada's currency should be pegged. Such negotiations not only were a cumbersome way of managing bilateral imbalances but also left Canada vulnerable to US pressure on a range of issues and raised Canadian nationalist concerns about American interference in Canadian sovereignty. The introduction of a floating rate provided a way to cut Canada loose from these problems. In Louis Pauly's words, it acted as a kind of "buffer" in the Canada-US relationship.[7]

The country's relationship with the US influenced Canada's exchange rate regime choices in one further way. Although the decisions to float in both 1950 and 1970 formally contravened the Articles of Agreement of the International Monetary Fund (IMF), the Canadian government avoided international censure in each instance because the US supported its position. Like their Canadian counterparts, US officials appreciated how a floating exchange rate helped ease adjustments in the bilateral Canada-US economic relationship without needing to resort to capital controls or other alternative mechanisms. US businesses also shared with Canadian business a lack of concern about the float. In both 1950 and 1970, the sympathy of the US government and US businesses for the introduction of a floating Canadian dollar was augmented by the fact that the float produced an upward, rather than a downward, movement in the Canadian currency. The few times when US policy-makers expressed concerns about Canada's floating exchange rate – notably in the early 1930s, 1961–62, and the mid-1980s – occurred as the currency was moving in the other direction.

THE EMERGENCE OF THE NAMU DEBATE

Given the longstanding preference of Canadian policy-makers for a floating rate, what explains the sudden emergence of the NAMU debate? The second half of the book examines the politics of the NAMU debate. To begin with, it highlights that supporters of NAMU are right to associate the new popularity of their proposal with the free trade era and the creation of the euro. However, the connection is not just that these developments have raised the profile of the issue on the Canadian political agenda. The political sources of support for NAMU also share similarities with those that drove the creation of the FTA in the 1980s and the euro more recently. In particular, NAMU has been promoted by a group of prominent Canadian economists who have seen it as a way to advance the kind of "neoliberal" goals that drove the initiative to create the FTA in the 1980s. They link NAMU to such neoliberal objectives as the acceleration of regional economic integration, the imposition of greater wage and price discipline within the domestic economy, and the introduction of "neo-constitutionalist" measures that lock in fiscal restraint and the promotion of price stability as the primary goal of monetary policy. These arguments echo the "neoliberal" case for the euro in Europe.

But Canadian supporters of these arguments have encountered much more domestic opposition than did European backers of the euro. The opposition has also been much more widespread than that encountered by Canadian neoliberal supporters of the FTA in the 1980s. Some of the most prominent opposition has in fact come from expert economists and policy-makers who share the general neoliberal values of these NAMU supporters but continue to believe that a floating exchange rate is an important tool for balance of payments adjustment, particularly since Canada and the US still experience distinct external shocks. They also highlight that the FTA and its successor, the North American Free Trade Agreement (NAFTA), have no provisions for free labour mobility or inter-country fiscal transfers which might help Canada adjust to such shocks in the absence of exchange rate adjustments or flexible domestic wages and prices. The fact that NAMU might force these alternative adjustment mechanisms to be put into place has also revived political concerns about Canadian sovereignty that were expressed in periods when Canada had a fixed exchange rate with the US.

Another argument voiced by neoliberal opponents of NAMU is that it would not bring any greater price stability than Canada already has. In the European context, neoliberals' enthusiasm for the euro in many countries has stemmed from the prospect that the European Central Bank – modeled as it is on the inflation-fighting German Bundesbank – would offer more "disciplined" monetary policy than their own national monetary authorities have provided. This argument has much less appeal to neoliberals within Canada who believe that the Bank of Canada's anti-inflation credentials have been stronger than those of the

US central bank since the late 1980s. This distrust of US policy-making has led them to continue supporting a floating exchange rate that can preserve Canadian monetary autonomy.

The NAMU proposal has also not received much support from the Canadian business community. Its advocates had hoped that the Canadian private sector would see closer monetary links with the US as a way to eliminate bothersome currency-related costs in an age when Canada-US commerce is expanding very rapidly. To be sure, some business leaders have backed NAMU for this reason. But in contrast to their strong support for the FTA in the 1980s, the major business associations in Canada – even the most internationally-oriented ones – have been unwilling to endorse NAMU. In keeping with their views since the 1930s, Canadian businesses have not seen the building of closer monetary ties with the US as a cause meriting their strong support. Some of the implications of NAMU – particularly its potential impact on Canadian banks' competitiveness vis-à-vis US counterparts – have also provided specific sectors with reasons to oppose the idea.

The Canadian left has also been unwilling to support the NAMU idea. Since it opposes neoliberal values and earlier lobbied against the FTA, this opposition is hardly surprising. But it does pose an interesting contrast with Europe where many social democrats and labour leaders have supported the euro. The rationale for this European support varies from country to country, but one common thread is a belief that the euro may help build a more united Europe in which social democratic values hold a prominent place. This basis for supporting monetary union makes little sense to the Canadian left, which has long associated closer economic integration with the United States with a downward harmonization to US standards in such areas as labour legislation and social policy.

Finally, nationalist arguments have attracted much more widespread support in the NAMU debate than they did at the time of FTA debate in the 1980s. In addition to the nationalist concerns of the left, many Canadians more generally have seen the Canadian dollar as an important symbol of sovereignty and national identity. Also prominent has been the worry that the common currency for North America would very likely be the US dollar, and that Canada would be given very little influence over its management. Even many neoliberal economists and business leaders have cited these broader nationalist concerns as the most important reason for their refusal to back NAMU.

Supporters of NAMU have tried to address the last concern by arguing that Canadians should not underestimate the willingness of the US to endorse a NAMU in which Canada is granted a significant voice. This possibility briefly seemed worth discussing in 1999 when US Congress began to hold hearings on the question of whether it should be encouraging foreign countries to adopt the US dollar. This was in fact one of the developments that helped put NAMU on the Canadian political agenda. But it quickly became apparent that US politicians were not willing to provide much support for the idea of a regional monetary union. In the context of Canada-US relations, and true to historical pattern, US policy-makers and businesses have not seen the floating Canadian dollar as much of a problem that needed fixing. They have also been concerned that NAMU might entangle them politically in alternative adjustment mechanisms that were undesirable from a US perspective. Faced with the fact that NAMU could only come into being if Canada unilaterally adopted the US dollar, many Canadians who might have been more sympathetic to the idea have turned against it on nationalist grounds.

There is, however, one group within Canada that has been relatively unconcerned by the outcome of the US debate: Quebec sovereigntists. Along with some neoliberal economists, they played a lead role in first putting the idea of NAMU on the Canadian political agenda in 1999. They have nationalist reasons for their position: NAMU is seen as a tool for easing the path to Quebec independence. In both the 1980 and 1995 referendums on Quebec's political future, many Quebec voters were nervous about the risk of currency instability if Quebec moved to independence. To counter this fear, sovereigntists insisted in both referendums that an independent Quebec would retain the Canadian dollar. But this prediction was questioned constantly by federalists, often with considerable success. If Canada – or a future independent Quebec – were to join a North American monetary union, many sovereigntists believe that Quebec sovereignty would then be perceived as a less risky option from a monetary point of view. Not only would the US dollar, or a new North American currency, provide a better guarantee of currency stability in the event of Quebec independence, but a sovereign Quebec would be less vulnerable to Canadian pressure if it no longer used the Canadian dollar.

Given this motivation for backing NAMU, the question of representation within the governance of a regional monetary union is a much less significant one for Quebec sovereigntists. It would of course be desirable from their standpoint to have representation. But already in the 1995 referendum, many leading sovereigntists had endorsed the idea of unilaterally adopting the Canadian dollar without expecting any representation in the Bank of Canada. It was a short step from that position to endorse NAMU with or without a voice in its management.

The support that Quebec sovereigntists have given to the NAMU proposal echoes that of European groups such as Scottish nationalists for the euro. It is also reminiscent of the stance that Quebec sovereigntists adopted in the FTA debate in the 1980s when they emerged as one of its staunchest supporters on the grounds that North American free trade would reduce their dependence on the rest of Canada. But they have been less able to influence the Canadian debate on this issue. The kinds of alliances they made with the Canadian business community and neoliberals in the rest of the country to promote the FTA are less easily forged on the NAMU question. Quebec sovereigntists can also no longer count on the support of the commodity-exporting provinces that were enthusiastic champions of the FTA. Given the fact that the floating exchange rate has often buffered them from external shocks, these provinces are more wary of the NAMU proposal. In these circumstances, Quebec sovereigntist support for NAMU has not been very influential to date within the Canadian polity as a whole. Indeed, if anything, it has reinforced opposition to NAMU in federal government circles that are hostile to the idea of Quebec sovereignty.

PROSPECTS FOR NAMU:
IS THE LOONIE REALLY DOOMED?

What then are the prospects for NAMU? This book's analysis suggests that they are much less promising than many NAMU supporters argue. Some believe that "a common currency has the potential to make the transition from political issue to policy reality in much the same way as Canada-U.S. free trade did in the 1980s."[8] But the politics associated with the NAMU debate in Canada are quite different from those that accompanied the introduction of the FTA. To be sure, there are some important parallels: both initiatives have been supported by a coalition of neoliberals and Quebec sovereigntists. But support for NAMU is much less consistent in neoliberal circles where the longstanding arguments in favour of a floating exchange rate remain influential and are now reinforced by nationalist concerns specific to the NAMU proposal. In regional terms, Quebec sovereigntists also no longer find commodity-exporting provinces to be the strong allies they were in the FTA debate. And neither group can count on much support from the business community which remains – true to historical fashion – willing to accept a floating exchange rate.

The argument that the creation of the euro is generating a push for currency blocs across the world also overlooks the fact that the politics of the NAMU debate in Canada are quite different from those of the euro debate in many European countries. It is true that support for NAMU from some Canadian neoliberals and Quebec sovereigntists *does* parallel some developments in the EU. But in addition to the split within Canadian neoliberal circles, two distinct features of the Canadian debate make the prospects for regional monetary union less likely in North America. First, in keeping with the history of its approach to Canadian exchange rate regimes, the US is a much less willing and accommodating partner in the monetary union enterprise than Germany has proved to be vis-à-vis smaller countries in Europe. Second, the important support for monetary union that came from many European social democrats and labour leaders is not present in the Canadian context.

This is not to suggest that the Canadian polity will never endorse NAMU. The NAMU debate has revealed that important groups in Canadian society now favour the idea and they will no doubt look for new opportunities to raise its political profile again. Neoliberal supporters of NAMU will continue to promote their ideas, and circumstances may unfold in which they find new support among the business and political elite as well as from expert groups that have long played an important role in Canadian exchange rate regime policy-making. Nationalist opposition to NAMU could also wane if the US showed more willingness to provide Canadians with a significant voice in the operation of a regional monetary union. NAMU might also come into place if Quebec sovereigntists succeed in creating a new country which adopts the US dollar, a development which would put pressure on the rest of the Canada to follow suit. But whether these scenarios or others come to pass or not, it is important to recognize that there is nothing inevitable about NAMU. The loonie is not "doomed" to extinction. Instead, like the FTA and the euro, NAMU is, and will continue to be, a political project whose success or failure will be a product of political struggles.

BROADER THEORETICAL IMPLICATIONS OF THE CANADIAN CASE

The concluding chapter addresses a more theoretical question: what is the significance of Canada's longstanding preference for a floating exchange rate for the broader literature on the politics of exchange rate regimes? Canada's preference challenges the common argument that countries with very open economies will generally favour fixed exchange rates or monetary unions with their closest commercial partners. As noted above, this argument is based on the assumption that internationally-oriented private sector actors will push strongly for these exchange rate regimes, an assumption that is not borne out in the Canadian case after 1914. Although private sector preferences have played a role in determining Canadian exchange rate regime choices, they have been much more context-specific than allowed for by the dominant deductive models employed in most existing literature on the politics of exchange rate regimes.

The Canadian case also supports the argument that state policy-makers often have a considerable degree of autonomy from domestic interests in exchange rate policy-making. In this regard, some scholars who have analysed the preferences of state policy-makers in such contexts of autonomy suggest that these preferences are shaped by partisan concerns or survival-maximization strategies to stay in office. But this study suggests that other influences have been more significant in the Canadian context. In keeping with the predictions of optimum currency area (OCA) theory, Canadian policy-makers' support for a floating exchange rate has partly reflected distinct structural features of the Canadian economy such as the composition of exports and the degree of wage and price flexibility. The Canadian experience also reinforces the growing body of literature which argues that ideas, beliefs, and identities play an important role in exchange rate policy-making. At the same time, it highlights how ideational influences, such as nationalism and neoliberal ideology, have affected Canadian exchange rate policy-making in ways that are often more complicated than this literature suggests.

Finally, Canada's experience also has relevance for those concerned with the role of international factors in exchange rate regime policy-making. In the European context, the existence of a regional financial power and heightened international capital mobility are often cited as important factors that encouraged the move towards regional monetary union in Europe. In the Canadian context, these two external factors have also influenced exchange rate regime policy-making. But they have had the opposite effect, reinforcing the case for a floating exchange rate because of the content of US monetary policy, US exchange rate preferences, and sensitivities regarding the asymmetry of power in the bilateral Canada-US relationship. The case thus highlights once again the importance of recognizing the context-specific nature of external influences on exchange rate regime policy-making.

This examination of Canada's longstanding preference for floating thus contributes to the broader study of the politics of exchange rate regimes in significant ways. At the most general level, it highlights that exchange rate regime choices are not simply the product of the degree of openness of a country's economy, but rather are better analysed with a multi-level approach that examines not just domestic economic interests but also the preferences of state policy-makers and the influence of international pressures. More specifically, it identifies some key limitations of models that have been developed to explain the role of each of these levels of analysis in exchange rate policy-making. For this reason, the Canadian experience should be of interest not just to those curious about Canadian and North American affairs but also to a broader audience concerned with the politics of international monetary relations.

PART ONE

Canada's Exchange Rate Politics from 1850 to 1985

CHAPTER ONE

The Birth and Early Life
of the Canadian Dollar

What are the political determinants of the Canadian exchange rate regime? The first half of this book addresses this question by analysing the historical evolution of Canada's exchange rate regime from the mid-nineteenth century until 1985 when the Free Trade Agreement (FTA) negotiations began. The mid-nineteenth century is chosen as the starting point for this analysis because it marked the birth of the Canadian dollar. If we hope to understand the Canadian dollar's future, it should be useful to examine why it was created in the first place. As this chapter shows, the answer turns out to be a rather surprising one from a present-day standpoint.

The decision to create the Canadian dollar was taken in circumstances that were remarkably similar to those of today. In the 1850s, cross-border trade between the US and the Canadian colonies of Britain was expanding rapidly, assisted by a free trade agreement, the Reciprocity Treaty of 1854–66. Then as now, intensifying North American economic integration prompted Canadian policy-makers to consider closer monetary ties with the US. Today, the question is whether to give up the Canadian dollar in favour of a North American monetary union. Then, the issue was whether to create a new national currency in the first place; that is, whether to abandon colonial sterling standards in favour of a new national currency – the Canadian dollar – that was closely aligned with the US monetary system and would thus facilitate commerce. Ironically, then, support for the creation of the Canadian dollar in the mid-nineteenth century was associated with what we would call today a "continentalist" perspective.

But the continentalism of Canadian policy-makers during that era should not be overstated. There were important regional differences of opinion on the question of closer monetary ties with the US – differences that would remain a key feature of Canadian exchange rate politics, as we shall see. From the start, the creation of the Canadian dollar was also linked by many policy-makers to Canadian nation-building. This association only grew in the wake of the confederation of the colonies in 1867 when the consolidation of the Canadian dollar was seen as fostering a national market, bolstering the fiscal capacity of the state, and even cultivating a national identity. By the late 1870s, a significant political movement even emerged in the country calling for the introduction of a floating Canadian dollar on nationalist grounds. Although this movement was ultimately not successful, its arguments for a floating rate deserve attention because they were remarkably similar to those that would reappear in the twentieth century.

FREE TRADE AND CLOSER MONETARY LINKS: BACK TO THE FUTURE?

To understand the origins of the Canadian dollar, we must first examine the monetary systems of the Canadian colonies before its creation. In the early 1850s, the Canadian colonies were formally on local "sterling" standards, but their monetary systems were in fact very heterogeneous. Because the British government refused to produce a colonial coinage for them, the colonies were forced to rely for coin on imports of British and other foreign currency, particularly Spanish and US coin. These coins were not only heterogeneous in value but also of varied quality. As one banker from Galt put it at the time, "anything more *chaotic* than the currency of Canada it is hardly possible to conceive. A mere *jumble* in fact of the various coins of Christendom."[1]

All coins were then "rated" according to local sterling standards using the familiar terms of pounds, shillings, and pence. These standards acted purely as a standard of value since there was no locally issued coin that actually reflected their value. This was even true of British coin. In Nova Scotia, for example, the "Halifax standard" rated the English shilling at 15p at the time, instead of the 12p it would have been in Britain. To compound the complexity, the standard of each of the colonies was also slightly different; that is, foreign coins were assigned slightly different values in each colony. Particularly confusing was the fact that the exchange rate between the two dominant coins in circulation – British and US coins – differed slightly between each colony. In Nova Scotia, a British pound was the equivalent of US$5, whereas it was worth only US$4 in the Province of Canada created by the merger of Upper and Lower Canada in 1841. Each of the two rates was also different from the ratio prevailing in the United States itself where one British pound equalled US$4.86⅔.[2]

Because of constant shortages of imported coin, various paper notes and small denomination tokens were issued by the colonial governments as well as by municipalities and even private firms. These locally issued forms of money were denominated not just in the local sterling standard; they often included a reference to their value in US dollars because of the widespread use of US coin. This was particularly true in the Province of Canada where trade with the US was growing rapidly.[3]

In the early 1850s, the Province of Canada outlined an ambitious program of monetary reform designed to create a more homogeneous currency. The initiative was led by Francis Hincks, who dominated Canadian policy in this area in his roles as inspector general in 1848–51 and then prime minister in 1851–54. At the time of political upheavals of the late 1830s in Upper and Lower Canada, he had emerged as a strong liberal supporter of constitutional reform that ushered in responsible government, and had been elected to the first Legislative Assembly of the newly formed Province of Canada in 1841. Hincks's commitment to monetary reform was linked to his political principles. With the arrival of responsible government, Hincks did not see why the Province of Canada could not address its monetary problems on its own without British interference.[4]

In 1850, he introduced a legislative bill to allow the province to issue its own silver and gold coins. His goal was partly symbolic: the move would, he argued, be "a source of gratification and pride" to Canadians.[5] But the initiative had also long been demanded by local businesses on the economic grounds that it would reduce the colony's dependence on heterogeneous foreign coin and enable the government to manage the supply of coin more effectively. As the province's commercial and industrial economy grew rapidly after the late 1840s, the complexities associated with conducting business in the existing monetary system generated increasing frustration.[6]

In addition to proposing a new coin issue, Hincks also raised the question of Canada's monetary relationship with the US. When he had overseen the creation of a unified monetary standard for the new Province of Canada in 1841, Hincks had already proposed that the province adopt a decimal-based dollar standard modeled on that of the US as a way of simplifying and fostering trade with the province's southern neighbour.[7] At the time, trade with the US was complicated by the fact that the relationships of monetary values under the existing sterling standard did not correspond easily with those of the US dollar standard.[8] His proposal was opposed by those who remained attached to a sterling standard on sentimental grounds as well as by those who opposed the general idea of strengthening economic ties with the US. The British government shared both concerns and even worried that this monetary reform might lead to annexation by the US.[9] It insisted not only on a sterling standard, but one set with a rate that did not correspond with that in the US.[10]

Ten years later, Hincks's idea found more support. The British decision to abolish its Corn Laws in 1846 and reduce timber preferences throughout the 1840s sent economic shockwaves through the British North America colonies by ending their protected export market in Britain. Many colonial subjects now saw the US as the best alternative market, and trade with the US thus began to expand rapidly. Indeed, many prominent Montreal merchants even famously called for annexation with the US at one point in the late 1840s. As an "ardant imperialist," Hincks was a leading opponent of the annexation movement.[11] But he was deeply committed to – even "obsessed" with, according to one scholar – the project of expanding trade with the US in this period and he played an important role in the early stages of the negotiations that led to the Reciprocity Treaty of 1854.[12] In these new conditions, the idea of introducing a dollar-based monetary system became increasingly popular, particularly among the business class. In the early 1840s, a survey of local business had found just under half supported this option. By the time of another survey in 1855, the figure had risen to 100 per cent.[13]

When Hincks proposed his monetary reforms in 1850, he did not initially include the idea of adopting a decimal-based dollar standard. He suggested instead that the province's sterling standard be altered slightly to reflect the US practice of valuing one pound at $4.86⅔. Even this limited proposal, however, encountered strong resistance from the British Treasury. While agreeing that the existing colonial units of account should be eliminated, the Treasury argued that it would be better to replace them with a unified standard for all the British North American colonies, one based on the standard of British sterling and using British currency (at least until a common colonial coin could be created). This was, after all, the policy adopted by many other British colonies, and it had the advantage from the British standpoint of facilitating "the adjustment of Trade with the Mother Country."[14] The British Treasury also opposed Hincks's proposed coin issue on the grounds that it would infringe on the royal prerogative.

Although Hincks's act was passed by the provincial legislature and the local governor-general, the British Treasury succeeded in having the act disallowed by the British government. Hincks responded in 1851 by submitting a second bill to the provincial legislature. In this bill he conceded that the issue of coins would be subject to the Queen's approval. In fact, he argued that "it was not essential to us that we should have any separate coinage ... That was more a matter of national pride than anything else."[15] But apparently provoked by the Treasury's intransigence, Hincks now proposed a more ambitious US-style decimal-based dollar standard. The change was needed, he argued, because the goal of facilitating trade with the US was more important than that of expanding trade with the other British North American colonies. Indeed, at the time, trade between the Province of Canada and the United States was valued at £2.8 million, while that with other British North American colonies equalled only £300,000.[16] Hincks made the case for the reform in the following way: "With the people of the United States ... Canadians are brought into constant daily intercourse. They travel on the same Steamers and Railroad Cars – lodge at one another's Hotels and carry on a most extensive Commercial intercourse with each other. To have an entirely different Currency ... would be an intolerable inconvenience."[17]

Hincks's proposal was supported fully by the provincial legislature. One member of parliament even "congratulated the House on the fact that people can now talk of dollars and cents without imputations of disloyalty."[18] Fearing another showdown, the British government did not disallow this act, but instead asked the province to consider a compromise in 1852. It now accepted the principle that the province could issue its own gold and silver coin (subject to the Queen's approval) and even introduce the standard of value that Hincks had wanted. But it requested that the standard be named a "pound" and that new gold coins be called "royals" with the fractional silver coins called "half-crowns" and "shillings."[19] As an observer at the time noted, the British government "may have considered it [the proposal for a dollar-based standard] to have too Americanizing a tendency, and been afraid that it might prove 'the insertion of the *thin* end of the wedge.'"[20]

Hincks initially seemed willing to support this idea, arguing the names of the coins were "of little consequence."[21] He proposed a system of coins called "royals," "shillings," and "marks" which would be based on a decimal accounting system (there would be 100 marks in a royal and 10 marks in a shilling).[22] Hincks found little support for this idea in the legislature, however. Most members favoured a dollar-based system on the grounds that dollars and cents were "universally understood."[23] The broader public and business community shared this preference. As one historian notes, "the very general opinion of the press was fairly expressed by the Toronto *Leader* in the statement, that in a country like Canada, situated on the borders of the United States and with more than one-half of its trade carried on with that country, it is necessary to adopt the system in force there."[24]

Faced with these arguments, Hincks quickly dropped his proposal and an act was soon passed, in 1853, which allowed for the issue of silver coin and which legalized the use of a dollar standard of the kind Hincks had earlier proposed.[25] This dollar standard was not initially introduced as the exclusive standard of the province. The bill stated that public and private accounts could be kept in either the dollar-based standard or the old sterling-based one. Although this appeared to be a significant concession to the British view, Hincks was aware that if people had the option of using the dollar-based standard it would soon win out in practice because of its familiarity and convenience.[26] This prediction was quickly borne out. Already by 1855, one government report noted: "[the adoption of the dollar standard] has taken place already in many parts of Canada; merchants keep their books, railway boards transact their business, hotel-keepers and traders make out their bills, in dollars and cents; bankers place their dollar on their notes as a regulating unit; the reciprocity treaty will greatly increase our trade with the United States, and our people are daily becoming more familiar with the decimal system in use there. The County Council of Lambton has recently ordered that dollars and cents shall be adopted as the system for keeping the country accounts, levying rates, etc."[27]

The provincial government soon took further steps to solidify the new dollar-based monetary regime. In 1857, it declared that the dollar standard would become the exclusive standard of the province; in other words, the use of dollars and cents was now mandatory. The next year, the provincial government issued the first silver provincial coins denominated in this standard (which carried the monarch's image and a wreath of maple leaves). These monetary reforms were a key part of a broader project in the late 1850s to create a more modern and efficient public accounting and fiscal system for the first time.[28] There was also symbolic value in issuing the new coins, as Hincks had initially recognized. Ever since 1853, there had been calls for the Province of Canada to issue its own coin for this reason. One banker summed up the case in 1855: "While every petty state in Europe and Republic in South America can boast of a currency of its own, it is at once marvellous and humiliating to think that a country filling so large a space in the map of the world ... and containing such an enterprising and energetic population, with powers of self-government, should not, with the exception of the penny token of the Upper Canada Bank and the *sou* of *Bas Canada*, have a single coin it can call its own."[29]

Despite these various reforms, the Province's coinage system retained some of its heterogeneous qualities. Old private copper coins and bank tokens that were denominated in the obsolete system of reckoning continue to be used – despite a formal ban – because of a shortage of low denomination coin. Not until the 1870s were they replaced by new standardized low denomination coin issued by the state.[30] The new Canadian silver coins also were not issued in large enough quantities to displace British and US coins, which remained the most common silver coins in use. US coins, in particular, came to dominate the circulation in the 1860s for reasons explained below.[31]

REGIONAL DIVISION AND THE MONETARY STANDARD DEBATE AT CONFEDERATION

The Province of Canada was not the only British colony in North America to introduce a decimal-based dollar standard in this period. New Brunswick adopted an identical one on an optional basis one year earlier in 1852 and made it compulsory in 1860 when the colony began to issue its own corresponding coins.[32] Nova Scotia, British Columbia, Manitoba, and Prince Edward Island also embraced decimal-based dollar standards in 1860, 1865, 1870, and 1871 respectively.[33] The British Columbian and Nova Scotian governments chose to value the dollar standard in a slightly different way than the others. In British Columbia's case, the difference was very small: a British pound was valued at US$4.85 instead of US$4.86⅔. But the difference was much larger in Nova Scotia where the government retained the old value of the Halifax standard in which a British pound equalled US$5.[34]

Nova Scotia's decision to continue to link its monetary standard to sterling reflected the fact that its economy was deeply integrated into an Atlantic mercantile system that operated on a sterling basis. While the fortunes of the Province of Canada were increasingly tied to the US economy, the success of almost all businesses in Nova Scotia was dependent on the colony's economic relationship with the British West Indies. The latter acted as the central market for the colony's fish catch and for the wholesale shippers in the Nova Scotia carrying trade, both of which, in turn, were critical for the local shipbuilding and lumber industry.[35]

When Nova Scotia joined New Brunswick and the Province of Canada to form the new federation of Canada in 1867, the former's distinctive monetary system posed a dilemma for the new federal government. Most people agreed that the new country would need a unified monetary standard. Indeed, the prospect of currency unification had been one of the chief selling points for the cause of Confederation in the two Maritime provinces.[36] The difference in Nova Scotia's standard of value – for example, 75 cents in Nova Scotian currency was equivalent to only 73 cents elsewhere[37] – had already been causing economic inconvenience in the region. Nova Scotian merchants complained that their money was not always accepted at par outside the province, while businesses in New Brunswick reported large financial losses when they did accept the depreciated Nova Scotian currency at face value.[38] The new federal government also found immediately that the Nova Scotian monetary standard complicated its own fiscal operations, such as those for tax collection and postal services. As the frustrated finance minister, John Rose, put it, "Were they [the government] to collect postages, customs duties, etc., at one rate in Nova Scotia, and at a different rate throughout all the rest of the Dominion?"[39] Indeed, the federal government had even felt compelled to circulate a special issue of five-dollar notes in Nova Scotian currency – and payable only in Halifax – that were worth only $4.86⅔ in the rest of the new country.[40]

If Canada needed a single monetary standard, which one should it be? Many Nova Scotians wanted the rest of Canada to adopt their standard because it facilitated Nova Scotia's trade with sterling-based countries and colonies abroad. They also argued that the adoption of the Canadian standard would effectively devalue their currency slightly.[41] One Nova Scotian MP even complained that the change would hurt Nova Scotian contractors on the Inter-Continental railway who had counted on profiting from the fact that they could pay workers in Nova Scotian currency while receiving income in Canadian currency.[42]

Politicians outside of Nova Scotia, however, had little desire to change the standard they used, particularly since it facilitated commerce with the US. But because Confederation was already very controversial in Nova Scotia, they recognized the political difficulties involved in pressing the issue too vigorously.[43] Eighteen of the nineteen MPs elected from Nova Scotia in the first federal election of 1867 were opponents of Confederation and anti-Confederation candidates received 60 per cent of the vote in the province. In these circumstances, as one MP from Quebec put it, the federal government needed to "to hesitate before they again furnished the opponents of Confederation with a weapon against it."[44] To avoid a fractious debate, Canadian policy-makers stumbled upon an ingenious solution.

During the same year as Confederation, an important international conference was held in Paris that recommended the creation of a kind of worldwide monetary union to bolster global commerce. This was not a monetary union in the sense we think of today involving the replacement of national currencies with a new supranational form of money. Instead, the conference simply suggested that countries across the world link their existing currencies to a common gold-based monetary standard that was tied to the value of the French five franc coin. Each member country would also allow gold coins from other member countries to circulate in its territory.

This proposal provided a way for Canadian policy-makers to sidestep the domestic disagreement over the monetary standard. The very first monetary legislation passed after Confederation included a clause allowing Canada to join the Paris initiative, provided that US Congress also chose to do so. This measure was very cleverly crafted to enable the government, in Rose's words, to be "relieved from the embarrassment of making a choice between the two courses."[45] It achieved this purpose for a simple reason. If the US embraced the Paris proposal, its monetary standard would be adjusted in a way that fit well with Nova Scotia's standard. In these circumstances, the rest of Canada would then happily defer to Nova Scotian preferences. But if the US refused, Nova Scotia would have to embrace the rest of Canada's standard. In this way, Canadian policy-makers avoided making a decision on this contentious issue by leaving the choice in US hands. This effort to "depoliticize" the question of the external monetary standard provided an early example of a pattern of Canadian exchange rate policy-making that would reappear at various key moments in the country's history.

What choice did the US government make? It soon became clear that the Paris proposals would not be adopted by the US or indeed by most other countries. As a result, the federal government decided in 1871 to end Nova Scotia's distinct standard. The initiative was led once again by

Hincks, who had reappeared as finance minister in October 1869 (a post he held until 1873) after a fifteen-year stint as governor of Barbados and British Guiana. While acknowledging that Nova Scotia's standard facilitated trade with Britain and many of its colonies, he noted that the rest of Canada could not adopt it because it would be "at variance with that of the rest of the continent." He reiterated his long-standing view that the object of currency reform must be "to have an assimilated currency throughout the whole of this continent." In his words, "we were too small a people to hope to have a Currency differing from other nations. It was especially necessary to assimilate the Currency with that of the United States."[46]

Many Nova Scotian politicians now accepted this outcome for the simple reason that it put an end to the economic inconveniences of having a separate monetary standard from the rest of the country.[47] Some even embraced the move on more political grounds. As one Nova Scotia MP put it, the move was a "most important measure, being nothing less than one of the first steps towards making us one people." Some politicians in the rest of the country made the same point. As an MP from Hamilton argued, the experience of using a common money would "make the people of the Dominion feel more like one people."[48]

NATION-STATE BUILDING AND THE CONSOLIDATION OF THE NATIONAL CURRENCY

The divisiveness of the debate about the monetary standard highlighted that the desire of Canadian policy-makers to develop closer monetary links with the US in this period should not be overstated. A second indication of Canadian reticence was the federal government's decision after Confederation to eliminate from domestic circulation the US silver coin which had long played a significant role in the Canadian monetary system. At a cost to the government of $118,000, five million dollars' worth of US currency was taken out of circulation in 1870–71 with the help of the private banks.[49] At the end of this laborious operation, the legal tender of US silver coins – indeed, all foreign silver coins – was ended. Why were Canadian politicians so keen to remove US coin after its use had been so common for decades?

The question is a particularly interesting one because the Canadian decision differed greatly from initiatives in many countries in continental Europe at this time. In 1865, France, Belgium, Switzerland, and Italy had created the Latin Monetary Union (LMU) which established a

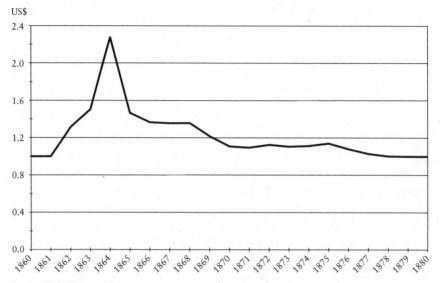

Figure 1
Canadian–US dollar exchange rate 1860–80
Year-end spot rates

Source: Global Financial Data

common monetary standard and allowed each members' coins to circulate in the other members' territories. Sweden, Norway, and Denmark soon followed suit when they established the Scandinavian Monetary Union (SMU) between 1873–75. In both cases, these initiatives were designed to bolster commerce among the member countries. Canadian politicians (outside of Nova Scotia) had already demonstrated their desire to foster commerce with the US by adopting a similar monetary standard as that country. With US coins circulating widely in the country, they seemed in fact to have created a de facto "monetary union" of the European kind – albeit a unilateral one. But instead of embracing this situation, Canadian policy-makers now actively rejected it. What explains this decision?

One explanation is that the US coins had come to be seen as a "silver nuisance" after they lost their convertibility into gold at the beginning of the US civil war in 1860. (The value of the US currency vis-à-vis the Canadian dollar – which remained on the gold standard – is shown in Figure 1). Because US silver coins had long been accepted at face value in Canada, speculators sent enormous sums of these coins to Canada during the 1860s in the hopes of turning a quick profit. Canadian

merchants soon realized that they should no longer accept the depreciated silver coins at face value but instead assign them a discount (e.g.,
20 per cent). These discounts quickly caused inconveniences, especially
since they were unevenly applied. Labourers were particularly hard hit
since some employers began to pay wages in the depreciated coin. In
these circumstances, the Canadian government faced strong domestic
pressure to eliminate US coins from domestic circulation. In Shortt's
words, "thus did the American Civil War result in the distinct separation of the currencies of the United States and Canada."[50]

At the same time, the expulsion of US coin was also part of the new
post-Confederation enthusiasm for "nation-building." As one member
of parliament put it in 1869, "We had heard a good deal lately about
adopting a national policy, and was it not humiliating that we should be
compelled to carry on the commercial transactions of the country in a depreciated foreign currency? If we were to be a nation, we should have a
currency of our own."[51] Canadian policy-makers also did not share the
kind of internationalist sentiments that had played a role in encouraging their European counterparts to create monetary unions. The SMU,
for example, drew strength from the "pan-Scandinavian" movement at
the time, while the LMU was supported by countries which had close
political ties to France. In Canada, while there were some policy-makers
who worried that removal of US coin might undermine Canada-US relations,[52] the concern met with little sympathy from other politicians, especially since the Reciprocity Treaty had ended in 1866: "the sooner we
ceased to express fears of offending the United States in legislating for our
advantage the better. (Hear, hear) We had heard so much of this sort of
talk lately that the Americans would begin to imagine that we could not
get on without them."[53]

The removal of US coin also helped strengthen the new Canadian
nation-state in a more concrete fiscal sense. Hincks noted that the circulation of US coin in Canada cut into the potential seigniorage revenue
that the government was earning from the issue of its own currency.[54]
At the time, the federal government faced difficulties financing its ambitious public works initiatives. The operation to remove US coin was
seen as an opportunity to increase the circulation of government-issued
currency. In fact, policy-makers were delighted to learn that the profit
earned on the issue of the new Canadian currency exchanged for the removed US coin more than offset the cost of removing the US coin in the
1870–71 operation.[55]

The desire to earn seigniorage also provided part of the rationale for another key initiative that helped consolidate the new national currency: the government's decision in 1870 to give itself the exclusive right to issue the one-dollar and two-dollar notes that dominated note circulation.[56] The government had, in fact, sought a monopoly over the entire note issue, but it had encountered stiff opposition from the note-issuing private banks as well as from politicians who had various reasons to fear stronger central government control over the currency. As a compromise, the government agreed to allow private banks to continue issuing higher denomination notes.[57]

The creation of the state-issued Dominion notes also served nation-building goals in a more symbolic sense. We have already seen that the creation of the independent coin issue in the 1850s had been associated with nationalist sentiments. The same was true of the new Dominion notes which were decorated with key personalities from the nation's history (e.g., Wolfe, Montcalm, Cartier), an image of railways, and even an allegorical figure pointing to Canada's location on a globe.[58]

Equally important, the note issue supported the government's goal of fostering a more integrated national market. Not only did the notes provide a "safe" currency for the poor, who might otherwise have difficulty discerning the trustworthiness of various privately-issued low denomination banknotes, but they were also accepted at the same value across the entire geographic territory of the nation. By contrast, the notes of the private banks often had different values in different locations because, until the government forced them to in 1890, not all banks had redemption offices in every province.[59]

At the same time that the Canadian national currency was being consolidated in these various ways during the 1870s, it was also being extended to the new provinces that joined Canada during that decade. In the case of Prince Edward Island (PEI), which entered the country in 1873, this was a simple task. It had already adopted a dollar standard identical to that of the rest of Canada two years earlier, and Dominion notes and coins were easily introduced there.[60] When British Columbia entered in 1871, the task was more difficult. US currency had come to dominate that colony's monetary system in the wake of the 1858 gold rush. The colony's governor had even issued notes in US dollars in 1861 in order to increase their acceptance, a move that provoked an objection from the British government. After the colony introduced an independent dollar-based monetary standard in 1865 (that differed slightly in value from the Province of Canada's), US coin continued to dominate the monetary system and, due to the province's remoteness from the rest of the country, this situation remained after the colony joined Canada. It was not until 1881 that the federal government finally harmonized the province's monetary standard with the rest of Canada and began sending large quantities of Canadian coin to the province. With the completion of the Canadian Pacific Railway in 1885, the dominant role of US currency in the province's monetary system finally ended.[61]

THE NATIONAL POLICY AND AN EARLY CASE FOR A FLOATING EXCHANGE RATE

The efforts of the federal government to consolidate a more territorially standardized and exclusive national currency within the country were paralleled in many other countries at this time. Policy-makers across the world shared the belief of their Canadian counterparts that these monetary reforms were an important part of the task of building a modern nation-state.[62] In some countries, however, nationalists went one step further. In addition to supporting a consolidated national currency *within* the country, they called for a new exchange rate policy which would end the convertibility of the national currency into gold. This move, they argued, would insulate the country from external monetary influences, discourage international trade, and enable the government to manage the currency actively to serve domestic needs.

This kind of thinking also found many supporters in Canada, particularly around the time of the introduction of the National Policy of 1879. The National Policy established a high tariff which was designed, at least in part, to develop a stronger domestic market and a more inward-looking development strategy. At the time, many Canadians argued that the National Policy should also have a monetary dimension involving the inconvertibility of Canada's currency into gold. Their arguments are worth exploring briefly, especially since their endorsement of a floating exchange rate foreshadowed Canadian policy for much of the twentieth century.[63]

The leading proponent of this policy was Isaac Buchanan, a very prominent Ontario merchant who had been elected to the first parliament of the Province of Canada in 1841 and had also been president of both the Toronto Board of Trade and the Hamilton Board of Trade. Buchanan had in fact been a critic of both the gold standard and free trade with Britain for several decades. He associated these policies with

"English political economy," which he believed was designed to central-
ize the world's manufacturing industry in England, while inhibiting industrialization and the development of an internal national market in
countries such as Canada. He preferred a "Patriotic or Social Economy" that was based on similar ideas as those of the economic nationalists Thomas Attwood in England or Henry Carey in the US (with
whom he corresponded regularly in the 1870s).[64]

Buchanan and his supporters advocated a state-issued inconvertible
currency partly because it would discourage trade. As William Wallace,
an Ontario MP from South Norfolk and the lead advocate of inconvertible money in the federal parliament, put it in 1880: "Money which is
not exportable, which cannot be sent to buy foreign goods, is the truest
and best system of protectionism."[65] Equally important, they believed
that this currency arrangement would allow the federal government to
pursue a more activist monetary policy designed to maximize economic
growth and full employment. When Canadian currency was convertible
into gold, the country's supply of money fluctuated according to Canada's external payments position. These fluctuations were particularly
severe for a commodity-exporting country such as Canada because the
prices and market conditions of raw materials were often volatile. Indeed, for this reason, Carey went so far as to argue in an 1873 letter to
Buchanan that "*no country that exports raw materials can maintain a
specie currency and all efforts at so doing, whether by yourselves or by us,
must prove failures.*"[66]

Buchanan believed that Canada's balance of payments should not be
allowed to determine domestic monetary conditions, especially given that
"the internal transactions of a country are calculated to be at least twenty
times the amount of its exports."[67] If the link to gold were broken, he argued that money could be managed to serve domestic needs: "Canada is
possessed of untold wealth in the wonderful energy of her population,
and in the boundless resources of her soil, and forests, and minerals,
which only want the institution of full patriotic money to develop
them ... [Money] should be something capable of being expanded permanently to the extent which the wisdom of Parliament sees to be required
for the full employment of the people, and the development of the productive resources of the country."[68] Another supporter of an inconvertible national currency put the case against the gold standard in a similar
manner: "Let those who do a foreign trade transact their own business; it
is not for the mass of people to be inconvenienced – nay, impoverished,
and peradventure, ruined – because the foreign liabilities of a mere

fraction of the population have to be discharged in a costly metal. To an agricultural community the hard-money basis is a positive injustice."[69]

These arguments in favour of a Canadian inconvertible currency often drew inspiration from the issue of inconvertible greenbacks by the US government during that country's civil war. Buchanan and his supporters argued that the US example showed how this monetary reform could indeed discourage international trade and promote domestic growth.[70] Greenbacks had of course been issued not for these purposes but rather to support the war effort. Buchanan noted, however, that a Canadian equivalent – "beaverbacks," he called them[71] – could have these explicit goals. As one of his supporters noted, "there is a difference between the Canadian beaverbacker and the United States greenbacker. The greenback was issued truely for the preservation of the nation in a war which destroyed much property, while the beaverback would be issued to assist in developing the wealth and resources of Canada."[72]

In addition to these economic arguments, advocates of inconvertible money suggested that it would also strengthen the Canadian national identity. Buchanan argued that "money should be a thing of, or belonging to a country, not of or belonging to the world." Because the gold standard rested on a cosmopolitan form of money, it was in his view "disloyal" and "unpatriotic" (not to mention "unChristian").[73] Wallace made a similar argument in the House of Commons: "If a man has $1000 in paper money, the value of which exists only in the country of its creation, while it may not be worth ten cents outside that country, he has an incentive to support its institutions, in addition to his patriotism, because he knows if the country goes down his money will be valueless. But the man with a $1000 of gold in the bank, which he knows will be taken in any part of the world, can readily withdraw it and leave his country if it should get into difficulty; he is not obliged to fight its battles."[74]

Political interest in an inconvertible currency reached a peak in the late 1870s. The arguments in favour of a more expansionary and domestically-oriented monetary policy resonated with many Canadians in the context of the economic depression of that time. Supporters of an inconvertible currency also found a political opportunity to press their case when the government was forced to renew the charters of the private banks in 1880. Buchanan mobilized his supporters through a body called the National Currency League which had branches in Toronto, Hamilton, and St Catherines. It held meetings throughout 1879 demanding that the government assume a monopoly of the note issue and make this currency inconvertible into gold.[75]

Because the Conservative government elected in 1878 had drawn support from supporters of the League, it undertook initiatives designed to appease the currency reformers.[76] The issue of Dominion notes was increased from $12 million to $20 million, and the required gold backing for the banknotes was lowered (a move that freed up $2 million of gold reserves for the government to use for other purposes). In addition, the private banks were required to keep more of their reserves in Dominion notes (up to 40 per cent from 33.3 per cent) and the government took over the issuing of the five-dollar note.[77] Although these initiatives were welcomed by leaders in the currency reform movement,[78] they were in fact very limited steps. Canadian currency remained convertible into gold and private banks retained the right to issue notes above five dollars (a situation that would last until the Bank of Canada's creation in 1934). What explains the government's caution?

The League had provoked vociferous opposition from supporters of the gold standard who referred to its members as "rag-baby" people.[79] Shortt notes that the League's proposals particularly "antagonized the whole banking and financial world."[80] The financial elite worried that an inconvertible currency would lead to inflation and monetary instability as governments were tempted to print money and the currency became the target of speculators.[81] They also feared that the abandonment of the gold standard would disrupt Canada's international commerce on which their business depended heavily. The Canadian banks at this time were unusually oriented to trade, with few long-term ties to, or investments in, domestic manufacturing. The "conservative nationalism" of the National Policy had been less threatening to them because the tariff was designed partly to generate revenue that could help to build railways and other infrastructure that supported Canada's external commerce.[82] But the proposal to create an inconvertible paper currency represented a more radical move that appeared in the words of one critic "to raise an impassable barrier between the Dominion and the outer world, to prevent exportation and importation, or all foreign trade."[83]

These criticisms of the League's case were politically decisive. Goodwin argues that the power of the bankers reflected their "strong position" in Canadian society at the time. He also notes that they were able to dominate monetary policy discussions throughout this period because "monetary theory was a subject which laymen could not master easily … Before the professional economists were present in universities and government the bankers themselves were the best qualified experts on banking."[84] Even if professional economists had been more present in Canadian public debates at the time, however, most of them would likely have sided with the bankers. Few economists of that era took seriously the idea that the government could play an active role in promoting macroeconomic outcomes through discretionary monetary and/or fiscal policy. This was a doctrine that did not gain popularity among mainstream economists until the interwar period.[85]

The political weakness of populist movements that supported the interests of the poor in Canada at this time also worked in the bankers' favour. In many countries during the pre-1914 period, support for inconvertible currencies was strongest among these groups because the poor often bore the brunt of the automatic adjustments of the gold standard. When a country encountered a trade deficit, the gold standard induced domestic deflationary pressures which forced wages downwards (or generated unemployment if wages did not fall). The poor were also often affected disproportionately when government spending was cut. As Eichengreen has argued, these policies were politically viable in many countries during the nineteenth century only because the poor did not yet have a full voice in the political arena.[86]

In Canada, Buchanan's ideas also found their greatest support "among the masses" during the 1870s.[87] Indeed, Buchanan made an explicit effort to attract working class support for his proposals when the government's opposition to them became clear.[88] But populist movements had limited political influence on the government in this period. Their weakness can be attributed partly to the electoral franchise, which still applied property rules for federal elections.[89] Laxer also argues that populist movements "were seriously divided by ethno-national issues" along French and English speaking lines.[90] Not until the interwar period did Buchanan's goals begin to be realised in Canada and other countries, as we shall see in the next chapter.

CONCLUSION

This analysis of the birth and early history of the Canadian dollar in the nineteenth century provides some preliminary insights into the political determinants of Canada's exchange rate regime. To begin with, supporters of NAMU today may be encouraged by the fact that the free trade and deepening economic integration with the US generated domestic political demands for closer monetary ties during the 1850s and 1860s. Although the demand was for a currency modeled on that of the US rather than full monetary union, the motivation was similar to one articulated by NAMU advocates today. Policy-makers and businesses sought to facilitate cross-border commerce by reducing currency-related transaction costs. The case for closer monetary ties was also strengthened by the fact that economic integration was encouraging widespread unofficial "dollarization" within Canada. A similar case is made by NAMU advocates today, as we shall see.

More discouraging to NAMU supporters may be the fact that political support for the creation of the Canadian dollar was also linked from its very origins to nationalist sentiments. The link was partly at the symbolic level: the issuing of a national currency was associated with national sovereignty and identity. The consolidation of an exclusive and homogeneous national currency was also connected with nation-building in a more concrete economic sense through its strengthening of the national market, a collective economic experience, the fiscal capacity of the state, and – for Buchanan and his supporters – the state's ability to serve the macroeconomic needs of its citizens. As we shall see, the nationalist significance of the Canadian dollar has reemerged as an important issue in the NAMU debate.

Two other features of Canadian exchange rate policy-making in this period are important to highlight. The first was the regional divisiveness of the debate about the monetary standard at the time of Confederation. As we have seen, many Nova Scotians did not share the "continentalist" perspective which had encouraged the creation of the Canadian dollar during the 1850s, and 1860s, because their relationship to the international economy was quite different from those of other regions. This kind of split between different regions of the country on the question of the exchange rate regime would reappear many times during the twentieth century. Canadian policy-makers would also continue the pattern of coping with this split by trying not to take responsibility for the choice of an exchange rate policy. In 1867, they did this by deflecting the ultimate decision for the monetary standard onto foreigners. During much of the twentieth century, Canadian policy-makers would see the embrace of a floating exchange rate – in which the market, rather than politicians, determined this sensitive price – as another means by which to avoid a divisive domestic political debate.

Another rationale for the floating exchange rate also made an early appearance in this period. Buchanan and his supporters highlighted how an inconvertible national currency could bolster the economic autonomy of the nation as well as its capacity to pursue domestically-oriented macroeconomic policies. As we have seen, these arguments found some support among farmer and labour groups – as they would again in the interwar years – but they had little impact on government policy. Committed to the liberal orthodoxy of the gold standard, governing elites worried that a floating exchange rate would provoke domestic inflation as well as currency instability that would disrupt the internationally-oriented nature of the Canadian economy. Although they had little influence in the pre-1914 years, Buchanan's macroeconomic arguments foreshadowed a central argument that Canadian policy-makers would put forward for embracing a floating exchange rate for much of the twentieth century.

CHAPTER TWO

The Floating Rate of the Interwar Years

Since the time of its creation until 1914, the value of the Canadian dollar was firmly fixed to gold. In retrospect, this attachment to a fixed exchange rate represented an unusual era in Canadian history. Since 1914, there have only been three brief periods when Canada again embraced this exchange rate regime: 1926–31, 1939–50, and 1962–70. A floating exchange rate has been in place at all other times. What explains the long attachment of Canadian politicians to a floating exchange regime? This chapter begins to explore this question by examining the early years of the floating exchange rate regime in the interwar period.

When Canada introduced a floating exchange rate for the first time in 1914, there were few indications that this initial move marked the beginning of a new way of thinking about exchange rate policy. As the first section of this chapter highlights, the decision was prompted simply by the pressure of war finance, and Canadian policy-makers made clear that they hoped to return to the gold standard as soon as possible. Although some groups associated with labour and farmers dissented, governing elites remained committed to the pre-1914 orthodoxy and the gold standard was restored in 1926.

The circumstances surrounding the reintroduction of a floating exchange rate regime in 1931 were quite different. To be sure, this move too was in response to an unexpected emergency: the international financial crisis of the time. But, as is explained in the second and third sections of the chapter, government policy-makers quite quickly began

to express the view that the floating currency should not be just temporary. They advanced a number of reasons why they were now willing
for the first time to consider a floating exchange rate as an appropriate
exchange rate regime for Canada: (1) it helped them to avoid taking
sides in an intense domestic political debate about the appropriate level
for the exchange rate; (2) it provided greater monetary autonomy for
the country; and (3) exchange rate movements helped facilitate balance
of payments adjusments. The fourth section then shows how these reasons, in addition to the relative stability of the floating rate, also help
explain why Canadian policy-makers embraced a freely floating exchange rate for the rest of the decade until 1939. Despite the creation of
the Bank of Canada, which allowed policy-makers to manage the value
of the Canadian currency more actively, they chose to leave its value almost entirely to market forces.

FROM FLOATING BACK TO THE GOLD STANDARD:
1914–1931

Canada moved to a floating exchange rate with the Finance Act of
1914, which enabled the federal government to suspend the convertibility of Dominion notes into gold and to make advances of Dominion
notes that were not backed by gold to the private banks. Had Isaac
Buchanan still been alive, he would surely have applauded this act. But
the rationale for its introduction was quite different from his own. The
act was simply designed to address the fact that the onset of World War
One had triggered capital flight and runs on the country's banks.
    Although the floating exchange rate regime had been introduced as
an emergency measure, it lasted for twelve years. Like most of their
counterparts in other countries, however, Canadian policy-makers retained what one scholar calls a "gold-standard mentality" throughout
this period; that is, their objective was to return to the gold standard as
soon as economic conditions made it possible.[1] Not only was the gold
standard seen as the monetary regime that would best facilitate international commerce, it was associated with price stability and monetary
discipline. Canadian policy-makers had little interest in taking advantage of the floating exchange regime to pursue the kind of activist
domestically-oriented monetary policy that Buchanan and his supporters had advocated. As one scholar puts it, "The loss of autonomy in internal monetary policy [associated with the gold standard] ... either
was not recognized or was not considered too high a price to be paid."[2]

There was one prominent set of political forces that dissented from this liberal orthodoxy. At the end of World War One, populist political parties representing farmers and labour – particularly from the west of the country – suddenly achieved political prominence, disrupting the elite-dominated two-party political system of the pre-1914 period. These parties came to power in three provinces (including Ontario in 1919), and the farmer-dominated National Progressive Party won one-third of the seats in the 1921 federal election, including almost all seats in prairie provinces.[3] Politicians in these parties called for the creation of a central bank that would pursue an activist monetary policy aimed at promoting economic growth and smoothing out the business cycle. Under their "managed currency" policy, exchange rate stability would be sacrificed to this goal of a domestically-oriented national monetary policy. In fact, they hoped that the central bank would actively manage the exchange rate in the interests of the country.[4]

These ideas resembled the thinking of the National Currency League.[5] Their new political influence made it more difficult for the governing elite to restore the gold standard, particularly since this could only be done via a deflationary policy that restored prices to their pre-war levels. Between 1921 and 1925, a Liberal minority government was in power, and it remained in place only because of the support Prime Minister Mackenzie King acquired from the Progressive Party.

The Relative Stability of the Float

Governing elites also accepted a floating exchange rate for such a long time after the war because it proved much less disruptive to international commerce than had been predicted in the debates of the 1870s. Canada's exchange rate remained in fact quite stable throughout the period of floating. During the war, the Canadian dollar hardly changed in value vis-à-vis the currencies of the country's two major economic partners, the US and Britain. When the British pound fell approximately 30 per cent vis-à-vis the US dollar during 1919–20, there was a period of brief instability when the Canadian dollar also depreciated, although to a lesser extent (about 18 per cent against the US dollar). Sterling then recovered much of its value in 1921 and so too did the Canadian dollar, returning to a discount vis-à-vis the US dollar of only 5 per cent. Between 1921 and 1926, the Canadian dollar was quite stable once again, and it returned to par around the time that sterling went back formally on gold in 1925 (see Figure 2).[6]

Figure 2
Canadian dollar in terms of us dollar and pound sterling, 1914–39
Average annual rates

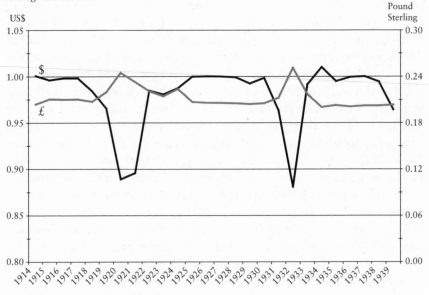

Source: Statistics Canada

Given the absence of significant currency instability for most of the 1914–26 period, there were few protests from the private sector about the floating exchange rate. The only serious complaints I have found in the Canadian federal government archives came during the brief 1919–21 period when the Canadian Importers Association objected to the impact of the depreciation on its members' businesses.[7] It is also clear that currency instability proved disruptive in some border regions where US dollars were widely used. Nearly thirty years later, one federal politician recalled how poorer citizens were taken advantage of at that time: "if you happened to go in with a few fish scales in your hair or a few hayseeds you were given 10% [discount when paying with US currency]. But if I were making a transaction and if I got a businessman in the town who was well acquainted with the banker and who knew local conditions better than I did, I would get 15 or 18%."[8] Merchant associations in US border towns such as Buffalo also began to charge discounts on Canadian coin in 1919.[9]

For the most part, however, the floating rate did not appear very disruptive to Canada's international commerce. Indeed, Canada's trade and investment relationships with the outside world grew rapidly during the 1920s, especially those with the US. Particularly striking was the growth of US investment, especially foreign direct investment. By 1926, US companies owned approximately 30 per cent of all Canadian manufacturing and 32 per cent of all Canadian mining and smelting operations.[10] As these numbers grew, so too did the proportion of Canada's trade that took place within these large multinationals. This too diminished the pressure for a fixed exchange rate. From the standpoint of these firms, the impact of exchange rate fluctuations was easily offset through intra-firm pricing mechanisms and transfers of funds.

Why was the value of the Canadian dollar so stable vis-à-vis the US and British currencies in this period? The pattern of short-term capital flows played an important role. While many countries experienced disequilibrating short-term capital flows in this period that contributed to currency volatility, the Canadian experience was quite different because of the existence of a large number of Canadian-issued "optional payment bonds" that were payable in either Canadian dollars or sterling. When sterling depreciated, Canadian investors would export capital to London – thus pushing the Canadian dollar down – in order to purchase these bonds in sterling because their price was then lower than bonds purchased in the Canadian market at the same time, and as they were still payable in Canadian dollars (because of the optional payment feature) profit would result. When sterling appreciated, the opposite would occur. As a result, the Canadian dollar would move in tandem with sterling.

Did government intervention in the foreign exchange market also foster exchange rate stability? The finance minister reported in 1918 that the government had been attempting to keep the Canadian dollar stable for some time by intervening in foreign exchange markets through its agent, the Bank of Montreal. But interventions were small, and the main effect was simply to smooth out daily fluctuations. When the Canadian dollar depreciated sharply in 1919–20, the government attempted briefly to defend the currency through informal requests to financial institutions not to facilitate certain kinds of capital outflows. But the request had little effect on the behaviour of these institutions.[11]

The difficulties involved in regulating the Canadian dollar's value no doubt encouraged Canadian authorities simply to accept a floating exchange rate. Even British officials and financiers who wanted to fix the Canadian dollar to sterling in the early 1920s were forced to acknowledge how difficult the task would be. They hoped to fix currencies throughout the British Empire to sterling in order to bolster trade with the Empire and strengthen the international role of sterling and London's financial markets. But even they recognized it would be much more difficult to fix the value of the Canadian dollar than that of the currencies of other parts of the Empire, such as Australia, New Zealand, or South Africa. In a memo written for Canadian authorities in 1920, the lead advocate of Empire currency cooperation, J.F. Darling of the Midland Bank, explained the problem. While Canada's exports to and imports from Britain had been roughly equal in volume in 1913, the latter now dwarfed the former. These trade patterns, he argued, "are so one-sided that the feasibility of stabilization becomes lessened unless as part of an Imperial scheme with a state bank, with offices over the Empire, holding all the banking reserves, and thus forming a pool through which adjustment would at once be affected." If Canada was to consider joining a broader imperial scheme of this kind, it would require a major reorientation of the focus of Canadian banks away from New York towards London. Here is how Darling described the challenge involved: "An Anglo-Canadian Exchange Scheme would require a good deal of thinking out in conjunction with the Canadian authorities ... I do not see how it could be accomplished unless there were a clean cut-away from the United States. Canadian banking cash reserves are mainly held in New York and consequently New York is the ultimate Clearing House for Canadian transactions. From the point of view of the Empire this is undesirable, and the decision of Canada to cut the American dollar and link up with sterling would be an event of the greatest importance in both Canada's future, and that of the Empire."[12]

The Gold Standard Restored

Although Canadian policy-makers restored the gold standard in July 1926, their enthusiasm for a new exchange rate regime should not be overstated. When Britain had returned to gold in 1925, Canadian policy-makers had been advised by leading private bankers not to follow its lead on practical grounds. Many of them continued to oppose the move in 1926, arguing that the gold reserves of the country were not large enough to maintain a link to gold. The initiative to restore the gold standard at this time also attracted opponents who worried about its deflationary consequences.[13] Even a Conservative politician such as Sir Henry Drayton – who had been finance minister briefly after the war – attacked the governing Liberal party in 1925 for moving too quickly to return to gold on this basis:

Reduce the purchasing power of your people. Close factories. Injure your mixed farming industry. Injure your national pay-roll on which in the last analysis all purchases, foreign as well as domestic, rest, and you will cut down the demands for foreign exchange arising from the purchase abroad all right. But stick to this policy of the King government long enough and you will ruin your country and drive your people out ... The unfortunate thing is the cure is much worse than the disease. An active, fully employed, people, with a currency depreciated in the exchanges, but as good as ever at home, are much better off than those faced with unemployment and difficulty in living, with a currency temporarily or even permanently at premium.[14]

In the end, the timing of the 1926 decision simply reflected the fact that the renewal of the Finance Act in 1923 had outlined a three year deadline for the restoration of the gold standard. The move was also made easier because the Progressive Party's influence had declined dramatically after the 1925 elections.

Once the country was back on gold, Canadian policy-makers also did not show much of an inclination to defend the new exchange rate. When the Finance Act was renewed in 1923, it continued to allow the government to advance unbacked Dominion notes to the private banks, but now on an indefinite basis. Yet with the country back on gold, the federal government should have been very careful to limit these advances in order to guarantee that credit conditions in the country reflected the country's level of gold reserves. In fact, however, it *increased* advances to banks between 1927 and 1929. Curtis argued that this policy reflected ignorance of monetary principles rather than a deliberate effort to sabotage the gold standard: "I believe that the country has never realized just what it did when it passed the Finance Act. The thing occurred so easily, so gently, that I do not think the true significance of that thing has ever been appreciated or recognized."[15] Bryce notes, however, that the government had received advice to stop or at least constrain its advances at the time the gold standard was restored, and it had simply chosen to ignore the advice.[16]

Whatever the case, these advances did soon influence the monetary standard. As interest rates in New York rose to as high as 8 per cent in 1928, the banks found it very profitable to borrow Dominion notes at the Department of Finance's rate of 5 per cent, convert them into gold, and invest in New York. This practice quickly drained the government's already small gold reserve, prompting it to ask the banks to stop redeeming Dominion notes into gold. This request signalled the de facto termination of the gold standard in January 1929 since Dominion notes were no longer convertible.[17] But because the Canadian dollar remained near par until September 1931, many people still considered Canada to be on the gold standard at this time.

Among those holding this view were some Americans who supported an initiative at this time to encourage the Canadian currency to be accepted at par in their country. This initiative was an interesting one because it sought to create a de facto currency union of the SMU/LMU type in which the currencies of the US and Canada co-circulated. The idea had in fact been first put on the US political agenda by Canadian businesses who complained in 1928 that their country's currency was not always accepted at par in the US. In an era when Canada-US trade, investment, and tourism linkages were expanding rapidly, many Americans soon took up the cause on the grounds that "it would be the finest kind of an inter-American 'gesture of friendship' between the two countries if Canadian money were to be accepted in the United States as freely as American money has long been accepted in the Dominion."[18] This "injustice to Canada" was soon decried in newspaper editorials as far away as Louisville, Kentucky.[19]

Initially, the US government responded to this chorus of support by declaring the issue to be a private one, and they asked the American Chamber of Commerce to consider addressing it.[20] But the US Department of Commerce soon suggested that the Federal Reserve Board should take some formal action to address the situation because of the level of Canadian concern.[21] Many Federal Reserve Board officials were sympathetic to the cause, but they were also very wary of committing US Federal Reserve Banks to any requirement to accept Canadian currency at par in the absence of a broader initiative to guarantee the future stability of the Canadian dollar. As an internal committee investigating the issue noted, "it appears inadvisable to endeavor to exchange Canada and United States *currencies* at par without making similar arrangements to maintain *exchange* at parity between the two countries."[22] Indeed, Federal Reserve Board officials were well aware in 1929 that Canada was no longer formally on the gold standard and that issues of Dominion notes had often been in excess of the appropriate level since 1926.[23]

In April 1930, the Federal Reserve Board finally issued a formal statement noting that the discount on Canadian dollars was often as high as 10 to 20 per cent across the United States and that "this is regarded as excessive and has given rise to some feeling in Canada, especially as

United States currency is generally accepted at par in Canada."[24] To address the situation, it sent notices to all banks in the US asking them to accept the Canadian paper currency at the par value "except in the event of extreme fluctuations in exchange rates."[25] To encourage this practice, the regional Federal Reserve Banks agreed to cover the costs of shipping Canadian paper currency from the private banks to their offices where it would be converted at current *market* rates of exchange (minus a small exchange charge). The Board argued: "if member [private] banks cooperate in this matter by extending a similar service to their customers, Canadian tourists travelling in this country will find American merchants willing to accept Canadian currency at or near par."[26] Although the Canadian government was careful to take no formal position on the issue, officials in External Affairs noted privately that they were very pleased by the Fed's final decision.[27]

This de facto monetary union soon unravelled when Canada left the gold standard formally and its currency fell in value vis-à-vis the US dollar in late 1931.[28] The catalyst for the Canadian dollar's depreciation was Britain's decision to abandon gold and allow sterling to depreciate in September 1931. This decision had been emulated by many other national governments and financial markets quickly anticipated that the Canadian government would follow suit. In the face of considerable speculative selling, the federal government was hard pressed to defend the currency with its small gold reserves. On 19 October 1931, the federal government sought to curtail further capital flight by restricting the export of gold, thus formalizing the country's departure from the gold standard. The Canadian dollar then depreciated by approximately 15 per cent by the end of the year.[29]

THE DECISION TO FLOAT IN 1931–33:
RESPONSE TO A DOMESTIC POLITICAL STALEMATE

Although the Canadian government's decision to leave gold at this time was not unusual, its introduction of a "free float" that lasted until 1939 was more unique. Many other countries that left gold in 1931 soon repegged their currencies to a major currency such as sterling. Even those countries which adopted an independent floating exchange rate generally employed a "dirty float" when the government intervened in foreign exchange markets to manipulate the rate. As it had in the 1914–26 period, however, the Canadian government made very little effort to manage the exchange rate throughout this period. As Plumptre noted, "the Canadian dollar had remained, up to the outbreak of war, almost the only completely uncontrolled currency in the world."[30] What explains this choice?

During the 1931–33 period, the decision partly reflected a domestic political stalemate within the country. The question of the exchange rate was a highly controversial one in Canada in these years. On one side were those who either opposed the abandonment of the gold standard altogether or preferred to see only a limited depreciation vis-à-vis the US dollar (which stayed on gold until 1933). Among the strongest proponents of this view were members of the Canadian financial community. As in the pre-1914 period, they feared that a large depreciation would generate inflation and capital flight as well as undermine Canada's creditworthiness abroad. They also worried that a depreciation would increase the cost of servicing US dollar-denominated debts which had accumulated dramatically during the 1920s. This latter concern was not restricted to the financial sector. Over 80 per cent of the bonded debt of Canadian corporations was payable, solely or optionally, in a foreign currency. So too was over 50 per cent of the debts of various governments at all levels: federal, provincial, and municipal.[31]

The fact that a significant depreciation would discourage imports also brought many importers into the same political camp.[32] Some with close economic ties to the US also feared that a sharp depreciation vis-à-vis the US currency might disrupt trade and investment flows across the border more generally. Indeed, some analysts highlighted that a significant depreciation might also provoke US trade retaliation.[33] By early 1932, US Congressional committees were already studying ways of protecting US business from the depreciation of foreign currencies, and the US Chamber of Commerce demanded such protection at its annual meeting in May of that year. When the Chamber followed up with a report later in 1932, it specifically identified a number of sectors in which Canadian exports to the US had increased because of the Canadian currency's depreciation. At the time, the Chamber recommended the introduction of a special tariff – as other countries such as France had recently introduced – that would apply to countries that were using depreciation as a competitive tool.[34] Although the Chamber's suggestion was resisted by US government officials, the threat of increased US protectionism was clearly quite real.

On the other side of the debate were those who advocated a large depreciation. Most of the people in this camp called for the Canadian government to match sterling's devaluation and then fix the exchange rate vis-à-vis sterling or even join an initiative to create an Empire currency. This position was particularly popular among farmers in the West and elsewhere. Western wheat farmers had been among the strongest advocates of a significant depreciation since the onset of the Great Depression in 1929. They had been hit particularly hard by the collapse of wheat prices and they hoped depreciation could boost their competitive position as well as the prices they received for their goods in Canadian dollars. The currencies of their leading competitors abroad – Argentine and Australian farmers – had left gold in 1929–30 and had depreciated as much as 40 per cent and 46 per cent respectively by the end of 1932.[35]

The call for a link to sterling was also taken up in the early 1930s by businesses in many other sectors across the country who faced competition from sterling area countries – i.e., countries whose currencies were pegged to sterling. This included not just various commodity exporters in sectors such as dairy, fruit, and livestock farming, as well as forestry. It also included many manufacturing firms, both exporters and import-competing firms.[36] Even prominent figures with the large sector of US-owned manufacturing firms, such as the president of Dodge Manufacturing Co. of Toronto, advocated a sharp depreciation. Indeed, by January 1933, he warned the government that its failure to endorse this move was creating frustration among businesses across the country and "is creating an antagonism towards the present administration, which to my mind will destroy the Party."[37] At first sight, the involvement of US-owned firms might seem surprising given their close ties to the US. But they had often established production in Canada primarily to sell to the protected British Empire market. Although they imported parts and equipment from the US, their exports were focused on sterling area markets; indeed, they were frequently banned from exporting back to the US.[38]

Those advocating a link to sterling also highlighted how this exchange rate policy would foster trade and investment with Britain and the wider sterling area. This argument held considerable weight after the US's 1930 Smoot-Hawley tariff had shut many Canadian exporters out of the US market and the 1932 Ottawa conference had strengthened Canada's trade links with the Empire. Canadian borrowing in New York had also dried up after Canada left gold, leaving Britain as Canada's most promising source of foreign capital.[39]

The case for a link with sterling was also sometimes couched in pro-Empire and anti-American sentiment. In advocating for the sterling link, the president of the National Dairy Council even suggested to the government in 1932 that Canada's currency be renamed the "crown" to highlight its significance to the "mass of the people." He argued: "They [the people] have a very deep rooted habit of measuring our dollar against the American one, and seem to forget that our own unit is always worth 100 cents *here*, whatever the foreign position. The new scheme would enable the Government to explain the happening much more effectively, and would give tangible evidence of the separation of our standard of value from American dominance."[40] This proposal seemed to revive the ideas of British authorities from the early 1850s.[41]

We have seen how Canadian exchange rate policy had traditionally been dominated by financial interests. In this highly politicized context, their influence was challenged. Within the federal government, the exporters' cause was taken up particularly strongly by the minister of trade and commerce, H. Stevens from British Columbia. Indeed, to increase pressure on his cabinet colleagues, he actively solicited letters in late 1932–early 1933 from Canadian exporters in which they described the competitive difficulties they faced because of depreciations abroad.[42] Stevens also made links to British financial figures, such as J.F. Darling and Leo Amery, who were promoting the idea of an Empire currency, or at least a kind of fixed exchange rate between the Canadian dollar and sterling.[43]

In the federal parliament, the case for a significant depreciation was taken up strongly by many opposition politicians, especially those on the left who had been calling for a managed currency throughout the 1920s and now pointed to the precipitous decline of Canadian incomes (by about 48 per cent between 1929 and 1933) in the face of deflationary pressure abroad.[44] Prominent radical MPs such as Agnes McPhail reminded the government that the famous economist John Maynard Keynes had urged countries to abandon the gold standard in this context.[45] Other left-wing politicians, such as G.G. Coote, highlighted the distributional consequences of efforts to slow the Canadian currency's depreciation: "If government policy is exercised to artificially improve the rate of exchange, that is, to hold up the dollar, in effect this should be regarded as a sort of forced contribution from those who are producing for export, to government, municipalities, corporations and individuals for whose benefit the rate of exchange is being artificially held up."[46]

The case for depreciation was also strengthened by the fact that even some figures in the financial establishment supported it. One of the earliest advocates of depreciation was S. Randolph Noble of the Royal Bank, a banker with enormous experience in international issues. In late

September 1931, he wrote to Prime Minister Bennett urging that Canada leave gold and depreciate the currency substantially. In a context where the US and France were mismanaging the gold standard with excessively deflationary monetary policies, Noble argued that Canadian politicians should stop worshipping the monetary regime. What was needed, in his view, was a policy that would allow Canada to gain "absolute control of its own price level."[47] This case against the gold standard echoed some complaints that had been heard in parliament that Canada had simply become a thirteenth Federal Reserve District.[48]

Noble also disputed the prediction that depreciation would produce a domestic financial panic and capital flight, arguing that "we are already off the gold standard and, moreover, were off it during the whole of 1929, so that the public have not been taught to regard it as sacred, as is the case in England."[49] Unlike many other bankers, he did not think the move would produce inflation because the Depression conditions would constrain price increases. In a February 1932 memo, Noble acknowledged that he was advocating a "managed currency" along the lines that Keynes had proposed in his 1923 *Tract on Monetary Reform.*[50] In that work, Keynes had famously critiqued the gold standard on the grounds that exchange rate stability was not always compatible with the goal of domestic price stability. In these circumstances, Keynes had advocated prioritizing "internal stability" over "external stability."

By March, Noble recommended a formal tie to sterling because the Canadian dollar had depreciated by approximately the level he thought appropriate. He also made a more political case for the move: "It is unnecessary for me to mention that the Middle West is being deluged with misinformed and misleading propaganda against the banks and the Government, which would be absolutely silenced by such a move."[51] Noble's arguments were taken up the next month by another Royal Bank official, Graham Towers, who would soon become the first head of Canada's central bank. In a memo to Josiah Stamp of Britain, a copy of which reached Bennett, Towers argued that the link to sterling would boost domestic agriculture and industry. He also highlighted the broader macroeconomic case for this exchange rate regime: "If an early upturn in the United States is not to be anticipated, we should take steps to avoid further useless deflation in this country."[52]

Both he and Noble argued that the fears of US dollar–denominated debt holders, in both the public and private sector, were overstated. Because the devalued Canadian dollar would boost the domestic economy, governments should soon find their fiscal position considerably

improved as tax revenue increased and social service spending declined
(particularly unemployment relief). They would thus be in a good fiscal
position to handle the increased foreign debt servicing costs.[53] Others
noted that the healthier domestic economy would also help private sector debtors repay their higher debts.[54] It might even be possible to provide public compensation to those private debtors who were severely
affected by the depreciation.[55]

But the fear of higher indebtedness remained politically significant in
influencing federal government policy in this period.[56] After reading
Towers's memo, Bennett noted to a Department of Finance official in
April 1932: "The question is not a simple one; it is: would the benefits
accruing to Canada through improvement in conditions by inflation
compensate for the loss sustained in the purchase of exchange to meet
our foreign obligations, private, public, and corporate?"[57] Canadian
policy-makers also worried that a large depreciation might undermine
investor confidence. This fear stemmed partly from what Bryce calls
their "debtor mentality – the concern to protect the country's credit rat-
ing."[58] Canadian officials were also aware that the country was uniquely
vulnerable to capital flight because of the enormous cross-border securities trade in optional payments bonds and because of the large volume of
liquid balances held by US branch plants. As the 1940 Royal Commission on Dominion-Provincial Relations – or Rowell-Sirois Commission –
noted in describing the views of policy-makers during the Depression:
"Normally the movements in the optional-pay securities and the branch
plant balances are akin to the operations of a huge equalization fund
which smooth out temporary or small scale fluctuations in the exchange.
Under some circumstances, however, they constitute a serious danger
since anything that causes foreigners to take an extremely pessimistic
view of Canadian conditions may precipitate a large withdrawal of capital which might shatter the Canadian financial system and completely
destroy Canadian credit, both internally and abroad."[59]

Faced with these competing arguments and interests, Bennett's government confronted a difficult political situation. It was clearly impossible to choose an exchange rate that would not be politically
controversial. Because the Canadian economy was such an open one,
many groups had a deep stake in this choice. The fact that the Canadian
economy was divided economically along regional lines only compounded the political problem. The strongest supporters of a large depreciation were commodity exporters who were concentrated in the
West and the Maritimes, while many of the most vociferous opponents

of such a policy – financial interests, in particular – were concentrated in central Canada.[60] The controversy thus had the potential to inflame regional tensions, just as the choice of a monetary standard had at the time of Confederation. And regional tensions were already very high because the Depression had been experienced so unevenly in a geographical sense, with the West hurt much more than central Canada.

In this circumstance, the government found it easiest to sit on the fence and let the exchange rate float freely. When the free float produced a depreciation equal to roughly half of sterling – just as it had after the war – the desirability of this choice was only reinforced. As the minister of finance, Edgar Rhodes, noted in March 1933, this "halfway" value "may be working out a not unsatisfactory compromise between those of our national interests which would be benefited by close and stable relations with sterling, and those on the other hand which would be seriously harmed by a heavy and fluctuating discount in terms of New York."[61]

When the US left the gold standard in April 1933, the political tension surrounding the exchange rate question finally eased. The Canadian dollar continued to float halfway between sterling and the US dollar, but now at a value which reflected an *appreciation* vis-à-vis the US dollar and a *depreciation* against sterling. Indeed, the new values of the three currencies were now very close in relation to each other to what they had been before 1931 (but at reduced gold values). This change suddenly pleased all of the main groups who had been involved in the political debates over the exchange rate question over the previous two years. The depreciation against sterling helped the key exporting sectors whose main competitors had currencies tied to sterling, while the appreciation against the US dollar pleased those who held debts denominated in that currency.[62]

W.C. CLARK AND THE MACROECONOMIC CASE FOR FLOATING

Support for a floating rate in the early 1930s did not stem only from the efforts of the federal government to balance competing domestic interests. This exchange rate regime was also backed on more principled grounds by some prominent professional Canadian economists who found themselves with a significant role in Canadian exchange rate policy-making at this time. We have seen how Canadian exchange rate policy before 1931 was dominated by the views of private bankers. This

situation suddenly changed as exchange rate issues became more politicized in the context of the Great Depression and policy-makers recognized that managing rates had become an important task of public
policy. Because there was no one in the civil service with expertise in international monetary issues, Canadian policy-makers looked for advice
to a new generation of professional economists that had emerged within
the Canadian universities.[63]

The most important of these economists in the early 1930s was
William Clifford Clark. He had studied economics as an undergraduate
at Queen's University and then as a graduate student for three years at
Harvard with professors such as Frank Taussig (although Clark never
completed his Ph.D.). He then taught economics at Queen's in 1915–23
where he showed a particular interest in monetary, banking, and international trade issues. After working for a private business in the US, he
returned to teach at Queen's in 1931–32.[64] His official involvement
with the federal government began in the lead-up to the 1932 Ottawa
conference on Empire trade relations. Currency relations were on the
agenda of the conference, and top government officials had quickly recognized that there was no civil servant competent to advise politicians
on the issue. In his role as undersecretary of state for external affairs,
O.D. Skelton – himself an economist – was the chair of the interdepart-
ment committee preparing for the conference, and he approached
Clark, his former student at Queen's, to ask if he was willing to prepare
some briefing papers for the government on the issue.

Even before Skelton approached him, Clark had been in conversation
with Bennett as early as March 1932 about what exchange rate regime
might be most appropriate for the country.[65] He was very willing in mid-
1932 to accept Skelton's request and soon found himself appointed a special advisor to the Canadian delegation to the conference. Two months
later, Prime Minister Bennett invited Clark to become the deputy minister
of finance.[66] He accepted in early November 1932 and remained in the
position until 1952. Under his leadership, the department emerged as the
central economic policy-making body within the government.

In his first formal role advising the government in mid-1932, Clark
provided a very detailed economic defense of the floating exchange rate
in a remarkable 196-page memo he wrote after soliciting advice from
economists across the country.[67] The memo rejected the idea that Canada should tie its currency to either the US dollar or sterling, and advocated a managed floating exchange rate that would keep the value
of the Canadian dollar between that of the US dollar and sterling. His

arguments are worth describing in some detail because they represented the first detailed justification of a floating exchange rate regime within government circles, and because they would be echoed in government circles long after this.

One of Clark's rationales for this policy was that it provided a way of reconciling Canada's close economic ties with both the US and the sterling area. Clark noted that Canada had a strong interest in exchange rate stability because of its very high dependence on foreign trade and borrowing. The difficulty, however, lay in choosing which of these two trading partners to fix to. The United States accounted for 46 per cent of Canada's exports and 68 per cent of its imports, and had become the major source of foreign capital for Canada during the 1920s. Volatility in the Canada-US exchange rate would disrupt trade relations with the US and undermine US investor confidence. At the same time, exchange rate stability vis-a-vis sterling was also important since the Canadian economy relied for 33 per cent of its exports and 20 per cent of its imports on Empire countries – and he predicted these numbers would rise in the wake of the Ottawa conference. With New York basically closed to new borrowing in the early 1930s, London might once again become the country's main source of foreign capital. Faced with this dilemma, Clark concluded that a managed floating exchange rate keeping the currency's value between sterling and the US dollar, as it had been since 1931, would serve the country best. As he put it later in a November 1933 memo to Bennett: "in view of our important commercial and financial relations with both the United States and Great Britain, this compromise seems to have been a not undesirable one."[68]

Clark's more important argument in favour of a managed float was that it would provide Canada with monetary autonomy. His preference for monetary autonomy reflected a distrust of both US and British monetary policy-making. Like Towers and Noble, his case against tying to the US dollar was that US authorities had shown an inability to address their country's deflationary monetary conditions: "if we do really tie ourselves to the American dollar we will subject our Canadian economic structure to all the oscillations of a monetary unit which has shown no capacity for stability – worse still, has in recent years shown little but a tendency to appreciate."[69] He also did not trust the British government's commitment to provide stable monetary conditions.

Clark argued that Canada needed to carve out an independent monetary course. In an earlier memo to Bennett in March 1932, he had already made the case for a floating rate: "Do we want to be dependent on any other country in so far as a monetary standard goes or does wisdom lie rather in complete independence and flexibility, – freedom to change our minds and adjust ourselves to changing situations as they arise?"[70] In this more detailed memo in mid-1932, he repeated this case with more vigour:

> The arguments against a tie-up with New York and with London constitute the case for retaining our national autonomy in monetary matters for the present at least. In particular, neither alternative offers any real assurance of price stability or the restoration of our prices to a level at which the burden of fixed debt resting upon the industrialist and taxpayer will be appreciably mitigated. Either would subject our economic system to the possibility of external shocks that might conceivably be sudden and violent. Neither would offer us in the way of exchange stability anything more than approximate stability with a part of the world. There is much to be said against entering into hard and fast monetary agreement in the present state of uncertainty. If we retain our independence, we may choose our own objectives and plot our own course towards them.[71]

It is important to emphasize that Clark's case for monetary autonomy did *not* stem from a desire to pursue an activist domestic monetary policy aimed at promoting full employment or domestic growth. He endorsed the orthodox view that monetary policy should be designed primarily to maintain price stability. Both at this time and later during the 1930s, he rejected calls for more activist policies designed to promote a domestic expansion on the grounds that they would be inflationary. Indeed, at one point in 1936, in warning about the dangers of inflation, he sent the minister of finance a marked copy of Andrew White's *Fiat Money Inflation in France* – a well-known book that describes the disastrous experience of the *assignats* during the French revolution – and noted "this book, I think should be made required reading for all Members of Parliament."[72]

Still, Clark's endorsement of monetary independence was a bold one at the time. Stamp reported that the Canadian bankers he had talked to at this time ruled out the idea of a deliberate float "on the ground that Canada would not be regarded by the world as having any experience of these matters, and her position would neither be understood nor trusted."[73] Towers was one of the bankers with this view at the time: "Canada has had little experience along these lines, and there might conceivably be a general lack of conviction in respect to our ability to achieve satisfactory results. Further inflationary pressures might be feared ... There is no reason to believe that we would manage our own currency any better than sterling will be managed."[74] Even radical politicians such as McPhail were calling for a peg to sterling rather than a floating exchange rate. His view was, however, shared by other economists such as Frank Knox who noted in 1934: "For the smaller countries to keep their currencies at fixed ratios of exchange to the currencies of the great powers, is to keep open the channels by which economic fluctuations are spread between countries ... One of the most important ... measures [to insulate] is a variable exchange rate."[75]

In addition to endorsing monetary autonomy, Clark also discussed at some length one other macroeconomic rationale for a floating exchange rate. At the time, a number of economists were arguing that Canada should begin using exchange rate adjustments to offset external shocks to the economy. The most prominent proponent of this view was A. Wynne Plumptre, an economist at the University of Toronto who had studied with Keynes at Cambridge. Plumptre highlighted that Canada's balance of payments was subject to very large fluctuations because of the size of capital flows in and out of the country and because of its role as a resource exporter, for which world prices were unstable. Regarding the latter, approximately one-third of the country's national income came from exports in the early 1930s, of which about two-thirds involved raw materials such as foodstuff, newsprint, lumber, and minerals.[76] If the country maintained a fixed exchange rate, the only way it could adjust to these frequent changes in the balance of payments was through changes in domestic monetary conditions. When resource exports collapsed as in 1929–31, the entire country was forced to undergo a painful deflation to restore the external balance.

In Plumptre's view, it made more sense in this kind of context – particularly when the balance of payments shocks were only temporary – to adjust to the external shock through exchange rate manipulation. A depreciation of the exchange rate would more quickly and efficiently restore the external balance by promoting exports and discouraging imports. As he put it in 1932, Canada faced a choice "either to seize the [balance of payments] tail and stabilize it, perhaps under a heavy weight of gold, a policy which will necessarily result in severe oscillations of the body economic; or else we may try to influence the position of the body by gentle but firm pressure upon an exchange rate tail, the width of whose wags we hope to be able to restrain within reasonable limits."[77]

Plumptre went even further to argue that, even in the absence of an external shock, exchange rate policy could be used to serve domestic monetary goals. In the context of a depression, he argued that a conscious depreciation of the currency could provide an important stimulus to the domestic economy. Indeed, in an open economy which was dependent on raw materials exports, monetary authorities might find it more effective to influence the domestic money supply by this tool of exchange rate management than by more traditional methods such as open market operations. In his words, "the foreign exchange rate is and must be the monetary key to the level of prices and prosperity in a country such as Canada [i.e., a raw materials exporter]. Such a country stands self-condemned if, in a period of depression, it has not canvassed the possibility of utilizing the exchange rate remedy."[78]

One other reason that traditional methods of monetary policy were quite ineffective in Canada was the absence of a Canadian money market at the time. Domestic interest rates were highly influenced by conditions in New York markets where Canadian banks held the bulk of their liquid reserves. Plumptre in fact argued that a floating rate – along with the creation of a central bank – might help to build up a local money market independent of New York by encouraging banks to keep their liquid funds at home. This, in turn, would help domestic monetary authorities to exert more influence over domestic monetary conditions by open market operations or discount rate changes.[79]

Throughout the 1930s, Plumptre's arguments in favour of an activist exchange rate policy were shared by other Canadian economists, politicians on the left, and even some business leaders.[80] Some economists, such as Queen's economist John McDougal, also made the important point that a deliberate depreciation could be used to offset the fact that Canadian wages were downwardly inflexible. Foreshadowing arguments in the postwar years, he suggested that this strategy was necessary because "the sheltered and protected classes would resist any reduction in their money rates of remuneration until they were forced to accept them by the threat of unemployment." The move would also share the burden of adjustment more equally across the country. During the Great Depression, McDougal noted the standard of living of those who remained employed had often improved when prices fell more than wages. A more conscious policy of devaluing the currency would have produced less unequal experience:

our economic institutions are so ordered as to resist any spreading of the strains of depression and/or deflation over the whole community ... If that is so, then it ought to be a major object of policy to minimize the dislocation of sectional price levels. I can conceive of no single policy which would accomplish that end more quickly or more surely than a controlled depreciation of the Canadian dollar in terms of other currencies. A direct attack on the money rates of pay of the sheltered classes seems totally impossible. It is probably too much to hope that even the indirect attack of tariff reductions on the eve of the depression would be socially acceptable. I trust, therefore, that when we next face depression we shall stand ready to use this weapon of depreciation as the necessities of the case may demand.[81]

In his 1932 memo, Clark made it clear that he was sympathetic to Plumptre's case for activist exchange rate management as a means of adjusting to balance of payments shocks. His case is worth quoting at length:

our national economy is subject to a substantial degree of instability arising out of the importance of agriculture on our national life and the effect, on the yield of our exports, of the wide swings in world prices for raw and semi-raw materials which bulk so large in our total exports. The possible reaction of this instability on the problem of monetary aims needs to be considered. In the first place, it makes more difficult the stabilization of the general level of internal prices ... The second difficulty is that economic instability is likely to make the maintenance of exchange stability difficult and painful. For under a policy of fixed exchanges, an upset in the country's balance of payments due to a crop shortage, or a change in foreign demand for one or more of the country's important products may have to be corrected by the painful process of restricting credit and reducing prices and personal incomes. This process appears the more ruthless when it is realized that many of the disequilibria in international balances of payments are of a temporary nature. The question may be raised whether the policy of exchange stability in some case does not involve the payment of too high a price for the advantage gained ... The effect [of Plumptre's suggestion] would be to cushion the shock to the economic structure of any adverse circumstances that tended to produce a sharp reduction in the national income from exports ... With imports restricted and exports stimulated, the country's balance of payments would be restored to equilibrium by the direct and easy process of exchange rate depreciation rather than by the slower and more painful process of gold outflow, credit restriction and reduction in the general level of prices and incomes.[82]

At the same time, however, Clark also expressed some reservations about Plumptre's arguments: "Such a policy sounds plausible, but, as its sponsor admits, it is subject to several objections; (1) as a deliberate national policy it is new and untried; (2) incompetence on the part of the monetary authority or inability to withstand pressure from sectional interests might result in a continuous policy of exchange rate depreciation with resulting internal inflation; and (3) exchange rate depreciation would raise the question of the effect of such depreciation on past, present, and future borrowing."

He also suggested that Plumptre may have overstated the instability of Canada's balance of payments during normal times. More generally, Clark worried about a permanent policy of exchange rate manipulation because "the great importance both of foreign trade and of foreign investment to Canada makes exchange stability a specially desirable monetary objective for us." Summing up his view, Clark wrote the following: "Conscious manipulation of exchange rates has been suggested as a national policy for Canada in order to ease the shocks of fluctuations in the national income due to weather vagaries or other uncontrollable external factors. There may be occasional conjunctures of economic events when allowing the currency to depreciate may be the least of several evils but the erection of exchange rate variation into a permanent national policy would be of doubtful wisdom."[83]

THE CREATION OF THE BANK OF CANADA AND THE FREE FLOAT

If Clark presented these rationales for a policy of managed floating, how did he in fact propose to control the currency's value? At the time of his mid-1932 memo, he suggested that capital controls could play a role. He wrote: "whether or not we remain upon the gold standard, some conscious control of capital movements is desirable. For substantial periods during the last few years Canada has been able to maintain the gold standard only with strain; that strain has been due probably not so much to the types of uncontrollable instability referred to above as to capital movements ... The justification for national control of capital movements is to be found in the fact that the effect of international borrowings and repayments is not confined to the individuals concerned but is exerted upon exchange rates, gold movements, and thereby the whole structure of Canadian industry and agriculture."[84] Clark's endorsement of capital controls was echoed by Plumptre and others at the time.[85]

But it had already become clear that the federal government was unlikely to introduce capital controls. Like Canadian officials in 1919–20,

Bennett had briefly attempted to curtail the Canadian dollar's depreciation in December 1931 through informal controls on capital outflows. Canadian bankers had been asked to stop Canadians from buying foreign securities and from repurchasing Canadian securities abroad. Although the bankers initially agreed, their commitment quickly waned when it became clear that some investment bankers opposed the initiative and that the embargo was not being consistently applied.[86] In January 1932, Bennett also considered issuing a public appeal to Canadian holders of optional payment bonds to accept payment only in Canadian dollars, but the banks convinced him that this would have little effect and would undermine the standing of Canadian securities abroad.[87] Bennett abandoned the idea, concluding: "We still live in a selfish world."[88] By late 1933, Clark too noted how difficult it would be to control financial transactions in and out of the country.[89] Analysts at the time also highlighted that efforts by the federal government to control provincial borrowing abroad might not be constitutional.[90]

If capital controls were ruled out, what about managing the Canadian dollar's value through intervention in the foreign exchange market as the government had attempted around 1918? Both Towers and Stevens initially suggested the creation of a fund of foreign exchange reserves for this purpose as the way to guarantee a fixed link between the Canadian dollar and sterling.[91] But others pointed out that the idea was not very practical. Typical was the view of the British authority Leo Amery who reminded Stevens that this kind of fund would be effective only if it was extremely large, given the scale of trade and capital flows in and out of the country. In Amery's view, the value of the Canadian dollar could only be managed effectively with a more significant institutional change such as the creation of a central bank.[92]

Clark and others shared this view. Clark had in fact been pushing for the creation of a Canadian central bank as far back as 1918 when very few other members of the establishment had been willing to consider the idea.[93] In the early 1930s he found more allies. The need for institutional reform had been highlighted for Bennett in late 1931 by the Queen's University economist W.A. Mackintosh in a confidential memo that discussed Noble's September 1931 advocacy of depreciation: "There is little that the government can do at the moment but allow depreciation to continue as the market dictates ... Frankly, if, as the memorandum suggests, we are embarking on a system of managed currency, it should be clearly borne in mind that we are attempting to manage it without any rudder. However, as we are already afloat we had probably better sail with the breeze and construct a rudder as soon as possible rather than try to put back to shore."[94] A similar sentiment was expressed by many in the business community. As a Montreal businessman, Mark Fisher, put it, the debate about what level to set the exchange rate "was purely an academic one ... since there was no machinery for doing it in any case." He continued: "This huge country is drifting without steering gear ... She has no one to set a course and no machinery for keeping a course."[95]

Fisher was in fact testifying before the Royal Commission on Banking and Currency which was established by Bennett in March 1933 to explore the idea of creating a central bank. Clark had encouraged Bennett to take this step by making his acceptance of the post of deputy minister of finance in 1932 conditional on Bennett's willingness to create a central bank (as well as the creation of unemployment insurance, a promise Bennett did not keep).[96] But Bennett did not in fact need a lot of convincing. He had already become interested in the idea of a central bank as a means to deflect criticism of his inaction in addressing economic problems during the Depression.[97] He also found appealing the notion that a central bank could regulate the external value of the currency more effectively by centralizing the country's foreign exchange and gold reserve for intervention purposes and by regulating credit conditions in the country in a centralized manner.[98] In addition, Bank of England officials – who also favoured the creation of the Bank of Canada – pointed out that a central bank could help stabilize the exchange by co-operating with foreign central banks.[99] Bryce argues that Bennett had in fact first become interested in the idea of a central bank in late 1931 after the US Federal Reserve had refused his request for an exchange stabilization loan on the grounds that such loans were only made to central banks.[100]

The Royal Commission was quite a landmark in the country's history since it represented what one scholar calls "the first really comprehensive attempt made by Canadians to analyse critically the workings of their own monetary and banking system."[101] During the hearings, most of the Canadian banking community – with some notable exceptions such as Towers – opposed the creation of a central bank. But the idea was supported by many other groups, ranging from professional economists to radical Western populists. The former were influential not just in the hearings but also behind the scenes. For example, Plumptre – a strong supporter of the central bank – was chosen to act as the secretary of the commission. In its final report, a majority of the five members of the royal commission came out in favour of the creation of a bank. They included Lord Macmillan of the UK (who chaired the commission), Charles Addis of the Bank of England, and John Brownlee, the premier of Alberta. The other two members – the banker and former finance minister William T. White and the Montreal banker Beaudry Leman – opposed the idea. Bennett's government quickly embraced the majority view and appointed the thirty-seven-year-old Towers as the first governor of the new Bank of Canada. Clark played a major role in drafting the Bank of Canada's legislation and it is not surprising to find a passage noting that one of the key purposes of the bank was "to control and protect the external value of the national monetary unit."[102] Soon after the bank began operations in March 1935, parliament also strengthened its ability to meet this goal by creating an exchange fund that the bank would manage.

With these reforms, the country finally had the institutions to regulate the exchange rate more effectively. It is odd, then, that the bank did very little for the rest of the decade to take up this task. The Canadian dollar floated freely for the duration of the decade, and the exchange fund was hardly used up until the outbreak of war in 1939.[103] How do we explain this inaction? One explanation is that the Canadian dollar's free float was remarkably stable between 1934 and 1939 (see Figure 2, page 42). While other countries with floating rates experienced considerable exchange rate volatility in the 1930s, the Canadian currency remained roughly at par with the US dollar and slightly below par with the pound throughout the period.[104] This exchange rate stability was partly attributable to the stability of the US dollar–sterling exchange rate. Towers also attributed it to the pattern of equilibrating capital flows associated with the large number of optional payments bonds which, as he noted, was "a feature of our financial economy which is not found in any important degree in any other country."[105] In the late 1930s, Towers even argued that these equilibrating financial movements were generated *only* when the exchange rate was allowed to float freely. In other words, he cited the equilibrating pattern of capital flows as a reason not to intervene to influence the Canadian dollar's value. When the Canadian dollar fell slightly below par with the US dollar in April 1938 and Towers was under pressure to manage the exchange rate more actively, he resisted this pressure with this argument: "A premium on U.S. dollars encourages capital and other movements which tend to reestablish equilibrium and therefore one should hesitate to oppose an upward movement in the U.S. dollar rate ... We, therefore, would not recommend any attempt now to stabilize the exchange rate at par, or at any definite level, either by direct intervention in the exchange market or by means of monetary policy (which would involve some degree of contraction)."[106]

The importance of the de facto stability of the Canadian dollar in this period was that it lessened the case for active foreign exchange management. At the time of the 1933 royal commission, some domestic groups had noted that exchange rate volatility could be disruptive to their international operations.[107] Policy-makers, including Clark as we have already seen, also believed that the Canadian dollar's value should be kept relatively stable vis-à-vis Canada's major economic partners because of Canada's extensive international economic involvements. Indeed, the degree of openness of the Canadian economy at this time is worth recalling. By the mid-1930s, 30 per cent of the net value of all Canadian production was exported, a level not matched by any other major industrial country at the time. Also unequalled was the high portion of industrial production – 25 per cent – involving branch plants of foreign corporations. Canada was also a major importer and exporter of other kinds of capital, and its net interest and dividend payments were the largest in the world. In addition, levels of tourism were surpassed only by France.[108]

Given the stability of the Canadian dollar vis-à-vis sterling and the US dollar, why did Canadian policy-makers not simply fix the currency formally? The question almost never arises in the archival documents of the time. The only example I have found was a brief discussion in 1936 at the time when the US, Britain, and France agreed to stabilize the exchange rates between their three currencies. This Tripartite Agreement has been seen by some historians as a precursor to the 1944 Bretton Woods Agreement. As we shall see in the next chapter, Canadian policy-makers became strong supporters of the latter. But they chose not to join this earlier initiative for reasons that Towers outlined in memos he wrote to Clark and Finance Minister Dunning soon after the agreement had been announced.

Towers argued that Canada would derive few direct benefits from joining. If the agreement successfully stabilized the relationship between the US dollar and sterling, he noted that the Canadian dollar would likely be stabilized, too, without the need for any formal commitment by Canada. Such a commitment would also bring some costs since it would infringe on Canada's freedom to alter its exchange rate in response to changing economic conditions. It would also require new arrangements to be put in place to monitor, and perhaps control, cross-border capital flows.[109]

If these practical concerns argued against Canada joining, Towers did acknowledge that Canada's participation might help the broader goal of promoting global monetary stability. Anticipating arguments in the lead-up to Bretton Woods, he wrote: "We know that the arrangement is a most laudable attempt to achieve something that will be highly beneficial to the world at large, and not least to Canada. Each addition to the ranks of the co-operators counts for something psychologically, if in no other way; and it is conceivable that inclusion in the group would inspire greater confidence in Canada, if, in due course, membership implies a form of currency respectability." At the same time, however, he was not confident that the stabilization initiative would succeed. In the event that it failed, he noted "no great good would have been done by our joining the group."[110]

Although Towers's memo highlights his desire to preserve the option of using exchange rate movements to address economic problems, he and other Canadian policy-makers remained quite reluctant to embrace the kind of activist exchange rate changes that Plumptre had advocated. The issue arose in both 1935 and 1938–39 when there were public calls for a deliberate depreciation to raise domestic prices and help domestic groups such as Western wheat farmers. In both cases, these calls were resisted and Canadian policy-makers stuck to the free float. They were very conscious at these moments that any deliberate exchange rate choices would produce a wide range of domestic winners and losers.[111] Given these distributive consequences, they feared such a move might ignite the kinds of political controversies that had flared up during the 1931–33 period. By 1940, even Plumptre acknowledged that the Bank of Canada's passive exchange rate policy was understandable in these circumstances: "The economy is one of considerable complexity and wide variety of economic interest. Positive policies and bold strokes of statesmanship are, under present circumstances, likely to set up or aggravate centrifugal tendencies among the various groups, areas, and provinces that make up the country."[112]

Canadian policy-makers were also concerned about the possible US reaction to a deliberate depreciation strategy. This concern had arisen in the early 1930s, but it was now intensified by the signing of the US-Canada Trade Agreement of 1935 which included a clause noting that the agreement could be terminated by either government "in the event that a wide variation occurs in the rate of exchange between the currencies of Canada and the United States of America."[113] When a managed depreciation was being discussed in 1938–39, the deputy governor of the Bank of Canada opposed the idea partly because it might bring about the end of this trade agreement.[114]

One further objection was that the predicted economic benefits of depreciation were overstated. At the time of the 1935 debate, the new Bank of Canada's chief of research, Alex Skelton (son of O.D. Skelton), noted that the benefits of a depreciation for local producers might be offset as increased Canadian exports lowered world prices in sectors such as wheat, metals, and newsprint where Canada controlled such a large share of world production. He also argued that depreciation would produce only a temporary competitive advantage for Canadian firms since it would likely generate a rise in domestic prices. More generally, he worried that a strategy of boosting short-term competitiveness via exchange rate depreciation might undermine long-term competitiveness of Canadian firms by discouraging necessary adjustments to changing market conditions: "not only does depreciation check the evolution of natural tendencies and the adoption of the existing economic structure to changed conditions, but it encourages developments on a temporary and artificial basis which must ultimately collapse. Vested interests are created, and the pressure to perpetuate them constantly beclouds the future stability of the currency ... unhealthy expansion in uneconomic industries is stimulated."[115]

Skelton and other policy-makers also reiterated the point put forward by Clark earlier: that Plumptre's strategy might provoke capital flight and undermine Canada's reputation among foreign lenders.[116] Towers even expressed a fear that this policy might undermine the broader economic confidence of the general public: "It is important to remember that there are very few instances of a country depreciating its currency unless subject to considerable pressure because of an unfavourable balance of trade or an outward movement of capital. Deliberate currency depreciation by a country enjoying a strong balance of payments position ... might react so unfavourably upon public confidence as to cause an actual fall in economic activity and a decline in real national income."[117]

Some of these economic arguments against a deliberate depreciation highlighted the general conservativism of economic policy-makers towards activist macroeconomic management. Although the government had deliberately expanded the money supply in 1932 and 1934, further such moves had been resisted. In addition to reflecting their conservative inclinations at this time, the reluctance of Canadian officials also reflected worries that efforts to boost domestic aggregate demand in the open Canadian economy would simply attract imports which could generate a vicious cycle of depreciation and inflation.[118]

CONCLUSION

What explains the new Canadian interest in a floating exchange rate regime in the interwar years? There was not in fact much enthusiasm for this regime before 1931. The introduction of a floating exchange rate between 1914 and 1926 was seen by the governing elite of the time only as a temporary measure made necessary by the problems of war finance and postwar international economic instability. To be sure, labour and farmer interests in this period reiterated some of the arguments against the gold standard that Buchanan had advanced. But their political influence was limited to delaying the return to gold. And even then, the delay also simply reflected a recognition of the difficulties associated with regulating the exchange rate in the absence of capital controls or a central bank, as well as the fact that the stability of the floating exchange rate reduced business pressure for a quick return to gold.

When a floating currency was reintroduced in 1931, it was again simply an emergency measure, responding this time to the international financial crisis of that year. But quite quickly, the view of Canadian policy-makers began to change. It helped that the floating rate did not generate much currency volatility. Even more important, however, was the fact that a floating exchange rate came to be seen in a more positive light as a regime worth endorsing. Three rationales for supporting a floating exchange rate emerged in this period and remained influential for the rest of the decade (as well as subsequent decades, as we shall see). First, a free float provided a way for Canadian policy-makers to "depoliticize" the question of the appropriate level for the exchange rate, an issue that was enormously controversial because of Canadians' diverse and extensive international economic relationships. Second, the professional economists who assumed prominent positions in exchange rate policy-making for the first time in this period argued that a floating exchange rate would enhance Canadian monetary autonomy in a context of financial openness. Although government policy-makers remained wedded to the orthodox notion that the prime purpose of monetary policy was the maintenance of price stability, they recognized that a floating exchange rate – rather than the gold standard – might provide the better means to achieve this goal, since it could insulate Canada from disruptive monetary developments abroad, such as the US deflationary pressures in the early 1930s.

Finally, some influential economists also now endorsed the idea that a floating exchange rate could play a useful role in assisting adjustments to balance of payments disequilibria. As Carey had noted in the nineteenth century, the availability of this alternative adjustment mechanism could be particularly important for a country such as Canada whose balance of payments fluctuated enormously in response to harvest conditions, commodity prices, and international capital flows. Some economists also suggested that exchange rate depreciations had an important role to play in offsetting the international competitive consequences of inflexible domestic wages.

This third rationale for a floating exchange rate was the most controversial in policy-making circles. Concerns were expressed that any deliberate use of a depreciating exchange rate to foster balance of payments adjustments might: (1) undermine investor confidence, (2) bolster inflation, (3) provoke US opposition and protectionism, (4) provide only short-term benefits to Canadian firms, (5) unleash domestic political controversy because of the differential impact of exchange rate changes across the country, and (6) undermine exchange rate stability, upon which the open Canadian economy depended. Each of these points would be raised again in subsequent decades as a critique of the floating exchange rate regime.

CHAPTER THREE

The Short-Lived Commitment to Bretton Woods

At the outbreak of World War Two, Canadian policy-makers abandoned the float of the 1930s and then played an important role in supporting the Bretton Woods negotiations which created a multilateral fixed exchange rate system for the postwar world. But their new commitment to a fixed exchange rate regime proved short-lived. In September 1950, Canada became the first country to reintroduce a floating exchange rate regime. Although the decision met severe criticism abroad, Canadian policy-makers did not back down and the country remained the only major Western country to contravene the Bretton Woods exchange rate rules throughout the 1950s.

This chapter seeks to explain why Canada abandoned the Bretton Woods exchange rate system more quickly than any other country. It begins by exploring the reasons why Canadian policy-makers endorsed a fixed rate first in 1939 and then again during the Bretton Woods negotiations. In discussing Bretton Woods, particular attention is devoted to a question that has received little attention in existing literature: why did Canadian policy-makers not give more support to the "key currency" plan, proposed as an alternative to Bretton Woods, which would have allowed for Canada's 1950 decision? The chapter then examines the 1950 move to reintroduce a floating exchange rate, highlighting how the choice reflected many of the same considerations that had led Canadian policy-makers to endorse a floating rate during the 1930s: (1) the prioritization of monetary autonomy and financial openness over fixed exchange rates, (2) the desire to use exchange rate movements to foster balance of payments adjustments, (3) the goal of depoliticizing exchange rate issues within the Canadian polity, and (4) the sentiment that a floating exchange rate need not be associated with currency volatility. Equally important, the decision was also facilitated by the fact that the US supported it for reasons that are explored in the final section of the chapter.

THE ONSET OF WW2 AND THE ADOPTION OF A FIXED EXCHANGE RATE

Although exchange rate policy had been very controversial in Canadian politics at various times during the 1930s, there was very little public debate about the decision to fix the Canadian currency vis-à-vis the US dollar and sterling in September 1939. The level that the government chose for the peg contributed to this. When Britain had entered the war, it had set its currency at a level that represented a 20 per cent devaluation vis-à-vis the US dollar. Canadian policy-makers chose a smaller 10 per cent devaluation to a rate just above US$0.90, a decision that helped to balance competing preferences of various domestic groups. But even in elite policy-making circles, the move to a fixed exchange rate provoked little comment or discussion. It was seen simply as a necessary part of the broader wartime emergency measures adopted at the time. This view was interesting in light of the fact that Canada had *abandoned* a fixed exchange rate at the start of World War One. What explains the difference?

The rationale for the 1939 decision was that Canada's exchange rate would otherwise become extremely volatile in the unstable wartime conditions. This volatility, it was feared, would have proven very disruptive to the country's international trade and finance.[1] Canadian policy-makers were particularly concerned about the risk of large-scale capital flight that would undermine the government's ability to pay for the war by borrowing funds domestically at low interest rates. Large capital outflows would also deprive the country of scarce US dollars that were needed to pay for crucial imports associated with the war effort. This fear of capital flight was much more pronounced in 1939 than it had been in 1914. As Towers noted, the difference partly reflected the fact that the Canadian government hoped to rely much more heavily on domestic borrowing during this war. The government was also worried that US investors now held a much larger number of Canadian securities than they had in 1914 and that these investors were likely to withdraw their funds when Canada entered the war.[2]

Concerns about capital flight not only prompted the government to stabilize the exchange rate. They also led to a much more dramatic policy change. For the first time in Canadian history, the government introduced a system of foreign exchange control which enabled it to regulate all of Canada's international economic transactions. Secret planning for this move had begun in early 1938 after Towers had become aware that the British were planning to introduce controls of this kind in the event of war. After undertaking detailed studies of the foreign exchange control regimes of many different countries, a small group of Bank of Canada officials prepared a fully developed plan which was then put into place by an Order-in-Council passed on 15 September under the War Measures Act, soon after war broke out.[3]

The introduction and administering of foreign exchange controls was a massive and complex operation. Towers was convinced that capital flight could be controlled effectively only if a system of comprehensive exchange control was put in place.[4] But he also recognized the enormity of this task in a speech to the Foreign Exchange Control Board (FECB) staff in 1940: "from some points of view exchange control in this country is more difficult, more upsetting in a way, than in almost any other country in the world ... because of our extremely intimate relations with the United States. It is almost like cutting a body in two to run the line of exchange control across our frontier."[5] In addition to the high level of trade and tourist traffic, the Canada-US economic relationship was characterized by extensive and complex cross-border investment relations that complicated this regulatory initiative. As Louis Rasminsky, the director of economic research for the new FECB, noted in 1941, the operations of US branch plants and subsidiairies posed a challenge to regulators: "Goods have moved across the border from parent [company] to child and child to parent without money necessarily changing hands – only a book entry to inter-company account. On the other hand, funds have been freely transferred from Canada to the United States and vice-versa to meet the need of one or other part of the organization, without these transfers being necessarily connected with specific shipments of goods or with the declaration of a specific dividend."[6]

More generally, many observers highlighted how the imposition of foreign exchange controls at the Canada-US border was an entirely new experience for Canadians and Americans, with all cross-border economic transactions now subject to regulation by the FECB. As one FECB official noted, "the truth is this; foreign exchange control is probably the most drastic set of regulations that has ever been imposed on the Canadian people ... It is a form of regimentation entirely new to our people."[7] For

·Americans, the new controls were also a confusing and worrying novelty. Indeed, their introduction initially provoked rumours that US tourists to Canada would have their money and even guns and cars confiscated, rumours that prompted Canadian officials to send out 75,000 explanatory circulars to US hotels, travel clubs, and tourist organizations.[8]

From the standpoint of exchange rate policy-making, the introduction of foreign exchange controls was enormously important since it allowed the government to regulate the exchange rate much more effectively than ever before. But policy-makers also made it very clear that the desire for exchange rate stability was *not* the primary reason for introducing exchange controls. More important had been the need to curtail capital flight directly in order to preserve the country's scarce foreign exchange reserves and the government's domestic borrowing capacity.[9] In a comment that foreshadowed developments in the early postwar years, Towers explicitly noted that the exchange rate motivation on its own would not have been sufficient for government to introduce the controls: "I put that as a factor of some importance to business, but not of course as a major thing which would make one decide on control. Stabilization of rates is very useful, but it is not so vital that one would embark on such a thing as exchange control for that purpose alone."[10]

The introduction of foreign exchange controls provoked remarkably little political opposition. Although the controls were cumbersome, they were accepted by most Canadians as a necessary cost of the war effort.[11] The only significant protest came from Quebec where Premier Duplessis objected to the fact that the federal government would now be regulating the Quebec government's foreign borrowing. Indeed, he called a provincial election within one week of the introduction of the foreign exchange controls after the Bank of Canada rejected his request for new funds. But his subsequent electoral defeat removed this source of opposition.[12]

SUPPORT FOR THE BRETTON WOODS EXCHANGE RATE REGIME

Although Canadian policy-makers initially saw the introduction of a currency peg as an emergency wartime measure, they soon became more enthusiastic about fixed exchange rates in the context of their involvement in the negotiations that led up to the 1944 Bretton Woods conference. British and American policy-makers were the clear leaders of these negotiations that began in 1942. But Canadian officials also played a significant role and they even advanced a formal Canadian plan for the postwar monetary world in July 1943. The plan, which highlighted their support for a postwar regime based on fixed exchange rates, was designed not just to influence the British and American nego-tiators but also US domestic opinion. As W.A. Mackintosh, a wartime advisor to the government, noted at the time, "the United States Trea-sury does not command a great deal of support either in the country or in Congress. Canada, on the other hand, has an almost embarrassingly high position in banking and financial circles in the United States and is not without reputation in Congress where we at least have no taint of the New Deal about us ... A Canadian plan would probably attract more support in the United States than a Treasury plan. It would give rise to no instinctive opposition such as a British plan."[13]

The enthusiasm of Canadian policy-makers for the creation of the Bretton Woods exchange rate regime is somewhat puzzling in light of Canadian exchange rate policy-making both before and after the war. We have already seen how Canadian policy-makers were unusually at-tached to a floating exchange rate regime throughout the 1930s, an atti-tude had even led them to reject participation in the 1936 Tripartite Agreement that is often seen as the precursor to the Bretton Woods Agreement. And we shall soon see how Canada became the first coun-try to abandon the Bretton Woods exchange rate regime in 1950 and adopt a floating exchange rate. What, then, explains their brief support for a fixed exchange rate system during this period?

It is commonly argued that Canadian policy-makers were influenced by their desire to avoid being forced into choosing to focus the coun-try's trade on either the sterling or the US dollar area. Not only did Canada traditionally have strong economic ties with both, but during the war the country had come to rely on exports to the sterling area to offset its imports from and debt payments to the US. In this context, it was extremely important for Canada that an international monetary system be built in which sterling was convertible into US dollars at a stable rate. More generally, there was a strong feeling that Canada would derive particular benefits from the growth of international trade and finance that would result from a more stable international ex-change rate regime.[14]

Rejecting the Key Currency Plan

This story is accurate, but it leaves unanswered a question that was raised by US opponents of the Bretton Woods agreement. Why did

Canada not give more support to their "key currency" proposal that provided an alternative way to stabilize the sterling–US dollar relationship? This proposal, widely supported by the New York financial community, had been put forward in the July 1943 issue of *Foreign Affairs* by John Williams, a Harvard economist and vice-president of the Federal Reserve Bank of New York. Instead of building the complex multilateral monetary order suggested by the lead British and US negotiators, Keynes and Harry Dexter White, Williams argued that it would be more efficient for the US simply to offer Britain a bilateral loan to restore the convertibility of sterling to US dollars at a fixed rate. In his view, this initiative offered a more realistic way to rebuild an open world economy because it would stabilize and free up the two most important currencies used in international trade and investment: "the essence of my idea is that what the nations really want and need is either dollars or sterling (at their option) in the final settlement of multiangular trade, and the real question is whether this or what the plans substitute for it (stabilization fund, exchange union, clearing union) is the more attainable and desirable objective."[15]

What was particularly interesting about Williams's proposal from a Canadian perspective was that he explicitly endorsed the idea that smaller countries which were highly dependent on world markets should be allowed to continue to vary their currencies' value. In his words, "I have long believed that the younger countries, whose economic conditions primarily reflect the conditions existing in the great world markets, for which they are only secondarily responsible, should be permitted to vary their currencies. It might help them somewhat, without too seriously affecting the larger countries."[16] His rationales for flexible rates for these countries were ones that Canadian policymakers would soon endorse in 1950. Williams argued that flexible rates would allow countries "to protect themselves so far as they can from short period fluctuations."[17] Countries would also be able to protect their policy autonomy in an atmosphere of capital mobility: "the internal monetary system can be protected from the deflationary effects of an otherwise uncontrollable capital outflow ... Moreover, if the system of flexible exchange is combined with internal money management, the possibility of effective internal control is enhanced by exchange variation. If, for example, ... the internal effects of discount rate changes or open-market operations are nullified by their opposite effects on international short-term capital movements, exchange variation would protect internal control from external interference."[18]

At the core of Williams's proposal was a critique of the idea that all countries should be governed by the same rules with respect to exchange rate arrangements. This idea had been prominent during the gold standard era and he believed that it was being mistakenly endorsed again by Keynes and White. He argued, as Canadian policymakers also would in 1950, for a more differentiated system: "There are grounds for thinking that we do not need or want any single pattern of compromise in all countries such as the gold standard pattern was before the war. Different kinds of countries require different kinds of monetary systems." [19]

This vision should have been very attractive to Canadian policymakers. Under his proposal, they could have adopted the same position they had at the time of the 1936 Tripartite Agreement. Indeed, Williams made it clear that his proposal was designed to build directly on that agreement.[20] Canada could benefit from the stabilization of the sterling–US dollar relationship, while at the same time retaining freedom of action vis-à-vis Canada's own exchange rate. But during the Bretton Woods negotiations, Canadian policy-makers refused to endorse Williams's ideas. In fact, Louis Rasminsky, Canada's lead policy-maker on these issues at the time, went out of his way to write to Williams in mid-July 1943 and criticize his ideas. This letter was strongly endorsed by W.C. Clark.[21] Rasminsky followed up this letter with a more public attack on Williams's ideas in a high profile article in the July 1944 issue of *Foreign Affairs*, an article which impressed both White and Keynes.[22]

Canadian Embedded Liberalism

Rasminsky's ideas are worth exploring because he would remain a very influential figure in Canadian exchange rate policy-making until the early 1970s. During the 1920s, he had studied economics as an undergraduate student at the University of Toronto (where he had been a classmate of Plumptre) and as a graduate student at the London School of Economics. In 1930, he had joined the League of Nations's Economic and Financial Section where he specialized in banking and currency issues for the rest of the decade. Clark had long been impressed with Rasminsky's work and in 1940 he and Towers succeeded in recruiting Rasminsky into the Canadian civil service. He was formally hired to work with the Foreign Exchange Control Board, but he quickly emerged as the lead policy-maker within the government on international monetary issues and the Bretton Woods negotiations.[23]

Although economists who had worked for the League often had a rather orthodox outlook, Rasminsky made clear that he felt classical liberal economic ideas were outdated in the early 1940s. In discussing how a League of Nations report should be written in May 1942, he noted: "It should recognize what seems to be the basic fact which must condition the whole of our thinking about the economics of the post-war world, namely that this is in fact a revolutionary war and that the object of economic policy after the war will not be to make the institutions of a capitalist or semi-capitalist society work with a minimum of friction but to make sure that ... the fruits of production are widely distributed ... This point of view [must be] kept constantly in the foreground."[24] In the monetary realm, he noted in 1944 how this new political environment meant that governments would no longer be willing to sacrifice the goal of full employment to that of exchange rate stability as they had under the gold standard: "If one thing is clear about postwar economic policy, it is that the primary objective of all governments will be to maintain employment at high levels. This aim will take precedence over exchange stability; and if exchange stability is desired, some technique must be developed to make the two aims compatible."[25]

Rasminsky's views were in fact quite typical of other Canadian policymakers at this time. In a prominent December 1941 memo about postwar planning, the Department of Finance's Robert Bryce, who had studied with Keynes and is credited with bringing his ideas to Canada after Bryce entered the department in 1938, noted: "It does not take a political expert to forecast that following an Allied victory, many nations will embark upon 'New Deals.' Quite apart from the development of socialism itself, the social temper seems sure to require forthright and vigorous action to provide work and security under all circumstances."[26] In the monetary realm, Bryce, who also played a role in developing Canada's policy during the Bretton Woods negotiations, echoed Rasminsky's views: "Nations and their governments will be less willing than ever to sacrifice domestic price levels or interest rates, much less production and employment, in order to maintain exchange rates ... It seems obvious that the reestablishment of the gold standard in anything like its old form is not going to be an issue at all after the war. Monetary conditions and monetary policy are now recognized as too important and too close to the heart of fiscal sovereignty to be entrusted to any automatic or even semi-automatic system."[27]

Even the head of Canada's central bank had come to embrace this line of thinking. In 1942, Towers argued that a key benefit of the British and

US proposals was that they would provide policy autonomy to governments to address unemployment in an aggressive fashion: "[Countries] would have no legitimate excuse for failure to tackle energetically their domestic problems. I hope ... that those domestic problems will, in fact, be tackled in a really bold fashion. One thing seems certain, namely, that with the experience of war fresh in their minds, and the recollection of the pre-war depression close in the background, people in this and other countries will be extremely impatient with any state of affairs which involves unemployment on a material scale for any appreciable length of time."[28] It is worth noting that Towers's enthusiasm for activist domestic policies was somewhat unusual in central banking at the time. Indeed, when Towers's name was floated as a possible successor to Montague Norman as the head of the Bank of England in 1944, many Bank of England officials were opposed on the grounds that he was "too Keynesian."[29]

These quotes highlight how Rasminsky and other Canadian officials clearly shared the kind of "embedded liberal" ideology that inspired both Keynes and White at this time. This term is often used to describe the worldview which sought to reconcile the rebuilding of a multilateral liberal world economy with the new interventionist priorities of the embryonic Keynesian welfare state.[30] The prominence of this ideology among British and American negotiators gave Canadian policy-makers an important reason to back the Bretton Woods proposals. Plumptre, for example, who was one of the Canadian delegates to Bretton Woods and worked as financial attaché at the Canadian embassy in Washington during the Bretton Woods negotiations, later put it this way: "I myself am a wild radical at heart and my sympathies were with the New Dealers with whom I happened to be working."[31]

The embedded liberal orientation of Canadian policy-makers also provided incentive to oppose the key currency plan. Although Williams himself rejected many aspects of the pre-1930s economic orthodoxy, his key currency proposal was strongly backed by the New York financial community whose members generally wanted the gold standard restored. Even if some more conservative Canadian policy-makers had been sympathetic to this goal, they had to recognize that it was not compatible with domestic political priorities within Canada. Indeed, by late 1943 and early 1944, polls were showing that the socialist CCF (Cooperative Commonwealth Federation created in 1935) was the most popular federal political party and it was voted into office in Saskatchewan in 1944.[32] At the time of the Bretton Woods conference,

Towers told a British colleague that he was convinced the CCF would either win the next election with a majority or at least be in a position to dictate the policies of the Canadian government.[33] In 1944–45, the federal government responded to the changing political mood by introducing a number of new nationwide measures that helped to build a welfare state and it committed to countercyclical fiscal and monetary policies designed to maintain a high and stable level of employment and income in its 1945 *White Paper on Employment and Income*. Even the Conservative Party accepted the new full employment goal.[34]

More generally, if Canada backed the key currency proposal, it risked undermining the careful efforts that had been made during the Bretton Woods negotiations to build closer British-American economic cooperation. If Williams and the bankers succeeded in torpedoing the Bretton Woods negotiations, this cooperation might collapse since the key currency proposal had few supporters in Britain. This was an outcome that Canadian policy-makers were determined above all else to avoid. They also worried that the defeat of the Bretton Woods proposals would signal a broader unwillingness of the US to assume an economic leadership role after the war. As Clark put it to Rasminsky in August 1943: "if, as a result of the arguments made by Williams et al. and the prejudices and propaganda of bankers and politicians, the chances of getting a currency plan through are so slim as they now seem to be, what in Hades chance have we of getting the United States to do what it should do in connection with long-term lending?"[35]

Specific Arguments against the Key Currency Plan

If Canadian policy-makers had these broad reasons to oppose the key currency plan, they explained their opposition to Williams in more specific terms. Rasminsky asked him to consider whether there were political benefits in having a multilateral body such as the International Monetary Fund (IMF), rather than the US, give advice to debtor countries. He also suggested that it would be harder to mobilize domestic support within the US for a loan to Britain than for more general support of the IMF. In addition, Rasminsky expressed his worries that the key currency approach would not do enough to promote multilateralism and it might in fact lead to various 1930s-style bilateral agreements among monetary authorities to hold each others' currencies.[36] Finally, it appeared to him that Canada and other small countries "would have to become monetary satellites of one or other 'key' currency. This is an unenviable position which we should seek to avoid."[37] His worries in this respect are worth quoting at length:

it is difficult to see where the smaller countries fit it. I have the uneasy feeling that the "key currency" approach is the monetary counterpart of the Great Power doctrine of international organization generally. This approach seems to accept, if not to encourage, the splitting up of the world into economic blocs. It implies a sterling area with a group of satellite countries revolving around the United Kingdom and a dollar area with a group of satellites revolving around the United States ... Is it expected that Canada will obtain her American dollar requirements from the United Kingdom, explaining what the dollars are needed for (an explanation to which the British would be entitled since they would be ultimately responsible for the repayment of the dollars)? Or is it expected that Canada would finance the British deficiency of Canadian dollars by accumulating sterling, while the Federal Reserve System and the American Treasury finances the Canadian deficiency of US dollars by accumulating Canadian dollars? Canada would not be able to offset the one against the other.[38]

Clark strongly endorsed these arguments, and he wrote Williams that the key currency approach was not bold enough in its approach to promoting a stable and multilateral monetary order. He noted that the multilateral vision outlined by Keynes, White, and Rasminsky was a key precondition for broader international cooperation on trade, investment, and political issues after the war. Without this kind of bold approach, the world risked ending up in a permanent transition period that went "from bad to worse."[39] In a letter back to Rasminsky and Clark in August 1943, Williams strongly rejected the idea that his proposal would lead to bilateralism. He also repeated his argument that a country such as Canada might want more exchange rate flexibility than the Bretton Woods framework would provide: "I have wondered whether the next five years may not be the formative period, particularly for the growing countries and whether they ought not, therefore, to be careful to insist upon a sufficient degree of freedom of action."[40]

If the key currency proposal was not bold enough for Rasminsky and Clark, what about this fact that it would provide postwar Canada with more freedom of action to vary its exchange rate? As we have seen, Canadian policy-makers had already made clear their view that domestic priorities could no longer be sacrificed for exchange rate stability. They were clearly more willing than ever to accept the idea that deliberate exchange rate movements could be used to preserve monetary policy autonomy as well as to facilitate balance of payments adjustments. Indeed, on the latter point, Bryce went beyond Plumptre's ideas of the 1930s, arguing that exchange rate movements could help the country adjust not just to *external* shocks, but also *internal* price and wage movements – a point McDougal had earlier suggested, as noted in the last chapter. During the debate in 1938–39 about a deliberate depreciation, Bryce had noted that this kind of exchange rate policy could help the country adjust to the likely introduction of "contributory social insurance" programs.[41] Because these programs represented a tax on payrolls and wages, they would likely increase Canadian production costs which, in turn, could undermine the international competitiveness of Canadian-based firms. Anticipating arguments later in the postwar period, Bryce noted that a deliberate depreciation would help to offset the impact of this change.

Given these ideas, one might have predicted greater sympathy for Williams's proposal to allow countries such as Canada to maintain a flexible exchange rate. Rasminsky did acknowledge this benefit of the proposal, but he argued that Canada's freedom would continue to be constrained because US producers would object if Canada varied its exchange rate for competitive gain: "so far as the American wheat states are concerned, the Canadian dollar is in fact a 'key currency,' and so is the Argentine peso and so is the Australian pound. If postwar monetary organization were limited to a stabilization of the dollar-sterling rate and Canada or Australia obtained a competitive advantage over American wheat producers by currency depreciation, is it at all likely that the latter would be satisfied with the explanation that these were not 'key currencies'?"[42] In testimony to a House of Commons committee in early 1944, Clark also noted that Canada could be harmed if countries other than the UK and US were allowed to engage in competitive depreciation.[43]

More generally, Rasminsky noted later – just after Canada's 1950 decision to float – that Canadian policy-makers had decided that "the major objectives [of Bretton Woods] were considered by Canada to be so desirable, both for the world as a whole and for Canada in particular, that we assumed the obligation to operate on the basis of a fixed parity even although we realized this might involve us in considerable difficulties."[44] In an article in *Foreign Affairs* in October 1944, even Williams was forced to acknowledge Rasminsky's point that the key currency plan "has become overlaid with secondary, and not strictly relevant, considerations, such as the Great Powers doctrine versus the United Nations Doctrine, a gradual versus a once-for-all approach, and perhaps others."[45]

This did not stop Canadian negotiators from lobbying for a degree of exchange rate flexibility during the Bretton Woods negotiations. When White's April 1943 plan proposed that a country could change its exchange rate only with the approval of 80 per cent of the votes of the governing board of the Fund, Canadian policy-makers argued that this provision was "too rigid" and Rasminsky lobbied White in June to allow depreciations of up to 10 per cent.[46] When writing Canada's formal July 1943 proposal, Rasminsky then chose to echo Keynes's April 1943 idea that countries should be allowed to depreciate their currencies by up to 5 per cent in the event of current account problems and suggested that changes of up to 10 per cent should be allowed in certain circumstances.[47] Not surprisingly, they were pleased when the final IMF Articles of Agreement allowed changes of up to 10 per cent at each country's discretion, and also noted that the IMF would approve larger changes if they were required to correct a "fundamental disequilibrium."

The Importance of Capital Controls

The final reason Canadian policy-makers were willing to accept constraints on their freedom of action in exchange rate policy was that the Bretton Woods agreement endorsed the use of capital controls. Both Keynes and White had outlined in their early drafts that controls on capital flows would be a permanent feature of the multilateral order being constructed. They hoped that capital controls would help governments defend fixed exchange rates against the kind of "disequilibrating" and speculative capital flows which had been common in the interwar years. Equally important, capital controls would provide governments with greater autonomy to pursue domestically-oriented macroeconomic policies. This new endorsement of capital controls reflected a dramatic rejection of pre-1930s thinking, but it was very widely shared in the early 1940s.[48]

Canadian policy-makers also endorsed this view. As early as 1942, Rasminsky noted that both he and Towers believed that the British and US proposals for the postwar monetary order would only work with a general system of capital controls, and that they both supported the idea.[49] Here, for example, is a speech that Graham Towers made in 1942 to a study group in the Canadian Foreign Exchange Control Board: "I think it is the generally accepted opinion nowadays, amongst those who are giving serious consideration to the subject, that private movements of capital between countries cannot be allowed to take place for some time after the war except under license. It is realized that countries which have to tackle serious domestic problems, countries which are liable to be somewhat short of foreign resources, cannot have their problems aggravated by the desire of individuals to shift their money from point to point around the globe for reasons which are in no way related to the investment of capital in new productive enterprises."[50]

In their formal July 1943 proposal, Canadian policy-makers followed the Keynes and White drafts in permitting countries to use capital controls.[51] They also made clear that Canada intended to retain its wartime capital controls after the war ended, particularly because of the fear that US investors might sell their Canadian securities, thereby upsetting the market for Canadian government securities. By the time of Bretton Woods, Towers also told a British colleague that he was worried about the likelihood of US investors pulling out of Canadian investment once an election gave the CCF power in Ottawa.[52]

Their 1943 proposal also backed White's idea that countries be encouraged to cooperate in enforcing each others' capital control regimes.[53] The proposal had emerged in response to Keynes's early observation that Britain could only control capital movements effectively if it had a system of comprehensive exchange controls that covered current account payments. Since US officials did not want Britain to retain its exchange controls after the war, they had suggested in 1942 that this might be avoided if the US helped to enforce British capital controls by refusing to accept capital inflows that contravened those controls and by sharing information about British financial holdings in the US.[54]

From a Canadian perspective, this US proposal was very attractive since it might allow Canada to loosen or even abandon its cumbersome wartime exchange controls. As late as March 1944, Rasminsky continued to push for this idea to be explored in internal discussions of postwar planning: "Could we dispense with this [comprehensive foreign exchange controls covering current accounts after the war] if U.S. authorities co-operated by giving us information regarding security transactions and bank balances of Canadians? What type of information would we require?"[55] Around this same time, the FECB began to investigate whether this kind of cooperation might make it easier after the war to eliminate the programs of mail censorship to and from the US, as well as the searching of travellers leaving Canada.[56] In the end, however, White was forced to withdraw his idea in the face of opposition from the New York financial community. By the time of the Bretton Woods conference, the US officials had made it clear that they were no longer interested in backing cooperative initiatives to control capital flows in these ways. If Canadian officials hoped to control capital flows effectively, they would thus have to leave their system of exchange controls in place. As we shall see, this policy would soon provoke widespread domestic opposition.

EXPLAINING THE 1950 DECISION TO FLOAT

If Canadian policy-makers had good reasons to back the Bretton Woods exchange rate regime, why did they soon become the first country to withdraw from this regime by introducing a floating exchange rate in September 1950? In the months leading up to the 1950 decision, Canada was experiencing enormous inflows of speculative capital, primarily in the form of Americans buying Canadian government securities. Defending the currency's value required an accumulation of reserves which threatened to fuel already existing inflationary pressures in the domestic economy. Most observers expected Canadian policy-makers simply to repeg the Canadian dollar at a higher level in response to the market pressures – a move that would have discouraged further inflows and also helped to curtail inflationary pressures. The Canadian government had, after all, already twice shown its willingness to adjust the value of its currency peg. In July 1946, it revalued the Canadian dollar 10 per cent to parity with the US currency; a move that marked the first exchange rate adjustment by an IMF member. Then, three years later at the time of sterling's devaluation, the government had adjusted the dollar's peg again, this time downwards 9 per cent.

The decision to float instead was a very unexpected one at the time.[57] Even the Canadian bankers, who were suddenly called upon to create a market in foreign exchange for the first time since 1939, were surprised by the decision and they found themselves scrambling to find older staff who remembered the techniques of foreign exchange trading.[58] The decision to float also shocked and angered senior staff members at the institution created by Bretton Woods, the IMF. In particular, its director of research E.M. Bernstein highlighted that the IMF's Articles of Agreement did not permit member countries to float their currencies (even temporarily). He and others subjected Louis Rasminsky, who had been Canada's executive director to the IMF since 1946, to a four-hour grilling on the morning of 29 September during which he was told that Canada's action was "piratical" and that it would undermine the credibility and purpose of the Fund. Although Belgium had briefly experimented with a floating exchange rate a year earlier, Rasminsky reported

that Bernstein was particularly worried about Canada's decision because it was a major trading country and because "Canada's ethical position rated above all others."[59] This last statement likely referred not
just to the fact that Rasminsky had played a widely respected role during the Bretton Woods negotiations, but that he had also led an important defense of the stable exchange rate system when Belgium had asked
the IMF to accept its decision a year earlier. Although the US and other
members allowed the Fund to issue a statement accepting the Belgian
move as "an appropriate step in view of the exigencies of the situation," Rasminsky had strongly – and unsuccessfully – opposed this approach, arguing that it undermined "respect" for Fund obligations.[60]
Now, Rasminsky – along with other prominent Canadian officials who
had supported the Bretton Woods exchange rate system, such as Towers
and Clark – supported the floating of the Canadian dollar.[61]

Depoliticizing the Exchange Rate

What, then, explains the Canadian decision to float the currency? To begin with, it is clear that Finance Minister Abbott saw the introduction of
a floating exchange rate as a way to "depoliticize" the exchange rate
question within Canadian politics. At the time of Canada's 1947 balance
of payments crisis, the government had been severely criticized for induc-
ing the crisis by revaluing the Canadian currency to par with the US dollar a year earlier. Whether this criticism was deserved or not, it had, in
Rasminsky's words, "introduced the exchange rate into the field of domestic controversy."[62] Abbott worried that any decision to revalue the
dollar again (especially if par with the US dollar was chosen as the new
rate) could also soon be subject to the same kind of intense criticism. As
Rasminsky reported to US Treasury Secretary John Snyder, "The criticism
which was engendered [in 1947] was bitter and extreme and Mr. Abbott
feels that he simply could not face Parliament and the public and again
announce a return to parity unless he were thoroughly convinced that
this was the right rate for Canada. He is not convinced of this."[63]

He was not convinced, because of the uncertainty of international
economic conditions. The very openness of the Canadian economy ensured that it could be subject to many different kinds of external shocks
which were hard to predict. The volatility of capital flows across the
Canada-US border was a particular source of concern. As Rasminsky
told the IMF Board, Canada was a rather unique country because "it is
a foreign country but one which American investors regard as not quite
foreign even under conditions of control."[64]

Another key source of uncertainty was the direction of US monetary policy. The float would enable Canada to avoid importing US inflation which was showing signs of accelerating with the onset of the Korean War.[65] It would also enable Canadian policy-makers to tackle domestic inflationary pressures in a more active way at a time when it was unclear whether the US Fed would do the same. Since 1944, the Bank of Canada had kept interest rates at a stable and low level of 1.5 per cent, with the primary goal of supporting government bond prices.[66] With inflationary pressures rising, however, the bank wanted to move towards a more active monetary policy. Very soon after the floating rate was introduced, the interest rate was increased to 2 per cent.[67] It is understandable then that foreign officials such as George Bolton at the Bank of England interpreted the Canadian float as a sign of distrust in US monetary policy.[68]

These rationales for the float reflected the continuing commitment of Canadian policy-makers to the idea that exchange rate movements had an important role to play in preserving monetary policy autonomy and facilitating balance of payments adjustments. This commitment had already been revealed in the 1946 and 1949 exchange rate adjustments. The 1946 revaluation had been designed to prevent US inflationary pressures from entering Canada when the US abolished its wartime price control system.[69] Plumptre notes that the idea of deliberately adjusting the exchange rates to serve Canadian economic objectives was "quite novel at the time."[70] The subsequent devaluation in 1949 had been designed to help Canada's trade position adjust to sterling's 30 per cent depreciation at the time in a manner that minimized domestic unemployment.[71] What was new in 1950, however, was the argument that a float represented a better method for facilitating necessary exchange rate movements given the domestic political controversies that *deliberate* adjustments of the peg could generate.

A similar rationale for the floating exchange rate had been provided in an internal Bank of Canada memo of January 1949, which was the first within the bank to advocate a floating exchange rate.[72] The author of this memo is unnamed, but it has been attributed to James Coyne who would soon become governor of the bank in 1955. The memo noted that changes in the value of the Canadian dollar played an important role in helping the Canadian economy to adjust to changing US economic conditions. If the US experienced deflation or a recession, for example, the memo noted that "it would almost certainly be necessary for the Canadian exchange rate to decline in order to facilitate whatever adjustments might be necessary in the Canadian economy, assuming it would continue to be an object of policy to maintain reasonable full employment in Canada." But if the exchange rate was fixed, the necessary change in the exchange rate might not happen because the government could find its decision subject to political pressures: "whatever might be the expert opinion, action would be affected by the state of public opinion and by the state of Government inertia. And if and when action were taken, it would be regarded, correctly, as a deliberate act of policy which would find many critics."[73] The introduction of a floating exchange rate would, Coyne implied, help avoid this difficulty.

This desire to "depoliticize" the exchange rate issue in 1950 was not a new one. As we saw in the last chapter, Canadian policy-makers had seen a floating rate during the 1930s as a way to insulate themselves from the domestic political struggles that could be unleashed by deliberate exchange rate adjustments. When the exchange rate had been fixed in 1939, its value had also been chosen carefully to avoid a divisive domestic debate. Canadian policy-makers then resisted further changes during the war for fear of arousing domestic political debate. For example, when capital inflows in 1943 led some to believe the US would press for a revaluation of the Canadian dollar, Rasminsky argued against any exchange rate change on the grounds that it "would lead to sectional difficulties." He told Canadian officials to remind their US counterparts of "the difficulties connected with deliberately choosing a low sterling rate; the possible political debate between East and West which would follow; and the dangers involved in letting the exchange rate become a political football."[74] A year later, there had been considerable debate about whether the dollar should be revalued to par with the US dollar. Although many in the government favoured the move, it was again rejected for fear of political opposition from the Western provinces.[75]

The experiences with exchange rate adjustments after the war only reinforced the point that deliberate exchange rate changes could be politically controversial. The 1946 appreciation had created political difficulties for the federal government not just because it had subsequently been blamed for the 1947 balance of payments crisis. It had also provoked opposition in Newfoundland at a sensitive time when the British colony was considering joining the Canadian federation. The colony had long used Canadian currency, and Newfoundland exporters – especially in the fish sector – complained that the Canadian dollar's appreciation hurt their export earnings. The move rekindled discussions that had taken place since the 1930s about whether Newfoundland would be better served with an independent currency.[76]

The 1949 devaluation had also generated considerable debate within Canada. While some favoured an even larger devaluation for competitive reasons, others – including the powerful minister of reconstruction, C.D. Howe – had strongly opposed any depreciation on the grounds that it would increase the price of imported machinery.[77] True to historical pattern, Canadian officials chose to lower the Canadian dollar by a value that left the currency's value between that of the US dollar and sterling.

As we have seen, this fear of unleashing domestic political battles over exchange rate questions was clearly at the front of Abbott's mind at the time of the float.[78] And it continued to provide a justification for a "free float" throughout the 1950s, as one internal 1957 memo within the Bank of Canada by J.F. Parkinson (who was Rasminsky's alternate as Canada's executive director in the IMF) made very clear:

there can be no rate of exchange which can simultaneously satisfy the requirements of all the separate economic groups in the country. No given rate of exchange could be regarded as "ideal" to such separate groups as: exporters, importers, industries meeting foreign competition, consumers, tourists, shipping interests, firms borrowing abroad or investing abroad, institutions paying interest on debt held abroad or redeeming foreign debt, etc., etc. The choice of any specific rate of exchange, or the decision to raise or lower the market rate must mean a decision to favour or discriminate against some of these groups ... The appropriate character of the chosen rate [if a fixed rate was adopted] would be a matter of public and Parliamentary concern and discussion. Conflicting representations would probably be put forward as to the rightness and wrongness of the target rate, based upon the separate interests of various regional and other economic groups concerned. Exchange rate policy might well become a matter of public controversy, as it was between 1946 and 1950. There is nothing wrong with this, of course, but the disadvantages are obvious.[79]

Rejecting Tighter Capital Controls

But the desire to depoliticize the exchange rate does not provide a full account of the 1950 decision. It leaves unanswered the question of why the Canadian government rejected the IMF staff's advice to tighten Canadian capital controls as a way of coping with the crisis. If the government discouraged capital inflows with controls, IMF officials pointed out that there would be no need to change the value of the Canadian dollar.[80] In his presentation to the IMF Executive Board, Rasminsky gave three reasons why the Canadian government rejected this advice.

To begin with, he argued "from the technical standpoint it would impose a tremendous, if not impossible, administrative burden on the Foreign Exchange Control Board in determining what inward movement of capital to license."[81] Bernstein had argued that Canada should be able to curtail the bulk of the capital inflows by restricting the sale of Canadian government securities to US nationals through a licensing system. Another IMF staff member noted that Canada could force banks to hold 100 per cent reserves against deposits created from acquiring US dollars.[82] But Rasminsky remained unconvinced, arguing that it was extremely difficult in the Canadian context to distinguish between speculative and "productive" capital inflows: "The attempt to distinguish between what money would be desirable for productive investment would, in the Canadian situation, be impossible to exercise for one shades imperceptibly into the other. What about trading in outstanding securities? I believe we would put ourselves in an extremely difficult if not impossible situation."[83]

Second, Rasminsky noted that controls on capital inflows "might place Canada in a position of creating an atmosphere of hostility toward American capital through administrative action. This Canada did not wish to do, particularly in view of the economic expansion it faced and the need for outside capital to finance continued development."[84] This concern not to alienate American investors and US corporations had in fact been very prominent throughout the short history of Canada's exchange control regime. Very soon after the introduction of controls in 1939, the government had emphasized that there would be no restrictions on income earned from Canadian securities by non-residents and profit remittances from US subsidiaries in Canada. As Clark explained in 1940, "Canada has tried to conduct its affairs, even under the extraordinary pressures of the present war, in such a way as to continue to be worthy of the confidence of foreign investors."[85] Even when capital inflows from the US in 1943 threatened to increase Canada's foreign exchange reserves beyond limits agreed to with the US, Rasminsky had argued against controlling them partly on the grounds that this would involve "breaking the link with American security markets which may be very useful to us post-war."[86] In the postwar years, this same attitude continued, and Canada's Foreign Exchange Control Act of 1946 empowered the government to control only the export of capital, not its import. Implementing the kinds of controls advocated by the IMF would thus have marked a sharp break from past practice and would have undermined the goal of trying to attract US investment. It was not realistic, Rasminsky told the IMF staff, "to shut off the flow of US capital and to hope that the tap could be turned on again at some future date. It would be most difficult to maintain friendly rules towards one group of capital exporters and to maintain hostile rules against other groups."[87]

Finally, Rasminsky noted that "the temper of opinion in Canada and in the Government was against direct controls or interference."[88] This statement was an interesting one. During negotiations leading up to Bretton Woods, government officials had been very supportive of the view that capital controls had a central role to play in preserving postwar exchange rate stability and national policy autonomy.[89] And indeed at the end of the war, they maintained foreign exchange controls for the purpose of controlling capital flows, arguing that Canada was particularly vulnerable to capital flight because of its debtor status and the fact that a large portion of Canadian securities were held by US residents. As Finance Minister Ilsley put it in 1946: "We cannot leave ourselves in a position where our choice of domestic economic policies has to be influenced by the consideration that one policy or another may lead to capital withdrawal by foreigners or capital flight by Canadians."[90] In the same year, Towers echoed this view: "I fail to see how, in the existing state of world affairs, a commitment can be taken to maintain exchange rate stability with the sword of uncontrolled capital movements hanging over our head."[91]

But this decision to maintain foreign exchange controls encountered much stronger domestic opposition than similar ones in other countries at the time. When the Liberal government introduced the 1946 Foreign Exchange Control Act, it met stiff resistance from the opposition Conservative Party as well as from many Liberals, resistance which forced the government to accept a three-year time limit on the bill.[92] When the act was renewed in 1949 for two more years, the opposition intensified. Enthusiasm for controls was also clearly waning in the government by this time. When the Canadian dollar was devalued in 1949, a Canadian official noted that one reason the prime minister supported the move was that "we wish ultimately to get rid of the exchange controls. If we do not move the rate we shall put off the day of relaxation still further."[93]

What was the case against exchange controls? Some Conservative MPs critiqued them on the broad ideological grounds that they were "totalitarian" and reminiscent of the practices of Hitler's Germany or Stalin's Russia.[94] In the words of the Conservative finance critic J.M. Macdonnell, "we should not consider them [foreign exchange controls] merely as powers which are exercised by amiable and pleasant gentlemen who have shown great discrimination and moderation in the use of them, but as powers which may not always be exercised by those same pleasant gentlemen, which may sometime get into the hands of people we may not find so agreeable and so pleasant and who may find these powers most convenient for purposes of their own."[95] Conservative MP John Diefenbaker even reminded parliament that Hayek's recently published *The Road to Serfdom* had described foreign exchange controls as "the complete delivery of the individual to the tyranny of the state, the final suppression of all means of escape – not merely for the rich but for everybody."[96] To defenders of the foreign exchange controls, these arguments seemed overblown. As one CCF MP put it, "There must of necessity be certain restrictions in this and other lands if we are to have any freedom at all. Apparently what my honourable friend regards as freedom is a thing which has robbed most people in this country of any freedom at all."[97]

The more influential arguments against foreign exchange controls highlighted the more practical costs they imposed. We have already heard Rasminsky's concern that the controls discouraged American investment. Macdonnell reiterated this point: "as long as we have this situation where people put their money in and have it impounded, then we shall have a brake on investment."[98] Another argument was that foreign exchange controls were "a frightful nuisance to a businessman and to individuals," particularly in the context of the close commercial ties between Canadians and Americans. As Conservative MP Jackman put it, "The board seems to think that business men have no more to do than to sit in their offices and fill out forms."[99] Opposition in business circles stemmed not just from the inconvenience of having to fill out various forms. Plumptre noted that opposition to foreign exchange controls was in fact concentrated in Montreal and Toronto business circles, particularly among those involved in the financial sector whose business in cross-border securities trading was inhibited by controls: "It is not surprising that people who make their living by providing the country with a market for securities, both within the country and abroad, lose patience with the controls and the controllers and want to get rid of both."[100] Highlighting another concern of the financial community, Jackman noted how the controls were preventing Canada from becoming a substantial international financial centre in a broader sense: "May I point out that already Canada has become the third or fourth largest trading nation in the world and the amount of foreign exchange bills resulting from that trading is substantial. But these bills are now all cleared through New York, and a commission is paid to those engaged in financial business in that centre. If we were able to do without control in this country there is the possibility that just as other centres in Europe such as Paris, Brussels and Berlin did at the time when London was the paramount financial centre, so we might on this continent become a financial centre of some importance, and thereby add to our national income."[101]

If a fixed exchange rate could only be maintained with foreign exchange controls, many Conservative politicians began to question whether this exchange rate regime was worth the price. As early as 1947, one Conservative MP argued that, if a stable currency could be achieved only by "depriving people of this country of the control of their property, and as a result, of their movements ... then I am opposed to a stabilized exchange."[102] By 1949, Macdonnell was attacking the government's "fixation with fixing," arguing that the currency's value should be "decided, not by the judgment of this person or that person, but by the only financial judgment – the state of trade throughout the world. Unless this happens we shall just sink deeper and deeper into a mass of controls."[103] The same view began to surface within government policy-making circles. Coyne's internal January 1949 memo that first advocated a floating rate highlighted how this exchange rate regime would diminish the need for tight exchange controls, a development that in turn might help the goal of attracting US investment which he saw as crucial for Canada's ability to promote growth in the coming years: "A freely moving rate would reduce the psychological atmosphere of restrictionism and control, particularly in the eyes of non-residents, and would almost certainly make non-residents more interested in the idea of investing capital in Canada, both short-term and long-term and both in securities and in direct business enterprises."[104]

Questioning of the Bretton Woods Case for Fixed Rates

These last arguments were particularly interesting because they highlighted how the idea of a floating exchange rate had begun to attract a number of domestic advocates in advance of the 1950 decision. Although the Conservative Party had backed the Bretton Woods Agreement when it was signed, its members began to reevaluate their support for its exchange rate rules in light of Canada's experiences since the war. By the time of the 1949 election, the Conservative Party was even calling for the introduction of some kind of a floating exchange rate in its election promises.[105] Its case for a floating exchange rate was not just that it would enable a relaxation or elimination of foreign exchange controls. Many Conservative politicians had also begun to argue that a floating exchange rate would allow market forces to determine the value of the Canadian dollar in ways that encouraged more appropriate and timely adjustments in the balance of payments. After the 1949 devaluation, one Conservative MP summarized this case well: "If we had not retained foreign exchange controls after the war there would have been no problem of devaluation harshly and ruthlessly confronting Canadian industry overnight. Our dollar would have been fluctuating in accordance with the balance of our import and export trade, and would have been regulating that balance automatically from day to day."[106] In the same manner, Jackman argued that a floating exchange rate would "bring about self-righting devices which are good for any country, and which are even necessary, because if a correction does not take place at the appropriate and natural time, then the correction will very likely have to take place at a subsequent and perhaps much more painful time."[107] Similar arguments in favour of a floating exchange rate were also put forward by Coyne within the Bank of Canada: "it is preferable to have a natural [exchange] rate which could move up and down from time to time as economic conditions might require."[108]

Figures within the business community had also begun to press for a floating exchange rate for the same reasons. Like Conservative politicians, the business community had been largely supportive of the Bretton Woods agreements in 1944. This had even been true of members of the Canadian banking community such as Hackett who had refused to back Williams's key currency plan on the grounds that it would promote bilateralism.[109] But by the late 1940s, the views of business had begun to change.

As early as October 1947, the president of the Robert Simpson Company had written privately to the prime minister that a floating rate would foster appropriate balance of payments adjustments:

I believe the artificial values of various currencies have had an effect opposite to that it was hoped to bring about. Whereas it has been confidently hoped that rapid recoveries would be made if the various currencies were stabilized, actually the artificial situation created by such "stabilization" has hindered international transactions and has resulted in a crisis which only radical revaluation of currencies can correct ... Some exchange variations will no doubt in some respects respond to wise measures of control in both countries affected in any given transaction. The situations with which we are now faced, however, are too complex and intricate to find their solutions in control measures alone.

He had also noted one further rationale that recalled Bryce's earlier point that exchange rate movements could be used to offset higher domestic production costs: "If our policy in respect to the value of the Canadian dollar were realistic we could then afford to meet any reasonable demand of labour for higher wages."[110]

By the time the floating rate was introduced in 1950, Muirhead reports Canadian businesses widely welcomed it: "business leaders were overwhelmingly convinced that the country should not repeg the dollar under existing conditions. Many in fact felt it desirable to have the rates of all, or at least most, countries fluctuating freely *vis-à-vis* one another in a permanent system."[111] This business support for the float was striking given that they knew the float would generate an appreciation of the Canadian currency which could hurt their competitive position. But, because of the booming US market at the time, those in the tradable sector were not terribly concerned about this implication. As one Bank of England official reported after a trip to Canada in the fall of 1950: "There is considerable confidence in the ability of Canadian exports to hold their present position in the U.S. markets ... There seemed to be an assured market for everything that Canadian industry could make."[112]

Why were these supporters of a floating exchange rate not more concerned about the broader potential drawbacks of such a monetary regime? After all, almost all economists at the time of the Bretton Woods conference believed that the experience of the 1930s had entirely discredited floating exchange rate regimes. This exchange rate regime was associated with competitive devaluations, currency instability, and disequilibrating speculative financial flows. But the Canadian experience with floating in the 1930s had been different from that of many other countries. The floating rate had not been deliberately manipulated by Canadian policy-makers to bolster national competitiveness. Its value had also been remarkably stable throughout the decade after the 1931–33 depreciation. Perhaps most significantly, Canadian policy-makers associated the "free float" of the 1930s with *equilibrating* capital flows. As we saw in the last chapter, Towers noted that episodes of capital flight were quickly ended when the floating currency depreciated, thus lowering the price of Canadian securities and ending the panic selling. Even as late as 1938, Towers was arguing that capital exports could be stopped through a devaluation of the Canadian currency in the event of war.[113]

It was this experience that domestic advocates of a floating exchange rate – both Conservatives and those in the government – drew upon in advancing their case.[114] Rasminsky did the same when he was given the task of defending Canada's decision to IMF officials. When Bernstein predicted that Canada's decision to float would encourage more destabilizing speculative capital flows, Rasminsky replied that this had not been the case for most of the 1930s: "this course of action is not new and unknown, and in the past it has not caused evil consequences."[115] Indeed, supporters of the float argued that it would reduce speculative capital flows by ending the kind of one-way speculative bets that were encouraged under a fixed but adjustable exchange rate regime. As W.A. Mackintosh put it, "Any renewed pressure of capital imports, speculative or otherwise, will be met by the elastic resistance of a moving rate which will reduce the prospect of speculative gain. There will no longer be an authority accommodating enough to hold the new rate so that the speculator may withdraw his capital and realize his gains."[116]

In making these arguments, Canadian advocates of floating rates were breaking new ground in challenging the assumptions of the Bretton Woods architects. While some advocates were careful to argue that their advocacy of a floating rate was only applicable to the distinct circumstances of Canada, others launched a full assault on the Bretton Woods fixation with stable exchange rates.[117] These arguments in favour of a floating rate were in fact very similar to those put forward by Milton Friedman a few years later in his famous 1953 article that is widely cited as the first prominent case for floating exchange rates in the postwar period.[118] Friedman himself claims to have influenced the Canadian debate through his advocacy of floating in an April 1948 radio debate with Mackintosh and the deputy governor of the Bank of Canada, Donald Gordon: "Apparently, this was the first time that Donald Gordon ... had ever heard this solution put forward seriously and he and I had a vigorous argument about it. This discussion played a major role in the adoption of floating rates by Canada on September 30, 1950."[119]

Friedman overstates his influence not just because a number of Canadians had already been advocating for a floating rate before this debate. Equally important, the government's decision to float the currency in 1950 did not necessarily reflect the fact that it had been entirely convinced by these economic arguments in favour of floating.[120] To be sure, we have seen that some officials in the Bank of Canada shared these views. But they were viewed a little more skeptically by the most influential policy-makers – particularly Towers and Rasminsky – who were nervous about the prospects for currency instability in a floating regime. When the currency was floated, the government initially retained the exchange control regime for this reason. As Towers made clear in a memo at the time, he worried about the fact that Canada might be vulnerable to large swings in capital movements: "I do not dare to recommend the abolition of exchange control ... Without controls, we are fully exposed to the vagaries of U.S. investors."[121]

These fears about a floating exchange rate had also been clearly voiced outside the government in advance of the 1950 decision. Politicians on the left, for example, opposed floating and the abolition of foreign exchange controls on the grounds that "money and exchange should not be left to be gambling instruments for anybody."[122] Social Credit MPs shared this view, as MP Victor Quelch highlighted: "To my mind the only people who have any need to fear a foreign exchange control board are those who indulge in speculation in foreign exchange ... The people who make a living by gambling in foreign exchange will be opposed to the measure because the only thing they do is for themselves and not for the good of the country."[123]

In the end, however, these fears about currency instability proved unfounded. After appreciating to just above par with the US dollar by early 1952, the rate fluctuated between $1.02 and $1.06 from 1952 until the end of 1960, a pattern that some noted was in fact more stable than the Canadian dollar's movement during the previous five years of the "fixed" rate (see Figure 3).[124] As one Bank of Canada official concluded by 1954: "Movements in the rate have taken place slowly in a broad market, and this, together with the development of adequate forward exchange facilities, has reduced the problem of rate uncertainties to negligible proportions. Certainly the risk of exchange rate fluctuations has not had any apparent adverse effects on the growth of Canada's foreign trade in the past three years."[125]

It is important to note that the stability of the exchange rate was not a product of government intervention in the currency market, which was very limited in this period.[126] It was also not influenced by the government's foreign exchange controls. Indeed, the government chose to abolish the country's foreign exchange control system in December 1951. In addition to leaving several hundred employees out of work, the decision made Canada the first IMF member to abandon an existing foreign exchange control regime.[127] The decision reflected not just the government's recognition that the feared destabilizing capital movements had failed to materialize. Towers and Rasminsky also

Figure 3
Canadian dollar in terms of US dollar and pound sterling, 1945–62
US$ monthly rates; sterling avg. annual rates 1945–49

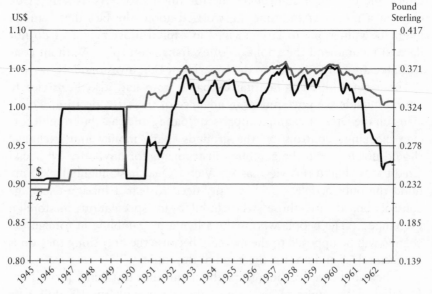

Source: Statistics Canada/Bank of Canada

worried that the decisions of the FECB might become increasingly inconsistent as controls were loosened and officials had more discretionary power.[128] Their most interesting rationale for abolishing the controls, however, was that the floating exchange rate could now regulate capital outflows just as effectively as formal controls. As Rasminsky put it, "It would seem to be more prudent to allow an increase in the premium on the American dollar to exert its influence on reducing capital withdrawals rather than to employ direct methods."[129] This argument resurrected the point Towers had made in the late 1930s that capital flows in and out of Canada had tended to be equilibrating in a floating exchange rate regime.

Indeed, Bank of Canada officials soon noted that the reemergence of equilibrating capital flows of the kind that had existed in the 1930s was in fact one of the major benefits of the floating rate system in the Canadian context. By contrast, they noted that capital flows had tended to be disequilibrating during the period when the exchange rate had been fixed between 1939 and 1950.[130] This lesson – that floating produced equilibrating capital flows – was the exact opposite of that put forward at Bretton Woods. Its advancement by Rasminsky highlighted the extent to which Canadian policy-makers increasingly embraced not just the political but also the economic case for floating. During the interwar period, equilibrating capital flows had been associated with the large volume of outstanding public and private sector optional payment bonds. By the 1950s, large numbers of these bonds had been retired, but the enormous cross-border trade in securities continued, now focused primarily on outstanding Canadian government bonds.

A Sympathetic International Environment

To explain the 1950 move to a floating exchange rate, one final influence deserves mention: the international political context. As noted above, Canada's decision formally contravened the IMF Articles of Agreement. For this reason, Canadian policy-makers recognized the importance of receiving some form of international endorsement of the move. Even the strong advocates of a floating rate in the Conservative Party suggested that Canada should first push for a change in IMF rules before this exchange rate regime was introduced.[131] The IMF decision to endorse Belgium's request for a temporary float a year earlier (a float that in the end only lasted two days) proved to be a key development. Although Rasminsky had opposed this endorsement, he also recognized at that time that it changed the domestic political context in Canada:

I saw Gutt [the IMF managing director] this morning and told him that I wanted him to know that I was worried about the repercussions of this decision in Canada. I reminded him that the question of fluctuating vs. stable exchange rates had been an election issue and had come up at various times in Parliament, and that the Minister of Finance had stated that fluctuating exchange rates were incompatible with our obligations under the Fund Agreement. He was now confronted with a formal decision by the Fund, in the case of Belgium, praising the adoption of fluctuating exchange rates and not indicating any incompatibility with the Fund Agreement ... I said that so far as I was now concerned, I could no longer advise the Canadian Government against any course of action on the ground that it was inconsistent with the provisions of the Fund Agreement.[132]

Still, Canadian officials went to considerable lengths to ensure that international support existed for their policy change before it was made. A few weeks in advance of the 1950 Canadian decision, Rasminsky approached Gutt at the annual IMF/World Bank meetings and found him sympathetic to the arguments for a float.[133] Particularly important was the task of assuring US support for the move. To this end, Rasminsky held meetings with US Treasury Secretary Snyder and US IMF representative Frank Southard in advance of the Canadian decision. At the key IMF meeting, the US did back the Canadian position (although Southard insisted that US support for floating was based on the assumption that this was a transition to a fixed rate[134]). This support – which was echoed by some other key countries such as Britain, the Netherlands, and France – guaranteed that the IMF simply agreed to take note of the Canadian decision rather than oppose it.[135]

What explained the US support? The Belgian precedent played a role: Rasminsky reports that Gutt told him on 9 September that "he did not see how the United States could oppose in view of their favorable attitude in the Belgian case."[136] Based on interviews conducted in Washington at the time, one analyst reported confidentially to the Canadian government that the US Treasury had in fact been supportive of the idea of floating rates in selected circumstances – particularly for currencies experiencing upward pressure – "for nearly three years."[137] In the Canadian case (as well as more generally as we shall see below), he noted that US officials saw the decision to float as a move that would help relax import and foreign exchange restrictions, as well as eliminate the unofficial rate for Canadian dollars that existed in New York.

The veracity of his report was reinforced by the comments of Southard at the key IMF Executive Board meeting that approved the Canadian decision. As Rasminsky noted, Southard argued that a floating rate was preferable to the IMF suggestion of tightening capital controls: "He shared the reluctance of the Canadian government to attempt the control of capital inflow before trying the expedient of a floating rate ... He did not think that the close capital relationships between the two countries should be tested by trying to turn off and on the beneficial capital spigots."[138] Capital controls were cumbersome for the large and growing number of US multinationals located in Canada. New York bankers also strongly welcomed the Canadian decision on the same grounds. Echoing the comments of Canadian proponents of the float, the *Wall Street Journal*'s editorial went further to argue that the decision highlighted the failure of the IMF to impose artificial stability.[139]

Rasminsky himself helped encourage US officials to see the float in this positive manner. He reminded Snyder that the Canadian decision would allow a loosening not just of capital controls but also the import controls and travel restrictions imposed during the 1947 balance of payments crisis. Indeed, when the government announced the float, it also announced that it would be removing all remaining import restrictions that had been introduced in 1947. It would also end the unofficial exchange rate that had existed in New York, thereby enabling "Americans in a position to withdraw capital from Canada to do so at the same exchange rate as is applied to all transactions."[140] In these ways, Rasminsky argued that Canada's floating currency would support the broader goals of the Fund, which were to promote convertible currencies and multilateral trade.

The objective of fostering Canadian trade liberalization was one that had attracted considerable attention in US policy-making circles at the time. In the wake of Canada's 1947 balance of payments crisis, US officials had secretly met with their Canadian counterparts to discuss a possible bilateral free trade deal – a deal that fell through when Canadian prime minister Mackenzie King backed away from endorsing it in 1948.[141] After this, the idea remained alive; in the summer of 1950, for example, US-based economist Michael Heilperin published a prominent article in the Canadian Institute for International Affairs's *International Journal* proposing a bilateral trade deal that would include not just trade liberalization but also the abolition of Canada's exchange controls. Because the abolition of its exchange controls would leave Canada vulnerable to balance of payments crises, Heilperin suggested that this deal would have to be accompanied by "a set of agreements which would come very close to establishing a monetary union between the two countries." He had in mind the creation of a joint board that "would aim at harmonizing the monetary policies of both countries" as well as an arrangement under which the US would agree "to hold indefinite balances of Canadian dollars, thereby forestalling any fears Canada might experience concerning a dollar shortage on currency account or a flight of capital from Canada to the United States."[142] Although Rasminsky and others made no reference to this proposal, they demonstrated a few months later that the floating of Canada's currency was in fact a much simpler way of fostering closer Canada-US economic ties.

Finally, US officials also felt that a floating Canadian dollar might help depoliticize the issue of the Canadian dollar–US dollar exchange rate within US politics. As noted above, an obvious alternative to a float would have been to repeg the Canadian dollar at a higher level, perhaps at parity with the US dollar. But Southard had advised Snyder that this option held some domestic political risks. As reported by

Rasminsky, he had said "that looking at the matter from an exclusively American standpoint the floating rate was preferable to parity. Parity, in his judgment, would have been regarded as more of a reflection on the U.S. dollar and as indicating a desire of the Canadians, 'our best friends,' to exploit the defence effort of the United States by getting better terms of trade."[143] Indeed, even when the floating rate was introduced, US officials made a point of telling the US press that "there is no suspicion that Canada is trying to take advantage of the United States defense effort."[144]

Canadian officials also recognized that the task of managing an adjustable peg could raise complications in the Canada-US relationship. If, for example, Canada tried to maintain the peg by accumulating foreign exchange reserves, Towers noted that the country's reserve levels would undermine its bargaining power with the US on issues such as defense production sharing and Canada's right to use tariffs to offset its deficit with the US.[145] The 1949 devaluation had also shown how complicated the process of repegging the exchange rate could be. In advance of the devaluation, the Canadian government had felt obliged to consult extensively with US – and British – officials. Although the US ultimately accepted the case for the 9 per cent devaluation, the process of consultation was cumbersome and provided US officials with opportunities to raise various other issues.[146]

If the US had a number of reasons to support Canada's 1950 decision to float, why did this support continue? When the IMF's executive board had decided not to oppose Canada's float at its September 1950 meeting, Rasminsky had assured the IMF that Canada hoped to return to a fixed exchange rate soon.[147] When the country did not do so, he was forced throughout the 1950s to continue to justify Canada's floating rate to the IMF. On these occasions, he reiterated his earlier arguments, reminding the executive board that Canada's floating rate had allowed the country to liberalize its trade and exchange controls and thus left it further ahead of most countries in meeting the IMF's overall goals of non-discrimination and convertibility – especially after Canada's exchange controls were abolished in December 1951. He also noted that Canada's experience had proven that a floating rate could be quite stable and that it would indeed curtail speculative capital inflows in the ways that had been predicted.[148] When sometimes pressed on the question of why Canada was not tightening capital controls, he continued to reject this option (sometimes with unusual arguments such as that in

1951 when he "questioned whether the manpower necessary to enforce such controls could be spared at this time of high employment"[149]).

These rationales were accepted by the US and other IMF members. By 1956, De Vries reports that the IMF had largely ceased to be concerned with Canada's float.[150] When the country's exchange rate regime became more controversial in the early 1960s, some policy-makers looked back to the 1950s with fondness and amazement. As Canada's finance minister in the early 1960s, Donald Fleming, put it in his memoirs: "Why the IMF tolerated this condition from 1950 to 1962 I will never understand. We simply 'got away with it' for twelve years."[151] In the early 1960s, one Bank of Canada official speculated that Canada's trading partners did not have a particular interest-based reason to object to the policy during the 1950s: "In a general world context of high employment and rapid growth, the Canadian dollar first appreciated against the U.S. dollar, then followed a relatively level course. Other countries had no grounds for seeing in the Canadian action a threat to their levels of exports, incomes and employment; in practice, such effect as there may have been was in the other direction."[152]

But Canada's float was also accepted because many US and IMF officials agreed with Rasminsky's arguments. Even Bernstein appeared to have been persuaded as early as January 1952. In discussing the European context at the time, he wrote a memo that endorsed temporary floating exchange rates on the grounds that they would encourage a lowering of trade restrictions and allow "natural" market pressures to accommodate balance of payments strains.[153] The memo was written at a time when British policy-makers were also considering the introduction of a float for reasons that were similar to those of Canadian policy-makers: it would allow Britain to eliminate exchange controls and loosen trade restrictions, as well as help the country maintain policy autonomy.[154] Although the idea was ultimately opposed by the British cabinet (particularly on the grounds that a floating rate would undermine sterling's position as an international currency), it is worth noting that the US Treasury was once again willing to endorse it.[155] In discussing Bernstein's memo in February 1952, Treasury officials supported its ideas and noted that they would *not* oppose requests from foreign countries to float, although they acknowledged that it was "unwise to announce in advance of requests to the Fund the receptiveness of the United States to proposals for the use of floating rates, or even to make this position known informally within the government." In October

1952, Southard confirmed in an internal memo that the US Treasury felt "our basic policy must and does admit the right of countries to adopt flexible rates under appropriate conditions."[156]

CONCLUSION

In the context of Canadian exchange rate policy during the twentieth century, the commitment of Canadian policy-makers to a fixed exchange rate between 1939 and 1950 was unusual. As we have seen, it emerged initially from a very practical concern about exchange rate instability in a wartime context and it was made possible by the introduction of wartime exchange controls. By the early 1940s, however, Canadian policy-makers had become strong supporters of the initiative to create a new postwar international monetary order that had a fixed exchange rate system at its core. This enthusiasm even led them to reject the key currency plan which would have enabled Canada to preserve the exchange rate flexibility it had embraced in the 1930s and would soon seek again in 1950.

As we have seen, Canadian support for the Bretton Woods regime stemmed primarily from a broader interest in seeing Britain and the US cooperate in building a more open multilateral world economy in which the Canadian economy could once again flourish. The country's willingness to sign on to the specific Bretton Woods provisions relating to exchange rate stability was, in other words, somewhat instrumental. Indeed, during the Bretton Woods negotiations, there were already signs that the Canadian support for a fixed exchange rate was tentative. Not only did Canadian negotiators push for an agreement that maximized their freedom to adjust the Canadian exchange rate – a freedom they quickly took advantage of in 1946 and 1949 – but they also expressed frustration with their cumbersome exchange controls that helped to maintain a fixed exchange rate.

Canadian enthusiasm for a fixed exchange rate proved short-lived. The 1950 decision to float surprised many observers at the time, but it is interesting that many of the reasons for the float were similar to those put forward during the interwar period. First, a floating exchange rate was seen as a useful tool for correcting balance of payments disequilibria. As in the 1930s, some argued that Canada's vulnerability to external shocks made this exchange rate regime particularly important for Canada. Others added the argument that a floating exchange rate could help compensate for changes in Canadian prices and wages.

Second, the float provided a way of preserving monetary policy autonomy in a context of capital mobility. During the Bretton Woods negotiations, Canadian policy-makers had suggested that they were willing to sacrifice capital mobility in order to reconcile their interest in monetary policy autonomy with their commitment to a fixed exchange rate. But when faced with the choice in 1950 of tightening capital controls or floating the currency, they chose the latter. It was a choice that Canadian policy-makers had made throughout the interwar period and one that Towers even anticipated in 1939 at the time of the introduction of exchange controls. In 1950, it reflected not just his and other policy-makers' desire for US investment but also widespread opposition to capital controls and exchange controls from the Canadian business community.[157]

Of course, Canadian policy-makers could have preserved both a fixed exchange rate and capital mobility if they had been willing to sacrifice monetary policy autonomy, as had been done under the gold standard. But no one seriously raised this option within Canada at the time. Canadian policy-makers embraced the commitment to monetary policy autonomy that Clark had put forward in the early 1930s in his defense of a floating rate. During the Bretton Woods negotiations, this commitment had in fact become much more ambitious as Canadian policy-makers expressed interest in more activist forms of domestic monetary management that would be designed to promote full employment. In practice, Canadian monetary policy remained quite passive in the early postwar years and the key concern of Canadian policy-makers in 1950 was very similar to that in the early 1930s: to insulate their country from monetary instability south of the border. While Clark had worried about importing US deflationary policies in the early 1930s, the fear in 1950 was of Canada's vulnerability to inflationary pressures emanating from the US. This concern to insulate Canada from US price movements remained a key rationale for the floating exchange rate throughout the 1950s.[158]

These two macroeconomic rationales for the float had first been put forward in Canadian policy-making circles by expert economists in the 1930s. Since that time, these experts had become even more influential in Canadian exchange rate policy-making. Visiting Canada in March 1951, one Bank of England official wrote privately about the existence of a kind of "Ottawa 'Brains Trust'" in which he included, among others, Towers, Clark, Rasminsky, Plumptre (then head of the economic division in the Department of External Affairs) and Bryce (then assistant deputy minister of finance). He described them as follows: "My first general impression was of the extraordinarily high quality of the

'Brains Trust.' The atmosphere is slightly academic but, nevertheless, very real and quite different from what I had experienced in Washington. Continuity in political direction over the last fifteen years has left the Bank of Canada and the top level Civil Servants relatively free from the major preoccupations over internal political questions."[159]

While they had considerable leeway to determine Canadian policy vis-à-vis exchange rates, their autonomy should not be overstated. We have noted the importance of business support for the decision to float in 1950. Equally important, we have also seen how Canadian policy-makers continued to fear the domestic political struggles that could be unleashed by deliberate exchange rate adjustments. Their desire to "de-politicize" the exchange rate as an issue in Canadian politics provided an important rationale for the float, as it had in the 1930s.

During the interwar period, support for a floating exchange rate had also been bolstered by the fact that this exchange rate regime was not associated with much currency instability. The memory of this interwar experience was also important in generating support for the 1950 decision. Since this experience with a floating exchange rate did not accord with the conventional Bretton Woods view of the interwar years, it gave strength to Canadian critics of the Bretton Woods exchange rate system. Their arguments helped to pave the way for the 1950 decision by making the option of floating more intellectually respectable. Although key policy-makers were not entirely convinced of these arguments at the time of this decision, they became more so once the experience of floating seemed to prove the arguments correct.

If political support for the float was similar to that in the interwar period in these various respects, one final political factor accounting for the 1950 decision needs to be mentioned: the importance of US support. Since Canada's decision to float broke IMF rules, Canada needed international support for this move in a way that was not true in the pre-1939 period. The US provided this support because US officials agreed with their Canadian counterparts that a floating exchange rate was preferable to the maintenance of exchange and capital controls. Both Canadian and US policy-makers also saw the float as a tool for resolving payments imbalances between the two countries in a manner that did not require complicated bilateral political negotiations. Not until Canada began to pursue a deliberate competitive depreciation strategy in 1961–62 did the US finally begin to demand that Canada abide by the Bretton Woods rules and reestablish a fixed rate, as we shall see in the next chapter.

CHAPTER FOUR

From Fixed back to Floating Again: 1962–1985

Although Canada's decision to float its exchange rate in 1950 was presented initially as only a temporary one, this exchange regime remained in place for twelve long years. In 1962, however, the country rejoined the Bretton Woods exchange rate regime. This chapter begins by highlighting how the decision to peg the Canadian currency to the US dollar did not reflect a long or careful reevaluation of the costs and benefits of a fixed exchange rate regime among Canadian policy-makers. Instead, it was taken in a very hurried fashion in response to a foreign exchange crisis and was designed primarily to restore the confidence of financial markets.

Then, from this inauspicious birth came only a short life. There were already discussions about abandoning the peg by 1968, and two years later Canadian policy-makers restored a floating exchange rate. As with its 1950 decision, Canada's move to a floating rate in 1970 was a bold one in an international context. It contravened the IMF Articles of Agreement and it provoked considerable foreign anger once again. As in 1950, Canadian officials stuck to their decision and the US ultimately backed them. Between 1970 and the start of the negotiations in 1985 that led to the Canada-US Free Trade Agreement, the float was then never seriously questioned in Canadian policy-making circles. But Canadian officials no longer accepted a pure "free float" as they had for most of the interwar and 1950–62 periods. Instead, they often tried to influence the currency's value through foreign exchange intervention and changes in domestic monetary policy. Despite this difference, the second half of this chapter shows how the floating exchange rate regime was supported for two main reasons that were reminiscent of those in previous eras: it bolstered monetary autonomy in the context of financial openness and it facilitated balance of payments adjustments.

THE MOVE BACK TO A FIXED RATE IN 1962

The Canadian government's decision to peg the Canadian dollar in May 1962 came roughly one year after it had launched a strategy of deliberately driving down the value of the floating Canadian dollar. This strategy reflected its frustration with the Bank of Canada's tight monetary policy at the time. The bank had begun to raise interest rates after the mid-1950s, adopting an increasingly aggressive anti-inflationary stance. This policy shift was closely associated with the preferences of James Coyne, who had replaced Towers as governor in 1955. While Towers had generally resisted the use of high interest rates to contain inflation, Coyne – who had become disillusioned with Keynesianism – did not.[1] His anti-inflation policy marked the first time that the Bank of Canada had pursued this kind of activist interest rate policy in an environment of a floating exchange rate and open capital account regime.[2] The result was one familiar to students of open macroeconomic theory today: high interest rates attracted capital inflows which drove up the currency's value, thereby reinforcing the contractionary effects of the tight monetary policy as the tradable sector experienced new competitive pressures.

Although these causal links had not yet been formally modeled within the economic profession in the late 1950s,[3] they were increasingly drawn by Coyne's critics at the time. Canadian policy-makers, as well as many economists outside government, argued that the country's recession after 1957 and its growing trade deficit had been worsened by the high level of the Canadian dollar. And they highlighted how the high dollar – which reached a peak just above $1.06 in August 1957 – had been generated by capital inflows attracted by the Bank of Canada's tight monetary policy. If Coyne would only reduce interest rates, they implored, the country's economic prospects would be significantly brightened under the combined stimulus of these rate cuts and a lower dollar.

Coyne, however, who had little formal training in economics, was not willing to accept these arguments.[4] Because of his determination to control inflation, he refused to lower interest rates. He also called into question the link between capital inflows and his monetary policy stance. In a series of high profile speeches between late 1959 and early 1961, he argued that capital inflows had been encouraged by the country's trade deficit, as well as by government regulatory and tax policy that had been too friendly to foreign capital. In increasingly nationalist language, he called for inflows to be stemmed through regulatory changes that would lessen Canada's dependence on foreign borrowing and foreign corporations, and strengthen a more independent form of Canadian economic development.[5]

In his December 1960 budget, the Conservative finance minister Donald Fleming showed a willingness to discourage capital inflows by eliminating various exemptions that had enabled non-residents to avoid paying the full 15 per cent withholding tax on new Canadian securities. But he was not willing to go as far as Coyne's recommendation to discourage foreign capital through regulatory means. His own officials warned that more heavy-handed proposals might induce serious capital flight from Canada and make future borrowing abroad more difficult. In the words of Plumptre, who was now assistant deputy minister to Fleming, "we must also remember that capital inflow cannot be turned on and off at the will of the recipient country. This whole field needs a much lighter hand and more refined touch than Mr. Coyne seems to be disposed to apply to it." He went on to attack Coyne as "not only an ardent nationalist, but also an interventionist and protectionist."[6] Fleming was also clearly uncomfortable with Coyne's approach, worrying that discouragement of foreign investment would "produce a 'little Canada,' cut off from many of the contacts with the outside world that have enriched our national life."[7] When his limited moves had little impact, Fleming considered moral suasion, urging private banks on one occasion in May 1961 to reduce their foreign borrowing. But again the results were disappointing.[8]

Unable to persuade Coyne to lower interest rates and unwilling to control capital flows more vigorously, Fleming turned to the strategy of deliberately devaluing the dollar as a means of promoting economic recovery and addressing the country's trade deficit. The strategy was implemented primarily by talking down the dollar through public statements, beginning in June 1961.[9] This policy of deliberately depreciating the currency in a floating exchange rate regime was a novel one for Canadian policy-makers. Throughout the interwar years and in 1950–60, Canada's floating exchange rate regime had been a relatively "free float." Although the idea of deliberate depreciation had been discussed in the past, most notably by Plumptre and others in the 1930s, it had always been resisted. In opposing the government's decision, Coyne reiterated some of the earlier objections, arguing that the strategy was a "dangerous drug" and "sleight of hand" that would simply fuel inflation and leave unaddressed the core problems of the Canadian economy.[10]

Restoring Confidence

The government's policy proved to be short-lived. As some analysts had warned in the 1930s, what began as an orderly depreciation soon turned into a serious run on the currency and the government began to intervene in foreign exchange markets to *stem* the downward speculative pressures against the currency. The intervention became very extensive in April 1962 when speculation intensified dramatically, encouraged no doubt by the fact that a federal election campaign was underway in which the government was promising increased spending. Between October 1961 and the end of April 1962, the country's Exchange Fund had spent $500 million – or about one-quarter of its reserves – in defending the currency.[11]

With the currency entering a free fall (see Figure 3), Canadian policymakers turned to the idea of fixing the exchange rate as a way of restoring confidence and preventing further depreciation. The rationale was summed up well by Louis Rasminsky, who had become governor of the Bank of Canada in July 1961 (a position he would hold until 1973): "the best way to eliminate uncertainty was to declare a par value and create a situation where government was formally committed."[12] But this decision was hardly a unanimous one. At a crucial late April meeting, Fleming found that his senior officials in the Department of Finance could not agree on how best to respond to the foreign exchange crisis. He decided to back the idea of a currency peg, despite the fact that he had publicly rejected it earlier in the month on the grounds that the currency's fluctuations were not large and that the early postwar experience with a fixed rate had not been a positive one. The question of what rate to choose then immediately arose and the decision, once again, was taken in a hurried fashion. Fleming chose the rate of 92.5 cents simply as a compromise between the competing proposals of his advisers.[13]

He then presented the idea to Prime Minister Diefenbaker, who agreed to it only very reluctantly. Once cabinet had approved the idea at a 2 May meeting, Diefenbaker even changed his mind, believing that the decision to peg at 92.5 cents would contribute to his defeat in the election to be held on 18 June. He said later that he should have just let the currency continue to fall and "nobody would have cared."[14] In the end, he accepted the new fixed rate only because Fleming convinced him that it was too late to reverse the decision.[15] The decision to peg the currency did not in fact cost Diefenbaker the election; his party was re-elected, albeit with only a minority government. But he was right that the opposition Liberals did try to undermine the government by attacking the 92.5-cent dollar, labelling it the "Diefenbuck" during the election campaign.[16]

Although the currency had been fixed in order to re-establish confidence, this goal was not realized immediately. After Diefenbaker's re-election, pressure on the currency continued, and the government was forced by late June to consider further measures. One option was to abandon the fixed rate, but this was ultimately deemed too risky. The introduction of exchange controls was also discussed, but judged too impractical. In the end, the government adopted an emergency plan involving a combination of temporary tariffs, cuts to government spending, higher interest rates, and foreign loans from the US, IMF, and Bank of England.[17] With these measures, the crisis passed.

The argument that a fixed exchange rate could help restore the confidence of financial markets was an interesting one in light of the history we have examined. It called into question the frequently made case that a floating exchange rate was best suited to induce *equilibrating* capital movements in the Canadian context. To be sure, some analysts, such as Peter Cornell in the Bank of Canada, stuck to this position, opposing the idea of a fixed exchange rate on the grounds that it would likely encourage the kind of disequilibrating short-term capital movements that had characterized the 1945–50 period.[18] This line of argument, however, found few supporters in a period when a floating exchange rate was associated with increasingly disequilibrating capital flows. Not only had capital inflows between 1957 and 1961 exacerbated Canada's balance of payments difficulties by pushing the dollar up, but capital outflows had reinforced the currency crisis in the lead-up to the 1962 election.

Although the decision to fix was taken in a hurried fashion in the midst of a currency crisis, it was one that had attracted a growing number of important supporters during the previous year. As early as the summer of 1961, prominent Bank of Canada officials, including Rasminsky, had begun to favour it.[19] So too had Plumptre who explained his rationale in an August 1961 memo that was designed to lay the basis for a discussion of the issue with Fleming and Rasminsky. Already at that moment, even before the 1962 exchange rate crisis, he was arguing – as were Bank of Canada officials[20] – that a fixed exchange rate could help restore some stability in a context where confidence in Canada's economic situation had deteriorated: "I believe that there may be some advantages attaching to elements of stability and certainty in present economic and political circumstances which did not exist formerly. At present there is far more doubt and uncertainty about the pace and direction of Canada's economic growth than there was a few years ago. The fact that the U.K. is negotiating with the E.E.C. has recently added a new and important uncertainty regarding our future. The Canadian trading community might welcome a new element of certainty in regard to the exchange rate where they were formerly quite happy to put up with some uncertainty."[21]

Although Plumptre did not mention it explicitly, perhaps the most important source of uncertainty was the highly public and bitter dispute between Coyne and the government which had ended the previous month with the governor's resignation from the bank. The government had in fact demanded Coyne's resignation on 30 May 1961 and been initially refused. The government had justified its demand by pointing to a controversy over the details of Coyne's pension, but this specific dispute marked the culmination of the ongoing tense debate between Coyne and the government over the direction of Canadian monetary policy. Indeed, after the government's request for Coyne's resignation was initially turned down, Fleming pointedly introduced an expansionary budget and made his first public announcement of the new strategy to talk down the dollar. Coyne finally agreed to step down on July 14 only after a Senate committee had concluded that he had been involved in no wrongdoing on the pension issue.

International Pressure

Plumptre and Bank of Canada officials also cited a second reason for their support of a fixed exchange rate: foreign governments were increasingly unwilling to accept Canada's anomalous exchange rate regime.[22] Plumptre attributed this new foreign pressure partly to Canada's changed position in the world: "In the immediate post war world, when Canada was in a uniquely favoured economic position and when we were distributing military and economic aid in very large amounts, other countries were quite willing to put up with abnormal actions on our part."[23] But the more important reason for the changed foreign opinion was opposition to the government's new strategy of deliberate depreciation. While many foreign governments had been willing to look the other way when Canada had a "free float" in 1950–60 – particularly one that had initially appreciated and then remained at a relatively stable and high level – they were not prepared to tolerate currency manipulation designed to gain competitive advantage in international markets. This was, after all, exactly the kind of policy that the Bretton Woods exchange rate system had been designed to prevent.

The government's currency policy had raised the ire of many foreign governments, including the US. IMF officials were also understandably upset by it. As early as July 1961, Canada's exchange rate policy became the subject of a special IMF Executive Board meeting and Canada was pressed to restore a fixed exchange rate at a board meeting in February 1962. IMF staff strongly shared the view of Coyne's critics that Canada's economic problems were caused by the country's high interest rates, which had attracted large capital flows and pushed up the value of the Canadian dollar.[24]

The Canadian experience in fact helped prompt two economists working at the IMF, Robert Mundell of Canada and Marcus Fleming of Britain, to develop the soon-to-be-famous "Mundell-Fleming" model that analysed macroeconomic policy choices in a context of a floating exchange rate regime with high capital mobility.[25] The model updated the point that Clark had made in 1932: that if Canada wanted monetary policy autonomy in an atmosphere of capital mobility, it had to embrace a floating exchange rate. But it analysed how a much more activist approach to interest rate policy than Clarke had envisioned would work in a context of a floating exchange rate and capital mobility. While fiscal policy would be quite ineffective in this environment, they showed that monetary policy would be very powerful because the impact of interest rate changes would be reinforced by exchange rate movements. By attracting capital inflows, a restrictive monetary policy of Coyne's type would generate an appreciation of the currency which could have just as much, if not more, of a dampening effect on the domestic economy as the initial high interest rates themselves. In these instances, the exchange rate would no longer necessarily be playing the useful role of helping the domestic economy adjust to external shocks, as Canadian supporters of a floating rate had long argued. It might instead represent a shock itself, contributing to the external imbalance, as Canada had discovered in the late 1950s.

At this same time, Mundell highlighted a second reason that Canadian policy-makers needed to be careful in using a floating exchange

rate to achieve specific macroeconomic purposes. He developed a point
that Canadian policy-makers had long been forced to recognize: Canada was really a "multi-regional" country whose various regions had
quite different economic structures and were affected by exchange rate
movements in quite different ways. In this context, he noted that a domestic monetary policy designed to promote national employment
might induce exchange rate movements that had quite different impacts
across the country. A currency depreciation used to offset the impact of
a negative external shock to one part of Canada might be inappropriate
for the macroeconomic needs of another region.[26] Although Mundell
was not the first to make these points, he developed them in a much
more theoretically sophisticated manner with his "theory of optimum
currency areas" (which would later be cited as one of the reasons he
won the Nobel prize in economics). The theory discussed how various
criteria could help explain whether a group of countries was well suited
to form a currency union. In the case of North America, he even speculated about whether the continent would be better served with two currency regions that were divided not along the existing North-South
national lines, but according to an eastern zone and a western zone.

How important was international pressure in influencing the decision
Canada took to restore a fixed exchange rate in May 1962? It certainly
presented a different external context than that which had existed during the 1950s. Rasminsky told the IMF Executive Board at the time that
it played some role in influencing Canada's decision, although he stated
that the main motivation had been the desire to restore the confidence of
the markets.[27] Cabinet members also mentioned it as one of several reasons to support the move at their 2 May meeting.[28] Fleming also made
clear that his decision to pick a rate of 92.5 cents instead of 90 cents was
driven by fear of generating further US anger about Canada's exchange
rate policy.[29] Even the rate of 92.5 cents produced considerable protest
in some parts of the US, such as in the Pacific Northwest where the lumber industry complained about the devaluation and began calling for
quotas on Canadian lumber exports in late 1962.[30]

The Role of Domestic Interests?

In his August 1961 memo, Plumptre mentioned one further rationale
for a fixed exchange rate, one related to domestic politics: "now the
Minister has taken a position regarding the level of the exchange rate
at a particular moment of time, he may find it difficult, perhaps

increasingly difficult, not to take a position regarding the exchange rate at every moment of time."[31] The argument was an interesting one in light of the analysis of previous chapters. We have seen how an important rationale during the 1930s and 1950s for a floating rate was that it would depoliticize the exchange rate as a domestic political issue. But as Plumptre pointed out, echoing comments of those critical of deliberate depreciation proposals in the 1930s, it could only play this role in the case of a relatively "free float." With a dirty float of the kind that Fleming had introduced, the exchange rate had been brought back into the arena of domestic politics. Indeed, Fleming himself had seemed to recognize this danger in an April 1962 speech: "Canada's international economic relations are, I believe, more complex and, in relation to our size, more extensive and pervasive than those of any other country … Canada might be regarded as a classic example of a country for which, because of the diversity of our international interest and obligations, it is extremely difficult to devise and pursue an exchange rate policy that may be regarded as completely satisfactory from every point of view."[32] In this new context, Plumptre suggested that the adoption of a fixed exchange rate – one that was firmly fixed – might actually serve to insulate the minister from exchange rate politics more than the dirty float did since it would not require a continuous judgment about what rate was most appropriate.

What other domestic political pressures might have encouraged the move to a fixed rate? There was no clear unified voice emerging from the business community on the question of a fixed versus floating exchange rate regime. At the 2 May cabinet meeting, some government members had predicted that "the proposed step would be popular in Canadian financial circles."[33] It was true that some financial figures, such as the chief economist of the Toronto Dominion Bank, A. McLeod, had pushed for a fixed rate as early as 1960 on the grounds that the floating rate generated uncertainty that hurt business planning.[34] But another government minister noted that there was in fact no consensus among Canadian financiers on the question of the relative merits of a fixed or floating exchange rate regime.[35] The president of the Montreal Stock Exchange, Eric Kierans, attacked the government's decision to peg the currency in the midst of the electoral campaign.[36] The president of the Royal Bank of Canada, W. Earle McLaughlin, had also been strongly critical of the idea of a fixed exchange rate earlier in the year on the grounds that it was likely to be associated with either the reimposition of exchange controls or the loss of domestic monetary autonomy. McLaughlin had also pointed out that a fixed exchange rate would likely be adjusted frequently, resulting in a more unstable exchange rate than a floating rate: "Canadian experience since the end of the Second World War suggests that the greatest range of fluctuation in rates of exchange will occur in the long run with so-called 'fixed' rates of exchange."[37]

Some policy-makers also suggested that manufacturing interests would favour a fixed rate. One official in the Bank of Canada argued in late 1962, for example, that the new fixed rate was well suited to an era in which importance of commodity exports within the Canadian economy was diminishing and that of industrial production was growing, because manufacturers needed more stable market conditions.[38] A comprehensive survey of members of the Canadian Manufacturers Association soon after the peg was announced confirmed that some members did indeed favour the fixed rate because it provided greater certainty in predicting costs and export receipts, as well as in planning long-term investments in certain product lines. But the survey also revealed that a large percentage of the respondents had no strong opinion on the question.[39]

One might have predicted that more business leaders in the tradable sector would in fact have *opposed* a fixed rate since it closed the option of further competitive devaluation. The government had, after all, been actively talking down the dollar in an effort to improve conditions in sectors that had been hurt by the high dollar of the late 1950s: exporters and businesses competing with imports. But businesses in tradable sectors noted that depreciation had not always helped them. One business leader in the manufacturing sector noted that depreciation often increased costs of production because of the high dependence of many Canadian exporters on imported parts and machinery, a point raised earlier in 1949, as we have seen, by C.D. Howe. Another reason that depreciation was not necessarily beneficial to exporters was highlighted by representatives of the pulp and paper sector. Echoing Skelton's comments in 1935, they noted that Canadian businesses were world price-makers in many commodity sectors because they dominated world markets; in these cases, the depreciating Canadian dollar only caused a decline in world prices. Even those in the tradable sector who benefited from the depreciation had been forced to recognize that Canada's floating exchange rate could cut both ways. While it made possible the depreciation in 1961–62, the floating rate had left them vulnerable to the appreciation of the currency in the late 1950s, an appreciation that had prompted many of them to pressure the government for a lower dollar or tariff protection by 1960.[40]

Two domestic groups that *did* strongly oppose the fixed rate were the Canadian Labour Congress (CLC) and the CCF.[41] Although they had little influence on Canadian exchange rate policy-making at this moment, their position was noteworthy in light of the fact that some politicians on the left had defended a fixed rate at the time of the 1950 decision. The CLC and CCF now rejected a fixed rate for the same reason that many of their predecessors had opposed the gold standard during the interwar years: it would prevent the government from pursuing an expansionary monetary policy that promoted growth and full employment. This defense of monetary policy autonomy was also particularly interesting since the Bank of Canada under Coyne's leadership had used the autonomy provided by the floating rate to pursue an overly *restrictive* monetary policy. While this experience had left many analysts and government policy-makers with a more skeptical view of the benefits of monetary policy autonomy,[42] the CLC and CCF remained optimistic.

Capital Controls, Monetary Autonomy, and the Fixed Rate

Finally, it is worth highlighting that some academic economists, such as Ed Neufeld, echoed McLaughlin's fears that the fixed rate would likely require capital controls – which Neufeld opposed – given the vulnerability of the Canadian balance of payments to rapid changes, particularly in capital flows.[43] This prediction highlighted the important point that the decision to fix was taking place in a very different context from that of 1939–50 when a strict capital control regime had been in place. The 1962 decision clearly did not reflect a new willingness to use capital controls; as we have seen, there was strong resistance to their use in the lead-up to the decision and the option was also rejected a few months later when the peg came under severe downward pressure.[44] But without capital controls, the fixed rate could only be maintained for a prolonged period by adjusting domestic economic conditions in ways that maintained external balance.

There were two principal ways to facilitate such adjustments. One was by encouraging business and labour to work together with the government to facilitate the appropriate wage and price movements. Weeks after the fixed rate had been introduced, Rasminsky "urged that cabinet should consult with business and labour" to find "methods other than exchange rate depreciation" for addressing the country's payment deficit.[45] But it was hardly surprising that this call led to few results. Canada did not share the kind of centralized corporatist arrangements which existed in many small, open European economies and which facilitated cooperation between government, business, and labour. Neither business nor labour organizations were centrally organized across the country, and collective bargaining processes were what a Royal Commission later called "among the most decentralized in the world."[46] The federal nature of the Canadian state also ensured that provincial cooperation would be required to make such arrangements work.

The other principal option was the more blunt, macroeconomic one of gearing domestic monetary policy towards the goal of maintaining external balance. Given the longstanding commitment of Canadian policy-makers to monetary policy autonomy, this option was difficult for them to swallow. But they were left little choice. This became apparent in the mid-1962 currency crisis that followed the decision to fix. Having rejected capital controls and a devaluation, the government in June 1962 was forced to curtail the downward pressure on the currency by tightening fiscal and monetary policy.[47]

The issue arose again one year later in quite a different context, one in which the US was increasingly concerned about *its* payments deficits vis-à-vis Canada and other foreign countries. To reduce capital outflows that were contributing to these deficits, US policy-makers imposed the Interest Equalization Tax (IET) on all foreign borrowers in US domestic securities markets in July 1963. Because of the dependence of Canadian borrowers on New York borrowing, the move provoked a collapse of Canadian share prices and selling of the Canadian dollar. Desperate to restore confidence, and unwilling to abandon its currency peg, the Canadian government pleaded for an exemption from the US measure. The US agreed only after the Canadian government made a commitment to prevent the country's foreign exchange reserves from rising above the current 1963 levels.[48] From the US perspective, this commitment guaranteed that Canada's capital imports would not contribute to US balance of payments problems in the future. From a Canadian perspective, however, it meant the acceptance of an external constraint on Canadian monetary policy. When inflation began to rise in 1965 and after, the Bank of Canada was constrained in its ability to increase interest rates since the resulting capital inflows would have increased the country's reserves.[49]

In making this commitment, the Canadian government had explicitly chosen to prioritize the free flow of capital across the Canadian border over monetary policy autonomy. Indeed, it had rejected an initial US suggestion that Canada could be exempt from the IET if it imposed its own quotas on Canadian borrowing in the US. The Canadian government's refusal to introduce this kind of capital control reflected not just Canadian business opposition but also the political difficulties involved in controlling the largest borrowers abroad at the time: the provincial governments. Some provincial governments had found US investors more willing to support their increased spending than the small tightly-knit Canadian financial community, a development that left them very wary of any effort to control foreign borrowing. The Quebec government, for example, had turned to the US to finance the nationalization of Hydro-Québec when Canadian banks had refused in 1962.[50]

The choice of accepting a constraint on domestic monetary policy autonomy instead of using capital controls to maintain the currency peg was apparent again at the time of the next currency crisis in 1968. This crisis had been provoked partly by the announcement of another US program designed to curtail capital exports, this time aimed at the activities of US multinational corporations, banks, and non-bank financial institutions.[51] In February 1968, the Canadian government did give serious consideration to the idea of floating the Canadian dollar as a way of responding to the speculative pressure against the currency. But Rasminsky convinced government ministers that the US would respond to this move by revoking the exemption from the IET.[52] Instead, as in 1962, the government defended the Canadian dollar by raising interest rates and by accepting international loans from the US, IMF, Bank for International Settlements, and some European central banks.[53]

In this crisis, the government did undertake some informal moves to discourage US subsidiaries from exporting capital in abnormal amounts to their head offices in the US. But the idea of implementing more serious formal controls on capital outflows was rejected once again, despite some interest in the idea from Rasminsky and loud calls for such controls from opposition politicians in the left-wing New Democratic Party (NDP), successor to the CCF. As they had in 1963, Canadian officials also pressed for an exemption from the US controls. US officials granted this request in early March, seeing it as a better alternative than a Canadian devaluation which might have increased speculative pressure against the US dollar. In return, the Canadian government agreed to hold its dollar reserves in US government non-liquid securities.[54] This exemption – along with the austerity programmme and foreign loans – helped end the currency crisis.[55]

THE FLOATING EXCHANGE RATE REGIME
RESUMED IN 1970

On 1 June 1970, Canadian policy-makers concluded that they were no longer willing to subordinate monetary policy to the goal of maintaining a fixed exchange rate. They reached this conclusion in a situation very similar to that of late 1950. Capital inflows were putting strong upward pressure on the currency at a time when domestic inflationary pressures were building. In the absence of capital controls, the currency peg could be preserved only by reducing interest rates (which would slow or reverse the capital inflows) or by increasing foreign currency reserves (which would result from efforts by Canadian authorities to sell Canadian dollars in foreign exchange markets to offset the upward pressure on the currency). Either option would generate further inflationary pressures.[56] In this context, the government decided that the reintroduction of a floating rate was the more attractive choice.

Rejecting Capital Controls

As in 1950, the decision subjected Canada to strong international criticism from IMF staff and foreign governments. Although the Canadian government declared the float to be temporary, it still left Canada in contravention of the IMF Articles of Agreement. Foreign critics were much more concerned with the systemic implications of Canada's float than with its specific economic impact. Canada's move took place at a time when there were serious concerns about the sustainability of the Bretton Woods exchange rate regime. In the eyes of many foreign observers, Canada's decision to float helped to undermine the fragile international commitment that remained to the regime.

Key US officials – including Paul Volcker in the Treasury and especially Federal Reserve Chairman Arthur Burns – were particularly angry that they had not been consulted more extensively in advance of the decision, given its wider implications.[57] It is true that Liberal prime minister Pierre Trudeau had made the decision very quickly and had then instructed his officials to float the currency almost immediately in order to minimize the need for further defense of the peg.[58] This approach ensured that there was little time for consultation with US policy-makers, leaving them understandably annoyed. One Canadian official, R.W. Lawson, reported Burns's views in the following way: "He said that he was surprised that the Government of Canada could be so naïve as to suppose that it could make exchange rate decisions on a unilateral basis. Canada was lucky, he said, that cool heads had prevailed in Washington that week-end or we would have had reason to worry about our currency being too weak on the exchange market rather than too strong."[59] When this official reminded Burns that an appreciating Canadian dollar would help the US economically, Burns made it clear that he was worried about the wider implications of the Canadian move.

As in 1950, foreign critics of the float wondered why Canada was not trying to defend its fixed exchange rate by controlling the capital inflows that were putting upward pressure on the currency. The government had already been informally discouraging capital inflows by encouraging Canadian firms to borrow at home in early 1970.[60] But foreigners thought the Canadian government should consider more formal controls on the ability of Canadians to borrow abroad and even perhaps a broader system of exchange controls.[61] Both options were urged on Canada by IMF staff as an alternative to the float, as well as by foreign officials at a BIS meeting on 6 June and an OECD Economic Policy Committee meeting on 15 June.[62]

Canadian officials flatly rejected these options. They reminded their BIS colleagues of "the practical impossibility of foreign exchange control in Canada, certainly in peace time, because of the length of our border and the magnitude and closeness of our economic and financial connections with the U.S."[63] Formal controls on foreign borrowing – particularly the large borrowing of provincial governments – were also deemed impossible on more political grounds. As Lawson told the OECD committee:

The difficulty with this lies in the nature of the Canadian state. Under the Canadian federal system, the provinces have a good deal of autonomy, and their free access to new issue markets abroad to supplement their borrowing in Canada has never been challenged. The distribution of functions in Canada is such that the provincial governments have major responsibility in many of the areas in which expenditures are rising most rapidly ... In the current state of federal-provincial relations in Canada, intervention by the Government of Canada to restrict the access to foreign capital of the provinces of Canada would have been a political decision with repercussions far beyond the balance of payments.[64]

Instead of controlling provincial borrowing directly, Volcker wondered why Canadian officials did not restrict capital inflows by simply ending the exemption Canada had earlier demanded from the US IET. Once again, according to Lawson's account, Canadian officials explained that the Canadian federal government could not initiate this move because it would raise too many political difficulties in its relations with the provinces: "In respect of the IET exemption we explained the difficulties that stand in the way of the Government of Canada taking action to reduce the availability of financing to the provinces and municipalities. In the present state of Federal-Provincial relations and in the light of developments in the Province of Quebec such action does not seem possible on political grounds." Canadian officials also pointed out how difficult it was to micromanage the country's balance of payments through these kinds of initiatives relating to Canada-US negotiations on issues such as the IET: "Our bilateral arrangements with the United States were not of a character which made it easy to use them for purposes of short-term adjustments in payments positions."[65]

Although some US officials were not happy with the Canadian decision to float, the US government ultimately accepted it. Much of the officials' initial anger, it appeared, had concerned the lack of consultation. As in 1950, the idea of tightening controls on economic transactions across the Canada-US border was not a terribly popular one in US business circles. The *Wall Street Journal's* editorial writers, for example, had welcomed Canada's float, arguing that fixed exchange rates often encouraged inflexibility and controls. An editorial in the *New York Times* took a similar position.[66] More generally, the Nixon administration itself was becoming increasingly opposed to the whole US capital controls program of the 1960s. With the Canadian government refusing to control capital flows, Canada's float was also reluctantly accepted by the IMF Executive Board and OECD, although only on the understanding that it was temporary.[67]

Domestic Arguments for and against the Floating Rate

The float did not turn out to be temporary. Why did Canadian officials not simply re-peg the currency at a higher rate after the initial float? Indeed, why had they not simply revalued the Canadian dollar to a new level as an alternative to the float itself in June? This option had been rejected on similar grounds as in 1950: it was too difficult to decide on an appropriate level given the economic uncertainties of the time. Particularly difficult to predict were economic developments in the US, most notably the prospects for renewed US inflation.[68] In this context, the exchange rate peg might need to be adjusted frequently if Canada was to protect its monetary policy autonomy, an option that was politically unattractive for reasons that Canadian policy-makers had noted in the past.

A confidential Department of Finance memo from 1969 made the case well. It noted that governments under the Bretton Woods system had been reluctant to adjust exchange rate pegs as these changes always had an adverse effect on at least some domestic groups because of their impact "on the terms of trade, on the general level of prices and on the relative structure of prices and incomes." Although the memo stopped short of recommending a float, it argued that the introduction of an automatic crawling peg might reduce political resistance to necessary exchange rate adjustments. The argument was very similar to the defense of floating offered in the 1950s and the 1930s: "governments will find themselves being 'nudged' by the market and they will be in a position to point to market forces as being the responsible causative agent of change. Some of the political difficulties may therefore be mitigated."[69]

Underlying the case for a floating exchange rate regime was the re-emergence of the longstanding idea that exchange rate movements were needed to preserve the country's monetary policy autonomy. During the previous few years, there had been growing support inside and outside the government for a floating exchange rate for this reason. Since the late 1960s, a growing number of bankers and academic economists had endorsed a floating rate on the grounds that it would insulate Canada from accelerating US inflation associated with the Vietnam War. It would also provide the Canadian government with greater freedom to pursue a more restrictive monetary policy designed to tackle Canadian inflationary pressures.[70] The prominent economist Harry Johnson also reminded Canadians of why their country's last experience with a floating rate had ended badly: "What went wrong was not the system, but the Governor of the Bank of Canada; and the floating rate predictably permitted him to maximize the damage done by a tight money policy in a period of mass unemployment."[71]

Johnson also argued that an appreciating exchange rate might help discipline domestic actors by bringing "pervasive competitive pressures to bear on Canadian wage and price fixing."[72] This form of discipline would be more effective, he felt, than the use of consumer credit controls or incomes policy, each of which was unworkable and/or inefficient. Indeed, the government had tried and failed to secure agreement from business and labour for voluntary wage and price guidelines in 1969–70.[73] Johnson's argument signalled a return to the classical liberal notion that an exchange rate regime should be used to *constrain* domestic wage and price increases, as under the gold standard, rather than accommodate them as "embedded liberals" in the early postwar years had suggested. This "neoliberal" argument would soon gain more supporters.

Although they made strange bedfellows with bankers and neoliberal economists, NDP politicians and others on the Canadian left were also strong supporters of a floating rate at this time. We have seen how they had earlier opposed the decision to fix the exchange rate in 1962. At the time of Canada's 1968 currency crisis, they had continued to push for a floating rate – along with capital controls – as the best way for the government to "gain control of our economy."[74] In 1970, they strongly supported the move to a floating rate on similar grounds. As Tommy Douglas put it, "we favour a floating exchange rate because we believe that an unpegged rate will provide Canada with a measure of monetary independence."[75] The most important virtue of monetary policy autonomy from the standpoint of NDP politicians was that it enabled expansionary policies rather than the restrictive policies favoured by other supporters of floating. And while Johnson hoped an appreciating currency would discipline domestic actors, Douglas reiterated the embedded liberal view that a floating rate would help *compensate* for Canadian wage and price changes: "there are few countries in the world which are as dependent upon the export trade as Canada and by allowing the Canadian dollar to find its own level we shall automatically compensate for any change in our price levels greater than those of our trading partners."[76]

While some supporters of the floating rate within the government shared the views of the bankers and neoliberal economists, others were sympathetic to this embedded liberal rationale for a float. Among the most prominent was Eric Kierans, who had earlier attacked the Conservative government in 1962 for its decision to fix, and was now minister of communications. Beginning in 1969, he pressed Prime Minister Trudeau to reinstate the float in order to allow the government to pursue a more expansionary policy.[77] The fact that supporters of floating such as Kierans hoped this exchange rate regime would loosen economic policy discipline made officials in the Department of Finance and the Bank of Canada nervous.[78]

One further justification for the float was that it would reduce the need for the kinds of bilateral agreements with the US relating to balance of payments management that had proliferated since the early 1960s. These related not just to the various exemptions from US capital controls and associated restrictions on Canada's reserve holdings. To prevent Canadian borrowing in the US from being relent to third countries, US authorities had also insisted that the Canadian government prevent Canadians from engaging in this kind of "pass-through" activity.[79] In effect, the move put the Canadian government in the role of enforcing US capital controls on Canadian soil. Indeed, in the mid-1960s, US Treasury had even briefly suggested that it might be useful to begin to present US and Canadian balance of payments vis-à-vis the world in an integrated way to help justify the special exemptions granted to Canada under the capital controls program. Not surprisingly the idea was rejected by Canadian policy-makers.[80]

These agreements had become a source of considerable resentment within Canada, especially in an era when Canadian nationalism was on the rise. Critics regarded them as a sign that Canada was moving "towards a colonial monetary system" that was designed to support the US dollar and its balance of payments.[81] Even Harry Johnson – usually known as a strong critic of Canadian economic nationalism in this period – played to these nationalist sentiments in advocating a floating exchange rate: "The period since 1962 has been characterized by a series of financial agreements obtained by the Canadians from the Americans at considerable expense to Canadian sovereignty, designed to preserve economic interdependence from the more ominous assaults of American balance-of-payments controls on U.S. foreign investment. With a floating Canadian dollar, transactions with Canada could not accentuate the American payments deficit, and the sorry state of American restrictions applied initially to Canada and then relaxed by special arrangement after a frantic trip to Washington by Canadian officials would not need to be re-enacted."[82]

We have noted already how Canadian officials were also frustrated that these agreements did not permit balance of payments adjustments to be made quickly or efficiently. They may also have seen a floating rate as a tool to reduce frictions with the US more generally. In explaining the decision to float, one *Globe and Mail* reporter raised this issue: "the primary factor seems to be the effect Canada's rising reserves is having on relations with the United States." By floating the currency, he argued that Canada "should head off Congressional criticism" at a time when the US was taking a tough stand on trade issues vis-à-vis such sectors as crude oil and automobiles.[83] This rationale, if indeed it was influential, was reminiscent of some Canadian thinking at the time of the 1950 float.

The decision to float in June 1970 did not meet with everyone's approval. The opposition Conservatives strongly attacked the government's move on the grounds that it broke IMF rules and that Canada's fixed exchange rate since 1962 had been good for the country's economic growth.[84] A major part of their criticism, however, was simply an attack on currency appreciation and its impact on the export sector rather than on the floating exchange rate regime itself. While Johnson had welcomed the fact that an appreciating currency might help discipline domestic firms, the Conservatives joined many exporters, especially in the farming, fishing, and paper and forestry sectors, in criticizing the government for the currency's upward movement.[85] One US researcher in the Fed noted that these protests were particularly loud because many export-oriented firms in Canada had made substantial investments in the mid-to-late 1960s without recognizing that the Canadian dollar had been undervalued in real terms in that period.[86]

Stemming the Currency's Appreciation in the Early 1970s: A Dirty Float

The federal government was also very concerned in the early 1970s about the impact of the appreciating Canadian dollar on the competitiveness of Canadian firms and on the overall level of employment and output. The concern was more intense than in 1950 because of the uncertain economic environment of the time. In an effort to soften the blow of the currency's appreciation to the domestic economy, the Bank of Canada linked the decision to float with a lowering of the bank rate from 7.5 per cent to 7.0 per cent.[87] Finance Minister Edgar Benson also made a point of highlighting, when introducing the float, that the Exchange Fund would be used "to moderate any appreciation of the Canadian dollar."[88]

In addition to intervening in foreign exchange markets at various moments throughout 1970–71, the Canadian government tried to minimize the currency's appreciation by urging Canadians – particularly provincial governments, provincial hydro companies, and municipal governments – to reduce their foreign borrowing.[89] As the currency continued to rise in the spring and summer of 1971 (see Figure 4), the federal cabinet and minister of finance began to consider more formal measures designed to influence capital movements, including capital and exchange controls, a dual exchange market for capital and current account transactions, and even initiatives that might encourage the US to end the IET exemption.[90]

Figure 4
Canadian–US dollar exchange rate, 1970–2005
Monthly rates

Source: Pacific Exchange Rate Service

The Nixon shock of August 1971 – in which the US ended its currency's convertibility into gold and pressed its allies to revalue their currencies – then created new uncertainties. Nixon's treasury secretary initially made it clear that the US wanted the Canadian dollar to be repegged at a rate of $1.05.[91] This marked a substantial appreciation from the level of 95 to 99 cents at which the rate had floated since mid-1970. Canadian officials opposed this strongly and successfully. At the December 1971 Smithsonian meetings where a new set of fixed exchange rates was established among the major industrial powers, Canada was granted an exception. Although the US endorsed Canada's float, it did so only on the condition that Canada's intervention in the foreign exchange market was limited to maintaining orderly conditions.[92]

IMF officials and many foreign governments continued to pressure Canada to restore a fixed rate throughout 1972, but US policy-makers backed the Canadian preference for floating.[93] It helped that the currency had risen above par and continued to move in an upward direction, but US officials also applauded the fact that the Canadian dollar – as in the 1950s – did not float in a volatile manner that could disrupt trade or financial flows (see Figure 4).[94] US businesses appeared to back this judgment. A survey conducted by the Federal Reserve Bank of Boston, for example, showed that New England businesses were not opposed to the float.[95] In commenting on this research, a senior VP at Morgan Guaranty Trust Co. provided the following explanation: "the exchange risk of doing business in Canada is not thought of as being in the same category of concerns as those involved in sterling, Deutschemarks, or yen, or in fact any other currency situation. By and large, and over time, people doing business across our northern border have just not bothered to hedge against loss from the exchange rate which can be expected to go up and down but never get so far away from the starting point as to leave them permanently damaged."[96]

While remaining committed to a floating rate, Canadian policy-makers continued to consider various ways to curtail the currency's appreciation.[97] Their concerns about the competitiveness of Canadian firms were only reinforced by the fact that Canadian production costs were beginning to rise more quickly than their American equivalents.[98] Between October and December 1971, the ministry of finance even drafted detailed legislation for the introduction of controls on capital inflows and the issue was raised again in June 1972 as the dollar continued to appreciate.[99] The month before, at an expert conference on international monetary reform, Finance Minister John Turner even publicly raised the question, "Have we gone too far in permitting and promoting the free flow of international capital?"[100] In early-to-mid 1972, there was also serious consideration of the idea of introducing a dual exchange rate system.[101]

In the end, however, the dollar's appreciation was tempered primarily through interest rate policy. This strategy stayed in place after the oil shock of 1973 put further upward pressure on the Canadian dollar (because Canada was a net exporter of energy), driving the currency to just above $1.04 by April 1974. Although this policy curtailed the rise of the dollar, it also constrained monetary authorities from attacking inflation as vigorously as they had hoped.[102] In this context, the floating exchange rate did not in fact provide as much monetary policy autonomy that some of its supporters had initially hoped.

The Monetarist Shift and the New Anti-Inflation Program

Not until late 1975 did the Bank of Canada finally focus monetary policy more exclusively on domestic goals and leave the exchange rate to fluctuate on its own. This shift resulted from the bank's decision to adopt a new strategy of "monetary gradualism." The strategy was designed to contain inflation by slowing the growth of the domestic money supply and it marked an important shift in the goals of Canadian monetary policy. As we have seen, some supporters of the 1970 float – generally on the left – had hoped it would permit monetary policy to be focused on the kind of full employment goals that had been endorsed in the early postwar years. But the bank now sided with the neoliberal view that the policy autonomy provided by a floating rate should be used more exclusively to defeat inflation. As Robert Campbell puts it, "the Governor of the Bank of Canada effectively moved Canada back into the pre-Keynesian monetary era."[103]

The ascendancy of this perspective partly reflected the growing disillusionment with Keynesian policies in Canada and across the Western world at the time. These policies were seen as ill-equipped to address rising inflation and were even blamed for contributing to it. According to some critics, Keynesian thinking had encouraged politicians to endorse growing government deficits which were increasingly paid for by monetary expansion. Within the discipline of economics, a "rational expectations" revolution was also underway which undermined the Keynesian notion that there was a long-term trade-off between inflation and unemployment. By highlighting how experiences of inflation over time may encourage people to adjust their expectations, this new economic analysis suggested that activist macroeconomic management could encourage higher and higher levels of inflation. To break these inflationary expectations, many economists argued that authorities would have to re-establish their credibility and reputation for producing stable money by a strong commitment to price stability.

Monetarists argued that the key tool for achieving this goal was to introduce monetary targeting; that is, establishing stable targets for the growth of the money supply. At the time, this view was put forward most forcefully by Milton Friedman who argued that the key determinant of the price level was the rate of growth of the money supply. In Canada, the monetarist position had a growing number of supporters within the Bank of Canada, including the deputy governor, George Freeman. It was also advocated strongly by some prominent economists outside of government, such as David Laidler, and most notably Thomas Courchene of the University of Western Ontario.[104]

The new priority of containing inflation did not just reflect the changing ideological landscape. It was also seen by top policy-making officials within the federal government in a more practical light as a means to maintain the international competitiveness of Canadian firms. In an era when tariffs were falling with the implementation of the Kennedy and Tokyo Rounds of the General Agreement on Tariffs and Trade (GATT), Canadian wages could not be allowed to continue to grow more quickly than those in the US without there being corresponding productivity gains.[105] Domestic inflation levels surpassing those in the US had produced an increasingly large appreciation of the Canadian currency in "real" terms (i.e., the rate adjusted for inflation differentials between the two countries) since 1972 even though the government had succeeded in preventing a dramatic increase in the "nominal" (i.e., the market) value of the currency.[106] Even those who did not subscribe to the "neoliberal" monetarist mantra thus had a reason to support the bank's new policy. Bringing down the inflation rate at this time was what Kate McNamara has called a kind of "competitive liberalism."[107]

An alternative route to restoring competitiveness, of course, might have been to encourage the currency to devalue in nominal terms. This option was considered in 1975 but rejected on the grounds that it might simply increase inflation and thus erode any initial competitive edge gained from the devaluation. In this context, policy-makers worried – as had observers in the 1930s, and Coyne had in the early 1960s – that Canada might end up experiencing a kind of wage-price spiral involving accelerating inflation and depreciation of the dollar.[108] The better option, it was felt, was to try to attack inflation directly. To reinforce the bank's policy, the federal government introduced other initiatives designed to contain inflation at this time, including not just restraints on government spending but also an ambitious system – one unprecedented in Canada – of three-year mandatory wage and price controls that covered the government and larger firms.[109]

With monetary policy now focused on domestic objectives, the Canadian dollar was left to fluctuate more freely than it had in the early 1970s. This decision initially only compounded the competitive problems of the Canadian tradable sector. The new, more restrictive monetary policy attracted capital inflows in 1976 which kept the Canadian dollar above par, despite the fact that Canadian inflation and wage cost increases continued to be higher than their US counterparts. But as the inflation differential remained and the current account deficit grew, the dollar began to fall in nominal terms in late 1976.[110] By early 1979, it had fallen quite dramatically to 83 cents.

The Long Nominal Depreciation

This nominal depreciation was now welcomed by many in the federal government. The task of controlling inflation was proving difficult and the currency movement provided a much simpler mechanism for adjusting Canadian costs relative to those in the US.[111] There was, of course, the risk that the nominal depreciation might exacerbate domestic inflationary pressures, thereby making these relative cost gains only temporary. But this risk was reduced somewhat by the fact that government's wage and price controls were helping somewhat to keep inflationary pressures under control.[112] Still, Bank of Canada officials were particularly worried about this risk and they intervened in foreign exchange markets as early as 1977 to slow the dollar's fall. By April 1978, the bank even announced that it "was giving high priority in its conduct to the external value of the Canadian dollar" and its intervention continued in a more aggressive manner during 1978 and 1979.[113]

When the US central bank suddenly introduced a much more restrictive monetary policy than Canada's in late 1979, the Bank of Canada became even more concerned about defending the Canadian dollar. Indeed, by 1981–82, the goal of stabilizing the Canadian dollar vis-à-vis the US dollar became the *primary* focus of the bank's monetary policy. This was not a formal peg; the bank noted publicly that it did not have a precise exchange rate target in mind and the exchange rate itself continued to fluctuate between 78 and 84 cents during these two years.[114] But the new principal focus on stabilizing the currency's value was important in signalling the formal abandonment of the bank's post-1975 "monetary gradualism" strategy.

The change of policy stemmed not just from the bank's fear of the inflationary consequences of depreciation. Also significant was the fact that the relationship between Canadian inflation and the growth of the money supply that the bank had been targeting had broken down by 1981–82, thus discrediting its "monetarist" strategy. Shadowing the US dollar provided a new method for constraining inflation: it enabled Canadian monetary authorities to import the dramatic monetary restraint program of the US at the time.[115] This strategy was similar to that of many small European countries that pegged formally or informally to the German Deutschemark (DM) in the 1970s and 1980s as a way of importing German monetary stability.[116] It was, however, an important departure for Canadian monetary authorities who had valued their autonomy from US monetary policy for most of the post-1931 period. Even when a fixed rate had been adopted in 1939–50 and 1962–70, Canadian monetary policy-makers had made clear their dissatisfaction at having to import US monetary preferences.

This new policy was deeply unpopular. The Bank of Canada had chosen to stabilize the currency vis-à-vis the US dollar at a moment when US monetary policy became extremely tight. As nominal interest rates rose as high as 22 per cent, this choice generated a sharp recession in Canada and provoked very strong opposition in many quarters of Canadian society, including among business leaders and provincial premiers.[117] Canada's economic troubles had been worsened by the fact that European countries and Japan were allowing their currencies to devalue vis-à-vis the US dollar in this period. The Canadian dollar was thus appreciating against the currencies of these trading partners, thereby exacerbating recessionary pressures in Canada.[118] Faced with enormous opposition, the bank's governor found himself compelled to defend this policy in ways that, in Howitt's words, thrust him "more actively into the political fray than at any time since the Coyne affair of the early 1960s."[119]

The policy did not last long. By late 1983–early 1984, with inflation subdued by the recession, the bank began to endorse a more expansionary monetary policy which included allowing the Canadian dollar to depreciate further. Elected in mid-1984, Conservative prime minister Brian Mulroney initially endorsed this lower dollar strategy, seeing it as a more popular alternative than higher interest rates. As John Crosbie had explained Conservative Party policy during the election campaign, "we opt for a lower Canadian dollar, and not higher interest rates which will ruin economic growth in this country."[120] By early February 1986, the Canadian dollar had fallen to US$0.69, a lower level than at any time in Canada's history.[121]

When compared with the value of the Canadian dollar in 1975, this new level for the exchange rate represented a very substantial nominal depreciation vis-à-vis the US dollar – about 28 per cent.[122] In *real* terms, however, the change was much less dramatic. In fact, the size of the nominal depreciation over the period almost directly matched the differential between Canada's inflation rate and that of the US.[123] The result was ironic in light of the goals of the monetarists a decade earlier. Far from allowing a decisive attack on inflation, the floating exchange rate had *accommodated* Canada's higher inflation rate vis-à-vis the US by allowing a steep decade-long nominal depreciation. Not surprisingly,

Canada's tradable sector had welcomed this result since it helped maintain the sector's international competitiveness. It also meant that Canadian policy-makers and societal groups had avoided the more serious "disciplinary" pressures to tackle inflation that would have existed if a fixed rate had been in place throughout this period. Canada had adopted a "soft currency" strategy, similar to that of Scandinavian countries in this period, in contrast to the "hard currency" approach of other European countries that pegged to the DM.

The fact that the long nominal depreciation of 1976–86 was accompanied by relatively little change in the *real* exchange rate may help explain why it did not provoke the kind of US opposition which had emerged during the 1961–62 depreciation. It might also account for why the depreciation was not accompanied by more domestic controversy. We have seen how a recurring theme in the history of Canadian exchange rate politics has been that significant changes in exchange rate policy often unleashed intense political controversy because of their differing impact on various domestic groups and regions. Particularly controversial have been exchange rate movements designed to accommodate *external* shocks, because these shocks have affected different regions in distinct ways, as Mundell highlighted. In this case, however, the nominal movement of the exchange rate was used to accommodate domestic price and wage trends that were experienced across the entire country and in ways that left the real exchange rate unchanged. This helped lessen the controversy – particularly that of an intra-regional nature – that was associated with the exchange rate movement.

There was one other factor that may have helped reduce intra-regional tensions associated with exchange rate movements throughout the period examined in this chapter. The creation of equalization payments between provinces in 1957 and the expansion of welfare state payments in the 1960s created a situation where income was now publicly redistributed spatially across the Canadian federation on a large scale.[124] The result was that the regional victims of exchange rate movements were now compensated to a greater extent by the public sector.

This method of addressing the political friction associated with Canada's "multi-regional" economy had in fact first been proposed in the wake of the exchange rate controversies of the early 1930s. One of the reports of the Rowell-Sirois Commission had noted that the decision not to tie the Canadian currency to sterling in the early 1930s had generated the need for larger inter-regional transfers of income by the federal government to help individuals and provincial governments in export regions.[125] Harold Innis had made a similar argument in 1943, after noting that the impact of the new enthusiasm for activist macroeconomic management would vary across Canada's different regions: "Each region had its conditions of equilibrium in relation to the rest of Canada and to the rest of the world, particularly in relation to Great Britain and the United States. Manipulation of a single instrument such as monetary policy implies a highly elaborate system to determine how far transfers between regions or provinces are necessary. Otherwise full employment will become a racket on the part of the central provinces for getting and keeping what they can. The provinces will require elaborate machinery to protect themselves against haphazard federal policies."[126] In the late 1950s, construction of this machinery had finally begun.

CONCLUSION

What have we learned about the politics of Canadian exchange rate policy-making in this brief survey of Canadian policy from the early 1960s to the mid-1980s? To begin with, the decision of the Canadian government to bring back a fixed exchange rate in 1962 did not reflect a serious re-evaluation of the benefits of a fixed exchange rate regime among expert groups, the government, or domestic interests. To be sure, the experiences with an overvalued exchange rate during the Coyne years and then the deliberate depreciation of 1961–62 had soured some important policy-makers on the benefits of a floating exchange rate, just as currency misalignments in the lead-up to the NAMU debate would, as we shall see. But the actual decision to fix was driven primarily by the government's desire, in the midst of a serious currency crisis, to re-establish credibility vis-à-vis the financial markets. This also foreshadows some of the interest in NAMU in 1999.

If Canadian policy-makers had endorsed a fixed rate in haste, they soon changed their mind. For those interested in the NAMU debate today, this shift was a particularly interesting one because the fixed exchange rate of 1962–70 resembled some of the conditions that would exist under NAMU. Unlike the 1939–50 period, the government made no adjustments of the peg in this period. The fixed rate was also maintained without the help of any capital controls. The fact that Canadian policy-makers soon chafed at the restrictions this monetary environment imposed should give pause to NAMU supporters.

One such restriction was the constraint on monetary policy autonomy. Without capital controls or adjustments to the peg, the government had to subordinate its monetary policy to the goal of maintaining the external balance. By 1970, Canadian policy-makers were no longer willing to bear this cost, particularly when it involved importing accelerating US inflation at the time. At the time of the 1970 decision, there was in fact little agreement about what the goals of monetary policy should be in the new floating environment. Some endorsed the embedded liberal vision that a more independent monetary policy could be used to promote full employment. But an increasingly prominent neoliberal perspective favoured a more restrictive policy designed to attack inflation. Between 1970 and 1975, neither group was satisfied, as monetary policy autonomy remained constrained by the government's desire, in a context of higher unemployment, to stop the Canadian dollar's appreciation from eroding the international competitiveness of Canadian firms. By 1975, those favouring a more restrictive, domestically-oriented monetary policy gained ascendancy, but their victory proved to be only partial. In 1976–86, Canadian inflation remained *above* that in the US and many Canadian policy-makers celebrated the fact that the floating rate permitted a large nominal depreciation to accommodate this inflation differential. Canada's inflation fighters also became increasingly less enamoured with the floating rate as the depreciation threatened to intensify inflationary pressure. Indeed, between 1981 and 1982, with the discrediting of their monetary targeting, they were even tempted to briefly endorse a loose and informal link to the US dollar as an alternative mechanism for introducing monetary discipline. This position foreshadowed a stance that would be taken again in the NAMU debate.

The exchange rate regime of 1962–70 also ensured that Canadian policy-makers lost the use of exchange rate adjustments as a tool for addressing balance of payments disequilibria. In the context of the Canada-US balance of payments relationship, this constraint prompted the Canadian and US governments to consider alternative adjustment mechanisms, such as restrictions on capital movements and rules relating to reserve holdings. The mechanisms generated growing frustrations on the Canadian side that also contributed to the 1970 decision to float.

In the post-1970 period, the floating rate was actively used for balance of payments purposes. Instead of a "free float," Canadian monetary authorities frequently managed the exchange rate in order to bolster the international competitiveness of Canadian firms. Rather than offsetting the impact of *external* shocks, exchange rate movements were used primarily to accommodate the (upwards) movement of *domestic* wages and prices. As demonstrated in 1962, 1969–70, and after

1976, Canadian policy-makers encountered significant political difficulties in trying to contain wages and prices in a more organized manner.
They saw exchange rate movements as a very useful tool to help compensate for this situation, although this strategy was criticized by many.

The decision to float in 1970, and the subsequent endorsement of this
exchange rate regime for the next fifteen years, thus reflected the renewed commitment of Canadian policy-makers to the two macroeconomic rationales for the float that had first been outlined in the 1930s.
Of course, these same macroeconomic results might have been achieved
through frequent adjustments of the exchange rate peg. But, as in the
past, Canadian policy-makers were well aware of the political difficulties involved – both within Canada and in bilateral relations with the
US – in trying to implement deliberate exchange rate adjustments, although these difficulties had been lessened somewhat with the expansion of a system of intra-regional compensatory payments within the
Canadian federation.

One final factor – US support – helps explain the Canadian decision to
resume its floating exchange rate regime. In the early 1960s, the US had
encouraged Canada to adopt a fixed exchange rate regime. This US pressure was noteworthy since it marked one of the few moments since the
early 1930s that US policy-makers became interested in Canadian
exchange rate policy. This interest had been provoked by the deliberate
depreciation strategy of the Canadian government during 1961–62. In
1970, however, US officials were more sympathetic to the need for a
float. The reasons were similar to those in 1950; US officials were not enthusiastic to see the use of capital controls to defend the fixed rate. The
fact that the float was now associated with an appreciation of the Canadian currency also helped reduce US opposition to the float. The 1961–
62 moment turned out to be an aberration. It was, however, one that
would be repeated in the mid-1980s, as we shall see in the next chapter.

PART TWO

Free Trade and the Emergence of the NAMU Debate

CHAPTER FIVE

The Exchange Rate Regime in the Free Trade Debate

The second half of this book examines the politics of the NAMU debate. NAMU supporters portray their proposal as a natural and obvious next step in the process of North American economic integration that began with the introduction of the Canada-US Free Trade Agreement (FTA) in 1989. They also highlight that interest in NAMU stems in part from a larger worldwide trend, prompted by the creation of the euro in Europe, towards the creation of regional monetary unions. From this perspective, the creation of NAMU is a very likely, if not inevitable, development. In this part of the book, however, the analysis of the politics of the NAMU debate suggests that the situation is more complicated.

Chapters 6–8 analyse the politics of the NAMU debate as it has unfolded since 1999. This chapter begins the analysis by examining exchange rate discussions that took place at the time of the negotiation and implementation of the FTA and North American Free Trade Agreement (NAFTA) in the mid-1980s to early 1990s. If NAMU is a logical extension of North American free trade, we should expect to find some discussion of the issue at the time that these agreements were created. As this chapter highlights, the issue did indeed receive some attention at this time. For the first time since 1970, Canada's floating exchange rate regime began to be questioned both in Canada and the US. Indeed, many of the prominent Canadian supporters of NAMU today first emerged as critics of the floating exchange rate regime in this period, and the arguments they put forward were very similar to those presented in 1999.

But the chapter shows that these critics of Canada's floating exchange rate regime ultimately had little influence in this period. Most supporters of the FTA and NAFTA *rejected* the idea that North American free trade required closer exchange rate cooperation, let alone monetary union. As a result, the FTA and NAFTA were established without even a limited initiative to stabilize exchange rates. The political forces that worked in favour of a continuation of Canada's floating exchange rate regime in this new free trade era were similar to those that had long encouraged this exchange rate regime in the Canadian context. Although the debates at this time did not lead to any change in Canada's exchange rate regime, they are important for us to examine. A decade before the NAMU debate took place, many of its battle lines were clearly drawn. And in many respects, so too were results.

US INTEREST IN LINKING EXCHANGE RATES TO THE FREE TRADE NEGOTIATIONS

The decision of the Canadian and United States governments to negotiate a comprehensive free trade agreement in 1985 marked an important turning point in economic relations between the two countries. If trade relations were to be transformed, it is not surprising that questions would also be raised about the exchange rate regime. We have seen how the connection between free trade and the Canada-US exchange rate regime had certainly been made in the past. When the 1935 Trade Agreement between the two countries had been negotiated, the US had demanded the inclusion of a clause that required Canada to maintain a relatively stable exchange rate. And further back, we have seen how closer Canada-US economic relations at the time of the Reciprocity Treaty of 1854–66 also acted as a prompt for Canada to conform its exchange rate regime more closely with the US dollar.

During the FTA negotiation, it was US policy-makers who first raised the exchange rate issue. The FTA was negotiated at a time when the exchange rate of the US dollar vis-à-vis other leading industrial countries had already become highly politicized within the United States. In 1985, the US was experiencing large current account deficits which were blamed partly on the fact that the US dollar had appreciated substantially against the currencies of the major US trading partners between 1980 and 1985. As demands for trade protectionism grew, the Reagan administration decided in 1985 to begin pressing for a major realignment of the value of the US dollar vis-à-vis the currencies of its major trading partners.

Initially, US political attention was focused mainly on encouraging the Deutschemark (DM) and yen to appreciate. The initial neglect of Canada's currency made some sense given that it had not depreciated to nearly the same extent as those currencies vis-à-vis the US dollar in the 1980–85 period; it had fallen about 14 per cent in nominal terms, or 6 per cent in real terms.[1] But as the DM and yen appreciated dramatically between late 1985 and early 1987, some US policy-makers began to examine the Canadian currency's value more closely. In particular, they were struck by the fact that the Canadian dollar had hardly appreciated at all in this period – from its low of 69 cents in early 1986, the dollar had risen to 73 cents by January 1987 – despite the existence of a large bilateral Canada-US trade imbalance. While some economists pointed to solid economic reasons – especially low commodity prices – to explain the Canadian dollar's value,[2] other analysts became convinced that the currency was undervalued in this period. Many in the US business community and US Congress shared this view.

The negotiation of the Canada-US Free Trade Agreement between 1985 and 1987 provided an opportunity to press the issue. The question of linking trade agreements to exchange rate issues was attracting more general attention at this time within US Congress and some parts of the US business community.[3] Like US negotiators in 1935, critics of Canada's exchange rate argued that a free trade agreement should not be signed without a guarantee that Canada would not manipulate its currency for competitive gain. Even some economists who were less critical of Canadian exchange rate policy, such as John Williamson, favoured the idea of combining the FTA with a more formal exchange rate relationship.[4]

Within the US business community, the National Association of Manufacturers was the most prominent group to take up the cause. It called publicly for the free trade deal to include a requirement for bilateral consultations if the value of the two countries' currencies changed dramatically.[5] The idea was also promoted by some key figures in the US Congress. In the House of Representatives, John Lafalce, a Democrat from New York, held hearings on the issue of including exchange rates within the FTA and he pressed the idea in many meetings with the chief US negotiator of the FTA, Peter Murphy.[6] The powerful Democratic senator Max Baucus also pressed for the Canadian dollar to be pegged within a "target zone."[7] Indeed, as the negotiations reached their final stage in early 1987, he argued that the exchange rate question was one of four issues that had to be addressed if the deal was to be acceptable to

US Congress: "In my judgment, the exchange rate issue should be addressed before any agreement is struck. The Canadian dollar currently is about 25 percent below parity, giving Canadian exporters a tremendous price advantage in the U.S. market. I do not want to go into the causes of the depressed Canadian dollar. I only want to note that an exchange rate that places U.S. producers at a disadvantage creates a bad climate for congressional approval of any free trade agreement."[8]

This domestic political pressure clearly had some impact on the US administration. In late 1985, just before the trade negotiations got underway, Canada's industry ministry, Sinclair Stevens, later recalled how US commerce secretary Malcolm Baldridge told him that a deal would not be reached unless the dollar appreciated to somewhere near the 90 cent mark.[9] Murphy also told his negotiating team in April 1986 that the Canadian dollar's movement was one of the major negotiating priorities, and a number of times during the negotiations he made a point of highlighting US Congressional concerns about the level of the Canadian dollar.[10] At a 20 May 1986 Senate Foreign Relations Committee hearing that took place one day before the preliminary trade negotiations formally began, Treasury Secretary James Baker also argued that Canada must stop what he called its deliberate policy of maintaining a weak dollar, a policy which he linked to Canada's trade surplus with the US. He added that Canada might have to accept a higher dollar if it hoped to join the "multilateral surveillance" process involving G-5 finance ministers and central bankers.[11]

THE CONTINUED COMMITMENT TO FLOATING IN CANADA

In the face of this US pressure, there was widespread speculation in Canada that Canadian policy-makers had agreed to a secret side deal on exchange rates that would keep the Canadian dollar at a high rate while the FTA was being implemented. This speculation was reinforced when the introduction of the FTA in 1988 coincided with an appreciation of the Canadian dollar that seemed to directly address US concerns. From a low of 69 cents in early 1986, the Canadian dollar rose to a high of 89 cents by December 1991. Even if a side deal was not part of the formal FTA negotiations, Laurie suggests that it still may have been reached at the G-7's February 1987 meeting in Paris when the "Louvre accord" was announced, as it established target ranges for the major currencies.[12] This speculation is understandable since the US had played the central role at the previous year's Tokyo Summit in expanding the G-5 finance ministers' meeting to include Canada and Italy.[13] And, as noted above, James Baker had stated publicly that the price of Canada's admission to the G-5 multilateral surveillance process would be some movement in the value of the Canadian dollar.

Suggestions that a secret deal on exchange rates was reached have been vigorously denied by Canadian policy-makers.[14] Some of those involved in the negotiations have provided some interesting details to back up their argument. Michael Hart, for example, argues that Finance Minister Michael Wilson was successful in persuading James Baker to back down from the goal he had outlined before the US Senate in May 1986 of pushing up the Canadian dollar.[15] John Crow, who was governor of the Bank of Canada at the time, also disputes the idea that Canada accepted an exchange rate target at the Louvre meetings. He notes that the exchange rate targets were agreed at a meeting of the G-5, which excluded Italy and Canada – indeed, the meeting took place before the Canadian representatives had even landed in Paris. The Italians were in fact so angry at their exclusion that their finance minister left the conference. Once the Canadians arrived, Crow reports that French officials did ask if they would like to join the agreement, but this offer was refused and the French accepted this decision.[16]

The exclusion of Canada and Italy from this decision-making was not so surprising. Although the 4–5 May 1986 Tokyo summit had agreed to create the G-7 finance ministers' group (which included Canada and Italy), it had also agreed to preserve the smaller G-5 group of finance ministers and central bankers, and it entrusted to this smaller forum the task of "multilateral surveillance."[17] This decision highlights that too much importance should not be placed on Baker's 20 May 1986 speculation that Canada would have to accept a higher dollar in order to be included in the G-5 process. This statement was uttered two weeks *after* the Tokyo summit decision at which Canada had already been accepted into the new G-7 finance minister ministers' group, and at which it had already been made clear that Canada would not join the smaller G-5 process at the Louvre.

Further evidence that no secret deal was reached at the Louvre meetings is Crow's report that the US Treasury continued to press in the fall of 1987 for a kind of fixed exchange rate arrangement that would prevent the Canadian dollar from depreciating. If a deal had been reached in February, there would have been no need for this further pressure. Crow also notes that Canadian officials once again rejected the idea and the US backed off. Here is Crow's analysis of the US thinking: "My own take is that the US Treasury negotiators were not particularly concerned to get a side deal but felt it was worth a try ... No doubt the Americans were curious to see how we would react to such a proposal." But Crow also notes that the rising Canadian dollar "might well have made the US side less aggressive in the actual bargaining than it would otherwise have been."[18]

If no secret deal on exchange rates was reached,[19] what reason did Canadian policy-makers have for resisting the idea of fixing the exchange rate in this period? In the lead-up to, and during, the FTA negotiations, many FTA supporters argued strongly in favour of a floating Canadian dollar on the grounds that it could play a crucial role in helping the Canadian economy adjust to the new continental free trade environment. The economic effects of the implementation of the FTA were hard to predict, and they argued that a floating rate was particularly important in guarding against a situation in which Canadian firms found themselves unable to compete in the new free trade environment. Here is how Richard Lipsey, the senior economic advisor to the C.D. Howe Institute in 1985, put it: "a flexible exchange rate is the ultimate protection against some of the disaster scenarios. What would happen, for example, if Canadian manufacturing industry found that it just could not compete and our exports fell dramatically while there was an associated flight of capital from Canada? The answer is that the exchange rate would fall until Canadian industry could compete and it no longer paid capital to flee the country. For example, many firms that could not export with a 75-cent dollar would find doing so profitable with a 65-cent dollar ... a free trade agreement with the United States would certainly be instituted in the context of a flexible exchange rate."[20]

This desire to keep the option of depreciation open was widely held among economists who supported the FTA negotiations. As Courchene put it a few years later, "virtually all advocates of free trade argued that a flexible exchange rate was the *sina qua non* of the Agreement" for this reason.[21] The idea that a free trade agreement should be accompanied by a floating exchange rate had also been endorsed by the important 1985 Royal Commission on Economic Union and Development Prospects for Canada, which had played the key role of putting the idea of a Canada-US free trade agreement on the Canadian political agenda. Commonly referred to as the MacDonald Commission, it had argued that a free trade agreement should be accompanied by a floating exchange rate partly because this exchange rate regime had "shock-absorbing benefits" that helped ease "our adjustment in the face of a 'boom or bust' in resource exports." More important to the commissioners, however, was the fact that a floating rate would allow Canada to secure monetary policy independence. As they put it, a floating exchange rate would allow Canada to "have a made-in-Canada macroeconomic policy."[22]

The commissioners' defense of monetary policy independence was interesting in light of subsequent developments. They acknowledged that many smaller European countries had decided to abandon monetary policy independence by pegging their currencies to the DM as a way of importing Germany's low inflation. But they pointed out that tying the Canadian dollar to the US currency would produce similar benefits to Canada only "if the US succeeded in establishing monetary stability and low inflation." Echoing the longstanding distrust of US monetary policy-making among Canadian policy-makers, the commissioners were not willing to give the US this vote of confidence: "Recent experience has demonstrated that Canada might not wish to be bound to developments in the United States."[23] The "recent experience" appeared to refer to the unpopular 1981–82 period when the Canadian dollar's informal link to the US had forced Canada to import the very high US interest rates. Indeed, the commissioners went out of their way to argue that Canadian monetary policy should be loosened to promote economic recovery, even if this produced a currency depreciation.[24]

To others, however, the benefit of a floating exchange rate was that it would allow Canada to pursue a more restrictive, rather than a looser, monetary policy than the US. Howitt, for example, highlighted how a fixed exchange rate would leave Canada vulnerable to importing US inflation, as it had been in the late 1960s.[25] The argument that a floating exchange rate would permit a strong made-in-Canada anti-inflationary monetary policy was taken up very strongly by John Crow when he became governor of the Bank of Canada in early 1987. After assuming the governorship, he outlined his determination to contain inflationary pressures that he argued were building in the Canadian economy. His tight monetary policy soon produced nominal interest rates that were much higher than those in the US at the time. Crow's obsession with conquering inflation at all costs reminded his critics of Coyne's earlier approach to monetary policy.[26] The parallel was particularly apt because of the international dimensions of Crow's policy. As in the Coyne period, high interest rates attracted capital inflows which pushed up the value of the Canadian dollar, thereby reinforcing the restrictive impact of the new policy. By December 1991, the Canadian dollar had reached a level of US$0.89.

The combination of tight money and the high dollar pushed the country into a deep recession in the early 1990s at the very moment that the free trade agreement was coming into effect. Canada's floating exchange rate was suddenly performing an opposite role from the one many FTA supporters had hoped for. Instead of cushioning Canadian firms from the new competitive pressures through a depreciation, the floating rate was reinforcing those pressures by generating a sharp *appreciation*. In these circumstances, the floating rate contributed to, rather than remedied, the kind of "disaster" scenario Lipsey had discussed in which Canadian firms were unable to compete in the new free trade world.

Although Crow and other Bank of Canada officials had anticipated an appreciation of the dollar, they appear to have been surprised by the extent of the currency's upward movement.[27] What had been difficult to anticipate was the scale of the capital inflows. These inflows encouraged a kind of self-reinforcing financial bubble; as investors were attracted by high interest rates, they pushed up the dollar, rendering their new assets even more valuable.[28] The bank did try initially to offset some of the upward pressure on the exchange rate,[29] but Crow made clear that he was not willing to sacrifice his pursuit of price stability to keep down the dollar's value: "I could not see how we could both have a properly credible monetary policy and arrange the value of the Canadian dollar in this way."[30] This set of priorities became particularly clear in early 1990 when the dollar fell briefly in response to the bank's temporary easing of monetary policy. Instead of welcoming this currency depreciation, bank officials worried that it might contribute to inflationary pressures and they reverted to a tight monetary policy.[31]

Years later, Crow highlighted his belief that the high dollar not only helped curtail inflation but also played a helpful role in accelerating the restructuring that Canadian businesses needed to undertake to compete in the new free trade environment. He explicitly attacked the way in which Canadians had come to see "a weaker currency as the escape hatch from a poor performance on inflation" in the past.[32] Unlike Coyne, Crow found support for his views among key figures within the federal government, most notably Finance Minister Michael Wilson, reflecting the ideological shift away from embedded liberal values that had been underway since the 1970s. As a member of the Opposition in the early 1980s, Wilson had been critical of the Liberal government's willingness to allow the Canadian dollar to depreciate since 1976, arguing that this soft currency option had discouraged firms from taking measures to improve their international competitiveness. When Wilson became finance minister in 1984, he initially endorsed the low dollar strategy because Prime Minister Mulroney had done so in the federal election campaign. But when the dollar fell to 69 cents in early 1986, Wilson made clear to Bank of Canada governor Gerald Bouey that he wanted to curb the dollar's fall. Then, when Crow became governor, Wilson fully backed the shift in the bank's policies.[33]

The rationale for a floating exchange rate put forward by Crow and Wilson echoed some of the more conservative views put forward at the time of the 1970 float, as well as in 1975 when monetary targeting had been adopted. But the rationale was quite different from the thinking that had endorsed the long depreciation after 1976. It was also very different from the recommendations of the MacDonald Commission only a few years earlier. In fact, the MacDonald Commission report had explicitly considered and rejected the approach adopted by Crow for defeating inflation. The commissionners had argued that future anti-inflationary initiatives should not rely exclusively on the blunt instrument of monetary restraint which was "likely to involve a severe and possibly extended recession" and produce "very substantial costs, many of which are borne by the weakest members of society." A less costly way of reducing inflationary expectations was to combine moderate monetary restraint with the kind of temporary wage and price controls which had been used in a relatively successful manner during the 1975–78 period.[34]

PRECURSOR TO THE NAMU DEBATE

As Canada was plunged into a deep recession in the early 1990s, Crow's policy provoked intense domestic opposition, including among the business sector. Critics argued that it was too radical and had been implemented at the worst possible time, just as Canada was struggling to adjust to free trade.[35] Amidst these points, there also emerged a critique of the role that Canada's floating exchange rate regime had played in this policy episode. For the first time in almost two decades, a genuine debate broke out among Canadian economists about the merits of a fixed exchange rate regime versus a floating one.

The debate is important because it foreshadowed the one that emerged around NAMU a decade later. Some of the central advocates of

NAMU after 1999 first put forward their critiques of Canada's floating exchange rate regime early in the decade, most notably the economists Thomas Courchene and Richard Harris.[36] Courchene had long been one of the leading analysts of Canadian monetary policy and we have already seen that he was a strong supporter of monetarism in the mid-1970s. Harris was also a well-respected economist who, like Courchene, had been a strong supporter of the FTA. Both linked their case for a fixed exchange rate to the fact that Canada was now in a free trade environment with the United States.

Both authors also endorsed a fixed exchange rate rather than NAMU. The reason was primarily practical: as Harris put it, "monetary union with the United States is certainly not a serious possibility at the moment."[37] There were, however, some other writers who went further and suggested that Canada embrace NAMU. Lucas and Reid, economists at the University of Saskatchewan and University of Alberta respectively, suggested that Canada adopt the US dollar and bargain for a place as a thirteenth reserve district with the US Federal Reserve system. Their proposal was put forward more in the context of the debate on Quebec's possible separation than on Crow's policy, although the latter crept into their analysis.[38] Herbert Grubel, an economist at Simon Fraser University, also put forward a proposal for NAMU, in some conference papers in 1992–93, although he notes that they were not initially well received.[39] He would emerge – alongside Courchene and Harris – as one of the lead proponents of the idea after 1999.

What was the case of these various authors against Canada's floating exchange rate?[40] In their view, this regime prevented Canada from benefiting fully from the new free trade environment. Not only did currency volatility inhibit cross-border commerce, but the floating exchange rate was also increasingly subject to misalignments. For example, Harris argued that between 1985 and 1988 the Canadian dollar had been undervalued and had thus provided protection for inefficient firms at the very time when they needed to be improving their productivity. Then, as the free trade agreement was being implemented between 1989 and 1992, the currency had become overvalued. This discouraged foreign direct investment into Canada and had prompted many firms to shut down Canadian plants and relocate production in the US.

Harris also reiterated a point made in the early 1960s: that the costs associated with a floating rate were becoming more significant as Canada moved from a resource-based economy to one based more on manufacturing and human capital. Floating exchange rates did not pose an enormous problem for the resource sector, because firms were selling standardized commodities in a well-organized spot market and most natural resource exports were priced in US dollars. Short-term swings in the Canadian dollar thus simply affected residual resource rents after nominal factor costs were paid. The manufacturing sector, however, required a more predictable cost structure because of its reliance on long-term bilateral contracts and high degrees of specialization. As he put it, "because contracts are normally stated in nominal amounts and are 'sticky' ... large swings in an exchange rate over a short period cause severe problems for firms and workers in sectors involved in international transactions."[41]

This argument was important in calling into question the longstanding view that the floating Canadian dollar provided a useful adjustment tool for the Canadian economy. This conventional view assumed that the exchange rate actually moved in the "right" direction to buffer the domestic economy from external shocks or to offset changes in domestic prices and wages. If, however, the exchange rate moved in the "wrong" direction, the floating currency regime, Harris pointed out, could itself become the source of an unpleasant shock to the domestic economy. As we saw in chapter 3, the overvaluation of the Canadian dollar in the late 1950s had led to a similar critique of the floating exchange rate.

Even if a floating exchange rate was not subject to volatility and misalignments, Courchene argued that its utility as an adjustment tool was becoming politically unacceptable within Canada in an era of intensifying North American integration. He noted a point we have observed throughout this book and that Mundell had also highlighted in 1961: in a highly regionalized economy such as Canada's, the impact of exchange rate movements varies enormously across the country. In Courchene's words, these movements are an "arbiter of regional fortunes." As each region within Canada traded increasingly with US counterparts, he argued – echoing Mundell – that "the 'optimal currency areas' become north-south cross-border regions, not the national economy."[42] In this context, exchange rate movements responding to sector-specific shocks in one part of the country would become even more controversial because they would disrupt these cross-border trading relationships. If, for example, an export boom in Ontario's auto sector put upward pressure on the Canadian dollar, businesses in British Columbia and Alberta would find this increasingly frustrating since it would undermine their ability to compete with western US states.

Courchene highlighted how, during Crow's era of tight monetary policy, the diverse regional implications of Canadian exchange-rate and macroeconomic policy had been particularly apparent. The inflationary pressures that Crow set out to conquer were much more present in Ontario than in the rest of the country. Many outside of Ontario felt the high dollar and high interest rates were quite inappropriate policies for the economic conditions they faced. This was particularly true of resource exporting regions which had been suffering from falling commodity prices at the time. This critique had even been anticipated by one of the research papers for the MacDonald Commission, which had noted that contractionary monetary policy was likely to impact much more heavily on resource exporting regions that would be hurt badly by a rising exchange rate.[43]

Lucas and Reid also contributed to this critique, arguing that western provinces had little to lose from the loss of Canadian monetary policy autonomy: "from a western Canadian perspective, the decision of the Bank of Canada to pursue a disinflationary policy in the 1980s despite the weak state of many of the western provincial economies and over the objections of the provincial premiers indicates that western Canadians have nothing to lose in this area." They went further, showing that inflation rates in the western cities did not correlate with those in Toronto and Montreal in 1975–90. Assuming that the bank would continue to focus on the needs of the latter, they concluded: "Bank policy will never be consistent with the needs of the western regional economies."[44]

If the exchange rate would no longer play a role as an adjustment tool, what did Courchene think would take its place? He argued that provincial fiscal policies could assume a larger role in helping Canada's regions adjust to external shocks under a fixed exchange rate. He also suggested that domestic wages and prices might become more responsive to international competitive concerns in a fixed exchange rate environment, as firms and workers were able to compare Canadian costs more clearly with those of their US counterparts.

This last suggestion related to a third argument in favour of a fixed exchange rate regime. Both Courchene and Harris argued that this regime would help impose a healthy market discipline within the Canadian economy. Courchene in fact suggested that the adoption of a fixed exchange rate might provide an alternative and less costly way to curtail inflation than Crow's approach for this reason. This argument was also made by the prominent economist Pierre Fortin, who endorsed a pegged exchange rate at this time.[45] Fortin argued that a currency peg, by making Canada-US cost comparisons more transparent, might help anchor Canadian wage and price expectations to the lower US inflation level without the need for so severe a monetary restraint as that employed by Crow. This was, after all, an approach adopted by smaller European countries such as Austria, which had pegged to the German Deutschemark and thereby succeeded in importing lower German price levels. To be sure, Fortin acknowledged that some Canadians did not think the US commitment to price stability was as trustworthy as the German Bundesbank's. But he argued that the recent record of the US was at least superior to that of Canada.[46]

Fortin argued that this strategy for containing inflation would be particularly useful in the Canadian context because of the difficulties of controlling wages and prices in Canada in a more organized manner. Many European countries were able to regulate wage and price rises directly through social partnership agreements between unions, firms, and the state. This approach relied, however, on a history of stable labour relations, a sense of mutual trust among all the social partners, and a national consensus on the need for full employment – none of which existed in Canada in the late 1980s and early 1990s.[47] It was true, he acknowledged, that the experience with temporary wage and price controls had been relatively successful, as the MacDonald Commission had also pointed out. But even these controls had generated inefficiencies over time and had encountered growing opposition. Indeed, when the idea of reimposing price and wage controls was raised by some at the height of Crow's monetary restraint, mainstream opinion had reacted negatively, as had the Bank of Canada and the Department of Finance.[48]

In terms of a fairer distribution of impacts, Courchene highlighted one further benefit of tackling inflation in this way. He noted that the tradable sector of the Canadian economy experienced the effects of Crow's tight monetary policy more severely than the non-tradable sector. It had to cope with not just high interest rates but also a temporary appreciation of the real exchange rate as the nominal value of the Canadian dollar rose more quickly than domestic wages and prices declined. The concentrated impact of Crow's policies was, in Courchene's view, unfair when the inflation being targeted had a domestic source.

The idea that a fixed exchange rate regime could be used to impose a kind of discipline on firms and workers foreshadowed the arguments of some NAMU supporters after 1999. It was not just workers and firms that would experience greater discipline under a fixed exchange rate regime. The fourth and final argument in favour of a fixed exchange rate was that it might impose new constraints on government too. Harris argued that greater price transparency between the US and Canada might put new pressure on Canadian governments to set tax levels closer to US standards. More importantly, a fixed exchange rate would bring greater discipline to Canadian macroeconomic policy. It would, for example, ensure that the impact of a lax fiscal policy was felt more quickly and directly. This kind of discipline, in turn, might help restore the government's credibility in the eyes of financial markets in a manner that was quicker than Crow's long and painful deflation. And the abandonment of the floating exchange rate would also constrain Canada's monetary policy-makers.

The fact that these authors saw this last implication in a positive light reflected their willingness to challenge the longstanding commitment of Canadian policy-makers to monetary autonomy. Having lived through the Bank of Canada's severe monetary restraint program, these critics of Crow's policies no longer saw the defense of monetary autonomy as such a virtue.[49] Their judgment echoed advocates of a fixed exchange rate in the early 1960s who had become disillusioned with Coyne's leadership of the Bank of Canada. Lucas and Reid's case for NAMU, however, even critiqued Canadian monetary policy *before* the Crow era. Noting that Canada had on average experienced higher inflation than the US between 1960 and 1990, they argued that NAMU would allow Canadians to import greater price stability from the US. They also highlighted the risks associated with the growing demands at the time from Quebec and other provinces for input in the decision-making of the Bank of Canada. Embracing NAMU would "eliminate the potential for greater political input into the design and implementation of monetary policy."[50]

These arguments in favour of a fixed exchange rate were strongly criticized on various grounds by two Canadian analysts who would emerge a decade later as the lead opponents of NAMU: Bill Robson of the C.D. Howe Institute, who had long been a prominent advocate of price stability, and David Laidler, an economist at the University of Western Ontario with similar views and who had been a supporter of monetarism in the 1970s along with Courchene.[51] To begin with, they argued that it would be very difficult to decide the rate at which to establish a peg, especially as adjustments to the new free trade environment were still underway.[52] They also questioned the idea that a fixed exchange rate would put an end to speculative financial flows which caused currency instability. They noted that a fixed rate would likely be an *adjustable* peg system which could encourage, rather than discourage, speculative financial flows, as had been witnessed in 1950 and 1970.

They also reiterated the familiar argument that a floating rate was needed to absorb external economic shocks given that the US and Canada were affected by external shocks in quite different ways. Without this tool, the adjustment burden would fall on domestic wages and prices, which were much less flexible than the nominal exchange rate. The result would be a much more painful and costly adjustment process. If Courchene felt that this macroeconomic role of a floating exchange rate was not always appropriate for all regions of the country, they reminded readers that external shocks under a fixed exchange rate would still provoke adjustments that involved the entire economy. If, for example, the government defended the currency peg with foreign exchange intervention or interest rate adjustments, the entire economy would be affected. Similarly, if foreign demand for forestry products increased, wages and prices across the Canadian economy as a whole would rise.

In addition, they questioned the argument that a fixed exchange rate could play a central role in constraining domestic inflation. It could perform this role, they argued, only if the peg was a credible one. But this would only be true if the domestic commitment to anti-inflation goals was firm. They recalled how Canadian policy-makers had been forced to tighten monetary policy soon after the 1962 peg had been introduced because it had not been perceived as credible. The episode highlighted that the significance of an exchange rate arrangement was easily overstated; what mattered more was the dedication of Canadian policy-makers to price stability.

Finally, they critiqued the idea that the goal of importing US price levels was a desirable one. In their view, the US central bank was an institution "that shows less enthusiasm for price stability" than the Bank of Canada recently had.[53] They also argued that US monetary policy was unlikely to change in this respect any time soon: "the shaky state of the US financial system and the fact that the United States' considerable – and growing – external liabilities are denominated in US dollars are two factors giving a potential inflationary bias to future US monetary policy."[54] This line of argument was echoed by other critics of a fixed exchange rate at this time. Economist Doug Purvis, for example, argued, "it is not clear that the historical record in the United States inspires the kind of confidence required to make this argument [for a fixed exchange rate] compelling."[55] Similarly, a Bank of Canada report rejecting the idea of a fixed exchange rate argued that the floating exchange rate had enabled the bank to be more aggressive in fighting inflation than the US had been.[56]

This debate about the virtues of fixed versus floating exchange rates was one that took place primarily among academic economists outside of government. It had no impact on Canadian policy-making in this period; the federal government and Bank of Canada remained committed to the floating exchange rate regime.[57] If there was a prospect in this period to mobilize a broad domestic opposition to the floating rate, it was diminished when the dollar began to decline in 1992. In response to the bank's loosening of monetary policy and speculative pressures generated by the 1992 European exchange rate crisis, the dollar fell from its high of 89 cents in December 1991 to 78 cents one year later. In contrast to its behaviour in early 1990, the bank did not resist this depreciation, recognizing correctly that there were few risks of inflationary pressures by this time.[58]

With the election of Jean Chrétien's Liberal government in 1993, the political context for exchange rate and monetary policy-making changed. The country had chosen a prime minister who had supported the dollar's depreciation when he was finance minister in the late 1970s.[59] During the 1993 election, the Liberals had also been critical of Crow's performance and they chose not to renew his appointment as Bank of Canada governor when his term ended the next year (and after he refused to accept higher inflation targets). In his place, the less doctrinaire Gordon Thiessen was appointed. The central architects of the "high dollar-tight money" policy – Crow and Wilson – were no longer in office.

THE NAFTA NEGOTIATIONS
AND THE EXCHANGE RATE ISSUE

If Canadian policy-makers remained committed to a float throughout this period, what about the US interest in a fixed exchange rate? Although US interest had diminished as the Canadian dollar rose in value during the late 1980s, the decision to negotiate NAFTA in 1991 provided an opportunity for the issue to be raised again. When US trade representative Carla Hills made her first appearance before Congress after announcing the proposed NAFTA in February 1991, Max Baucus immediately raised the question of whether Mexico, Canada, and the

United States should be creating a common currency, as European governments were doing. Although Hills rejected the idea entirely, one reporter noted "there is continuing unhappiness in some circles here that the Canada-U.S. deal didn't include a mechanism to ensure the value of the two currencies was kept within specific target zones. Although the value of the Canadian dollar has risen against its U.S. counterpart in the last year or so, Baucus and others complained the cheaper Canadian dollar gives exporters north of the border an unfair advantage over their American counterparts."[60] The National Association of Manufacturers also demanded once again that the new agreement "seek to prevent exchange-rate manipulation for a country's competitive advantage."[61]

The issue of whether NAFTA should be accompanied by formal exchange rate cooperation or a common currency along the European model was also addressed at a conference hosted by the Federal Reserve Bank of Kansas City in 1991. The conference brought together leading policy-makers and exchange rate specialists from all three countries and it revealed little enthusiasm for the idea. Mexican policy-makers outlined that they had no interest in linking NAFTA to the creation of a formal currency zone. They valued the fact that their floating exchange rate could help them adjust to external shocks.[62] Prominent US analysts, such as Martin Feldstein, noted that free trade areas did not need stable exchange rates since there was little evidence that exchange rate volatility disrupted international trade or financial integration.[63] Contributing to the skepticism was the Canadian critic of fixed exchange rates, David Laidler, who argued that a common currency would dilute national monetary sovereignty and would require much closer political cooperation.[64] Also, if exchange rates were no longer available as a tool of adjustment between the three North American countries, Laidler argued that the region would need to liberalize cross-border labour movements and/or create mechanisms for inter-country fiscal transfers. The importance of the exchange rate adjustment mechanism was also highlighted by other analysts at this time who noted that the three countries were far from an optimum currency area since they experienced uncorrelated economic shocks.[65]

As the NAFTA negotiations proceeded, some members of US Congress continued to press the administration to include exchange rates in the discussions. The issue became particularly prominent after Clinton's election when the new administration began to negotiate side-agreements relating to environmental and labour issues. Congressman John Lafalce once again took a lead role in raising the issue's profile. He organized a hearing in the Committee on Small Business in May 1993 in which he called for a separate side-agreement to be reached on exchange rates. The agreement would be, in his words, "an EC-like band as a guide that would trigger a consultation, coordination, and corrective mechanism if necessary." He explained his reasoning in the following way: "The exchange-rate relationship between the dollar and the peso will profoundly affect how any NAFTA operates and the distribution and nature of the benefits and burdens of NAFTA. Yet NAFTA establishes no mechanism to coordinate monetary policy between the United States and Mexico, nor does it provide for consultations or corrective measures if exchange rates are used to promote competitiveness."[66]

As this statement makes clear, Lafalce's interest had shifted away from the Canadian context to the Mexican one. Lafalce had been prompted to hold the hearing after Jorge Castaneda had told Lafalce's committee a few months earlier that the peso might be devalued shortly after NAFTA was passed, a result that Castenada had predicted would diminish the export gains of US businesses under the agreement. At the time, some people – recalling the earlier rumours about a secret deal on the Canadian dollar – were in fact speculating that the US and Mexico had reached an understanding to keep the peso at a higher value during the NAFTA debate.[67]

Lafalce found some support for his idea from the chair of the Committee on Banking, Finance and Urban Affairs, Henry Gonzales in a September 1993 hearing.[68] Echoing his earlier stance during the FTA negotiations, the prominent international economist John Williamson also endorsed the proposal to include a mechanism for stabilizing exchange rates within NAFTA.[69] The idea was also backed by a spokesperson for one of the leading US coalitions critical of NAFTA, Nikos Valance of the Fair Trade Campaign. Valance argued before a US Congressional committee in September 1993 that the absence of an exchange rate agreement opened the door to a devaluation of the peso which would not only hurt US exports to Mexico but would also put downward pressures on the wages of US workers trying to compete with Mexican producers. He speculated that an agreement on exchange rates had been deliberately avoided in order to allow US multinational firms to pressure the Mexican government for a peso devaluation and thus lower the wages of Mexican and US workers.[70]

But the idea of a side-agreement relating to exchange rates found little wider support. The Salinas government had no interest in the idea.[71] Within the US, exchange rate issues no longer generated the kind of interest they had provoked in the mid-1980s when US current account deficits had been growing rapidly.[72] The country was experiencing an economic boom for much of the 1990s and Lafalce was forced to acknowledge that the issue was "a perfect cure for insomnia for many members" of Congress. In addition, he noted that most US businesses seemed unconcerned by the prospect of a peso devaluation, a perspective that he guessed resulted from them being more interested in using Mexico as an export platform than as an export market for US-made products.[73] Economist Rudi Dornbusch also reminded members of Congress that the Mexican economy was vulnerable to quite different external shocks than the US because of the large role of oil exports in the Mexican economy. If the Mexican peso was no longer able to adjust to changes in oil prices, he suggested that the US might find itself helping finance Mexico's external imbalances in order to defend the currency peg.[74]

The fact that a stable Mexican peso might require US financial support became all the more apparent in the first months of NAFTA's implementation. The Mexican currency came under serious selling pressure in March 1994 in the wake of the assassination of the leading candidate for the upcoming Mexican presidential elections, and the US extended a $6-billion temporary credit to Mexico to defend the peso. The next month, the central bank governors and finance ministers of the three NAFTA countries went further to announce the creation of a permanent swap arrangement capable of mobilizing $8.8 billion to support each others' currencies. The arrangement included a $2-billion reciprocal swap arrangement which had been in place since 1962 between the US and Canada (but not drawn upon since the 1960s), as well as a credit line between Mexico and Canada which had first been established in 1991 and was now raised from $200 million to $1 billion. At the same time, the three countries announced the creation of a "North American Financial Group" that would consult on common financial and economic problems.[75]

These developments seemed to indicate that there was indeed some interest among the NAFTA partners in mechanisms that could stabilize exchange rates within North America. But this notion was quickly dispelled during the Mexican financial crisis of December 1994. Not only was the peso devalued massively by the Mexican government at the time, but the crisis also revealed the fragility of the US commitment to provide financial support to Mexico. Congress refused to endorse President Clinton's request for emergency financial assistance for Mexico during the crisis, forcing him to draw funds from sources that did not require Congressional authorization.[76] Opposition came from politicians who had already been suspicious of NAFTA on both the Republican right and the Democratic left. As one Texas Republican in the former camp, Steve Stockman, explained: "I've read the constitution and nowhere in this constitution does it talk about bailing out sovereign nations."[77] The whole episode made clear the lack of interest in any formal exchange rate arrangements or a common currency within the NAFTA region.

But the issue did not leave the agenda altogether. So severe was the crisis that some Mexicans began to debate whether their country should adopt the dollar as a way to maintain currency stability. In the US, too, there remained some interest in the argument that exchange rate instability in NAFTA necessitated the move to a common currency. The economist George von Furstenberg put the case in the following way: "separate currencies within a trading bloc are like loose cannons to be rolled about by the markets."[78] In Canada, Herbert Grubel argued after the crisis that Mexico could avoid future currency crises by abandoning the peso, and he predicted that the three countries of NAFTA would create a single currency by 2000.[79] Official opinion, however, showed little interest in these ideas.

CONCLUSION

Important precursors of the NAMU debate took place during the negotiations and implementation of the FTA and NAFTA. In the US, some politicians and business leaders expressed an interest in linking North American free trade to the establishment of more stable exchange rates – or even a monetary union – within the region. But true to historical fashion, the US interest in fixing the Canadian exchange rate was not terribly strong or sustained. It emerged from what Henning describes as an exceptional moment in US politics when broader concerns about the country's current account deficits in the mid-1980s briefly generated considerable domestic interest in the exchange rate policies of foreign countries. Once this broader concern faded, so too did the interest in regional exchange rate arrangements.[80] This absence of serious US interest in linking North American free trade and monetary cooperation foreshadowed developments during the NAMU debate.

A second important debate took place in Canada. In responding to US pressure, Canadian policy-makers were forced to make a serious defence of their commitment to a floating exchange rate for the first time since the discussions surrounding the 1970 float. They resorted to arguments that were familiar from previous eras, and that would appear again in the NAMU debate. At the time of the negotiation of the FTA, prominent Canadian supporters of the deal argued that a floating exchange rate was needed to facilitate balance of payments adjustments, particularly in the new and more uncertain free trade environment. They also argued that it made possible an independent monetary policy. While many European countries saw the fixing of their currency to the German DM as a way to import German price stability at this time, Canadian policy-makers highlighted that they continued to distrust US monetary policy in this period. Some argued that US policy was too restrictive, citing the high US interest rates of the early 1980s. Others thought the US central bank was not aggressive enough in attacking inflation.

In the wake of Crow's tight monetary policy, Canada's floating exchange rate became the target of domestic critiques among some Canadian economists who would emerge a few years later as the lead advocates of NAMU. Their arguments were similar to those that had surfaced in the early 1960s after Coyne's similarly tight monetary policy. In both eras, the value of monetary policy autonomy was questioned by those who were critical of the Bank of Canada's policies. The floating exchange rate was also seen to have exacerbated the country's economic troubles by generating currency volatility and misalignments. Also reborn was Mundell's earlier argument about the uneven regional impact of exchange rate movements. But these arguments had little impact on official opinion. And even in expert circles, they were hotly contested by economists who would soon emerge as key critics of the NAMU proposal.

CHAPTER SIX

The Neoliberal Case for NAMU and Its Reception

In 1999, Canadians began to debate the issue of North American monetary union in a very active manner. Given that the issue had received almost no attention before in the country's history, the sudden high-profile nature of the discussion was remarkable. The issue received extensive, often front-page, coverage in the country's newspapers. It became the subject of one of the CBC's weekly national phone-in programs. Canada's leading magazine, *Maclean's*, even ran a cover with a picture of George Washington in the middle of a Canadian coin and the headline "Say it ain't so" in July 1999. The question of NAMU was also the subject of many academic meetings as well as of parliamentary debate and Senate hearings. Leading political groups in the country weighed in with their opinions and pollsters quizzed Canadians for their perspectives.

The immediate catalysts for the debate are easily identifiable. Two distinct groups within Canada initially raised the idea in 1999: a small number of prominent Canadian economists and Quebec sovereigntists. Several other developments at the time ensured that their ideas received more attention than they might otherwise have garnered. The ten-year anniversary of the signing of the FTA was already encouraging widespread speculation about the future of North American integration in an era when commercial ties were deepening at a rapid pace. The creation of the euro that same year gave new attention and credibility to the idea of regional currency unions. At the same time, US Congress began to debate whether the US should be encouraging the emergence of a currency bloc across the Americas. Finally, the sharp depreciation of the Canadian currency's value from US$0.73 in the fall of 1997 to an all time low of US$0.63 one year later – a level at which it roughly stayed from 1999 through 2002 – undermined confidence in the currency and prompted new interest in its future prospects.

If this constellation of factors put NAMU on the Canadian political agenda, what kind of political support did the idea generate? What does an examination of the debate tell us about the likelihood that Canada might soon join a NAMU? NAMU supporters suggest that broad historical forces are on their side. They see the creation of NAMU as a logical, and even inevitable, development in this era of North American free trade and emerging currency blocs. There is no doubt that these factors helped put the issue on the Canadian political agenda. But the NAMU proposal has not yet managed to garner the same level of political support that the FTA earned in Canada in the 1980s or the euro project acquired across Europe more recently. Why not?

This question is addressed in the next three chapters. The analysis suggests that supporters of NAMU are right to argue that support for their idea stems from sources similar to those that supported the creation of the FTA and the euro. At the same time, however, the NAMU proposal has attracted influential political opposition, which raises substantial doubts about its political viability within the Canadian political context. Some of this opposition has reflected the enduring influence of features of Canadian exchange rate policy-making encountered earlier in Canadian history. Other sources of opposition have highlighted new concerns that are specific to the NAMU proposal.

THE ECONOMISTS' CASE FOR NAMU

This chapter begins by discussing the political reception of the case for NAMU that was presented by the group of economists who played a key role in raising the issue's profile. Two published works by prominent Canadian economists were particularly significant in generating widespread public interest in NAMU in 1999. The first was by Herbert Grubel, an economist at Simon Fraser University who was a well-known supporter of free market or "neoliberal" views and who had been a Reform Party MP between 1993 and 1997 (acting as finance critic for the party in 1995–97). In the previous chapter, we saw how he had already put forward a proposal for NAMU in 1992–93 in some unpublished conference papers. Now, he expanded his idea into a book published by the Fraser Institute, a right-wing think tank and advocate of neoliberal policy proposals, with which Grubel was closely associated. It was titled: *The Case for the Amero: The Economics and Politics of a North American Monetary Union.*[1]

The second work was published by the C.D. Howe Institute, a think tank that has been a staunch defender of free trade and is generally associated with neoliberal policy advice.[2] The publication was authored by Thomas Courchene and Richard Harris and was titled *From Fixing to Monetary Union: Options for North American Currency Integration.*[3] As we saw in the last chapter, Courchene and Harris had already highlighted their disillusionment with Canada's floating exchange rate during the early 1990s when they had each advocated a fixed exchange rate. Now they combined forces and went further in calling for a monetary union.

In these two publications, and in subsequent writings and public appearances, the authors advanced four central arguments in favour of NAMU, each of which had been foreshadowed in the writings of Courchene and Harris in the early 1990s. To begin with, Courchene and Harris reiterated and updated their earlier arguments about the costs of exchange rate volatility and misalignments. While their focus in the early 1990s had been the overvalued Canadian dollar at that time, they now worried that the Canadian dollar had become undervalued in ways that discouraged improvements in Canadian productivity by sheltering inefficient firms from market pressures. More generally, they highlighted how these episodes of exchange rate misalignment created an uncertain economic climate and discouraged investment, particularly in non-resource, human capital–intensive sectors of the economy.

By calling for a monetary union, as opposed to a fixed exchange rate, these authors highlighted one further efficiency gain that could be generated by the elimination of the floating exchange rate. All currency-related transaction costs could be eliminated in intra–North American commerce, including those associated with accounting and pricing in two separate currencies, and the conversion of currencies for individuals and firms.[4] The elimination of currency risk vis-à-vis the US would also produce deeper capital markets for Canadians and lower their borrowing costs. Over time, they argued, the elimination of separate currencies would also generate dynamic economic benefits in the form of deepening North American economic integration. Indeed, drawing on research of Andrew Rose and Jeffrey Frankel, some advocates of NAMU suggested that Canada-US trade might expand very considerably under a currency union, raising Canada's GDP by more than 30 per cent over ten years.[5]

Second, Courchene and Harris repeated Courchene's earlier critique of the Canadian exchange rate's role in fostering national macroeconomic adjustment. This role was hindered not just by exchange rate misalignments, but also by the fact that various regions of the Canadian economy experienced very different shocks and their business cycles were often not synchronized. As a result, when the exchange rate moved in response to shocks experienced by one region, it affected the others in ways that were not always appropriate to them. As each region became more integrated with US counterparts in the free trade era, these exchange rate movements were also increasingly disruptive to cross-border relationships. This latter point drew on a broader thesis Courchene had already been developing, that "Canada is less and less a single east-west economy and more and more a series of north-south, cross-border economies (with British Columbia also a Pacific Rim economy)."[6]

Courchene and Harris also noted that the implications for asset markets of using the exchange rate as a macroeconomic buffer deserved more attention. For example, a depreciation of the Canadian dollar to offset a negative external shock had the effect of making Canadian assets cheaper. This, in turn, could encourage foreign acquisitions of Canadian firms or make it more difficult for Canadian firms to raise new capital in the US. Thus, even if the buffering mechanism was performing a useful role, it could produce financial side-effects that were less desirable for the Canadian economy as a whole.

As part of their critique of the exchange rate's role as an adjustment tool, these authors also highlighted that Canadians could adjust to shocks in alternative ways within a North American monetary union. Courchene and Harris noted that existing public, nationwide automatic stabilizers – such as equalization payments, transfers within the tax system, and employment insurance – already played an important role in buffering region-specific and Canada-wide shocks. Provincial fiscal policies could also be used more actively. And of course, market mechanisms – internal migration and adjustments of domestic wages and prices – could play a larger role.

The fact that NAMU could encourage greater wage and price flexibility *within* the Canadian economy was in fact the third key benefit of this monetary regime for these authors. Workers and firms would be prompted to embrace greater flexibility because they would now experience more directly the international competitive consequences of their wage demands and business decisions. They would need to confront the impact of external economic shocks on their competitive performance in a more head-on fashion by embracing changes in prices and wages. This argument built on the case made by Harris, Courchene, and Fortin in the early 1990s about how a fixed exchange rate would help bring down Canadian inflation by imposing a form of discipline on Canadian price and wage expectations. But the rationale for discipline was no longer to restrain inflation in a less brutal manner than that chosen by Crow. Instead, it was articulated more as a critique of the rigidity of the Canadian economy. As one observer put it, this was a kind of "tough love" argument "to force Canadians to become more competitive."[7]

It was this case that Grubel took up in greatest detail. He reasoned that the depreciating Canadian dollar since the mid-1970s had allowed Canadian workers to demand nominal wage increases that were not matched by productivity gains in the tradable sector. Under NAMU, this would no longer be possible and labour market discipline would be restored, much as it had been in smaller European countries which had tied their currencies to the DM in the 1980s. Businesses would also no longer be able to hide behind the Canadian dollar's depreciation to delay needed productivity improvements or corporate restructuring. Indeed, Grubel suggested that the floating exchange rate's buffering mechanism had encouraged the Canadian economy to become overly reliant on natural resource production and had delayed its shift towards more high-technology industries.[8] He explicitly noted that his critique of floating rates was similar to that of orthodox thinkers in the 1930s who had argued against depreciation on the grounds that it distorted prices by affecting the entire national economy instead of just an ailing sector.[9]

The fourth and final purported benefit of NAMU was that it would help constrain the macroeconomic activism of the Canadian state. In the realm of monetary policy, Grubel hoped that the common currency of NAMU would be managed by a North American central bank that was – like the European Central Bank – politically independent and mandated to pursue price stability. In the fiscal policy realm, he picked up on Harris's point from the early 1990s that greater price transparency between Canada and the US might encourage Canadian governments to lower taxes to US levels. In addition, Grubel hoped that the federal government's fiscal behaviour would be constrained by a European-style "Stability and Growth Pact" which limited the size of budget deficits and public debt carried by members of the monetary union.[10]

The benefits of these constraints on government policy were partly ideological for Grubel. He had long been highly critical of the postwar Keynesian view that monetary policy could be used to promote employment goals or economic growth. As he told the Canadian Senate, "I would like to have an institution that protects me against the future, when another generation of economists is rediscovering Keynesianism, or whatever threats there might be in the future."[11] NAMU could serve this role: "Canada is more likely to be protected from the adverse consequence of future misadventures in monetary policy as a member of a North American Monetary Union than if it had its own central bank exposed to influences by ambitious politicians and public opinion."[12]

NAMU supporters also argued that tying the hands of the Canadian government might boost the confidence of international financial markets in the Canadian economy. Without any prospect of made-in-Canada inflation or large government deficits, international investors might deem Canada a safer location for investment, thus lowering Canadian borrowing costs. Grubel, Courchene, and Harris also highlighted how NAMU would stave off a potential crisis of confidence in the Canadian dollar in the future. In the wake of the global financial crisis of 1997–98, the risk of currency crises was in the forefront of many people's minds. The power of global financial markets to attack national currencies – even those of countries whose economies seemed well managed – through sudden large-scale selling of the currency had been well demonstrated during the crisis. Courchene and Harris summed up the conventional wisdom of the time well: "As recent events have proven, currencies can decline precipitously even if economic fundamentals are sound on both the inflation and fiscal fronts."[13] As the Canadian currency sank to new lows below 65 cents in 1998–99, the risks seemed apparent.

Grubel, Courchene, and Harris in fact suggested that Canada might already be suffering from a less dramatic, but still significant, crisis of confidence in its currency. In the face of the volatility and depreciating value of the Canadian dollar, they argued that many Canadians were turning to the US dollar to conduct their economic affairs. This informal "market dollarization" was particularly noteworthy in the business community. Suppliers were increasingly invoicing in US dollars as an informal form of hedging. Some Canadian firms with close ties to the US markets were also reporting their earnings in US dollars. Some firms with major parts of their operations in the US, such as Nortel, had also begun to do all of their accounting in US dollars.[14] More generally, it was argued that many Canadian residents were shifting their assets into US dollars to insulate themselves from the depreciation of the Canadian dollar.

These practices led Courchene and Harris to worry that the Canadian economy was slowly embracing the US dollar as its de facto currency, as some Latin American economies had. If this was true, the parallel to the mid-nineteenth century period would have been a striking one. Recall how growing economic integration with the US in that earlier period encouraged widespread unofficial "dollarization" in Canada which, in turn, strengthened the case for breaking with the sterling standard and creating the Canadian dollar. In a similar fashion, Courchene and Harris argued that the case for a change in exchange rate regime was strengthened by the threat of growing informal dollarization. Before dollarization proceeded further, they argued that it would be better for Canada to push for a new North American common currency over which Canada had some control. Obtaining even a small voice within a formal monetary union would be better than the alternative of being left with no voice in a de facto dollarized economy.

As noted above, many of these arguments in favour of NAMU echoed those put forward by Courchene and Harris in their case for fixing the exchange rate during the early 1990s. Why did they now endorse monetary union instead? It may have been a response to the earlier criticism that some of the alleged benefits of a fixed exchange rate were overstated, because the currency peg might not be a permanent or credible one. Even Grubel levelled this criticism against their argument for a fixed exchange rate.[15] More importantly, Courchene and Harris highlighted how the growing power of global financial markets now made the case for monetary union much stronger than that of a fixed exchange rate. The various currency crises throughout the 1990s – from the European crisis of 1992–93 to the Asian financial crisis of 1997–98 – had called attention to the difficulties of maintaining a credible fixed exchange rate in the face of global market pressures.

THE DIVISION IN NEOLIBERAL CIRCLES

To those who had followed the debates about monetary union in Europe, many of these arguments in favour of NAMU were very familiar. They echoed what was often described as the "neoliberal" case for the euro.[16] That is, monetary union was seen as a project to reinforce various goals associated with neoliberal thought: the acceleration of international economic integration, the imposition of greater market discipline within the domestic economy, and the introduction of "neo-constitutionalist" measures that lock in fiscal restraint and the promotion of price stability as the primary goal of monetary policy.

If NAMU was a neoliberal project, one might have expected that it would find considerable political support in Canada. After all, neoliberal ideas have been increasingly influential in Canadian policy-making since the 1970s.[17] NAMU was also being portrayed by these thinkers as a logic extension of the FTA, which itself had been widely seen, both by supporters and opponents, as a mechanism to strengthen neoliberal policy goals in Canada. But Canadian neoliberals as a whole found themselves much more divided internally on the question of NAMU than they were on the FTA.

To be sure, in the world of formal parliamentary politics, it was members of the two political parties most sympathetic to neoliberal economics at the time – the Reform Party/Canadian Alliance and the Progressive Conservative Party – who displayed the greatest interest in discussing the issue (aside from the Quebec sovereigntist party discussed in chapter 8).[18] In the journalistic realm, the newspaper most closely associated with neoliberal ideas, *The National Post,* also gave the idea a great deal of attention. We have also seen how neoliberal think tanks such as the Fraser Institute and the C.D. Howe Institute sponsored the publication of the work of Grubel, Courchene, and Harris.

But economists and policy-makers in the Bank of Canada who often endorsed neoliberal economic ideas – including ex-governor John Crow – strongly opposed the idea. Their stance was dismissed by some on the grounds that the bank was simply concerned that NAMU would threaten its power and perhaps even its very existence.[19] But this view downplays the fact that the bank's position reflected a genuine intellectual split in neoliberal circles on the NAMU question. This split was evident elsewhere. After publishing Courchene and Harris's paper, the C.D. Howe Institute subsequently published prominent work strongly critical of the NAMU idea by economists with strong neoliberal credentials, notably David Laidler and Bill Robson, who had together criticized Courchene's and Harris's proposals for fixed exchange rates in the early 1990s.[20] Similarly, although some members of the Reform Party/Canadian Alliance and the Progressive Conservative Party were intrigued by the NAMU idea, the parties themselves were unwilling to endorse it. Even *The National Post* reminded readers of the complexity of the issue from a neoliberal standpoint when it commissioned a week-long series in December 2000 in which neoliberal guru Milton Friedman defended Canada's float in a debate with Robert Mundell.[21]

What, then, accounts for the split in Canadian neoliberal circles on the NAMU question? To begin with, neoliberal critics of NAMU argued that its potential benefits were overstated by Grubel, Courchene, and Harris. They highlighted that the immediate efficiency gains to be realized by eliminating currency-related transaction costs were quite small. While European countries were eliminating many currencies, Canada's commerce with the US involves only one currency change. They also questioned the relevance of Frankel and Rose's study to the Canadian situation, a point that Rose himself acknowledged at a Bank of Canada conference in 2000.[22] In addition, they argued that the volatility of the Canadian dollar was overstated, since most of its movements could be explained by commodity price trends and interest rate differentials between Canada and the US.[23]

Critics of NAMU also suggested that the evidence did not support the argument that Canada's depreciation had increased foreign takeovers of Canadian corporations.[24] Likewise, they argued that the "lazy manufacturing" thesis – that Canada's depreciating currency inhibits productivity improvements – was not supported by existing economic analysis. Even if it were true, they noted that governments could prompt firms to change their behaviour by less drastic measures than NAMU, such as raising taxes.[25]

The benefits to be gained from constraining Canadian macroeconomic policy via NAMU were also questioned. In the absence of EU-style fiscal rules, critics noted that NAMU would not necessarily bring greater fiscal discipline to governments, as the experience of provincial governments within the Canadian monetary union made clear.[26] More importantly, they argued that NAMU would not bring any greater price stability than Canada already had. In the European context, neoliberal enthusiasm in many countries for economic and monetary union (EMU) stemmed largely from the promise that the European central bank would offer more "disciplined" monetary policy than their own central banks had provided. This argument had much less appeal for neoliberals in Canada because of recent trends in Canadian and US monetary policy-making. As we have seen, when John Crow became governor of the Bank of Canada in 1987, the bank began to pursue a policy of zero inflation with a determination that even many neoliberals found too extreme. The low-inflation regime was then institutionalized in 1991 when the government established inflation targets (1–3 per cent) for the Bank of Canada. These targets bolstered the credibility of the Bank of Canada in international financial markets and successfully anchored price expectations in a floating exchange rate regime.

It was not at all clear that NAMU would provide a more stable domestic monetary environment, especially since Canada had had lower inflation than the US since the early 1990s.[27] Many NAMU critics believed that the US Federal Reserve's anti-inflationary credentials were weaker than the Bank of Canada's in recent years. As we have already seen in the last chapter, opponents of a fixed exchange rate in the early 1990s pointed out that the Bank of Canada's efforts to fight inflation in the late 1980s and early 1990s would have been inhibited by such a monetary regime since the Fed was less aggressive in its pursuit of price stability at this time. The same point was made again in the NAMU debate. For this reason, John Crow found himself opposed to the idea of monetary union in North America, while his admiration for constitutionally-mandated price stability might have made him a supporter of EMU in the European context.[28] Even the American economist Milton Friedman highlighted the poor historical performance of US monetary policy in advocating a floating rate for Canada: "If I were a Canadian, I would not regard that record as an adequate basis for committing the country to US monetary policy."[29] The case against tying up with the US was only strengthened after President Bush began to run up government deficits in 2001.[30]

This critique of NAMU thus reiterated the rationale that had been provided for Canada's floating exchange rate regime since the 1930s. The regime was necessary to preserve Canadian monetary autonomy. Bank of Canada governor Gordon Thiessen emphasized that monetary autonomy was desirable not just in order to have a made-in-Canada inflation rate. More important from his perspective was the fact that a floating rate permitted discretionary monetary management that was designed to influence aggregate demand: "Typically, economists express this [monetary] independence as the ability to choose one's own national objective with respect to inflation. I do not find this to be a particularly useful way of looking at autonomy ... The real essence of pursuing a separate monetary policy is having the option and the ability to respond to fluctuations in demand that are unique to our economy." As an example, he recalled how the bank had deliberately lowered interest rates during 1996–97 in order to offset the contractionary effect of the federal government's dramatic fiscal cutbacks in 1995: "Both market interest rates and the exchange rate moved down in response, helping to stimulate foreign and domestic demand and so moderate the effects of fiscal restraint on economic activity."[31] He noted that the bank no longer worried, as it had in the 1970s and 1980s, that this kind of deliberate effort to boost aggregate demand through monetary easing and currency depreciation would provoke inflation and further depreciation. The bank's credibility as an inflation-fighter – and the government's broader fiscal restraint program – had brought inflationary expectations under control.[32]

In addition to valuing national monetary autonomy, neoliberal critics of NAMU were also concerned with the economic costs of losing the exchange rate as a tool for facilitating balance of payments adjustments. They highlighted similar arguments on this point to those of Canadian policy-makers since the 1930s. A floating exchange rate helped cushion the impact on the domestic economy of external shocks. This method of adjusting one single price – the exchange rate – was much more efficient than the alternative option of changing millions of domestic prices and wages. In the absence of exchange rate movements, the inflexibility of many domestic prices and wages ensured that the domestic economy would experience considerable unemployment and losses in real output during the transition period before wages and prices adjusted to their proper level. In Thiessen's words, the adjustment process "will take longer, will be more difficult and will cost more over-all."[33]

This argument had impeccable neoliberal credentials because it was first popularized by Milton Friedman in 1953. As we have seen, NAMU supporters thought it overlooked the fact that exchange rates experience volatility and short-term misalignments which undermine the ability of this "price" to facilitate proper adjustments of the national economy. Equally important, they argued that Friedman and others had been too "Keynesian" in accepting the relative inflexibility of domestic prices and wages. One of their goals in advocating NAMU was, after all, to transform the monetary environment in a way that forced business and workers to become more "flexible" and responsive to changing economic conditions. As Mundell put it in his newspaper debate with Friedman, "the possibility of exchange rate changes has ... deflected attention of policy-makers from the vastly more important subject of flexibility of all individual markets."[34] Grubel, too, suggested that more attention must be paid to the issue of "the extent to which the flexibility of labour and other institutions are *endogenous* to the exchange rate regime."[35] But defenders of Canada's floating exchange rate thought this project was unrealistic and they suggested that there was no clear evidence, even in Europe as yet, to suggest that monetary union would have this kind of dramatic domestic impact.[36]

The case for a floating rate also built on Robert Mundell's 1961 theory of optimum currency areas, which explored whether a group of countries was well-suited to adopt a common currency. Critics of NAMU pointed out that Canada and the US did not resemble an "optimum currency area" (OCA) for a number of reasons. Unlike within the EU, there is no free labour movement between Canada and the US, nor any supranational fiscal mechanisms to help facilitate adjustment in the absence of the exchange rate tool. The two countries also experience external economic shocks quite differently because Canada is a net exporter of commodities, while the US is a net importer.[37] During the international financial crisis of 1997–98, for example, Canada's terms of trade fell because of the impact of the crisis on the country's commodity exports, while those of the US rose.[38] The rapid depreciation of the Canadian currency vis-à-vis the US dollar in the wake of the crisis was thus appropriate in the view of NAMU opponents because it facilitated adjustment to an external shock that had been experienced asymmetrically by the two countries.[39]

The Bank of Canada in 2001 made it clear that it would in fact be willing to reconsider its opposition to NAMU if the Canadian and US economies began to approximate an OCA more closely in the coming years. This position represented a slight softening of its initial rejection of the idea. The change coincided with the appointment of David Dodge as the bank's governor in February of that year, and may have reflected his influence. In a speech in June 2001, Dodge outlined the new position: "[At] some future time, the structures of our two economies could converge to a point that the benefits of a common currency could outweigh the macroeconomic costs of abandoning our flexible exchange rate. But it is also possible that those structures could diverge further. We simply do not know."[40] In an internal memo (obtained by a journalist under the Access to Information law), the chief of the bank's international section, James Powell, reiterated this position: "The line we have been taking here in International is that a common North American currency (or more likely dollarization with, hopefully, a Canadian seat in the Fed system), is not a wacky idea if the Canadian and U.S. economies become increasingly similar."[41] Dodge subsequently argued that he would be willing to discuss NAMU more seriously if free labour movement within North America was established. In the wake of the terrorist attacks of 11 September 2001, however, the prospects for this dimmed as the Canada-US border became more – rather than less – restrictive for the cross-border movement of people.

What about Courchene and Harris's argument about the inappropriateness of the exchange adjustment tool, given the regional diversity of the Canadian economy? John Murray of the Bank of Canada suggested that this diversity was overstated, arguing that Canada's six regions have more in common economically with each other than any single region has with the US economy.[42] At the 1999 Canadian Economics Association annual meeting, Laidler also strongly attacked Courchene's case that the Canadian economy increasingly resembled a series of regional economies bound closely to various counterparts in the US. Responding to the argument, Laidler noted that labour still cannot move across the border.[43]

Finally, these critics of NAMU also noted that there was very little evidence that informal dollarization was dramatically increasing in Canada, as proponents of monetary union had suggested. As Laidler and Poschmann put it, dollarization in Canada "verges on the trivial" compared to Latin American countries. Although it had increased slightly in the 1990s, levels of informal dollarization had in fact been higher in Canada two decades earlier.[44] There was also little reason to expect dollarization to become more extensive. In the mid-nineteenth century, dollarization had accompanied North American economic integration because the Canadian monetary system was already chaotic. But in the current period, Canada had a standardized currency and it was much more difficult to dislodge its use in a major way given the many "network externalities" which reinforce the continued use of existing currencies.[45] Only in countries experiencing very high inflation and/or very significant political and economic instability has widespread dollarization taken off. Robson and Laidler concluded: "There is nothing inevitable about a single currency in North America: Canadians can choose."[46]

BUSINESS INTERESTS AND THE NAMU DEBATE

It was not just Canadian neoliberals who were divided on the issue of NAMU. So too were Canadian businesses. In the late 1980s, the Canadian business community was overwhelmingly in favour of the neoliberal case for the FTA.[47] Business support for monetary union is much less strong. When Courchene and Harris's study advocating NAMU was released in mid-1999, a *Toronto Star* reporter asked prominent business lobby groups such as the Canadian Chamber of Commerce and the Alliance of Manufacturers and Exporters Canada (whose members include the largest exporting firms such as those in the auto sector) if they had been researching the issue or lobbying for it. The answer in both cases was no.[48] At that same time, a *Maclean's* reporter discovered that the Business Council on National Issues (BCNI) – a very influential body that represents the largest and most transnationalized sectors of Canadian business – had "studied dollarization in depth over the past six months," but the organization's survey of its membership revealed that most businesses opposed the idea.[49]

In the next two years, business interest in the idea grew somewhat. Some prominent voices in the Canadian business community publicly supported the idea, such as Sherry Cooper of BMO Nesbitt Burns and Larry O'Brien, the head of Calian Technology, an Ottawa high-technology company.[50] A *National Post*-Compass poll of 4,000 Canadian executives in mid-2001 also found 45 per cent in favour of NAMU (and 42 per cent opposed).[51] But the major business associations remained unwilling to endorse the idea. In 2002, the Canadian Chamber of Commerce declared its continued support for Canada's floating exchange rate, as did the BCNI (subsequently renamed the Canadian Council of Chief Executives).[52] The Conference Board of Canada also published a study in late 2001 that came out opposed to NAMU.[53] Even when business interest in proposals for deeper North American integration rose suddenly after the events of 11 September 2001, the idea of currency union rarely surfaced within these discussions.

The lack of enthusiasm among many Canadian businesses for NAMU was consistent with the relative absence of a private sector lobby for a fixed exchange rate throughout the postwar period. But one might have expected a change in views following the greater exchange rate instability since the mid-1970s. As Pierre Fortin noted, the Canada-US nominal exchange rate had fluctuated with a band of ±6 per cent between 1950 and 1975. Since then, however, the Canadian dollar had depreciated 28 per cent between 1975 and 1986, then appreciated 22 per cent by 1991, and then depreciated again by 23 per cent up until 2000. These large currency movements also took place at a time when Canada's international trade grew from only 25 per cent of GNP to over 40 per cent.[54] Grubel had argued in 1999 that the rapid expansion of Canada-US commerce should be creating a Canadian business constituency which supported NAMU. Monetary union would, after all, eliminate the various costs that they increasingly experienced in dealing in two currencies.

Courchene and Harris held out the same hope, ending their initial case for NAMU by calling on Canadian business associations to get involved in the debate.[55]

What explains the Canadian business community's stance in the NAMU debate? To begin with, the issue of eliminating currency-related costs in Canada-US economic relations was not one that generated much passion in Canadian business circles. One reason was the fact that so much of Canada-US trade is intra-firm trade. Since this trade can be handled simply as bookkeeping entries within a firm's overall accounting, a floating exchange rate is not perceived as a large inconvenience.[56] As economist Jack Carr noted, "General Motors imports engines from the United States. They do not repay their US parents in US dollars; they re-export finished cars. It is really mostly bookkeeping transactions that take place. Little exchange cost takes place there."[57] Canadian business is also well practiced at coping with a floating exchange rate through currency hedging and other mechanisms (although NAMU would of course eliminate the need for these costs).[58]

The position of Canadian business is not entirely unique. In Europe, there is not much evidence that businesses involved in cross-border European commerce backed EMU in order to reduce costs associated with handling multiple currencies. It was only in the European public sector that concerns about these costs were expressed strongly. Since the 1960s, European governments worried about how exchange rate volatility could disrupt the smooth functioning of the EU-wide Common Agricultural Policy.[59] These fears provided a key rationale for many Europeans to support fixed exchange rates within their region. In North America, no such supranational fiscal structures exist to generate the same concern.

Some analysts, including Grubel, speculated that another reason some Canadian businesses were wary of NAMU was that they had benefited from Canada's depreciating dollar.[60] Although this is no doubt true in some cases, many businesses highlighted that the impact of depreciation on their competitiveness had often acted as a "double-edged sword."[61] As Grubel acknowledged, depreciation provided few benefits to Canadian businesses either dependent on imports or adding little value to the product in Canada. This included firms in important sectors of the Canadian economy, such as automobile assembly, computers, and consumer products. Other businesses noted that the dollar's depreciation had had some negative impacts on their competitiveness because it hurt their ability to recruit and retain specialized experts.

Foreign-owned corporations were also sometimes less inclined to make new investments in their Canadian subsidiaries because the dollar's depreciation lowered the value of the Canadian subsidiary from the head office's point of view.[62] Because of these diverse effects of currency depreciation on the Canadian economy, it is very difficult to make generalizations about the impact of depreciation on the business sector. Indeed, Paul Bowles reports that the Canadian Manufacturers and Exporters (formerly the Alliance of Manufacturers and Exporters Canada) found its member firms to be "all over the place" in terms of their view of how a depreciating dollar affected their competitive position.[63]

If Canadian businesses' support for the floating rate reflected competitive concerns, their interest in NAMU should have increased when the currency appreciated suddenly from a level of 63 cents in 2002 to above 80 cents by 2004. Grubel in fact predicted this in 1999.[64] But his prediction was not borne out. Indeed, interest in NAMU waned considerably in this period. Some analysts noted that the negative impact on Canadian exporters of the appreciation was muted by the fact that imported inputs played an increasingly large role in their production processes – up from 26 per cent in 1988 to 33 per cent by 1999. The appreciation lowered the cost of these inputs, thus partially offsetting the effect of the currency's movement on export competitiveness.[65] Once again, analysts also noted how this sudden and dramatic currency appreciation was affecting Canadian firms in very different ways. Those commodity sectors that were heavily dependent on exports to the US, such as pulp and paper and mining, were clearly hurt by the appreciation. But sectors whose trade exposure was lower or who depended heavily on foreign parts and components were much less vulnerable, and some – such as construction, petroleum, and coal products – likely benefited from the appreciation.[66]

One final point needs to be made about Canadian business preferences. Canadian banks emerged as high profile opponents of NAMU.[67] Their prominent role in the debate partly reflected their expertise on monetary and financial issues. They advanced many of the economic arguments against NAMU just cited. But the Canadian chartered banks also had some more self-interested reasons to be opposed. NAMU would result in the loss of business associated with Canadian dollar foreign exchange trading. This is a market that has been overwhelmingly dominated by Canadian banks based in Toronto.[68] A similar fear has encouraged bank opposition to monetary union in some smaller European countries, such as Portugal.[69]

The more significant cost of NAMU was its potential impact on the ability of Canadian banks to compete with US banks. Since the late nineteenth century, banking had been one of the few sectors of the Canadian economy without a large degree of foreign ownership.[70] NAMU could change this situation dramatically. If NAMU was based on the US dollar – which seemed most likely (see next chapter) – the competitiveness of Canadian banks vis-à-vis their US counterparts would be undermined unless they could be assured of access to US dollar clearing systems and the US Federal Reserve's provision of US dollar liquidity and lender-of-last-resort functions. If this access was not guaranteed, Canadian banks would encounter strong pressure to merge with a US counterpart.[71]

CANADA'S LEFT? A CONTRAST WITH EUROPE

The split within neoliberal and business circles on the question of NAMU created quite a different political context from the debate on the FTA in the late 1980s. There was, however, one similar feature in the two debates. Those who had opposed the FTA also emerged as prominent critics of NAMU. An important feature of the earlier FTA debate had been the strong opposition of Canada's left to the agreement. An unusually broad-based, anti-FTA coalition had emerged, including prominent social democrats, the union movement, environmentalists, feminists, and native groups. Many of these groups also now voiced their opposition to NAMU.[72]

Although this feature of the NAMU debate parallels that surrounding the FTA, it provides somewhat of a contrast with the politics of EMU. To be sure, European feminists and greens often emerged as opponents of the euro.[73] But many social democrats and unions across Europe – though by no means all – were very supportive of the drive to monetary union. Indeed, Notermans notes that "social democrats have ranked among the staunchest supporters of EMU" and that this support has been crucial to the success of the initiative.[74] If this source of support for NAMU were present in Canada, the project would obviously have had a broader political base. In our efforts to understand the political viability of NAMU, then, it is important to explain the contrast.

The issue is particularly interesting given the widespread characterization of EMU as a neoliberal project. Why would some European unions and social democratic political parties endorse neoliberal goals? To begin with, many European social democrats embraced price stability as the prime goal of monetary policy when witnessing national Keynesian strategies produce serious economic and currency crises after the early 1970s. Some blamed these crises on the growing power of speculative financial flows. In this context, endorsing price stability – and eventually EMU – was seen as the only way to protect the country from speculative financial attacks, particularly after all capital controls were abolished across the EU during the late 1980s and early 1990s. In other situations (e.g., Sweden, Finland, Spain), the crises were attributed to the fact that social democratic governments lost control over wage demands – often in a context where postwar corporatist wage bargaining structures were breaking down or were already weak – thereby producing situations in which domestic expansionary policies rapidly produced vicious cycles of inflation and depreciation. Again, the pursuit of price stability was then accepted reluctantly as a means to restore a more stable macroeconomic environment by providing an external discipline on wage demands.[75]

If some social democrats only grudgingly embraced this new monetary framework, others were more enthusiastic. Some saw it as a way to lower interest rates by reducing risk premiums that the markets were imposing, a result that could improve their governments' budgetary positions considerably. Because this helped the fiscal position of governments and thus prevented cuts to the welfare state, Rhodes feels justified in describing EMU as more of an "embedded liberal" regime than a neoliberal one.[76] In other countries (e.g., Austria), social democrats and unions increasingly saw international competitiveness as the best means to achieve full employment – instead of counter-cyclical fiscal and monetary management – and they embraced monetary discipline for this reason.[77] Some social democrats also argued that neoliberal monetary goals could finally provide a stable macroeconomic environment in which progressive supply-side reforms could be undertaken to promote equity, growth, and employment. As Notermans puts it, "far from being a threat, EMU has provided European social democracy with a favourable institutional set-up from which to avoid the main problem that brought down its post-war model, namely the inability to prevent inflation in tight labour markets."[78]

The embrace of neoliberal monetary goals for these various reasons was a critical precondition for the decision of many European social democrats to support EMU.[79] But it does not explain this decision entirely. After all, many countries today – including Canada, as we have seen, but also European countries such as Britain and Sweden – have committed to price stability via a monetary regime of a floating exchange rate and inflation targets. From a social democratic stand-point, this would seem a more attractive choice for the reasons ex-plained earlier; it enables external economic shocks to be buffered by the exchange rate instead of by domestic wage and price flexibility. Why, then, have so many European social democrats embraced the more rigid monetary regime of EMU?

One answer is that the importance of preserving a national floating exchange rate as a buffer against asymmetric shocks is less significant for a core of EMU countries because they more closely meet OCA criteria. It is not coincidental that the three countries opting out of EMU – the UK, Sweden, and Denmark – are among the top five countries experiencing the most asymmetric shocks in the EU (the other two are Finland and Ireland).[80] In some cases, the choice also reflected the fact that neoliberal monetary goals in Europe have long been associated with a strategy of "importing" the Bundesbank's monetary stability, initially via pegged exchange rates to the German currency within the European Monetary System and now via EMU. For countries such as Finland with a long his-tory of inflation and depreciation, inflation targets were also deemed less credible than joining EMU. In countries with strong pro-European senti-ment, social democrats also found EMU useful politically since they could wrap their new commitment to price stability in a pro-European rhetoric and thus minimize potential opposition from the more tradi-tional left.[81]

Perhaps the most interesting reason, however, is that many European social democrats and unions do not see "domestic wage and price flexi-bility" as incompatible with their goals. In the Canadian context, this phrase is almost always used to mean labour market deregulation. In some European countries with strong corporatist traditions, however, social democrats and unions have a different perspective. They have seen EMU as an opportunity to reinvigorate corporatist social pacts in which cooperative wage bargaining, employment-friendly taxation schemes, and other social protection measures can assume a key role in the payments adjustment process. Finland provides perhaps the most interesting example from a Canadian perspective because it shares Can-ada's status as a significant commodity exporter. Despite facing highly asymmetric shocks vis-à-vis the EMU region, Finnish social democrats and union leaders embraced EMU partly for this reason.[82]

Finally, some social democrats and unions have embraced EMU be-cause they have seen it as a necessary step in the construction of a stron-ger EU in which social democratic goals have a prominent place. For example, many who are less enthusiastic about neoliberal monetary goals have still supported EMU because it is viewed as a mechanism for diluting the monetary influence of the neoliberal Bundesbank across Europe. Although the new European Central Bank (ECB) has a strict mandate to pursue price stability, they have hoped that European governments could influence the ECB's behaviour over time and that EMU would also encourage coordinated EU-wide expansionary fiscal policies. In some countries, such as Britain, unions also supported EMU because they believed it might help strengthen employment rights at the EU-wide level and lead to transnational wage bargaining (as pay structures between countries became more transparent).[83] In some poorer EU countries, EMU was also seen as an opportunity to press for larger intra-EU fiscal transfers. The Spanish government, for example, withheld its support for EMU until it received a commitment that a new EU "Cohesion Fund" would be created for this purpose.

With these explanations in mind, it is easier to understand why Canadian social democrats and unions have not followed many of their European counterparts in embracing the idea of a regional monetary union. In the absence of European-style social corporatism, they anticipate that the need for greater wage flexibility under NAMU will strengthen neoliberal initiatives to deregulate labour markets and cut entitlements to unemployment compensation.[84] As labour economist Andrew Jackson put it, "we need to control our currency if we are to achieve full employment on the basis of a different social model than that which exists in the US."[85] More broadly, labour leader Ken Georgetti argued that depreciation of the Canadian dollar since the early 1990s has enabled Canadian workers to avoid the fate of US workers whose wages have not kept up with productivity growth for much of the decade. If NAMU had been in place, competitive pressures would have put similar pressure on Canadian wages: "The key point is that having our own dollar has given Canadian workers, and Canadian society as a whole, some protection from free-trade-driven integration with the harsh US social model. Canadian workers have had little to cheer about in the 1980s and 90s, but at least the wages of the average worker have about kept pace with prices."[86]

It is also worth noting that the social democratic goal of full employment has been much more closely associated with floating exchange rates throughout most of the postwar period in Canada than in many European countries. Despite the considerable depreciation of the Canadian dollar since the mid-1970s, support for a "soft currency" policy option has also not been eroded by the kind of traumatic currency crises that many European countries experienced and that generated a "fear of floating" for many on the European left. Indeed, as we have seen, the most traumatic Canadian economic experience associated with the floating exchange rate in this period involved the strong *appreciation* of the Canadian dollar in 1986–91.

The left's distaste for Bank of Canada policy in the late 1980s and early 1990s might have led to an embrace of NAMU as a form of protection against a repetition of this experience. After all, it was the floating exchange rate that allowed the bank to attack inflation in such an aggressive manner in those years. As we will see in the next chapter, this is an argument that some Quebec sovereigntists have made in support of NAMU. It finds few echoes in the rest of Canada. The more common argument is the one advanced by Georgetti: "while the labour movement vehemently disagreed with the Bank of Canada's monetary policies during the 1980s, we recognize the value of having an independent policy."[87] After discussing how US monetary policy since the late 1980s has been more supportive of employment goals than Canadian policy, Jackson also argues: "One might suggest that the best case for dollarization is that we would get better monetary policy through the back door, but it would be better to learn from US experience and apply it to our own ends."[88]

Finally, Canadian social democrats and unions find it difficult to relate to the European notion that monetary union could help construct a stronger regional community in which social democratic values have a prominent place. Instead, they have long seen closer economic integration with the US as a threat to these values and associated it with a downward harmonization to US norms. The fact that NAMU might lead to pressures to intensify North American economic integration in other sectors, particularly with respect to labour mobility between the US and Canada, has only compounded these fears.[89]

In short, the floating exchange rate is associated by the left with the protection of the distinct Canadian social model with respect to not just labour market policy, but also social programmes, as well as tax and fiscal policies. As NDP MP Lorne Nystrom puts it, "a common currency means alignment of North American policies and ultimately a political union ... Ultimately, we would no longer be able to maintain a different social program structure, such as our publicly funded fully portable health-care system."[90] Jim Stanford, an economist with the Canadian Auto Workers, makes a similar argument, one that also echoes Bryce's ideas in the late 1930s: "Canada's relatively more interventionist social policies and labour market institutions provide Canadian workers and unions with a better opportunity to capture a larger share of the economic pie. Relative to productivity levels, this will tend to generate higher unit production costs ... in which case a depreciating currency is necessary to preserve the competitiveness of Canadian output."[91]

These critiques of NAMU have even been shared by more conservative analysts. The *Globe and Mail*'s editorial writers, for example, noted: "It is worth asking whether currency integration might be a first step toward greater political integration, or at least toward greater structural similarity in programs such as health care and social services."[92] The chief economist of the Bank of Nova Scotia, Warren Jestin, also noted that adopting the dollar would "inevitably influence fiscal policy: That would affect health care, social services and a broad gamut of things across the country."[93] When he was chief economist at the Royal Bank, John McCallum highlighted how Canada's willingness to embrace the exchange rate's role of cushioning adjustment was "an issue of a 'kindler, gentler Canadian society', unwilling to induce dramatic downward adjustments in resource-based provinces."[94]

Courchene and Harris have tried to assuage these fears by arguing that many of the social programs treasured by Canadians were introduced during the 1960s when Canada had a fixed exchange rate. If this exchange rate regime was not an impediment to their construction then, why should the experience with NAMU be any different, they ask?[95] They might in fact have made this point a little stronger. Elsewhere, they argue that the automatic federal stabilizers would need to play an important role – alongside provincial fiscal policies – in buffering region-specific shocks under NAMU.[96] They might thus have made a plausible case that NAMU will in fact require a *strengthening* of such stabilizers as employment insurance, equalization payments, and the national tax and transfer system.

NATIONALIST OPPOSITION TO NAMU

The preservation of the Canadian dollar was also associated by many on the left with the broader goal of preserving Canadian sovereignty and a distinct national identity.[97] They in fact found much more support for this argument from some neoliberal thinkers and members of the business community than during the FTA debate. In that earlier trade debate, neoliberal analysts and the business community often attacked the "economic nationalism" of FTA opponents. This time around, opponents of NAMU from these circles often made nationalist arguments a central part of their case for the preservation of the Canadian dollar. Robson and Laidler, for example, argued that a key reason to oppose NAMU was the link between a national currency and national sovereignty.[98] Among the business executives who told the *National Post*–Compass poll that they opposed NAMU, by far the most common reason given was a concern about Canadian sovereignty and national identity, rather than specific economic arguments.[99]

The role of Canadian nationalism in generating opposition to NAMU did not surprise advocates of monetary union. When outlining their case, they had anticipated that it would represent one of the key political obstacles to their proposal. In many European countries, nationalist opposition to EMU had often been a very potent force.[100] Its potency is hardly surprising since national currencies have historically been closely associated with national identities.

In Canadian history, for example, we have seen how Hincks saw the creation of the Canadian dollar standard and its associated coin in the 1850s as a matter of national pride. At the time of Confederation, the establishment of a unified monetary standard and the removal of US coin were also seen as important symbols in nation-building. The imagery on Canadian money has also long been used to project certain conceptions of the national identity. This began with the country's first coins and notes and then continued with new images in the 1930s. Canadian coins had had basically the same design since 1858: a monarch on the front and the word "Canada" on the back with a maple leaf wreath. The coins of 1937, following similar changes in Irish and New Zealand coin design in the 1920s and 1930s, now included images of the maple leaf, beaver, Bluenose, and caribou, as well as an uncrowned monarch, reflecting Canada's more independent status at the time.[101] The new Bank of Canada notes in the 1930s also included Sir John A. MacDonald and Wilfrid Laurier on the front of high denomination notes instead of royalty. The deputy governor of the Bank of Canada had considered placing other national heros on all the notes but concluded: "It might be difficult to scrape up seven or five others, even counting the 1st Governor General and Champlain. It would be invidious to select among Governor Generals if one goes further than the 1st."[102] The back of the notes included allegorical figures representing agriculture, electric power, travel, fertility, radio, commerce and industry, and security.[103] Various changes in coin and note design, reflecting changing images of the nation, have continued to the current day.

Some of the opposition to NAMU has highlighted this symbolic role of the national currency for Canadian nationalism. Nystrom, for example, has stressed his concern that "there would be no symbols of Canada on the currency ... The Canadian dollar is a factor of unity and cohesion."[104] Similarly, Goldfarb proposed that "currency is part of what helps connect us with our past. When we use our money, we are reminded of our national icons. If we adopt the US dollar, our children will associate with American presidents, the American eagle and the Lincoln Memorial."[105] Anne Golden of the Conference Board of Canada has also argued that as "the maintenance of a separate national currency has been synonymous, historically, with political independence, such a decision would be a momentous step for Canada, with major implications for our continued existence as an independent nation."[106] Even Milton Friedman chimed in to this debate: "Currency is a very important symbol of sovereignty. If a nation is going to stay a nation, it needs as many symbols of sovereignty as it can possibly have."[107]

Some NAMU supporters have tried to minimize Canadian nationalist opposition by stressing that Canada could still retain nationalist images on one side of the new common coins and notes.[108] They have also pointed to the example of the euro to suggest that national currencies need not any longer be considered a key symbol of the sovereignty of a nation-state. As Courchene put it: "the euro is also signalling that in a progressively integrated global economy, currency arrangements are emerging as one of those supranational or international public goods, an international public good that will be fully consistent with the 21st century notion of what national sovereignty will be all about."[109]

But national currencies have been linked to national identities not just through imagery on money and their symbolic value for national sovereignty. Particularly important in the twentieth century has been the sense that a national currency also provides a crucial economic tool for the national community to manage its own destiny. In other words, national currencies are seen as serving the nationalist value of "popular sovereignty."[110] In the Canadian context, this connection was first highlighted by Buchanan and his supporters in the nineteenth century. It then became widely accepted from the 1930s onwards as the concept of activist monetary management was endorsed.

From this perspective, the key challenge of NAMU is that it would prevent Canadians from choosing their own distinct monetary policy. This argument has particular resonance for Canadians because it seems unlikely that Canada would have much say over the management of a common North American currency. In Europe, the national central banks of each of the participating countries were initially each given an equal voice within the new European central bank that manages the new supranational currency. This made it much easier for EMU supporters to argue that popular sovereignty was not being abandoned, but simply pooled at the EU-wide level. Supporters in smaller countries have in fact been able to argue that their central banks acquired *more* say over monetary developments affecting their country than they had in the German-dominated European Monetary System.

Some supporters of NAMU hope that the US, like Germany, might agree to abandon its currency in favour of a new North American currency managed by a new North American central bank in which Canada has a significant decision-making role. But this argument has not persuaded many people, and most analysts have concluded that the much more likely scenario is one in which Canada adopts the US dollar and tries to negotiate an arrangement for it to become a thirteenth Federal Reserve district within the Federal Reserve System. Opponents of NAMU have highlighted how difficult these negotiations are likely to be, given the asymmetries of power between the two countries and the absence of a strong interest in the issue on the US part. And even if successful, Canadian policy-makers would still end up with very limited say within a US-dominated central bank, as I point out in the next chapter.

These political arguments have persuaded many Canadians to be skeptical of NAMU. Even prominent analysts who support NAMU on economic grounds – including Pierre Fortin and Robert Mundell[111] – have been swayed by these points to oppose the idea. Supporters of NAMU have tried to address this concern with several arguments that I examine in the next chapter. As I suggest there, however, these arguments have not been very convincing.

CONCLUSION

As we have seen, a small group of prominent Canadian economists played a key role in putting NAMU on the Canadian political agenda. They were in fact the same group who had critiqued Canada's floating exchange rate in the early 1990s. Many of their arguments for NAMU were similar to neoliberal ones that also generated much of the support for the euro in Europe. Neoliberal ideas were also highly influential in encouraging Canadian policy-makers to embrace the FTA in the 1980s. Given these parallels, the prospects for NAMU would seem bright.

But the neoliberal case for NAMU has proven much more controversial than neoliberal arguments for the FTA in Canada during the 1980s, or those backing the euro project in many European countries. To begin with, many of those supportive of neoliberal values have refused to support NAMU. They remain strongly committed to Canada's floating exchange rate regime, just as many neoliberal thinkers and policy-makers were at the time of the FTA's creation. At the core of their opposition to NAMU have been the two traditional defenses of Canada's floating exchange rate: (1) it helps preserve monetary autonomy and (2) it facilitates balance of payments adjustments. The case for monetary policy autonomy is premised primarily on a distrust of US monetary policy, a common feature of Canadian exchange rate policy-making since the 1930s. The need for a floating rate to ease balance of payments adjustments is justified with reference to the longstanding argument that Canada experiences distinct external shocks and has relatively inflexible domestic wages and prices. Also important have been fears that NAMU would require alternative adjustment mechanisms in the Canada-US context – such as freer cross-border labour movements or inter-country fiscal transfers – that are considered either politically unrealistic or dangerous to Canadian sovereignty.

The neoliberal argument for NAMU has also failed to pick up support from many other groups in Canadian society. The Canadian business community, which had been very supportive of the neoliberal case for free trade in the 1980s, has proven much less sympathetic to NAMU. Despite their increasingly close economic ties to the US, Canadian businesses have continued – true to historical fashion – to register relatively little discontent about Canada's floating exchange rate. Canadian banks also have important reasons to worry about the consequences of NAMU because of its potential impact on their business. In addition, the Canadian left has refused to follow many European social democrats and unions in backing the idea of regional monetary union. Finally, nationalist arguments against NAMU have attracted broader support than did the nationalist case against the FTA.

This analysis of the reception of the neoliberal case for NAMU casts considerable doubt on the political viability of NAMU within the Canadian political context. At the same time, these doubts should not be overstated. There appears to have been some softening of the initial opposition to the idea in the expert circles that have played a key role in the debate so far. Many within the business community also might be willing to support the idea more strongly if the idea were to gather more political momentum. Finally, the next two chapters also highlight how the broader role of nationalism in the Canadian debate is more complicated than this initial discussion suggests.

CHAPTER SEVEN

US Politics
and the Canadian NAMU Debate

As we saw in the last chapter, one of the most important arguments against NAMU has been that Canada would have little power in the governance of such a monetary union. Supporters of NAMU have tried to address this concern directly. Grubel has suggested that people should not underestimate the willingness of the US to endorse a new supranational North American currency and central bank in which Canada is granted a significant voice.[1] Even if NAMU were based on the US dollar, Courchene and Harris have suggested that Canada might still be able to secure considerable influence by negotiating a place as one of the Federal Reserve districts that comprise the federal structure of the US central bank. If Canada joined the US dollar zone as a new thirteenth Federal Reserve district, they ask whether its situation would in fact be as different as critics suggest from that of individual European countries. Harris makes the case in the following way: "An important issue relating to NAMU that remains a stumbling block for many Canadians is that the governance of North American monetary policy would reside in the hands of the US Federal Reserve. While this would surely be the NAMU reality, it does not differ that much from the reality facing any single country within the Euro zone. Consider the currency choices facing Canada and Britain ... In Canada's case, this means sharing a voting membership on a North American Federal Reserve with the 12 existing US Federal Reserve banks and the Mexican central bank. In Britain's case, this means joining the Euro with a similarly small voting share – one of twelve votes."[2]

This chapter examines US views on NAMU. In 1999, US policy-makers began to debate the idea of NAMU for the first time in the post-war period. The debate in fact centred on the question of whether the US should be actively encouraging countries in the Americas more generally to adopt the US dollar. The discussion attracted considerable attention abroad and generated widespread speculation that the US might consider backing a formal currency bloc in the region to match the euro zone emerging in Europe. Not surprisingly, these developments gave encouragement to NAMU supporters in Canada, who argued that the question of a regional monetary union was no longer a strictly academic one, but rather was one being debated actively in the US, as well as elsewhere across Latin America.[3] But in the first three sections of this chapter, I show how the content and outcome of the US debate was in fact far from encouraging from the standpoint of NAMU supporters. US policy-makers outlined firmly that they were not yet willing to provide *any* support for the creation of a regional monetary union.

What if US views changed in the coming years and the US became more willing to consider NAMU, at least in the form proposed by Courchene and Harris? Would these authors be correct that the federal character of the US central bank could make a North American monetary union based on the US dollar more politically palatable to Canadians? In the last two sections of the chapter, I point out that the federal character of both the US central bank and the new European central bank is in fact more complicated than Courchene and Harris's discussion implies. An examination of decision-making in these two bodies highlights how Canada's position as a thirteenth Reserve district would be considerably different than the position of individual European countries within the euro zone. I also discuss how the European Central Bank may not be a very good model to follow for those seeking to create an accountable central bank. These arguments suggest that the decision-making structures of the Fed are unlikely to help garner significant support from Canadians wavering on the NAMU question.

THE US INTEREST IN DOLLARIZATION DIPLOMACY

The post-1999 US debate about promoting use of the US dollar in the Americas was not the first in that country's history.[4] The issue had first arisen during the 1900–15 period when the US was suddenly expanding its economic and military influence across Central America and the Caribbean. In many of the countries where the US had new influence, the dollar's use was promoted within the local monetary system alongside that of the existing domestic currency.[5] The idea of promoting the dollar's use in Latin America reached a highpoint in 1915 when the influential US financial advisor Edwin Kemmerer put forward a proposal for creating "Pan-American monetary unity" at the Second Pan-American Scientific Conference. Under his proposal, all countries in the Americas would adopt a common monetary unit that was equivalent to the US gold dollar (he suggested that it might be called the "oro"). Each country would then allow other members' gold coins to be used within its territory. He suggested that each country's gold coins might bear the words "Pan-American Union" along with their value in "oro" to facilitate their widespread circulation. In practice, this proposal would have encouraged the wide use of US currency across the Americas because of the confidence the dollar commanded vis-à-vis locally-issued currency. Although this ambitious idea was discussed at the conference, it was never endorsed and US interest in this kind of proposal waned after World War One.[6]

When the idea of encouraging countries in the Americas to adopt the US dollar resurfaced in 1999, it assumed a more ambitious form. Proponents of "dollarization diplomacy" now hoped that foreign countries would dollarize *fully*; that is, abandon their national currencies altogether and adopt the US dollar as their exclusive currency. If the goal was more ambitious, the means of reaching it were less so. Advocates of the new dollarization diplomacy suggested that the US offer encouragement in more subtle ways than the gunboats of the past. The most prominent proposal was that the US could compensate foreign governments financially for most (85 per cent) of the lost seigniorage they incurred from adopting the dollar.[7] In 1999, a bill was submitted to both the US Senate and House of Representatives to empower the Treasury Secretary to act in this way, and hearings on this "International Monetary Stability Act" were held in 1999–2000. These hearings provoked a much wider debate within the US about the pros and cons of this kind of dollarization diplomacy. Some analysts even predicted the imminent emergence of monetary union based on the US dollar stretching from Santiago to Alaska.[8]

What was the initial catalyst that returned this issue to the US policy-making agenda? The prompt came from abroad. In early 1999, Argentine officials approached the US government to ask what kind of support the US might be willing to provide if Argentina adopted the dollar as its sole currency. Residents of Argentina had increasingly used the US dollar alongside the national currency since their country had created a currency board tied to the dollar in 1991. Their government was now considering "full dollarization" as a way of reducing the currency-risk premium charged by its foreign lenders. But Argentina's central bank president, Pedro Pou, highlighted that Argentinna's preference was to take this move in the context of a "monetary association treaty" with the US, rather than unilaterally, and he suggested that this treaty could provide the first step towards a monetary union throughout the hemisphere.[9]

Around the same time, the idea of adopting the dollar was also attracting attention elsewhere in Latin America. In Mexico, for example, the head of the Mexican bankers' association backed the idea in January 1999 and he was followed by the president of the country's most influential business lobby group two months later.[10] Although Mexican president Ernesto Zedillo rejected the idea at the time, his successor, Vicente Fox, endorsed the idea of creating a North American monetary union over the medium term soon after his election in 2000.[11] Even more dramatically, Ecuador and El Salvador took the plunge and implemented full dollarization in 2000 and 2001, respectively.

The new Latin American interest in dollarization partly reflected the fact that, in the context of financial liberalization and domestic economic and political instability, informal and partial dollarization had become quite extensive in many Latin American countries during the previous two decades. Many Latin American analysts saw full dollarization as a way to "import" monetary stability, attract foreign investment, deepen domestic financial markets, and promote capital accumulation. Interest in adopting the US dollar was also a product of the ascendancy of neoliberal monetary ideas across the region; it was seen as a way to constrain government intervention in the economy and impose greater market discipline on domestic workers and firms. In a world of high capital mobility, the move was also seen as a way to insulate countries from the kind of damaging currency crises that many poorer countries had experienced in the 1997–98 international financial crisis.[12]

The Argentine request prompted US government officials and members of Congress to begin investigating the issue. In Congress, Republican senator Connie Mack of Florida and his research staff became particularly enthusiastic about the idea and they played the lead role in launching Congressional hearings. His enthusiasm was shared by a number of witnesses called before Congressional committees. In the media, too, a number of prominent analysts highlighted the benefits of the proposal. And some officials at various Federal Reserve Banks also made supportive comments.[13]

The arguments in favour of promoting dollarization in the Americas were often quite similar to those put forward by US policy-makers in the early twentieth century. In that earlier era, US foreign monetary policy had been shaped heavily by liberal economists – such as Charles Conant, Jeremiah Jenks, and Edwin Kemmerer – who held a strong belief in the virtues of price stability and the gold standard. They argued that dollarization diplomacy would bring price stability to Latin America, which in turn would promote economic growth by fostering the confidence of foreign investors and encouraging the growth of domestic savings and financial markets.

Connie Mack and his staff echoed these arguments and were strong supporters of neoliberal monetary thinking. A banker before he entered politics, Mack himself had earlier been a supporter of US legislation to make price stability the principal goal of the Federal Reserve System. He explained his interest in promoting dollarization abroad as an extension of the monetary principles he backed at home: "Those of you who know me know that it's a long-standing aim of mine that the United States ought to seek not only to export our products but to export our principles as well ... in terms of global growth, our #1 export right now ought to be our principled approach to price stability."[14]

The interest of some US neoliberals in dollarization abroad also emerged out of the experience of the dramatic international financial crisis of 1997–98. During this crisis, many US neoliberal thinkers and politicians – including Mack – were very critical of the large loans that the IMF extended to crisis-stricken countries. Some of these critics began to look at dollarization as an alternative way of promoting monetary stability abroad that would no longer require this kind of international financial support. As Mack put it, "I see dollarization as an antipoverty, prodevelopment policy ... By eliminating the root cause of currency crises, widespread dollarization would eliminate the need for international institutions to make the complex and highly controversial interventions in national economies that have been an integral part of recent currency rescue efforts."[15]

In the early twentieth century, dollarization diplomacy also had some broader strategic goals, particularly the cultivation of a currency bloc that could rival European influence in the Americas. This issue now resurfaced with the creation of the euro by European Union countries. As influential Congressional staff members put it, "official dollarization would help the dollar remain the premier international currency, a status that the euro is now challenging. Dollarization by one or more large Latin American countries would significantly expand the number of people officially using the dollar, moving the population of the dollar zone ahead of the population of the euro zone for the time being."[16] More generally, the 1999 *Economic Report of the President* – which adopted a neutral stance overall on the question of dollarization diplomacy – noted that dollarization could contribute to the "power and prestige" of the US by strengthening the dollar's role as an international currency.[17] In addition, supporters of dollarization diplomacy noted that the process of sharing seigniorage with dollarized countries could be used as a tool of US influence over dollarized countries. The International Monetary Stability Act would have given the US treasury secretary enormous discretion to decide whether or not to share seigniorage with a particular government. In the words of the same Congressional staff members: "even if a country does fulfil all of the considerations, the Secretary can still deny it a rebate. The latitude that the Secretary has is one factor that should induce countries interested in official dollarization to cooperate fully with the United States."[18]

In addition to being driven by these ideological and strategic motivations, supporters of dollarization diplomacy also suggested that this policy would serve specific US economic interests by eliminating currency-related transaction costs. As Mack put it, promoting the dollar abroad "would help workers and businesses by stabilizing export markets and getting these markets to grow more quickly. It would help investors by reducing the need to hedge against currency risk when investing in emerging markets."[19] In an era when the US was trying to build a Free Trade Area of the Americas, this line of argument carried considerable weight. As one US financier put it in his Congressional testimony, "I suspect that simply switching to a common currency would promote hemispheric integration as effectively as would many thousands of man-hours devoted to the ongoing negotiations over a free trade agreement for the Americas."[20] Another supporter highlighted the particular benefits that would accrue to the US vis-à-vis its existing NAFTA partners: "No more surprise devaluations, no more 'competitive depreciation' tactics to gain a price advantage in shared markets, no more protectionist responses to exchange rate-induced market distortions."[21]

In the early twentieth century, advocates of dollarization diplomacy had also hoped it would provide US businesses with a competitive edge vis-à-vis foreign competition because of their familiarity with the dollar, as well as its availability to them. Deputy Treasury Secretary Larry Summers made this same point in his Congressional testimony in 1999 when outlining the pros and cons of the US promoting the dollar: "To the extent that dollarization helped to consolidate or expand our large role in Latin American markets, it might help to ensure that we continued to benefit disproportionately from their future growth."[22] The 1999 *Economic Report of the President* highlighted that US financial institutions might stand to gain particularly from dollarization.[23] Dollarized countries would be encouraged by the US to open up their financial sector to US financial institutions as a way of fostering a stable banking system. The International Monetary Stability Act in fact listed this as one of various criteria that the US Treasury Secretary would consider in determining whether a country should be "certified" to receive seigniorage revenue.[24] Once they were in dollarized Latin American banking systems, US banks would also have a competitive advantage because of their privileged access to the US Federal Reserve's resources.[25] Given these potential benefits, it was not surprising that some Wall Street interests testified in favour of dollarization at Congressional hearings.[26]

OPPOSITION AND THE SHELVING OF MACK'S BILL

While some within the US supported Mack's bill on these various grounds, others – including officials within the Clinton administration and the Federal Reserve – were more sceptical. To be sure, Larry Summers had shown strong interest in the idea when he was with the World Bank in 1993: "In the long term, finding ways of bribing people to dollarize, or at least give back the extra currency that is earned when dollarization takes place, ought to be an international priority. For the world as a whole, the advantage of dollarization seems clear to me."[27] But when he appeared before Congress in his position as deputy treasury secretary in 1999, Summers was not willing to endorse Mack's initiative, and he declared that the US would neither encourage nor discourage foreign governments from adopting the US dollar. Federal Reserve Chairman Alan Greenspan took the same position. These officials preferred what Cohen calls a policy of "passive neutrality" to one of "active encouragement."[28] And this view ultimately won the day. Mack's bill was shelved.

US policy-makers were partly wary of stirring nationalist sentiments across the Americas. Even Mack acknowledged that the issue of dollarization "touches on a nation's very sense of self: the way in which maintaining a separate currency underscores a nation's sovereignty ... It's a concern to which we must be sensitive."[29] He attempted to deflect the issue by highlighting that the International Monetary Stability Act did not pressure any foreign country to dollarize: "The plan I've set out is all carrot and no stick."[30] But given the history of the early twentieth century, many within the US were keenly aware that any effort by their country to promote dollarization in Latin American would likely generate criticism that the US was "reinventing colonialism."[31]

If countries did decide to dollarize fully, US policy-makers such as Summers also worried that "in difficult times, the loss of domestic monetary sovereignty would foster resentment and encourage policy makers to deflect blame for problems onto the United States."[32] From the standpoint of the citizens of a dollarized country, the problem would not just be that the US Federal Reserve determined their monetary conditions. In the absence of exchange rate adjustments, their domestic price and wages would be called upon to bear a larger share of the adjustment burden to distinct economic shocks (vis-à-vis the US). Since wages and prices are relatively inflexible in the short-term, the result would likely be higher levels of unemployment and lower levels of real output. Critics of dollarization argued that this radical new kind of market discipline might lead to severe social dislocation within dollarized countries. Indeed, many felt that these predictions were subsequently substantiated by Argentina's dramatic financial crisis in 2001–02, a crisis that was blamed at least in part on the country's largely dollarized monetary system.

Critics of dollarization diplomacy also noted that US monetary authorities would begin to feel political pressure to consider the monetary conditions and preferences of dollarized countries when setting US monetary policy. Indeed, there was widespread recognition among US analysts that the demands of a large country such as Canada for a decision-making role within the Fed would be quite legitimate if it adopted the US dollar.[33] There might even be self-interested reasons for the US to back such a demand, because of the impact that monetary developments in Canada would begin to have on the US monetary system. As the economist Fred Bergsten put it, these developments would "have a considerably greater impact on overall monetary conditions in the United States itself, requiring greater consideration thereof in the conduct of US monetary policy. At some point, we would have to contemplate accepting those countries as new Federal Reserve districts and giving them seats on the Fed's Open Market Committee."[34]

This prediction was used by some to strengthen the case *against* promoting dollarization abroad. In other words, the very fact that the adoption of the US dollar abroad might increase pressure on the US to open up the Fed to foreigners was cited as a reason for US policy-makers to *oppose* the idea. Within US policy-making circles, there was little desire to dilute the focus of US monetary policy in this way. Summers made clear in his testimony that the US would not adjust its monetary policy to reflect foreign concerns.[35] Greenspan also warned the Senate Banking Committee: "We have to be particularly careful to remember that our monetary policy is first and always for the United States."[36] Even Mack's International Monetary Stability Act stated clearly that the Federal Reserve would not be obligated to consider foreign economic conditions when setting monetary policy. In the words of the Congressional staffers, the Act "does not reduce the national sovereignty of the United States. The Act does not establish a supranational central bank like the European Central Bank, nor does it give dollarized countries seats on the Board of Governors of the Federal Reserve System."[37]

In discussing the prospects for dollarization in Canada and Mexico more specifically, the director of the Federal Reserve Bank of Atlanta's Latin American Research Group, Michael Chriszt, registered the same concerns: "The United States should also be wary of dollarization from the perspective of monetary policy. While the US Federal Reserve would not be legally compelled to consider the economic and financial conditions of dollarizing countries when developing and implementing monetary policy, ignoring such information would likely be difficult in practice, especially for North American neighbors. Such a development could potentially cause tension within NAFTA, something that is clearly not desirable for any of its members. Therefore, dollarization in North America is not likely to be considered optimal from the US monetary policy perspective."[38] Similarly, Sidney Weintraub and Christopher Sands summarized the prevailing view in Washington in 2002: "Canadians should not expect to gain favours or special leverage from a decision to use the US dollar. Some have suggested that Ottawa would insist on a seat for Canada on the Federal Reserve Board and a voice in US monetary policymaking if it replaced its currency with the US dollar. Yet California, with an economy larger than Canada's, is not guaranteed a seat of its own. Why should Canada receive any preferential treatment? ... The only realistic option for Canada if it wants to abandon its dollar is the unconditional adoption of the US currency with no special voice in the management of monetary policy."[39]

Some critics of Mack's bill also pointed out that, in the absence of wage and price flexibility, dollarized countries might have to turn to alternative adjustment mechanisms which could affect the US in other ways. Bergsten, for example, reminded Congress that if Canada and Mexico adopted the dollar, these countries might require *more* financial support from the US, rather than less, in order to compensate for the loss of the exchange rate tool of adjustment. The US might also find itself receiving more migrants from the countries in response to negative shocks to the Canadian or Mexican economies. Neither option was likely to be terribly popular within the US. Congress was in no mood to consider the creation of what Bergsten called "some form of fiscal federalism to provide an alternative adjustment device to compensate for the abolition of the exchange rate instrument between them and us."[40] On the labour mobility front, a central rationale within the US for NAFTA had also been that it would *reduce* migration from Mexico. But without the buffer of floating exchange rates between itself and its NAFTA partners, the United States government would likely be forced to address these issues and become more actively involved in the resolution of payments imbalances between the three countries. As Bergsten put it, "The United States would then have to participate more directly in the adjustment of the dollarized foreign economies to economic dislocation. In essence, we would either have to send more capital to them or accept more workers from them in case they ran into recession. This would not be totally different from the current situation, where the United States already takes some of the impact of adjustment vis-à-vis neighbouring countries via the exchange rate and the trade balance. However, the distribution of the effects would be different and the transparency (and hence political awareness) of the impact on the United States could become much greater."[41]

Bergsten's argument was particularly interesting in light of the history of Canada's fixed exchange rate during 1962–70. As shown in chapter 4, the existence of that fixed rate forced the US and Canada into a series of complicated negotiations over alternative adjustment mechanisms involving the control of reserve levels and capital flows. The negotiations were often frustrating for both sides, and by the end of that decade Canadian politicians in particular chafed at the constraints imposed. A floating exchange rate provided a way of "depoliticizing" the bilateral adjustment issue. Some similar problems had arisen in the 1939–50 period.

One other concern raised by critics of Mack's bill was that dollarized countries would likely encounter difficulties in addressing domestic financial crises because their national monetary authorities would no longer have an unlimited capacity to print money for lender-of-last-resort (LLR) purposes. In these circumstances, the US might be called upon to bail out troubled financial institutions abroad. This was hardly desirable from a US perspective. In the words of one official at the Federal Reserve Bank of

San Francisco, it would "expose the US taxpayer to losses stemming from the poor performance" of lending institutions in foreign countries.[42] Moreover, without any supervisory or regulatory authority over financial institutions in dollarized countries, US officials would be unable to evaluate their financial health in order to determine if assistance was indeed required. For this reason, in the context of NAMU, Chriszt noted that "clearly, US participation in a lender-of-last-resort function in a North American monetary union would require deep financial and regulatory integration." But he acknowledged that this was "something that is unlikely to be a near-term development."[43] Indeed, even the strongest supporters of NAMU in Canada have rejected this idea.[44]

Mack's bill had tried to avoid any commitment to LLR activities abroad by specifying clearly that the Federal Reserve was not obligated to serve as an LLR to any dollarized country and was not responsible for bank supervision abroad. But the US might find it politically difficult to sustain this position during a severe financial crisis in dollarized countries. This point was highlighted in the early twentieth century in Cuba, a country whose monetary system had become largely dollarized by the early 1920s. During a severe financial crisis in 1920–21, Cuban-owned banks had collapsed because they did not have access to the US Fed's discount window. Soon after, the Federal Reserve established agencies in Cuba to provide lender-of-last-resort facilities for institutions operating in that dollarized monetary system.[45]

This issue also apparently arose in the context of Argentina's discussions with the US in early 1999. According to some reports, Argentina's government indicated that it would be more willing to consider adopting the US dollar if the Federal Reserve would agree to assume some LLR functions for the Argentine financial system.[46] US policy-makers, however, made it clear that they were not prepared to consider the Argentine request. During the debate about the Mack bill, they took the same position. As Summers put it, "it would not, in our judgment, be appropriate for the United States authorities to extend the net of bank supervision, to provide access to the Federal Reserve discount window, or to adjust bank supervisory responsibilities or the procedures or orientation of US monetary policy in light of another country deciding to adopt the dollar."[47] The fear of creating unwanted expectations in Latin America concerning this role no doubt helps explain why key US policy-makers have been so careful not to endorse dollarization abroad in their official statements. As Greenspan noted, "we have to be careful not to be perceived as creating a safety net" for banks in dollarized countries.[48]

The debate about the Mack bill thus made clear that there was little interest within the US in helping dollarized countries either by offering them a voice in US monetary decision-making, by facilitating their external payments adjustment process, or even by extending lender-of-last-resort assistance to them. This was even true of most *supporters* of the Mack bill. In this context, US policy-makers took the view that any initiative to encourage adoption of the US dollar by offering to share seigniorage would be politically risky. It could both generate unwanted foreign pressure for this kind of assistance in the future and create foreign resentment if and when this assistance was not forthcoming. Underlying this view has also been considerable skepticism that dollarization would bring the economic benefits to foreign countries that Mack and his staff suggested, and a belief that exchange rate flexibility and discretionary domestic monetary policy remain important macroeconomic tools for countries across the Americas.

IMPACT ON THE CANADIAN NAMU DEBATE

The outcome of this debate was hardly encouraging for supporters of NAMU in Canada. Grubel's hope that US policy-makers might be willing to consider the creation of a new North American currency and central bank was revealed as far-fetched at the moment. The US debate had focused almost exclusively on the idea that monetary union in North America – or the Americas more generally – would take place on the basis of foreign countries adopting the US dollar.[49] Even those few US analysts who endorsed the idea of a genuine monetary union acknowledged its small chance of being implemented. As Chriszt acknowledges, "In the United States ... the idea of sharing monetary sovereignty is unlikely to gain support any time soon."[50] Courchene and Harris's proposal for Canada to become the thirteenth Federal Reserve district was also dismissed outright by US policy-makers. A public opinion poll conducted in the US in 2002 also confirmed that only 10.4 per cent of respondents agreed with the idea of creating a new North American currency with Canada and Mexico, while 83.5 per cent disagreed. These numbers even held up among Americans living in states bordering on Canada.[51]

The US debate highlighted that NAMU could come into being between Canada and the US only if Canada was willing to adopt the US dollar unilaterally. US policy-makers made it clear that they are not prepared to offer even small concessions – such as the sharing of seigniorage – to countries that would like to adopt the US dollar as their currency. When the issue was presented in this way, many Canadians who might have been more sympathetic to NAMU turned against the idea. Monetary union in these "quasi-colonial" circumstances, they argued, would not be worth it.[52] Leaving aside the question of lost seigniorage, symbolic considerations, and the need to develop new ways of providing lender-of-last-resort activities, the central cost was seen to be that Canadians would be left with no say over monetary policy. As Robson and Laidler put it, "Monetary policy is a key tool of macroeconomic management and a legitimate focus of interest by voters. Most people would agree that ... the makers of monetary policy should be ultimately accountable to voters for the goals they set and their performance in achieving them."[53] An internal Department of Finance report obtained in April 2001 by the *National Post* made the same point: "Dollarization is unacceptable to us. It would mean zero influence over monetary policy, zero democratic accountability and zero capacity to deal with crises."[54] Anne Golden of the Conference Board of Canada also made this issue the centrepiece of her opposition to NAMU: "the real issue at stake is sovereignty. By adopting the US dollar, we would relinquish a critical policy tool for managing our economy ... And without political accountability, it is implausible that most Canadians would knowingly surrender their ability to make monetary policy."[55]

Some NAMU supporters, such as Courchene and Harris, have still been willing to consider unilateral dollarization as a superior option to the present floating exchange rate.[56] But this argument has not attracted many. Even Robert Mundell, a very prominent critic of Canada's floating exchange rate, was not willing to endorse this and advocated instead a fixed exchange rate.[57] It is worth noting that Courchene and Harris also expressed support for a fixed exchange rate, as they had in the early 1990s. But they acknowledged that a fixed exchange rate would be credible in the eyes of global financial markets only with what they describe as a wholesale "policy paradigm shift" in Canada involving "full coordination of fiscal policy, both provincial and federal."[58] The difficulties of establishing a credible peg that is insulated from speculative attack left many – even Fortin who had earlier joined Courchene and Harris – to conclude that policy-makers face a two-corner world in which they must choose either monetary union/dollarization or a freely floating exchange rate.[59] Given the problems associated with the former option in the North American context, many Canadians endorsed continuation of the floating exchange rate by default.

In this way, the US debate had the effect of strengthening the case within Canada against NAMU and in favour of the status quo. Weintraub and Sands note that US policy-makers are not at all unhappy with this turn of events. They sum up the prevailing wisdom in Washington in this way: "Since the United States has nothing tangible to gain from the formal Canadian adoption of its currency, Washington policy-makers will be leary of offering any encouragement to Canada that could serve to draw the US government into a domestic Canadian debate over sovereignty."[60] The US approach was well summed up in January 1999 when one US official stated that the idea of NAMU would warrant serious talks only " 100 years from now."[61]

If the US debate did not help the case for NAMU in Canada, might it change in the future? It is obviously very difficult to predict the future direction of US policy in this area. But it is clear that sceptics of dollarization diplomacy have the upper hand. And the Argentine economic crisis has only strengthened their position because it undermined support for dollarization both within the US and across the Americas. If debate of the Mack bill is any guide, strong support is also unlikely to come from US economic interests in the immediate future. Although US advocates of the Mack bill highlighted how internationally-oriented US businesses – particularly in the financial sector – stood to gain from dollarization abroad, there was relatively little business lobbying on the issue.[62] Some Wall Street interests supported Mack's bill, but they were not strongly engaged in lobbying on the issue, and some even lobbied against the idea. Walter Molano of BCP Securities, for example, opposed dollarization in Latin America on the grounds that the existence of a national currency ensured that external creditors were often repaid in a priority fashion during debt crises because governments essentially imposed an inflation tax on the local population. He concluded: "Unfortunately, dollarization bumps local currency holders up the seniority ladder and allows them to be paid prior to the external creditors."[63]

For the purposes of this book, it is particularly important to note that US domestic economic interests have shown little interest in the question of the Canada-US exchange rate.[64] There was no business lobby arguing in favour of Mack's bill on the grounds that it would stabilize the Canadian dollar vis-à-vis the US dollar. Weintraud and Sands attribute the lack of business interest to the fact that so much Canada-US trade is intrafirm: "The costs of short-term exchange-rate volatility can be minimized through adjustments in transfer pricing."[65] The US business position was also consistent more generally with the postwar history of US policy towards Canada's exchange rate that earlier chapters examined.

In Europe, by contrast, Henning shows how German policy-makers – for various institutional and interest group reasons – have always been much more interested in limiting the fluctuations of their neighbouring countries' currencies. Even with this interest, most analysts agree that Germany accepted EMU only because of an unusual set of circumstances in which monetary union came to be seen as a trade-off for European (and especially French) support for German reunification in 1989.[66] In the North American context, Canadians thus face a particularly challenging task in trying to create a monetary union in which they have a significant voice. Not only have Americans not been inclined historically to see Canada's fluctuating exchange rate as a significant problem they hope to "fix," US policy-makers also have shown considerable resistance to the idea of sharing decision-making powers in a North American context. During the FTA negotiations, Canada faced enormous difficulties in its efforts just to create the binational dispute settlement process. Granting Canada a place in the Federal Reserve System would be a much more significant step and would likely require large concessions from Canada in other areas that could easily outweigh the perceived benefits.

The only development that seems likely to produce a change in US opinion would be the competitive threat of the euro. If the euro began to pose a more serious challenge to the dollar's international position, US policy-makers might begin to see dollarization diplomacy in a more positive light. The spread of the dollar's use might come to be seen as a way to preserve the benefits accruing from the issuance of an international currency. In this scenario, Canadian policy-makers might finally gain more negotiating leverage. This, at least, is a hope expressed by Grubel, Courchene, and Harris.[67]

CANADA AND THE FED: WHAT ROLE FOR A THIRTEENTH RESERVE DISTRICT?

Let us assume for a moment that US policy-makers *do* become more interested in promoting the US dollar's use in Canada at some future date and that they are willing to consider admitting Canada as a thirteenth Federal Reserve district. How much political support would this help secure for NAMU within Canada? Skeptics argue that Canada would still find itself in an American-dominated monetary union without much voice. As noted at the start of this chapter, however, Courchene and Harris think otherwise.

In particular, they suggest that Canada's position would be little different from that of each European country in the euro zone.

How valid is this argument? Courchene and Harris are certainly correct that the federal character of the US central bank makes the political "architecture" of North American monetary union easier to imagine. The US central bank is, after all, called the "Federal Reserve" because it is made up of twelve reserve banks, each representing a district of US territory whose headquarters are in the following cities: Boston, New York, Philadelphia, Cleveland, Richmond, Atlanta, Chicago, St. Louis, Minneapolis, Kansas City, Dallas, and San Francisco. Given this structure, it certainly seems plausible that Canada could simply become a thirteenth district. And the attraction of this scenario is that it would enable Canada to have a voice in the US central bank – which would be renamed the North American Federal Reserve under Courchene and Harris's plan – since district banks have a formal role in the policy-making of the Fed.[68] But how much voice would Canada have in the Federal Reserve in its role as a thirteenth reserve district? The question is in fact difficult to answer definitively because the nature of the Fed's federalism is more complicated than Harris and Courchene imply.

The key decision-making body in the Federal Reserve is the Federal Open Market Committee (FOMC) which meets every four to six weeks and controls the Fed's all-important open market operations, as well as its foreign exchange operations. The committee does indeed have twelve voting members. But only five of these votes are allocated to the presidents of reserve banks, while the remaining seven are assigned to the members of the board of governors of the Federal Reserve System who have been appointed by the US president (and confirmed by the US Senate) to fourteen-year terms. The allocation of the five reserve bank votes is also done in an interesting manner: the president of the Federal Reserve Bank of New York (FRBNY) has a permanent vote (and is also the vice-chair of the FOMC), while the other four votes are shared on a rotational basis among the presidents of the remaining eleven reserve banks (although all the presidents can attend all meetings).

As a result, if the Bank of Canada became the thirteenth reserve bank – as perhaps the Federal Reserve Bank of Ottawa, or even Toronto[69] – it would not be guaranteed the kind of voting share that Courchene and Harris suggest unless it secured the same permanent vote that the FRBNY has. If this proved politically impossible, it would have to lobby hard for the best placing within the rotational system involving the other reserve banks. At the moment, the reserve banks are placed in four groups, each of which runs its own system of rotation: (1) Boston, Philadelphia, and Richmond, (2) Cleveland and Chicago, (3) Atlanta, Dallas, and St Louis, and (4) Minneapolis, Kansas City, and San Francisco. Obviously, the second group would be the best to join because banks in that group have a chance to vote more often. But one could certainly anticipate resistance from those same banks since Canada's entry would dilute their influence.

There is a further problem. The reserve banks are not structured in a way that is designed to represent the broad "public" interest of the districts they represent. Each of the reserve banks is privately owned by commercial banks that exist within the district. The election of their boards reflects this with six of the nine board members elected by the private banks. Three of these six are supposed to be chosen by the banks to represent the public (and they may not be linked to private banks as officers, directors, or employees), but in practice these "Class B" directors (as opposed to the three "Class A" directors that represent private bank interests directly) tend to be dominated by officials of large manufacturing firms.[70] One consequence is that the voting patterns of reserve bank presidents – who are elected by this board – within the FOMC tend to be more conservative than the publicly appointed members of the federal board of governors.[71]

At the same time, even this skewed form of regional voice is diluted by the fact that the remaining three members of the reserve bank boards – who are also supposed to represent the public (and once again can have no link to private banks, even as shareholders in this case) – are chosen by the federal board of governors. The federal board of governors also designates one of its chosen directors as the chair of the board of the reserve bank and another as the deputy chair. Perhaps most important is the fact that, once the nine-member board of the district reserve bank has selected a president to represent it on the FOMC (for a five-year term), the federal board of governors also must give its consent to the person chosen. The result is described by Woolley: "since the [federal] Board, and especially the chairman, exercises a virtual veto over selection of district bank presidents, it is believed the district bank presidents are individuals who reflect the preferences of the Board – or perhaps of the chairman. In the eyes of some Federal Reserve officials, the presidents are essentially employees of the Board."[72] The power of the local board of the reserve bank is also restricted by the fact that, once selected, reserve bank presidents are not bound by the preferences of their board when they cast votes in the FOMC.

If Canada formed a thirteenth district represented by a reserve bank of this kind, this bank would hardly act as a representative of the Canadian public interest. Instead, it would be beholden to an odd combination of the preferences of Canadian private banks and the views of the US-appointed members of the federal board of governors. Needless to say, this would be a sharp break from current practice. The Bank of Canada is presently a publicly-owned institution whose governor and board members are all chosen by Canada's minister of finance. Moreover, none of its board members is allowed any connection to private banks. If the Bank of Canada were to act as a public representative of Canada's interests within the FOMC, it would need to preserve this public character. Whether this kind of arrangement could be negotiated as part of Canada's entry into NAMU is an open question. A concession to Canada along these lines might be welcomed by those Americans who have long sought to reform the reserve banks to make them more accountable to the public.[73] For the same reason, it might be resisted by others who fear that the structure of the reserve banks cannot be altered without upsetting the delicate political balance on which the Fed was founded. Perhaps a messy compromise might emerge in which Canadian banks play the same role as their US counterparts in selecting six of the nine board members, while the Canadian government was given the role of choosing the remaining three and also of approving the selection of bank president (instead of the US-controlled board of governors).

Decision-making within the Federal Reserve thus represents a rather odd form of federalism. Power is concentrated in the Washington-based board of governors, which has a majority voting block on the FOMC and also plays a role in the appointment of the reserve bank presidents and their boards. And to the extent that the reserve banks express regional preferences, the views of local private banks play the dominant role. This unique decision-making model is not a product of any formal constitutional federalism, but rather of a political compromise at the time of the Fed's birth in 1913. At that time, a broad consensus had emerged on the need for some kind of national central bank. But policy-makers remained very sensitive to longstanding fears in US politics about such a bank becoming controlled either by New York bankers or by politicians in Washington. The distinct structure of the Fed was proposed as a solution. The federal structure of regional banks supervised by the Washington-based governing board was designed to address the fear that New York bankers might dominate the new central bank, while the private ownership of these banks reassured those who feared Washington's control.[74]

But there remained strong disagreements between the New York banking community and many Republican politicians on the one hand, and some key Democrats allied with smaller banks and agricultural interests from the West, Midwest, and South on the other. The former preferred a small number of reserve banks and a federal governing board with few political representatives. The latter called for a large number of reserve banks – some people wanted as many as fifty – and very little role for private interests on the federal governing board. When Woodrow Wilson was elected president, his sympathies were with this latter group and he endorsed a governing board that was entirely politically appointed.[75] At the same time, he accepted the idea of a smaller number of reserve banks than some of his supporters were demanding. The 1913 Federal Reserve Act allowed for between eight and twelve such banks, and twelve were soon created by a committee after receiving submissions from thirty-seven cities which wanted to house these banks.

The issue of where final authority rested in the Fed – with the privately-owned reserve banks or the politically-appointed federal board – was not outlined clearly in 1913 and it remained very contentious for the first twenty years of the central bank's existence.[76] Not until the Banking Act of 1935 was it finally resolved. In the wake of the Great Depression, Roosevelt's New Dealers made clear their goal of asserting greater centralized political control over the financial sector, a goal that included an attack on the power of the privately-owned reserve banks of the Fed. Roosevelt initially wanted to eliminate their decision-making role altogether from the FOMC, but he agreed to a compromise which set up the current configuration of the FOMC with board members having a majority share of the vote vis-à-vis the reserve bank presidents. Two other changes reinforced this shift of power decisively to the Federal Reserve Board (which was now renamed the Board of Governors of the Federal Reserve System): (1) reserve banks could no longer authorize open market operations without the FOMC's approval, and (2) the board would now approve the selection of heads of the reserve banks (now called presidents instead of governors), as well as their budgets, and bank presidents could no longer be instructed by the boards of their banks to vote according to the latter's preferences. It was also at this time that the present rotation system for the reserve banks was established (although the FRBNY did not receive a permanent vote until a 1942 amendment). These changes not only asserted greater public control over the Fed but also centralized decision-making in Washington.

If the Bank of Canada were to join the Federal Reserve as a thirteenth reserve bank, it would be joining an institution whose history has left it with complicated decision-making rules. To be guaranteed a vote on the FOMC, Canada would need to lobby hard to receive the unique status for the Bank of Canada that the FRBNY has obtained. At the same time, Canada would also need to maintain some degree of control over the process by which the head of the bank and its board is selected. Since both of these demands might be difficult to obtain, Canadian negotiators would likely also press for an alternative mechanism for guaranteeing Canada a permanent vote on the FOMC: obtaining a Canadian representative on the board of governors.[77] Since the US president nominates the existing seven members of the board, Canada would likely press for a Canadian representative to be appointed by the Canadian government. Canadian negotiators would likely try to justify this demand on the grounds that the Fed's board of governors is supposed to be somewhat diverse in regional terms.[78]

This demand might be particularly important for Canadian negotiators because the board – rather than the reserve banks – is where power has been concentrated in the Fed since the mid-1930s. The board controls the budgets of the reserve banks and sets the salaries of their officers. It also has ultimate power over such things as the setting of discount rates and reserve requirements (although their contemporary significance is not large).[79] Canadian negotiators would also likely press for some say over the selection of the chair of the Fed (this person is currently chosen by the US president with Senate confirmation). The chair is a powerful figure, playing a leading role in FOMC meetings and also strongly influencing the allocation of resources within the board. Individual board members, for example, find themselves quite dependent on the chair because they are allocated no staff of their own except for one research assistant.[80] If it was not possible for Canada to play a role in the selection of the Fed's chair, Canadian negotiators could perhaps press for a vice-chair role on the FOMC to parallel that held by the FRBNY.

Ironically, then, the existence of the regional reserve banks themselves may be less significant to the question of Canada's voice within the Fed than Courchene and Harris suggest. To be sure, their existence would at least guarantee a Canadian voice of some kind. It would also provide a mechanism for ensuring that attention would be given to Canadian monetary conditions; the FOMC receives a "Beige book" in advance of its meetings which summarizes economic conditions in each of the existing reserve districts.[81] Each reserve bank board also selects one person – usually a prominent banker – to serve on the Federal Advisory Council which meets four times a year to make non-binding recommendations to the board. But the role of the head of a Canadian reserve bank might ultimately be less significant in projecting Canadian preferences within the Fed than a Canadian representative on the board and/or a Canadian role in selecting the Fed's chair.

COMPARING TO THE EUROPEAN CONTEXT

How does Canada's potential position within a North American Federal Reserve compare to that of European countries within the European Central Bank (ECB)? Courchene and Harris argued that it would be similar. Here again, however, the situation is more complicated than they suggest. To begin with, there are a number of reasons why member countries of the euro zone have greater influence with the ECB than Canada can anticipate within the Fed:

1 At the time of the euro's creation (and the time that Courchene and Harris were making their argument), the head of each national central bank within the ECB was guaranteed one vote on the ECB's key decision-making body, the Governing Council. There was, in other words, no system of rotation among these representatives of the kind that reserve banks experience within the US Fed. This also meant that the central banks of small countries initially had exactly the same voting share as their counterparts from large countries.

2 The national central banks were given a majority voting share on the ECB's Governing Council, instead of the minority share held by the US reserve banks on the FOMC. The ECB's Executive Committee was made up of only six members (the president, the vice-president, and four others), a number easily outnumbered by the twelve national central bank representatives.

3 The Executive Committee (each member of which serves non-renewable eight-year terms) was selected by unanimous approval of the national governments participating in the euro zone. This ensured that the governments of even small European countries had a veto power, a much more influential role than Canada is likely to obtain with respect to selection of the Fed's board of governors and chair.

4 Unlike the Fed's board of governors, the ECB's executive committee was given no say over the selection of the heads of national central

banks. Each national government instead retained control over the selection process of the head of its central bank.

In these ways, the ECB was established with a more decentralized federal structure that gave more power to the "regions" of the common currency zone than the Fed. In March 2003, faced with the prospect of the entry to the euro zone of a large number of East European countries, the EU Council of Ministers approved a change to this initial design. The new system of voting retained an executive committee of six members, but allowed the size of the Governing Council as a whole to expand to a maximum of twenty-one voting members. The remaining fifteen voting members were now to be national central bank governors selected on a system of rotation from groups of countries organized according to the countries' economic and financial significance within the euro area. The proposed groupings are organized in a way that gives larger countries a vote more often within the system of rotation than smaller countries. Even with this change, however, the ECB retains a more decentralized decision-making structure than the US Fed.

There is one further reason why individual European countries have more say in the ECB than Canada would likely have in a NAMU. The ECB must report to, and consult with, a number of pan-European institutions in which each country has a voice. The European Parliament must be consulted about the selection of the ECB's president and its executive council (although it is not empowered to reject nominations), and it receives the ECB's annual report and can ask its president or executive committee members to appear before its relevant committees. The ECB president also reports to the European Council and European Commission.[82] In North America, there are no equivalents of these kinds of pan-regional bodies to which a North American Federal Reserve could report. This reduces the opportunity for Canada to express its preferences. For example, the chair of the US Fed has since 1977 been mandated to report semi-annually to the US Congress, but could the chair also be required to report to the Canadian Parliament? Some, such as Laidler, Buiter, and even Courchene, are skeptical, and conclude that only Canadian representation in the Fed would likely give a voice.[83] These kinds of difficulties have led many critics of NAMU to argue that the common central bank would lack legitimacy and could only function credibly on a sustainable basis if North American political institutions were created.[84]

It is important, however, not to overstate the "voice" of individual European countries within the ECB. One reason is that national central banks are mandated not to consider their country's interests when participating in the ECB's decision-making. This mandate is reinforced by the fact that, in contrast to the practices of the Fed, the votes and debates in the Governing Council are kept confidential – national governments are unaware of how their country's central bank head is voting.[85] These provisions were explicitly designed to force ECB directors to adopt a pan-European perspective. Indeed, Dyson notes that even the seating arrangement in the Governing Council is designed to serve this goal: "its members sit in alphabetical order, by name not by country, and mixing national governors with executive board members in order to avoid any grouping in hostile blocks."[86]

It is also important that the ECB has been established in a manner that makes it relatively unaccountable to elected officials across Europe.[87] As we have seen, national governments certainly influence the bank through their control of the selection of the bank's executive council and the governors of the national central banks. But once appointed to their long terms in office, these central bankers are relatively autonomous from elected officials. I have already noted that the ECB engages in some reporting and consultative activities vis-à-vis the European Council, the European Parliament, and the European Commission. But ultimately, the bank's autonomy has strong legal protection. Article 107 of the Maastricht Treaty states: "neither the ECB, nor a national central bank, nor any member of their decision-making bodies shall seek or take instructions" from outside bodies. The Maastricht Treaty also states famously that the bank must make "price stability" its central goal. This mandate was, of course, agreed to at the time by national governments. But because it was set out in this international treaty, future governments will have a hard time altering it. It cannot, for example, be changed simply by a vote of the European Council of Ministers or the European Parliament.[88] Many analysts argue that this weak accountability to elected officials is a fatal flaw in the ECB's design. The comments of Pringle and Turner are typical: "The biggest threat to the euro and the EsCB arises not out of any faults with the 'internal' design of the system but with the absence of a mechanism for political accountability ... No central bank can operate in the long term in an environment that is not in tune with the public interest ... there is no accepted mechanism for ensuring its continued political legitimacy."[89]

These features of the ECB make it much less accountable to elected officials than the US Fed and the Bank of Canada within their respective domestic political settings. The latter are both creatures of a legislative body (i.e., the US Congress and the Canadian Parliament) which can at any moment change their mandate. In the case of the Bank of Canada, the Canadian government has even set out specific "inflation targets" for the bank to follow since the early 1990s. The 1967 revisions to the Bank of Canada Act also highlight that ultimate responsibility for monetary policy rests with the government, and the Bank of Canada's governor is required to consult regularly with the federal minister of finance for this reason. In the event of a conflict between the governor and the federal government, the minister is also empowered to issue a public directive to the governor (although this has never been done and it would carry high political risks for the government).[90] The Fed is not guided by any specific "inflation targets" set by Congress or the president, and this kind of "directive" power does not exist. But it, too, consults regularly with elected officials and it is keenly aware of its potential vulnerability to changes in its mandate.[91]

In sum, then, individual countries have more voice within the ECB than Canada would likely have within a North American Fed. But even this European institution is hardly a model to follow since it is seen by many to suffer from a serious "accountability deficit." Indeed, many of those who are critical of NAMU on this basis are also critics of the ECB for the same reason.[92] It is worth recalling, however, that the weak political accountability of the ECB is seen by some as a virtue in Europe. Many supporters of EMU have in fact backed the project precisely because it promises to insulate monetary management from political influence to a greater extent than before. Joining the euro zone has been seen as a way to "lock in" an approach to monetary policy that prioritizes price stability. For some, this goal stemmed from their commitment to the "neoliberal" idea that price stability should be the prime objective of monetary policy. For others, it reflected a more pragmatic desire for monetary "credibility" in the face of increasingly powerful global financial markets. The fact that a significant political constituency supported these views across Europe helped generate some of the support for the euro project. And from this perspective, the ECB will in fact be perceived as legitimate as long as it fulfills its technocratic task of preserving price stability.[93]

The same goals drive some of the supporters of NAMU in Canada, as we have seen. Grubel hopes that a future North American Fed would be guided by the same price stability mandate as the ECB. Courchene and Harris also predict that a North American Fed might have this kind of mandate, and they try to dispel fears about NAMU being unaccountable to Canadians on the grounds that the provision of price stability should increasingly be seen as an uncontroversial supranational "public good." As they put it, "if the mandate of this North American central bank were framed largely in terms of pursuing price stability, the actual voting share might matter less."[94] They also argue that Canadians must recognize how national sovereignty in monetary affairs is increasingly becoming a thing of the past. In addition to pointing to the growing power of global financial markets, they highlight the growing use of the US dollar by the private sector within Canada. In a context of creeping informal "dollarization," they argue that obtaining even a small voice within the Federal Reserve would be better than being left with no voice in a de facto dollarized economy.[95]

If there is indeed large support for these views, the debate about an "accountability deficit" may be less politically controversial in Canada than some NAMU critics suggest. The chief of the Bank of Canada's international section, James Powell, hinted at this point in an internal memo about NAMU: "[Common North American political institutions] might be preferable in order for the North American Monetary Authority to be accountable to some degree to Canadians. *However, this may not be important to people.*"[96] As Dyson suggests, what is really at stake is two competing visions of legitimacy. Supporters of the ECB and NAMU are suggesting that these regional central banks can be sustained by a kind of relatively narrow "technocratic conception of legitimacy."[97] Their critics have a broader "Lockean" concept of legitimacy which emphasizes how these central banks can only function credibly on a sustainable basis if they are supported by ongoing democratic accountability and consent.

CONCLUSION

Within Canada, one of the more influential arguments against NAMU has concerned the question of governance. Opponents have argued that NAMU will inevitably be based on the US dollar and that Canada will have little say in managing the union. As we have seen, key supporters of NAMU have attempted to address this issue in two ways. Some have suggested that the US may be more willing than Canadians think to embrace a supranational currency and central bank in which Canada has a voice. Others have argued that even a NAMU based on the US dollar might not be so undesirable since Canadians could secure a similar voice to that of many member countries of the euro zone if it became a thirteenth reserve district of the US central bank.

Neither argument has proven terribly persuasive. Canadians were provided an indication of US views towards NAMU by the debate that broke out in that country in 1999 over the prospects for a regional monetary bloc in the Americas. Although the emergence of the US debate initially boosted NAMU supporters in Canada, its content and outcome ultimately undermined their cause. US policy-makers made clear that they had no interest in considering a supranational currency and central bank in the region. Only a monetary union based on the US dollar was on the table. And they were not even willing to provide *any* support to foreign countries that might choose to adopt the US dollar. The notion that foreign countries might join the Fed's decision-making processes was sharply rejected and even more limited forms of cooperation – such as the sharing of seigniorage – were ruled out.

Even if US policy-makers were willing to extend the Fed to include foreign countries in the future, the European analogy is misleading since both the Federal Reserve and the ECB have more complicated decision-making rules than the comparison implies. The Fed's more centralized federal structure and the quasi-private nature of the reserve banks would complicate Canada's efforts to obtain influence comparable to that of individual European countries in the ECB. I have also noted that the ECB itself should not be held up as a model since many Europeans worry that it suffers from an "accountability deficit" vis-à-vis European voters as a whole. This feature of the ECB is already raising questions about its political future, and it has generated a broader debate about the means by which central banks are legitimized in democratic societies.

What does this analysis tell us about the prospects for NAMU? It highlights that NAMU supporters in Canada will remain vulnerable to the criticism that Canada may have only a very limited voice within NAMU. More generally, it undermines the argument of some NAMU supporters that their proposal is a natural response to a broad worldwide trend towards the creation of currency unions. No such trend is likely to develop in any major way in the Americas in the coming years, unless there is a sudden change in US behaviour. Even with more active US support, countries in this region may balk at joining a US dollar zone on the grounds that their potential voice in the governance of the Fed would be limited.

At the same time, the significance of this kind of Canadian opposition should not be overstated. This issue of accountability does not generate passion among all Canadians. As noted above, those who see monetary policy as a technocratic exercise are less concerned about the day-to-day

democratic governance of a monetary union. The issue has also resonated much less strongly in the one part of the country where discussions of sovereignty and nationalism are usually the most heated:
Quebec. Explaining this conundrum is the subject of the next chapter.

The significance of nationalist opposition to NAMU should also not
be exaggerated for one further reason. Opinion polls taken during the
height of the NAMU debate suggest that many Canadians did not in fact
see the future of Canada's currency in strongly nationalist terms. In late
1999, for example, a Maclean's/CBC opinion poll found that Canadians
remain generally quite nationalist, but were in fact almost evenly split
on the question of whether Canada would benefit (44 per cent) or lose
out (42 per cent) from having a common currency with the US.[98] A few
years later, in April 2002, a survey by the NFO CFgroup found even less
support for the Canadian dollar. Participants in the survey were presented with three options: (1) Canada adopts the US dollar, (2) Canada
adopts the US dollar along with Mexico, and (3) the three countries create a new common currency. Fifty-one per cent of participants agreed
that Canada should embrace at least one of these scenarios, while only
42.5 per cent preferred the status quo. The percentage of people who
agreed with the first (32.2 per cent) or second (30.5 per cent) scenarios
was not in fact terribly different from the percentage agreeing with the
last (34.1 per cent).[99]

At the time of the 1999 poll, one Maclean's reporter explained the
lack of strong support for the Canadian currency in the following way:
"No doubt much of it stems from the weakened state of the Canadian
dollar and a sense that Canadians are falling behind their American
neighbours in material terms."[100] The observation recalls a point noted
in the introduction to the last chapter: that some of the new interest in
NAMU was generated by the collapse of the Canadian dollar's value in
1998. As the currency's value fell to new lows, it ceased to be an object
of national pride for many Canadians. Indeed, already at the time of the
Mexican peso crisis in late 1994, foreign analysts had been ridiculing
the loonie as the "Hudson's Bay peso."[101] With this further decline,
many Canadians may have come to see their membership in the Canadian monetary community as a liability.

This observation points to a further way in which currency structures
and nationalism are linked. When a national currency has a stable and
strong value, it can contribute to national identities by acting as a symbol of the vitality of the nation and by creating positive collective monetary experiences among citizens. The postwar "D-mark nationalism"

in the Federal Republic of Germany provides perhaps the best example of this phenomenon. But when the value of a national currency does not have these characteristics, the opposite can happen. It may become distrusted and citizens may begin to resent their economic dependence on it. This helps explain why support for the euro has been quite substantial in some southern European countries whose currencies had a history of instability.

If some of the Canadian interest in NAMU also stemmed from such considerations, the Canadian currency's sudden appreciation from 63 cents to above 80 cents in 2003–04 may have helped push the issue off the Canadian political agenda. Some even anticipated this result at the height of the debate itself. Here, for example, is the prediction of Jeff Rubin of CIBC in 2001: "if the Canadian dollar rebounds to U.S. 75 cents, then this issue would disappear, because the vast majority of Canadians know in their heart if we lose the Canadian dollar we've lost a large part of our sovereignty. They only want the U.S. dollar because they're beginning to ask themselves the question: what's the point of having a national currency if it makes us poor every year?"[102]

CHAPTER EIGHT

Quebec Sovereigntists
in the NAMU Debate

This analysis of Canada's NAMU debate has not yet examined regional divisions. In the first half of the book, we saw how these divisions have been an important feature of the politics of Canadian exchange rate regimes since Confederation.[1] They also played a key role in the FTA debate in the 1980s. At that time, the FTA found strong support in Quebec, especially among sovereigntists, and in the commodity-exporting provinces of the country, while Ontarians were much more nervous about the potential consequences to their province's industrial sector. Do we see a similar pattern of regional divisions in the NAMU debate?

In the opinion polls discussed at the end of the last chapter, the pattern of support and opposition to NAMU was in fact quite similar across most of the different regions of Canada. The one exception came in Quebec, where support for NAMU was consistently higher than elsewhere in the country. In the 1999 poll, 50 per cent of respondents from Quebec agreed that a common currency with the US would be beneficial, while only 35 per cent disagreed. Opinion was more evenly split in the rest of the country. In the 2002 poll, at least one of the three options for NAMU was supported by 61.5 per cent of Quebec participants, while only 30.4 per cent endorsed the maintenance of the Canadian dollar.

As in the FTA debate, support for NAMU has been particularly strong among Quebec sovereigntists. The leadership of the sovereigntist movement in fact played the lead role, along with the economists discussed in chapter 6, in first placing this issue on the Canadian political agenda. In December 1998 – even before the publications of Grubel, and Courchene and Harris – the leader of the Bloc Québécois (BQ), Gilles Duceppe, suggested publicly that Mexico and Canada should consider adopting the US dollar.[2] Quebec's finance minister at the time, Bernard Landry, then took up the idea the following month, calling for a task force to examine the idea of a Canada-US currency union. In March 1999, the Bloc moved that a special committee of the House of Commons be established to consider the idea of a pan-American monetary union (a motion that was defeated by the government). Former Quebec premier Jacques Parizeau also began to support the proposal for Canada to adopt the US dollar in this period,[3] and Quebec premier Lucien Bouchard indicated interest in the idea during a trip to partially-dollarized Argentina in May 2000. Other prominent sovereigntists have continued to promote the proposal since this time.

Although the position of Quebec sovereigntists on NAMU is consistent with their support for the FTA, it raises some interesting analytical questions. The case for NAMU in the rest of the country has been associated with the neoliberal goals of trade expansion, domestic deregulation, and fiscal and monetary discipline. These objectives are not those we traditionally associate with the economic policies of nationalist movements, not to mention the social democratic values that have historically been associated with much of the Quebec sovereigntist movement. Equally intriguing is the fact that Quebec sovereigntists have argued that they would continue to favour NAMU even after Quebec became an independent state. Although the issuing of a national currency has traditionally been seen as a key symbol of the sovereignty of a nation-state, Quebec sovereigntists are explicitly forgoing the opportunity to create one after independence. Indeed, in public statements, the sovereigntist leadership has actively downplayed the significance of national currencies for national identities. How, then, do we explain the support of Quebec sovereigntists for NAMU? And what kind of impact does their support have on the NAMU debate in Canada and its political prospects?

THE LONG HISTORICAL ROOTS OF QUEBEC'S "NATIONAL CURRENCY" QUESTION

To understand the position of Quebec sovereigntists in the NAMU debate, it is necessary to explore the deep historical roots of the question of whether a future independent Quebec would create its own national currency. This question emerged as a central one in Quebec sovereignty

debates from the very origins of the modern Quebec sovereigntist movement in the 1960s. Réné Lévesque's dramatic departure from the Quebec Liberal Party in 1967 is widely seen as the key moment in the rise of
the Quebec sovereigntist movement as a significant political force. From
the very outset, Lévesque made clear his belief that a sovereign Quebec
should not have its own currency. Instead, he proposed a five-year experiment in which an independent Quebec would share a currency
union with the rest of Canada. The joint currency would, he suggested,
be managed by a central bank with a joint board of directors to include
the deputy ministers of finance of both countries as non-voting members. The top positions of the bank would be distributed proportion-
ately between the two countries, and the positions of governor and
deputy governor would alternate between each country's officials.[4]

Lévesque's vision of a Canada-Quebec monetary union immediately invited criticism. Initially, the sharpest criticism came from federalists, most
notably Robert Bourassa. Lévesque had hoped that Bourassa would join
him in leaving the Liberal Party, but Bourassa had refused on the grounds
that he disapproved of Lévesque's monetary ideas.[5] If Quebec sovereigntists wanted true political independence, Bourassa argued that they
should plan to create an independent currency. A monetary union with
Canada would, in his view, ultimately require some form of political
union both because common fiscal policies would be necessary and because the two countries would each need influence over monetary policy.
Would he have given his support if Lévesque had called for an independent currency instead? The answer was still no. The creation of a new
Quebec currency would, he argued, produce the risk of massive capital
flight and monetary instability. If these risks could only be avoided by
continuing to use the Canadian dollar, and this use of the Canadian dollar required political union, then Bourassa would remain a federalist. His
decision to back the federalist cause was thus justified on this very pragmatic ground that the monetary costs of true sovereignty would be too
high. Bourassa repeated these arguments in his political battles against
sovereigntists throughout the 1970s, often with considerable success.

Criticism also came from the ranks of sovereigntists. Conflict on the
issue broke out within Lévesque's newly-created Parti Québécois (PQ) in
1972, with economists such as Jacques Parizeau pushing for the idea of
an independent currency.[6] Even when Parizeau became finance minister
in the PQ government after its election in 1976, he and others initially
continued to express skepticism about the idea of monetary union.[7]
They argued much as Bourassa had: a monetary union with Canada

would force Quebec to coordinate fiscal and other economic policies with Canada in ways that would severely undermine the significance of sovereignty. In Parizeau's 1977 words, it "would put huge constraints on them and on us."[8] McRoberts also notes that many sovereigntists argued in favour of an independent currency on the grounds that "currency can constitute a tangible symbol of national status, to which citizens are daily exposed."[9] In addition, it was noted that an independent currency would provide useful seigniorage revenue to the Quebec government.[10]

Despite these arguments, the PQ continued to formally endorse the idea of monetary union. In fact, its proposals in this area became more elaborate. During the 1980 referendum on sovereignty, the party proposed that Quebec would continue to use the Canadian dollar and suggested the creation of a Bank of Quebec which would control the banking system and act as the government's fiscal agent. It proposed that the Bank of Canada and the Bank of Quebec would also come together in a new monetary authority which would make key decisions about exchange-rate and monetary policy. The party's 1979 White Paper titled *Quebec-Canada: a New Deal* suggested that the leadership of this authority would be "chaired alternately by a governor named by each government; the number of seats allocated to each party on the board of directors will be proportional to the relative size of each economy."[11] In the event of disagreement between the representatives of the two countries within the monetary authority, a newly created "Community Council" – involving cabinet ministers from both countries – would have the power to give guidelines to the authority. Only if negotiations with Canada over the creation of this monetary union failed, or reached an impasse, would Quebec create its own currency.[12]

Parizeau ultimately agreed to support these proposals, but other sovereigntists remained opposed. When the idea of economic association with Canada was endorsed at the PQ's 1979 convention, the resolution on monetary proposals provoked enormous debate. In Leslie's words, it was the only resolution "which appeared to be in any real danger of rejection ... There were some powerful speeches against it, and they were well received. Two attempts to break up the 12-part resolution to allow a separate vote on the currency issue [were] narrowly defeated – one by a vote of only 642 to 611."[13]

The PQ's monetary proposals in the 1980 referendum campaign also exposed the party to severe criticism from federalists. Bourassa spoke frequently during the campaign on his common theme that monetary union would ultimately result in a form of continued political union: "a common money means you must have a common fiscal policy, and that in turn means you must have a common collective Parliament to direct it. The concepts form a triangle whose points cannot be separated."[14] Other observers also ridiculed the PQ for not proposing an independent currency, making arguments very similar to those advanced by sovereigntist critics. Writing in the *Montreal Gazette*, Graham Fraser's comments were typical of many: "the idea of political sovereignty without the currency is a virtual contradiction in terms ... When the PQ gives up the idea of the currency for a sovereign Québec, it is seriously compromising the nature of the sovereignty it is seeking."[15]

Although their defeat in the 1980 referendum set back sovereigntists politically, the collapse of several efforts to renew Canadian federalism revived their cause by the early 1990s and a second referendum was held in 1995. In the lead-up to this referendum, sovereigntist leaders once again stuck to the position that a sovereign Quebec would use the Canadian dollar. Some also added a surprising twist to this longstanding proposal. They argued that Quebec should be prepared to unilaterally adopt the Canadian dollar in the event that Canada refused to negotiate the terms of a monetary union. This idea was first mentioned by the 1991 Bélanger-Campeau commission, which had been set up with representatives of all parties in Quebec and various interest groups to analyse Quebec's future.[16] The sovereigntists who in fact then picked up the idea with greatest enthusiasm were figures such as Jacques Parizeau – now head of the PQ and Quebec premier – who had been more supportive of the idea of creating an independent currency in the 1970s. They seemed to delight in making the argument that Quebec could continue to use the dollar whether Canada liked it or not.[17] Bourassa's case that a monetary union would require a political union because of the need for fiscal coordination was also now questioned more strongly. By way of example, Parizeau pointed to the Ontario NDP government at the time as having a distinctive fiscal policy within the Canadian monetary union.[18]

In some ways, the enthusiasm with which this idea was embraced by some sovereigntists was puzzling. Unilateral adoption of the Canadian dollar would, after all, prevent Quebec from having any say over the management of the currency: Quebec's monetary conditions would be set by the Bank of Canada. It would also prevent Quebec from demanding a share of the seigniorage earned from currency circulating in Quebec.[19] For these reasons, many sovereigntists refused to endorse the idea. This was true of both the Bloc Québécois (which had been created in 1990 by Lucien Bouchard as a sovereigntist party in federal politics) and the Action Démocratique du Québec (a more moderate nationalist party in Quebec politics). They each supported the idea that Quebec would form a partnership with Canada in which decisions over monetary policy would be shared in an arrangement very similar to that proposed in the 1980 referendum.[20] These ideas also found support among many PQ members.[21]

The general idea of sharing Canada's currency – whether unilaterally or through a negotiated monetary union – met much less opposition within sovereigntist circles than it had in the 1970s. The new consensus was reflected in the fact that the "o'" of the "Oui" signs in the referendum contained a picture of Canada's one-dollar coin (showing the face of the loon rather than the Queen). But the idea continued to be ridiculed by federalists. They were particularly scathing about the proposal to adopt Canada's currency unilaterally. Daniel Johnson, the Quebec Liberal leader, asked: "how can you tell Quebecers that a separate Quebec will give another country, a foreign country, Canada, the right to determine those elements of fiscal and monetary and economic policy?"[22] Similarly, Canada's finance minister at the time, Paul Martin, asked: "How can it be that the Quebec desiring independence not only wishes to use the currency of another country but also is prepared to turn all of the control and influence a country must have over its monetary policy over to that other country? This is the touchy situation in which Quebec will find itself, this is the fundamental tool it will have foregone ... When Canada is in a period of full growth, if there is a downturn in Quebec, monetary policy will be set in Canada to the detriment of Quebecers. Tell me, what point is there in becoming independent if the tools of independence are handed over to another? It is totally pointless."[23]

Although Quebec sovereigntists lost the 1995 referendum, it was a very narrow loss and the cause of sovereignty remained politically alive within the province. The monetary proposals of Quebec sovereigntists, however, shifted in an interesting direction. While still rejecting the idea of a Quebec currency, they began in 1998–99 to endorse the idea of North American monetary union. This new interest in North American – or even pan-American – monetary union partly reflected the emergence of a broader interest in this idea across Canada and the rest of the Americas in this period. But it also drew strength from the fact that many sovereigntists had endorsed the idea of adopting the Canadian dollar unilaterally in the lead-up to the 1995 referendum. If Canada were to adopt the US dollar, Quebec sovereigntists are very aware that they – like all Canadians – would have little say, if any at all, in monetary decision-making. In the 1970s, this situation would have caused more concern. But in the 1990s, many sovereigntists had already accepted this idea when they embraced the idea of adopting the Canadian dollar unilaterally. It was thus not a big step to begin to advocate the adoption of the US dollar.

This did not stop politicians in the rest of Canada from continuing to criticize their position. NDP MP Nelson Riis, for example, questioned why sovereigntists would support dollarization when the adoption of the US dollar would turn Quebec "into a banana republic."[24] Also prominent were pointed questions about the alliance with neoliberal economists that social democratic sovereigntists found themselves making in the NAMU debate.[25]

THE QUEST FOR POLITICAL SUPPORT
IN THE DRIVE TO INDEPENDENCE

Quebec sovereigntists, thus, present us with a puzzle. Throughout the nineteenth and twentieth centuries, most nationalist movements have expressed a desire to create a national currency when their state achieved political independence.[26] For over thirty years, however, Quebec sovereigntist leaders have emphasized that they do not want one. They have stuck to this position even in face of strong criticism from their supporters and opponents, both of whom have argued that this position is not compatible with nationalist values. In the current context of the NAMU debate, their position has also landed them in a strange alliance with prominent neoliberal economists in the rest of Canada whose views on many economic questions they would not normally share. What explains this pattern of behaviour?

The first answer is that Quebec sovereigntists have believed it would help them win more support for political independence. They have long recognized that much of the Quebec population may be fearful of the monetary instability that might result from the creation of an independent currency after political independence. Their opponents have been quite successful in exploiting these fears with predictions of large scale capital flight and a rapid depreciation of a newly created currency. As early as the 1970 provincial election campaign, the provincial Liberals produced a sample Quebec dollar bill and predicted the collapse of its value in an independent Quebec.[27] During the 1973 provincial election, Bourassa was also very effective in playing on popular fears that an independent Quebec's currency would depreciate in value vis-à-vis the Canadian dollar.[28] The political saliency of these predictions has also been reinforced by the capital flight generated by the election of the PQ in 1976, by Parizeau's speculations about the creation of a Quebec currency in 1978, and during the lead-up to the 1980 and 1995 referendums.[29]

Sovereigntists have seen their endorsement of monetary union as a way to allay these fears. In 1979, Lévesque put it this way to an interviewer when explaining the need for a common currency: "as you know this subject [of a national currency] belongs to an area about which, as a whole, public opinion very easily becomes nervous."[30] Similarly, in 1991, Parizeau acknowledged that "the creation of a Quebec currency invariably sparks widespread panic among people. It has never stopped me from sleeping but you have to live in the world you're in."[31] In 1994, the PQ also highlighted this point in explaining the need to keep using the Canadian dollar after independence: "maintaining a common currency would represent a significant guarantee of stability."[32] Indeed, it was revealed after the 1995 referendum that the PQ was prepared to devote large financial resources to defend the stability of the Canadian dollar in the event of a "yes" vote in order to calm the population's fears about independence. In an interview taped just before the referendum and to be shown after a victory, Parizeau stated: "We are the co-defenders of the Canadian dollar. I find the Canadian dollar admirable ... I will support the Canadian dollar, with the support of the Bank of Canada, with the Caisse de dépôt, with the federal finance ministry, with the Quebec finance ministry. Everyone supports this glorious Canadian dollar. We will never let it fall."[33]

This sovereigntist motivation also helps explain why federalists have been so critical of the idea that Quebec would continue to use the Canadian dollar. If they could convince the Quebec population that sovereigntists would in fact introduce a national currency, they would win political support, particularly among undecided voters. As we have seen, one way to do this was by questioning the sincerity of the sovereigntist commitment to the idea of a monetary union by arguing that it was not compatible with "normal" nationalist objectives. Another line of argument, especially prominent in the 1995 referendum debate, was that, even if sovereigntists were sincere in their commitment to a common currency, events would quickly force them to change their minds and introduce a national currency. This argument drew on the predictions of people such as Robson, who highlighted how capital flight might generate financial instability in Quebec which the government could most effectively handle by creating a national currency.[34]

If the promise to use the Canadian dollar was designed to calm Quebec fears of monetary instability, the more recent idea of endorsing a North American monetary union was potentially even more effective for this purpose.[35] An independent Quebec that adopted the US dollar would be better insulated from potential currency instability, because of the US dollar's wide use. This is not to suggest that the monetary change would be simple. Complicated issues would present themselves, such as Quebec's sudden need to access US-dollar payments systems and lender-of-last-resort facilities, as well as its need for adequate US dollars to facilitate the currency changeover. For this reason, the ideal scenario for sovereigntists would be one in which Canada adopted the US dollar before a Quebec referendum debate, thereby allowing these issues to be resolved in advance of Quebec independence.[36] More generally, however, under either scenario an independent Quebec would also be less vulnerable to Canadian pressure if it no longer relied on use of the Canadian dollar.[37] Indeed, if NAMU were not yet in place, Parizeau has noted that the threat to adopt the US dollar might provide Quebec with considerable bargaining power in negotiations with Canada.[38]

The endorsement of monetary union has been designed by sovereigntists to reassure not just Quebec citizens but also business interests outside the province. If political independence could be achieved in an environment of monetary stability, the confidence of foreign business interests in the new state would be enhanced and disruption to international economic relationships could be minimized. In justifying the need for a Canadian monetary union as far back as 1968, Lévesque highlighted the importance of ensuring continuity in Ontario-Quebec relations: "there is no good reason for precipitately severing the extremely intricate relationship between the two great financial markets of Montreal and Toronto ... unless we should be forced to do so, why destroy this financial mechanism by a monetary break-away, when the normal evolution of a common market inevitably would lead us toward setting up again sooner or later?"[39] Similarly, in 1980 PQ minister Claude Morin argued: "Think of the hundreds of millions of dollars that have been invested in Quebec in the past and now from people based elsewhere in Canada. They are very happy that it should be the same money. They told me so in Toronto. It would be very awkward for them to have to deal with another currency side by side; it would be awkward for us too."[40]

QUESTIONING THE ECONOMIC CASE
FOR A NATIONAL CURRENCY

Quebec sovereigntists have justified their rejection of a national currency not only on these short-term, strategic political grounds. They have advanced some broader arguments about why a national currency may inhibit, rather than contribute to, their goals over the longer term. Some of the arguments have been similar to those of neoliberal supporters of NAMU, although sovereigntists have given them a nationalist tenor. For example, some sovereigntists – including Bernard Landry – have embraced the idea that NAMU would force businesses to improve productivity, arguing that this would help boost the competitiveness of Quebec industry. This argument has provided an opportunity to criticize the gradual depreciation of the Canadian dollar vis-à-vis the US dollar since the late 1970s. In the words of BQ MP Richard Marceau: "it could be argued that if the crutch supplied by a Canadian currency that has been quietly devaluing for the last thirty years were eliminated, Quebec businesses would have a much greater incentive to invest in improving productivity."[41]

They have also argued that, from a Quebec sovereigntist standpoint, the growth of powerful global financial markets has diminished the benefits, and increased the costs, of having a national currency. The quest for an independent national monetary policy is said to be increasingly futile for small countries which find themselves ever more vulnerable to speculative financial attacks. They have also highlighted how the volatile exchange rate movements are often a *source* of external shocks to the domestic economy, rather than a means of adjusting to such shocks. In these new conditions, sovereigntists argue that a national currency is increasingly a liability rather than an asset. Joining a monetary union looks increasingly attractive since it can insulate smaller countries from the effects of speculative currency attacks and exchange rate volatility.

Although these arguments are contested by many economists, they certainly find enough support to give them value in the political arena. Lévesque in fact used these arguments as far back as the late 1960s in justifying his call for a monetary union with Canada: "Let us again recall – and it is not wrong to insist, given the strength of the illusions held by some on the subject – what a narrow margin for maneuver is retained in monetary matters by nations subject to the interdependence that is the rule in advanced economic systems."[42] In a key paper prepared for the

PQ in advance of the 1980 referendum, Bernard Fortin made a similar case, arguing paradoxically that a monetary union with Canada would provide the best way for Quebec to preserve a degree of monetary sovereignty in a world of speculative capital movements.[43]

These arguments have become more persuasive in the last decade as financial globalization has accelerated. In advance of the 1995 referendum, Parizeau – in contradiction to his 1991 statement above – sometimes justified the fact that he no longer favoured an independent Quebec currency on the grounds that this currency would be too vulnerable to speculative traders whose power had grown so much since the 1970s.[44] The more recent decision to back NAMU has also been frequently justified in this way. In 1999, Marceau argued that NAMU would insulate Quebec from the kind of speculative financial flows that were evident a year earlier in the Asian financial crisis. In his words, the US dollar is "a strong currency right close to home that provides a shelter when the world economy nose-dives."[45] Similarly, another Bloc member, Yvan Loubier, argued that a common currency is needed to counteract "unscrupulous speculators, who destroy national currencies, thus threatening the countries' economic future and job creation efforts."[46] The last quotation also highlights how some sovereigntists have been able to associate NAMU with social democratic values (i.e., a commitment to full employment), just as many European social democrats have done.

They have done this in another interesting way as well. As we have seen, some neoliberals in the rest of Canada see NAMU as a way to prevent the Canadian government from pursuing activist Keynesian-style monetary policy in the future. But sovereigntists are more worried about preventing a repeat of the Bank of Canada's aggressive zero inflation strategy of the late 1980s. As in many other parts of the country, this policy was very unpopular in Quebec, especially since it was seen as being designed primarily to counter inflationary pressures in southern Ontario.[47] Sovereigntists have argued that NAMU might result in a monetary environment more conducive to their social democratic goals of employment growth because American monetary authorities have taken a less rigid neoliberal monetary stance in recent years. In Marceau's words, "if the past is any indication of the future the American pro-employment monetary policy might be more advantageous for our economy than an anti-inflationary Canadian monetary policy designed to reflect the prerogatives of Ontario."[48] As we have seen, this prediction that NAMU might represent a "soft-currency" option is in fact one shared by Crow and other neoliberals who *oppose* NAMU.

Another economic argument in favour of NAMU relates to the changing pattern of Quebec's external trade. Since the introduction of the FTA in 1989, Quebec's economic links with the United States have grown dramatically and Quebec now trades more with the United States than it does with other provinces. Quebec sovereigntists have highlighted how this change strengthens the case for creating a monetary union with the US since currency-related transactions would be eliminated for US-Quebec trade.[49] The fact that NAMU should foster even more trade with the US is also viewed positively; sovereigntists have long been supporters of closer economic integration with the US, seeing it as a way to reduce Quebec's economic dependence on the rest of Canada. This was indeed the primary reason for their support of the FTA during the 1980s.[50]

At the same time that Quebec's economic ties with the US have intensified, Beine and Coulombe note that its business cycles – as well as those of Ontario – are becoming increasingly similar to those of the US. In this circumstance, Canada's floating exchange rate is of less value to these provinces, and may even be detrimental if it produces currency movements that respond primarily to the needs of the commodity-exporting provinces in the rest of the country.[51] Courchene and Laberge, for example, suggest that when the value of the Canadian dollar responds to commodity price shocks these changes tend to be disruptively pro-cyclical in the Quebec context; that is to say, they *reinforce* existing expansionary or contractionary tendencies in the economy.[52] These developments have provided a further economic rationale for Quebec sovereigntists to favour NAMU.

THE SYMBOLISM OF A NATIONAL CURRENCY

If these arguments explain the economic drawbacks of a national currency from a Quebec sovereigntist standpoint, we are still left with the fact that a national currency has long been seen as a potent symbol of sovereignty. Why have Quebec sovereigntists not seen it in this way? In the late 1960s, Lévesque argued that the issue was not significant for the Quebec population because it did not have a historical tradition of associating currency with national identities. Whereas European countries associated their currencies with "a whole slice of national culture," he argued that Quebec was different: "We, who at the moment have neither agencies nor specialists nor any cultural patrimony depending on an indigenous 'piastre,' have nothing to gain by insisting on an attribute of independence which evolution is in the process of turning into a liability."[53] According to Fraser, Lévesque also dismissed this issue as

insignificant in his discussions with Bourassa: "Monetary system, economic system, all this is plumbing. One doesn't worry about plumbing
when one fights for the destiny of the people."[54] He made a similar argument in 1979 in discussing the prospect for monetary union between
Canada and Quebec: "Looking at the European experiment, it would
seem to be a difficult thing to realize. It is not simple. But unlike the old
countries, we do not have that tradition of monetary sovereignty which
is almost related to the national image, which makes the franc, the
franc, and the lire, the lire."[55] In fact, he went further to suggest that
the desire for a national currency on symbolic grounds would represent
a kind of immature chauvinism.[56]

Lévesque's argument that Quebec nationalists have historically attached little symbolic value to the creation of a national currency was
overstated. We have seen how some sovereigntist supporters did want
the creation of a national currency for this reason in the 1970s. Historians have also noted other past moments when Quebec nationalists associated national identities with currency issues. In 1842, just after the
Act of Union had joined Quebec and Ontario (then Lower and Upper
Canada) into the new province of Canada, the new Province ended the
legal tender of pre-1792 French coins which had been commonly used
in Quebec. According to Shortt, many French Canadians reacted strongly
to this move, seeing it as "another blow dealt at their nationality." The
coins, he argues, had often been viewed "as part of that cherished nationality which marked his [French Canadian] independence of British institutions." He notes that many French Canadians were also sceptical of bank
notes at the time because they were issued by English banks and that tokens issued by the English-dominated Bank of Montreal in the late 1830s
had often been refused on "patriotic grounds."[57]

A century later, nationalist concerns were also raised in the debate
about whether the new Bank of Canada's notes should be bilingual or
not. When the bank was created in 1934, provision had been made that
its notes would be in either French or English. Quebec politicians had
pushed Prime Minister Bennett's government to endorse bilingual notes
instead, seeing this as a symbol of the equality of French and English. The
issue aroused considerable passion and Bennett's refusal to do so contributed to the growing unpopularity of his government in Quebec at the
time.[58] When Mackenzie King took over as prime minister, bilingual notes
were finally introduced. While this pleased many in Quebec (as well as
Bank of Canada officials[59]), it angered some in the rest of the country
who felt, in the words of a group of critics from New Brunswick, that

"the issue of bilingual currency will weaken the supremacy of the English language, the strongest tie that binds Canada to the empire."[60]

Although Lévesque overstated his case about Quebec sovereigntist views on currency issues, his arguments were interesting in that they deliberately tried to downplay the symbolic role of money. This approach has continued in more recent sovereigntist discourse. In particular, as European countries have succeeded in creating a monetary union, sovereigntists have increasingly cited this experience to highlight how the link between national identities and national currencies is no longer a necessary one. For example, in 1991 when defending the idea of a currency union with Canada, Landry argued that the European situation showed how monetary issues were mere technicalities of nation-building that would increasingly be managed by international bodies in the future. In his view, "sovereignty refers more to the style of life – language, education, health and environment, these types of things."[61] More recently in the NAMU debate, Marceau argued that the creation of the euro "demonstrates how closely the sovereigntist plan proposed in 1995 [a currency union with Canada] reflects the modern world!"[62]

NAMU'S DEMOCRATIC DEFICIT AND
THE GOVERNANCE OF THE BANK OF CANADA

What about the question of popular sovereignty? Are Quebec sovereigntists not concerned that Quebec would have little say over monetary policy-making in a future NAMU? Parizeau has sometimes suggested that the worldwide trend towards the creation of independent central banks makes this issue less significant today than in the past. The more prominent argument that he and others have made, however, involves a critique of the existing governance structures of the Bank of Canada. They note that the Quebec government has never had a formal say in the operations of the Bank of Canada. Joining NAMU without much formal say in its governance, they argue, will thus not represent much of a change from the Quebec government's standpoint.[63] This latter argument was also used in the lead-up to the 1995 referendum to explain why Quebec's unilateral use of the Canadian dollar would not result in any further loss of sovereignty.[64] As Parizeau put it in 1992, "a lot of people argue we wouldn't have any control over the monetary policy of the currency we employ. And that's perfectly correct. But, as far as I'm concerned, Quebec doesn't have any control over the policies of the Bank of Canada right now. So what have we got to lose?"[65]

The argument highlights an important point about the Bank of Canada's governance structure. In contrast to the US Federal Reserve, the Bank of Canada gives no formal role to regional voices across the country. All of its twelve members comprising the Board of Directors are appointed by the federal government, with no role given to the provinces in this process. Although board members are supposed to be selected to represent a variety of occupations, there is not even a formal requirement for regional diversity. In practice, the federal government has embraced an informal regional arrangement; two board members are from Quebec, two others are from Ontario, and each of the others is from one of the remaining provinces (no members are from the territories).[66] But the significance of this informal regional representation is undermined by the fact that the board has historically played a minimal role in influencing the bank's policy-making. Its members hold part-time positions that are not well paid, and they receive only three-year terms.[67] Power has instead – until very recently (see below) – been highly concentrated in the position of the governor of the bank. Although the board does formally select the governor, the federal government's approval is required; in practice, the federal government has played the key role in this selection process.[68]

Given that Canada is a federal state, the lack of regional input in Bank of Canada policy-making is somewhat odd. Many other federal states, such as Germany, Switzerland, and the US (although not others such as Australia), have central banks that embrace federal decision-making processes.[69] The situation is particularly unusual in Canada because the enormous regional economic diversity of the country has often generated quite distinct monetary and exchange rate preferences, as we have seen. Not surprisingly, the lack of regional voices in the Bank of Canada's decision-making structures has long been a controversial issue in Canadian politics. When a 1933 Royal Commission recommended the establishment of the Bank of Canada, a Quebec member of the five-person commission – Beaudry Leman – dissented, noting that more careful attention should be given to the constitutional complexities of establishing such a bank in a country with a federal political system. Mindful no doubt of the fact that the Quebec government opposed the bank's creation,[70] he added: "Regardless of the constitutional aspects of the question, if a central bank is to be a co-ordinating agency in this country, it would seem indispensable to ascertain beforehand that such an institution would be assured of the goodwill and co-operation of each and every one of the Provinces of Canada. Before a central bank can hope to speak with one voice on behalf of Canada, it would seem desirable that it should have authority to express the views not only of the Dominion Government but also those of all the Provinces."[71]

Despite Leman's views, the commission did not recommend a federal decision-making structure for the bank. The approach was not defended in the commission's report, and some have explained this on the grounds that the Bank of England officials who dominated the commission simply used their own bank as a model for that of Canada.[72] It is certainly true that the British chair of the commission, Lord Macmillan, showed a preference in the hearings for a centralized model.[73] It also no doubt reflected the view of the government and the commission that the bank should be a privately-owned institution that was insulated from sectional political pressures.[74] Also important may have been the fact that regional voices from the Maritimes and the Western provinces did not appear to lobby strongly for a federal decision-making structure. Although attacks against the financial dominance of the country by central Canadian interests were certainly voiced by many in these regions during the 1930s, I have been unable to find calls for a federal structure for the Bank of Canada in the commission's extensive hearings. By contrast, the fear of New York financial domination in other regions of the US played a central role in strengthening the case for a federally-structured central bank in that country. Particularly important in demanding the decentralized US Federal Reserve system were banks in US regions such as the Midwest which hoped this system could preserve their existing central role in various regional financial systems.[75] In Canada, by contrast, the banking system had long been much more centralized on a national basis via branch banking. As a result, there was no parallel to the regional bank lobby that existed in the US at the time of the Fed's creation.

After Leman's critique, the issue of the lack of regional representation in the Bank of Canada arose again in the 1960s. During the 1962 hearings held by the next Royal Commission into banking issues, the issue was raised by the Ontario government. It demanded that provincial governments be allowed to nominate directors to the Bank of Canada's board who would then formally represent them.[76] By the late 1960s, the Quebec sovereigntist movement was gaining in strength and it also demanded a new decision-making model for the Bank of Canada. As we have seen, if a monetary union was to be preserved with the rest of Canada after Quebec separation, the leaders of the sovereigntist movement asserted that Quebec must receive substantial representation within the Bank of Canada, a view they maintained throughout the 1970s and into the 1980 referendum campaign.

The Bank of Canada's decision-making model became controversial once again during the early 1990s when Crow's rigid anti-inflation policy was subject to enormous and potent public criticism. The power of regionally-based criticism of the bank's alleged focus on Ontario's inflation was reinforced by the fact that the country was experiencing a period of constitutional crisis when Westerners and many in Quebec were demanding a radical restructuring of the Canadian federation. In this context, many proposals were put forward to force the bank to listen more to regional perspectives.[77] Even the Quebec Liberal Party's 1991 Allaire report, commissioned by Bourassa after the collapse of the Meech Lake accord, argued for guaranteed regional representation in the Bank of Canada if the Canadian federation was to be renewed.[78]

In its September 1991 constitutional proposals, the federal government included a number of reforms designed to respond to this controversy. They included measures to require (1) the Bank of Canada governor to meet with federal and provincial finance ministers on a regular basis; (2) the federal government to consult with provincial governments when appointing Bank of Canada board directors; (3) appointment of the Bank of Canada governor to be ratified by the Senate (which itself was to be reformed by giving provinces more say in the appointments of senators); and (4) the creation of regional consultation panels, chaired by bank directors, whose membership would be chosen in consultation with provincial and territorial governments.[79] These proposals were soon dropped from the overloaded agenda for constitutional reform. A House of Commons subcommittee also took up the task of analysing as many as eight different models of governance for the bank, but it too ultimately endorsed the status quo in its 1992 report.

The Bank of Canada itself finally took up the task of addressing some of the criticism. In 1994, it endorsed the idea of decentralizing authority away from the governor by establishing a new six-member Governing Council which included the governor, the senior deputy governor, and four deputy governors selected by the board (but not with any formal regional representative criteria in mind). Three years later, the bank created five regional offices. The governor explained the rationale: "because Canada is such a large country with so many diverse economic regions, it is important that the Bank maintain contacts with the public that are country-wide and that involve two-way communication. We need to hear first-hand what is happening to the economy in every corner of Canada.

That is why, in 1997, we set up five regional offices, including one here in Halifax for the Atlantic region. Our representatives are in frequent contact with various local associations, businesses, community groups, government officials, colleges, and universities to give and receive information and to exchange views on the economy and monetary policy."[80]

The debate about NAMU, then, has come shortly after a historical moment when criticism of the bank's insensitivity to regional perspectives reached a peak. In this context, fears about an "accountability deficit" in NAMU are received less sympathetically in some parts of Canada since they are seen simply as replicating a longstanding deficit of this kind already present within the Bank of Canada. Although the bank has been trying to respond by decentralizing its decision-making, the issue remains one that NAMU supporters can draw upon to mobilize support. In Quebec, sovereigntists have done so with some success, using it to deflect some of the criticism that NAMU would leave Quebec with little voice over monetary policy-making. In internal memos that came to light in 2001, even Bank of Canada officials identified the need to improve the bank's image in Quebec, which had suffered during the early 1990s, if they were to successfully counter sovereigntist arguments in favour of NAMU.[81] While the distinct form of federalism of the US central bank may not help the cause of NAMU supporters, the absence of federalism in the Bank of Canada is doing so, at least in the Quebec context.

QUEBEC AND THE OTHER REGIONS

Has this issue influenced the debate on NAMU in other regions of the country? Since many in the Western provinces shared Quebec's concerns during the Crow period, one might have expected this issue to sway opinions towards NAMU in that region. To be sure, we saw in chapter 5 how some economists from the West did raise it in the early 1990s in support of their early case for NAMU. But the issue does not seem to have influenced broader public views in the West more recently. As noted at the start of the chapter, opinion polls do not show support for NAMU to be any higher in Western provinces than in Ontario.

A key reason may be that Westerners are concerned about one of the other issues raised by Quebec sovereigntists: the distinctive regional macroeconomic effects of exchange rate movements. Because Canada's floating exchange rate can help ease adjustments to external shocks in the commodity sector, the regions of the country most dependent on resource exports may have the most to lose from NAMU. We have certainly seen this regional division on the question of exchange rate adjustments emerge at other moments in Canadian history, most notably in the early 1930s when Western provinces were the most critical of the gold standard. There is some evidence that it is again influencing opinion in NAMU debate today. Analysts in the western part of the country have indeed highlighted the potential adjustment costs that their region would face if NAMU existed.[82] The 2001 *National Post*–Compass poll of business leaders also noted that support for NAMU was lowest in Atlantic Canada, a region where commodity exports are very significant.[83] In Quebec, some business leaders in the resource sector have also expressed their opposition to NAMU for this reason.[84]

The NAMU debate thus reveals a different kind of regional politics than the FTA debate of the 1980s. No longer do Quebec sovereigntists find the commodity-exporting provinces to be strong political allies in their quest to deepen North American integration in this area. While these provinces favoured closer trade and investment ties with the US, they have important economic reasons to be nervous about closer monetary links.

But could Ontario be a potential ally? Beine and Coulombe's analysis mentioned above suggests that Ontario may have similar macroeconomic interests as Quebec since its business cycle is also increasingly similar to that of the US. Indeed, Courchene and Harris predict that commodity-induced exchange rate movements should be provoking growing opposition to the floating exchange rate in both of these two provinces as their economic ties to the US become increasingly dense. But Ontario may have a little more to lose economically from NAMU than this analysis implies. At the moment, Canadian regions that experience a region-specific economic shock find its effects partly buffered by automatic, intra-Canada, public fiscal transfers working through the national tax system, the federal unemployment insurance program, and equalization payments. If NAMU produced greater adjustment difficulties in commodity-exporting regions, these pan-Canadian fiscal mechanisms might be called upon more extensively. In this case, Ontario (and Quebec) would, in effect, be assuming more of the fiscal burden of adjusting to commodity price shocks experienced in these other provinces.

CONCLUSION

The Quebec sovereigntist movement has played a major role in putting the question of NAMU on the Canadian political agenda. At first sight, sovereigntist support for NAMU appears odd. Historically, nationalists in most parts of the world have been strongly attached to the idea that their country needs its own national currency for both economic and symbolic reasons. Quebec sovereigntist leaders have rejected this position not just in the NAMU debate but through their long support for the idea that an independent Quebec would continue to use the Canadian dollar. They have stuck to this position in the face of severe criticism from their opponents and even some of their supporters in the 1970s. Indeed, at times, Quebec sovereigntists have seemed to relish in their rejection of traditional nationalist values. For example, when prominent Canadian politicians have rejected the idea of NAMU, Bernard Landry has criticized them for acting out of "narrow-minded nationalism."[85]

This chapter has highlighted that the monetary proposals of Quebec sovereigntists are less strange than they first appear. They are in fact driven by nationalist goals. One such goal is that of attracting wider support for the sovereigntist cause by calming domestic fears about the prospects for monetary instability after political independence. As global financial markets have become increasingly powerful, Quebec sovereigntists have also associated the creation of a national currency with fewer economic benefits and more economic costs from a nationalist standpoint. More recently, their decision to back NAMU has also partly reflected the changing position of Quebec's economy in North America, as well as arguments about the negative effects of Canada's monetary policy and its depreciating dollar on the Quebec economy. In addition, the creation of the common currency in Europe has reinforced their own longstanding case that the symbolic value of national currencies has been overstated. And finally, the lack of formal regional representation in the Bank of Canada has only reinforced the sovereigntist case for NAMU, even if it involved unilateral dollarization.

Some of these nationalist arguments against the creation of national currencies are not entirely unique. Secessionist groups in some European countries have also seen the creation of the euro as desirable for many of the economic reasons that Quebec sovereigntists have put forward. Prominent economists such as Alesina and Barro have also noted that the cost of separation for regions within European countries have diminished with the creation of the euro. They even write that "several commentators have noted that regional tensions within countries have been fueled by the monetary unification in Europe."[86] The Quebec sovereigntist position is therefore far from unusual in the contemporary world. Indeed, in developing these arguments against national currencies more than thirty years ago, the Quebec sovereigntist movement can be seen as a kind of pioneer of this distinct form of "economic nationalism."

Although Quebec sovereigntists clearly helped put NAMU on the Canadian political agenda, how does their support actually affect the prospects for NAMU? In one respect, it may make NAMU less likely to happen since it undermines support for NAMU among those who are opposed to Quebec sovereignty. Some analysts have suggested, for example, that the federal government's strong opposition to NAMU is driven partly by this motivation. As Gibson puts it, "Ottawa is so fixed upon making the world difficult for Quebec sovereigntists that they see a common currency as solving a problem they do not want solved."[87] Some of the economists who are supportive of NAMU on neoliberal grounds have also sought to distance themselves from Quebec sovereigntists on the issue.

At the same time, Quebec sovereigntist support for NAMU obviously provides an important base of political support for the idea within the Canadian polity. In the realm of Canadian trade policy, the sovereigntist movement's favourable view of North American economic integration helped generate important political support for the FTA in the 1980s. Will it have a similar impact on the NAMU debate?

To date, sovereigntists have faced the difficulty of finding political allies in the rest of the country on this issue. During the FTA debate, they made common cause with a broad coalition of business leaders, neoliberal thinkers, and the commodity-exporting provinces. In the NAMU debate, this coalition is weakened by the division within neoliberal and business circles and the fact that commodity-exporting provinces have reasons to support the floating exchange rate regime. Unless the political conditions in the rest of the country change, Quebec sovereigntists are unlikely to influence federal government policy on this issue.

There is another scenario, however, in which they could have significant influence. If political conditions *within* Quebec changed, and the province voted to leave the Canadian federation, an independent Quebec might quickly adopt the US dollar. At that point, pressure for the rest of the country to follow would be considerable. Ontario might not want to be stuck with a currency whose value was now more influenced by the other commodity-exporting provinces. Ontario's close economic ties to Quebec might also provide an incentive for its politicians to push Canada to follow Quebec's lead. At the same time, the other provinces might worry about Ontario's more dominant economic presence in the smaller monetary union.[88] More generally, the atmosphere of political uncertainty would create incentives to embrace a monetary regime that provided stability and credibility.

This scenario may in fact be the most plausible one under which NAMU could come into effect in the short to medium-term future. This conclusion is an ironic one in light of the arguments of NAMU supporters. If NAMU is implemented in the next five to ten years, it will likely not be the inevitable result of the pressures NAMU supporters point to: the deepening North American integration or a worldwide trend towards the creation of currency blocs. Instead, it will more likely be an outcome of a breakdown of the Canadian federation.

Canada and the Politics of Exchange Rate Regimes

Let us return to the question set out at the start of this book. Is the emergence of the NAMU debate a sign that Canada's preference for a floating exchange rate is finally coming to an end? It should be clear from the analysis in the second half of the book that the free trade era and the creation of the euro hardly make NAMU inevitable. It is true that some of the political developments putting NAMU on the Canadian political agenda – such as support from neoliberals and some secessionist groups – are similar to those that promoted the FTA and the euro. But NAMU advocates have been unable to find significant broader support for their ideas. In contrast to the FTA debate, neoliberal opinion remains sharply divided on the issue, and the business community and commodity-exporting provinces have been relatively uninterested. The NAMU proposal has also generated broader Canadian-nationalist opposition than existed at the time of the FTA negotiations, opposition only strengthened by the US discussions on dollarization. Unlike their European counterparts, Canadian supporters of regional monetary union have also not been able to count on the support of social democratic and labour groups.

This is not to say that NAMU could never happen. We have seen in the past how expert opinion has played a key role in this debate, and this could of course change under a new set of circumstances. Many within the business community might also be more enthusiastic in a changed political context. In addition, Canadian nationalist opposition may be more fragile that it appears, and it could lessen dramatically in the event of a future currency crisis or a change of US views, perhaps prompted by the competitive threat of the euro. And finally, the likelihood of NAMU would increase if Quebec separated from the rest of Canada, for the reasons mentioned at the end of the previous chapter.

Although NAMU is thus a possibility in the coming years, it remains an unlikely one, particularly in the absence of Quebec's separation. This conclusion is significant not just for those interested in Canadian affairs. It has broader theoretical relevance for the study of the political economy of exchange rate regime choices. As noted in the introduction, it is commonly assumed that countries with very open economies will favour a stable exchange rate.[1] With one of the most open economies in the industrial world, Canada has long been an exception to this rule with its preference for floating. If the analysis of this book is correct, this preference looks likely to continue for some time, even as Canada's integration with the US continues to deepen. What, then, is the broader theoretical significance of Canada's enduring preference for a floating exchange rate?

Within the last decade, political economists have begun to focus considerable attention on the politics of exchange rate policy-making.[2] Although scholars working in this field share the same substantive interest, they have developed quite different ways to analyse the topic. One difference is methodological; some of the literature employs a deductive and rationalist framework of analysis, while other analyses – such as this book – adopt a more historical and inductive approach. Another difference concerns the level of analysis chosen to explain exchange rate policy-making. Some analysts focus on the role of domestic interests; others concentrate on the preferences of state policy-makers; still others examine the influence of the international context. Each of these three levels of analysis is useful in explaining Canadian exchange rate regime choices. But they are useful in ways that are often quite different than the literature suggests. Examining these differences highlights the broader theoretical significance of the Canadian experience.

PRIVATE ECONOMIC INTERESTS
AND EXCHANGE RATE REGIMES

Let us begin by examining the insights of the literature that focuses on the importance of domestic interests. The most prominent analysis of this kind has been developed by Jeff Frieden.[3] Frieden's work is particularly important for our purposes because it represents the most sophisticated attempt to model analytically why countries with more open economies will favour stable exchange rates. He argues that private actors involved in cross-border transactions – international merchants, multinational corporations, international investors, and banks – will generally press for a fixed exchange rate regime because it will reduce uncertainty and transaction costs for their internationally-oriented activities. In a context of financial openness, they will also be less concerned that a fixed exchange rate undermines the ability of national monetary authorities to pursue an autonomous monetary policy. While this loss of autonomy is worrisome to businesses in the non-tradable sector that depend primarily on the domestic market, the interests of internationally-oriented businesses are spread across a number of markets.

Based on these predictions, Frieden concludes that "the higher the level of international trade and payments, the more economic actors with existing or potential global activities want exchange rate stability."[4] Although Frieden cites empirical evidence in Europe and Latin America to support his analysis, the Canadian case appears to be an anomaly. Throughout the period being studied, Canada's dependence on external trade has been unusually high and multinational corporations have played a larger role in the domestic economy than in most other Western countries. In addition, it has maintained an open capital account regime for the entire period being discussed here, with the brief exception of the 1939–51 period. And yet, historically and today, this highly open economic context has not generated significant political demands from domestic economic interests for a fixed exchange rate regime.

To be sure, this kind of lobby *was* present in Canada in the pre-1914 period. As we saw in chapter 2, it helps explain not just the commitment of the Canadian state to a fixed exchange rate before 1914 but even the creation of the Canadian dollar itself in the mid-nineteenth century. But the influence of this kind of private sector lobby for a fixed exchange rate became increasingly less apparent after 1914 and especially after the 1930s. At each of the key moments when Canada's exchange rate regime changed in the twentieth century, it is indeed striking that internationally-oriented businesses have not displayed a great deal of concern about transaction costs associated with the country's floating exchange rate. They did not even play much of a role in pressing for the 1939 and 1962 decisions to adopt a fixed exchange rate, nor in supporting the NAMU proposal in the current period.

Why are these businesses not more concerned about the uncertainty and transaction costs associated with a floating exchange rate? In a critique of Frieden's work, McNamara highlights how firms are unlikely to prioritize the goal of creating a fixed exchange rate in contexts where a floating exchange rate has not been very volatile. She also notes that multinational firms are often relatively unconcerned by currency volatility because they have developed ways of coping with currency risks. These points are used to explain her empirical finding that many internationally-oriented European firms have not shown a strong interest in lobbying for EMU.[5]

These points also are relevant to the Canadian situation. The fact that the Canadian currency has not fluctuated too dramatically during most of the periods of a floating exchange rate has dampened potential business opposition to this regime.[6] During the float of the 1930s and that of 1950–62, the Canadian dollar did not fluctuate enormously vis-à-vis the currencies of the country's major trading partners. The fluctuations became larger during the post-1970 float, but they were still less significant than those experienced by most other countries whose currencies floated in this period.[7] Canadian firms – particularly in the important commodity-exporting sector – have also long been skilled at using currency hedging techniques to minimize their exposure to future currency movements. Because they deal with longer-term contracts and more specialized production, manufacturers find it harder to hedge against currency volatility.[8] But their interest in a fixed rate has been blunted by the fact that an increasingly large proportion of Canada-US manufacturing trade has taken place within large multinational corporations where exchange rate movements can be offset by adjustments in transfer pricing within the company.

Frieden's model itself provides another possible explanation for the views of Canadian business. He notes that producers in exporting and import-competing sectors may prefer a floating exchange rate if they manufacture goods for which price competitiveness is key and/or exchange rate changes can be easily passed through to the consumer. These businesses – such as standardized manufacturers and those producing commodities – may want to keep open the option of using exchange rate depreciation for competitive purposes. These kinds of businesses have been quite important within the Canadian economy throughout the period being studied and they have certainly lobbied the Canadian government actively for a competitive exchange rate at various moments.

But the significance of this lobbying in explaining Canada's floating exchange rate should not be overstated. Canadian producers in the tradable sector have often highlighted that the dollar's depreciation can be a double-edged sword in its impact on their competitiveness. Reasons include their high import dependence, their status as foreign subsidiaries, their foreign currency indebtedness, and their position as price-makers in world markets. Even those in the tradable sector who might benefit from depreciation have not always been very enthusiastic about the float as they too have been forced to recognize that Canada's floating exchange rate can cut both ways. While it allowed a depreciation at some moments, a floating rate has also left them vulnerable to a currency *appreciation* at other times. Canadian businesses realized, in other words, that there is no necessary reason for preferences for a competitive exchange rate to translate into support for a floating exchange rate.[9]

More generally, the very openness of the Canadian economy ensured that many private interests beyond producers in the tradable sector had an interest in the level of the exchange rate. This price affected Canadian economic actors in many ways, ranging from its impact on domestic inflation levels to its effect on the relative value of their foreign investments. As Plumptre once noted, "the level of the foreign exchange rate exercises a pervasive influence throughout the economy. In the Canadian price system it is probably the most important price of all."[10] Given this diversity, it was inevitable that Canadian economic interests often had highly differentiated preferences vis-à-vis the level of the exchange rate. These differences were reinforced by the sectoral diversity and multiregional nature of the Canadian economy as well as by the fact that Canada had two major trading partners during the interwar and early postwar years whose currencies sometimes moved in different directions.

In this context, it was rare to hear a coherent private sector voice on the question of exchange rate policy. If the entire Canadian business community had been politically organized at the national level in a more coherent fashion, it might have been possible for a clearer view to be expressed. But the Canadian business sector has not traditionally been organized by inclusive and strong nationwide business associations.[11] Coherence in the business lobby has also been undermined by the fact that Canadian banks and manufacturing firms do not have the kind of close relationship that exists in countries such as Germany or Japan. Henning notes how this relationship in the latter countries has encouraged banks to share the competitiveness-oriented exchange rate preferences of manufacturing firms in the tradable sector. In countries where this relationship is less close, however, he notes that banks are more likely to view exchange rate issues in light of other objectives, including their impact on inflation. He cites Britain and the US as countries where this situation exists – Canada is another.[12]

For these various reasons, the Canadian private sector did not play a significant role in pushing for a floating exchange rate on the grounds that Frieden anticipates. At the time of key decisions to endorse a floating rate – such as the early 1930s, 1970, or during the NAMU debate – the private sector lobby for this outcome was not large. Indeed, there was really only one moment when the Canadian business sector expressed a strong and coherent preference for a particular exchange rate regime change. This came in 1950 when the business sector did support the move to a floating exchange rate regime. Its rationale at this moment, however, was quite different than the one Frieden suggests. The Canadian business community saw a floating exchange rate as a way to hasten abolition of the country's exchange and capital controls. This concern was far more important to businesses than concerns about either the competitive level of the exchange rate (the 1950 float generated an *appreciation*) or the transaction costs associated with a floating exchange rate. Business opposition to capital controls has in fact been consistent throughout the period covered in this study, and it thwarted government efforts in the interwar years and in 1970 to stabilize the exchange rate as well.

This is not the only rationale for business support of the floating rates. There are others, although they were less decisive in influencing Canadian policy-making. For example, Frieden assumes that internationally-oriented businesses will be less concerned with monetary policy autonomy because they are less dependent on the domestic market. But we have seen how Canadian banks supported the float at key moments, such as 1970 and during the NAMU debate, because they associated monetary autonomy with their preference for low inflation. During the NAMU debate, they also worried about its impact on their business in foreign exchange trading and financial intermediation.[13]

There is one final *indirect* way in which private sector preferences influenced Canada's preference for floating. Frieden is right that the openness of the Canadian economy encouraged many private actors to take an active interest in the level of the exchange rate. But as noted above, the very openness of the economy ensured that their preferences on this issue were often highly varied because of the diversity of their links to the international economy. In this context, the level of the exchange rate was often a highly controversial issue in Canadian politics. These controversies in turn frequently inflamed regional tensions because of the spatial concentration of specific sectors in different parts of the country. As far back as Confederation, Canadian policy-makers searched for ways to diffuse these exchange rate controversies. After the early 1930s, the floating exchange rate was often seen as useful for this purpose. By allowing the market to determine the currency's level, policy-makers distanced themselves from responsibility for the issue and insulated themselves from political struggles that would be unleashed by deliberate exchange rate adjustments.[14]

In short, the Canadian experience during the twentieth century does not provide a great deal of support for Frieden's model of the politics of exchange rate regimes. Frieden himself acknowledges that "there are somewhat heroic assumptions underlying these assertions" and "much nuance and complexity is still masked."[15] The Canadian case upholds this point and it reinforces McNamara's critique that private sector preferences are more context-specific. This is partly because specific environments will determine how important the costs of exchange rate volatility are for firms, or how a floating exchange rate will affect the competitiveness of the tradable sector. It is also because the choice of an exchange rate regime has implications not just for the kinds of transaction costs and competitive concerns that Frieden highlights, but also for many other factors, including macroeconomic outcomes, the value of foreign debts and assets, and the use of capital controls. The relative weight that private actors place on these various implications is obviously very hard to model since it will likely be, as Henning puts it, "highly situationally dependent."[16] This fact, when combined with the uncertainty over the costs and benefits of different exchange rate regimes, reinforces the argument that the domestic politics of exchange rate regime choice are best characterized by what McNamara calls a "highly unstable societal preference structure."[17]

The Canadian context also reveals that the significance of private sector preferences in the determination of exchange rate regimes should not be overstated. This result is in fact consistent with the conclusions of a number of other scholars who have argued that exchange rate regime policy-making is often quite autonomous from private sector interests. Some attribute this autonomy to the technical complexity of the issues involved. Others highlight the fact that the distributional effects of exchange rate regimes are often small or unclear from the standpoint of private interests. Even when these effects are substantial and clear, they are also focused at the macroeconomic level in ways that undermine effective collective action by private actors.[18] These various explanations – and the others just noted – are all relevant to the Canadian context.

The nature of Canadian political institutions has also been significant. The Westminster model of parliamentary government ensures that the majority governing party holds concentrated power between elections and that government ministers rely on a relatively unchanging civil service. In Coleman's words, the latter "is cast as an apolitical reservoir of policy expertise and advice" which enjoys "considerable discretion in formulating policy to be submitted for ministerial consideration."[19] As we have seen, Canadian exchange rate regime policy-making since the early 1930s has indeed been dominated by top expert officials in the Bank of Canada and Department of Finance. When formulating advice and policy, this group – what was called the "Ottawa Brains Trust" in the 1950s – has often been quite insulated from private sector lobbying.

THE PREFERENCES OF STATE POLICY-MAKERS

If Canadian policy-makers have often had considerable autonomy from private interests in choosing exchange rate regimes, it is important to analyse why they have generally favoured a floating exchange rate regime. How can we best explain their preferences? The broader literature on the politics of exchange rate regimes offers a number of potential answers to this question. One approach suggests that the preferences of policy-makers will be determined by the "partisan" leanings of politicians. This analysis assumes that left-of-centre political parties will favour growth and income distribution, while those on the right will be more concerned with price stability. Unfortunately, however, this approach does not generate consistent hypotheses about how these preferences translate into exchange rate regime preferences. While left-of-centre political parties might be expected to favour floating exchange rates to maximize policy autonomy, they may also see a fixed exchange rate as a way to establish credibility in the eyes of global financial markets.[20] In addition to this theoretical problem, empirical evidence from OECD countries after the early 1970s does not provide any clear link between partisan leaning and the choice of exchange rate regime.[21]

In the Canadian context, it is again true that exchange rate regime choices do not appear to have been influenced by a clear pattern of partisan preferences. To be sure, the choice of exchange rate regime has often been seen in partisan terms. But the link between specific parties and particular exchange rate regimes has not been consistent over time. For example, during the pre-1931 period, right-of-centre political parties supported a fixed exchange rate in the form of the gold standard, while more radical political parties often attacked it. During the early postwar years, however, the positions were reversed: the Conservative Party pushed for the float of 1950, while left-wing politicians opposed it. Positions had changed once again by 1962 when a Conservative government fixed the exchange rate, and the left-wing NDP opposed the move. When a middle-of-the-road Liberal government re-introduced the float in 1970, the NDP was once again keen and the Conservatives were initially skeptical. Since that time, however, all three parties have endorsed the floating exchange rate regime. They have stuck to this position in the NAMU debate, while supporters of NAMU have included both right-of-centre economists and left-of-centre Quebec social democrats.

A second explanation for the preferences of state officials is a "rationalist" approach which assumes that policy-makers are driven primarily by the goal of holding office. This literature examines how the preferences of these "survival-maximizing politicians" are influenced by different institutional and political environments.[22] For example, Bernhard and Leblang suggest that policy-makers may prefer a fixed exchange rate regime in contexts where there is intense intra-party or intra-coalitional conflict over monetary policy. In their view, such a regime may help manage this conflict.[23] We have seen, however, how the argument can work both ways. In the Canadian context, a floating exchange rate has often been seen as a way to defuse intense domestic political conflict over the exchange rate question.

Others working in this tradition have argued that majoritarian (single-member plurality) electoral systems encourage policy-makers to favour a floating exchange rate regime. Because the costs of losing office are very high in this kind of winner-take-all system, they argue that ruling politicians will place a high value on the role of discretionary monetary policy in generating support before elections.[24] This preference may be reinforced by the fact that these politicians are held more directly accountable for economic performance. In federal political systems, Hallerberg argues, floating exchange rates are also more desirable because fiscal policy is less useful as a form of national macroeconomic management, given that the fiscal policies of subnational governments cannot easily be controlled by the federal government. Hallerberg in fact cites Canada as an example of a "one party player, federal" political system in which these reasons generate a desire for a floating exchange rate.[25]

Hallerberg's causation is a deductive one rather than one drawn from research about the sources of Canadian exchange rate policy-making. The findings of this book, however, provide very little support for his causal link. It is true that Canadian policy-makers have displayed a very strong commitment to monetary policy autonomy and that this commitment, in turn, has played a key role in explaining their support for a floating exchange rate (particularly given the opposition of both the private sector and Canadian policy-makers themselves towards capital controls for all but the 1939–51 period). But Canadian policy-makers did not discuss this preference in the kinds of electoral terms predicted, and none of the decisions to introduce a floating exchange rate were taken in the immediate lead-up to an election. Indeed, the only change of exchange rate regime to take place during an election was the choice to *fix* the exchange rate during the 1962 federal election campaign. In the context of making exchange rate regime decisions, policy-makers also did not discuss how Canadian federalism was complicating their ability to use fiscal policy as a macroeconomic tool. Indeed, as we have seen, Courchene and Harris have suggested that federalism should make a fixed rate easier to manage in the context of a multi-regional economy. Federalism arose as an issue in exchange rate policy-making only in the context of discussions about implementing controls on capital inflows at various moments.

This study suggests that the more useful approach for explaining the preferences of Canadian policy-makers in contexts where they have had some autonomy from domestic (and external) interests is one that draws on a combination of structural and "ideational" influences.[26] Since the early 1930s, Canadian exchange rate regime policy-making has been strongly influenced by expert groups who have fairly consistently defended the need for a floating exchange on two grounds: (1) it helped facilitate adjustments to balance of payment disequilibria, and (2) it bolstered monetary policy autonomy in a context of financial openness. What explains the prominence of these two rationales?

In explaining the importance of the floating exchange rate as an adjustment tool, Canadian policy-makers have usually referred to two structural features of the Canadian economy. The first is Canada's vulnerability to frequent balance of payments fluctuations, especially because of its heavy reliance on commodity exports. The second is the relative inflexibility of domestic wages and prices, particularly given the absence of European-style corporatist wage-bargaining arrangements. Since Mundell's work in the early 1960s, the link between these two features of the Canadian economy and the case for the floating exchange rate as an adjustment tool has increasingly been framed in terms of the recommendations of optimum currency area (OCA) theory. Although Frieden argues that empirical evidence showing OCA criteria as an influence on policy-makers is "almost nonexistent," the Canadian case suggests otherwise.[27]

But this is not to suggest that this dimension of Canada's commitment to a floating exchange rate has simply been a product of the structure of its exports and its wage-bargaining institutions. Objective conditions can, after all, be interpreted in many different ways. Buchanan put forward similar arguments in nineteenth century and they were dismissed by elite groups who subscribed to the liberal economic orthodoxy of the gold standard era. These arguments achieved prominence only once they were given legitimacy by a class of professional economists who became influential in policy-making following the economic upheavals of the early 1930s. Even then, these arguments for a floating exchange rate continued to be contested at various moments, including in the recent NAMU debate. When the floating Canadian dollar has been subject to misalignments, some have highlighted how it is acting as a source – rather than a buffer – of external shocks to the domestic economy. Others have suggested that exchange rate movements were often too blunt an adjustment tool, given the regional diversity of the Canadian economy. Still others have questioned the desirability of accommodating – instead of disciplining – price and wage inflexibility with exchange rate movements. Despite these various critiques, Canadian policy-makers have remained largely loyal to the intellectual argument that a floating exchange rate is a useful mechanism for facilitating balance of payments adjustments.

One other factor has reinforced the influence of this argument. During the few moments when Canada has embraced a fixed exchange rate since the 1930s, Canadian policy-makers have often found themselves drawn into negotiations with the US on various issues relating to management of the bilateral balance of payments. This approach to addressing bilateral payments imbalances not only has been cumbersome but has touched on Canadian nationalist sensibilities, particularly given the asymmetries of power in the Canada-US relationship. In this context, Canadian policy-makers have come to see a floating exchange rate as a less politically-charged and more efficient way to resolve bilateral balance of payments problems. In the current era, this consideration has arisen again among those who worry that NAMU would force Canada to negotiate for deeper North American integration in order to compensate for the loss of the exchange rate adjustment tool.

The nature of Canada's relationship with the US also helps explain the second rationale for the floating exchange rate – the desire for monetary autonomy. The specific intellectual case for monetary autonomy has changed over time. In the 1930s, Canadian policy-makers remained wedded to the orthodox liberal notion that the prime purpose of monetary policy was the maintenance of price stability, and they felt that a floating rate enabled them best to meet this goal in the circumstances. By the start of the Bretton Woods negotiations, monetary policy autonomy was also valued because it would enable a more activist macroeconomic policy designed to promote growth and full employment. Then, beginning in the mid-1970s and particularly after the mid-1980s, Canadian officials followed their counterparts in other countries in embracing the neoliberal idea that the primary objective of domestic monetary policy should be price stability and they understood a floating exchange rate to serve this objective. Despite these intellectual shifts, one overriding rationale has been quite consistent: monetary policy autonomy is necessary in order to carve out independence from US monetary developments.

The enduring influence of this idea requires explanation. In part, it reflects the fact that Canadian policy-makers have had good reasons to be wary of US monetary policy-making at various key moments. But there have been other moments when Canadians have disagreed about why distance was needed from US monetary policy-making, with some seeing the latter as too inflationary and others as too restrictive. At these moments, the only point of agreement has been a kind of subtle nationalist distrust of US policy and a concomitant confidence in the ability of the Bank of Canada to pursue policies which address Canadian preferences in conditions of a floating exchange rate.[28] In the context of the NAMU debate, this nationalist sentiment has become much more overt when policy-makers, and Canadians more generally, have been faced with the prospect of a US-controlled monetary union and the loss of their national currency.

This aspect of the Canadian experience thus suggests that ideational influences matter, but not always in the ways suggested by the existing literature on exchange rate regimes. The most common ideational argument among scholars working on this topic has been that anti-inflationary goals or neoliberal monetary thinking will be associated with a preference for rigidly fixed exchange rates or monetary unions. The reasoning is that this kind of exchange rate regime can act as a "credibility" mechanism, precluding discretionary monetary policy in conditions of capital mobility and thus providing a guarantee of price stability.[29] This desire for credibility did play a role in explaining the Canadian decision to adopt a fixed exchange rate in 1962. But more recently, most Canadian neoliberals have embraced a *floating* exchange rate because it would give the Bank of Canada more policy autonomy vis-à-vis the US to pursue a vigorous anti-inflationary program. The Canadian experience thus highlights a key point noted by Freeman: "the 'strength' of inflation-averse parties in the country to which one pegs is a key element of the decision to fix one's own exchange rate."[30] The argument that anti-inflationary preferences lead to a preference for a fixed exchange rate rests on an often unstated assumption – drawn largely from the EU context – that the country to which the fix applies has firm anti-inflationary policies. Because they distrust the anti-inflationary credentials of US monetary authorities, however, many Canadian neoliberals have chosen instead to support a floating exchange rate. There is, in other words, no clear link between neoliberal ideology and exchange rate preferences. As Bowles notes, the link is instead a "contingent" one.[31]

The role of nationalism in this area of Canadian policy-making also highlights a kind of ideational influence that has received relatively little attention in the broader literature on the politics of exchange rate regimes. Thus far, in examining ideational factors, existing literature has focused primarily on the significance of economic expertise, as well as political-economic ideologies such as embedded liberalism or neoliberalism. As we have seen, this study confirms the importance of these influences. But it also points to the importance of nationalism – both that of state policy-makers and of the public at large – in explaining exchange rate regime choices. There is some recent research that has finally begun to analyse the significance of nationalism and national identities in explaining state policy towards regional monetary unions, particularly in the European context.[32] The Canadian experience suggests, however, that they can be significant in influencing not just monetary union debates, but also decisions to fix or float.[33]

At the same time, the Canadian case also shows how complicated the role of nationalism and national identities can be in the context of monetary union debates. Although the abandonment of a national currency can generate nationalist opposition, the strength of this opposition will depend on factors such as the currency's symbolic role in the nation, citizens' trust in its value, and the importance placed on democratic control of monetary policy. Equally important, nationalism can generate not just opposition to monetary unions but also support for them, as we have seen in the case of Quebec.

If ideational influences provide part of the explanation for Canadian exchange rate regime choices, this study also highlights that their relative importance is hard to specify precisely. In the Canadian case, it is analytically very difficult to unravel the link between ideas, beliefs, and identities on the one hand and various changing external and domestic interests and structures on the other. The Canadian evidence does, however, suggest that ideational factors influence behaviour in much more significant ways than simply by providing a "road map" or "focal point" for agents with fixed interests in contexts of strategic interaction or imperfect information, as rationalist scholarship assumes.[34] It shows instead that the very content itself of the interests of key Canadian actors has been, to use Blyth's phrase, "ideationally bound"; that is, it was capable of being transformed by various ideas, beliefs, and identities.[35] In this sense, the Canadian case provides support for the growing "constructivist" critique of rationalist analyses of the politics of exchange rate regimes.

INTERNATIONAL INFLUENCES

The Canadian experience also has relevance for one final set of arguments in the broader literature on the politics of exchange rate regimes: those which point to the role of international influences. We have already seen how the Canadian choice of a floating exchange rate has been influenced by such international factors as the content of US monetary policy and sensitivities to the asymmetries of power in the Canada-US relationship. Also important have been US preferences concerning the Canadian exchange rate regime. There have been very few moments in the twentieth century – the 1930s, 1961–62, and the mid-1980s – when US policy-makers have displayed much concern or interest in Canada's choice of a floating exchange rate regime. Usually, the US has been remarkably tolerant of Canada's float, even when it formally contravened the IMF Articles of Agreement during the 1950s and the early 1970s. In these latter instances, this US attitude helped insulate Canadian exchange rate regime choices from very strong opposition from IMF officials and foreign governments. This US attitude has continued during the NAMU debate as US policy-makers have given no encouragement to Canadian supporters of monetary union, an attitude that has once again reinforced the Canadian preference for floating.

The US role might surprise those accustomed to thinking that hegemonic states will help foster international monetary regimes or regional monetary unions. In the North American context, the US certainly fits the description of being a hegemonic state. But instead of acting in this leadership role, the US not only helped Canada *break* the rules of the Bretton Woods exchange rate regime in 1950 and 1970, but more recently provided little support for the idea of NAMU. What explains the longstanding US support for Canada's float, particularly given the fact that Canada has been such a major commercial partner of the US throughout this period?

One answer is provided by Henning, who notes that US policy-makers have consistently shown less interest in limiting the exchange rate fluctuations of their trading partners' currencies than have other leading monetary powers, such as Germany. He attributes this pattern of behaviour primarily to the weaker political voice of US manufacturing firms – who often have an interest in this issue – in this area of US policy-making. This weakness, in turn, he explains by pointing to the absence of close links between US manufacturing firms and US banks, whose influence is stronger in monetary policy-making but whose preferences are more ambiguous. Also important, he suggests, is the lack of clear lines of responsibility for exchange rate intervention between the US Treasury and the Federal Reserve, as well as the relative independence of the US central bank.[36]

This study suggests that other factors are also important in explaining US behaviour towards Canada's float. US sympathy for the introduction of a floating Canadian dollar in 1950 and 1970 was likely bolstered by the fact that the float produced an upward, rather than a downward, movement in the currency. In the few instances when US policy-makers took a strong interest in Canada's floating exchange rate regime, the Canadian dollar was moving in the other direction, thereby raising potential competitive concerns. Concerns about competitiveness, or the disruption caused by currency volatility, have also been diminished by the high proportion of Canada-US commerce that is intra-firm. Finally, as we have seen, US policy-makers have often shared their Canadian counterparts' view that bilateral payments imbalances are more easily addressed with a floating exchange rate than with capital controls or other adjustment mechanisms that might be cumbersome or politically controversial.

One other external influence on Canada's exchange rate choices deserves mention: the role of heightened international capital mobility. We have already seen how Canada has been subject to a high degree of capital mobility for almost the entire period we examined. And, as the literature predicts, it had the effect of forcing Canada to choose between monetary autonomy and fixed exchange rates long before other countries faced this choice.[37] As global financial flows have grown dramatically in recent years, however, many analysts have suggested that the choice facing countries has become even narrower. If a stable exchange rate is the goal, it is commonly argued that governments must embrace new monetary arrangements – such as monetary unions, currency boards, or dollarization – as a way of signalling to powerful global financial markets the seriousness of their commitment. The only other option is said to be a floating exchange rate.

Drawing on the European example, it is often predicted that the increasingly unstable nature of fixed exchange rates will prompt more and more countries to seek the security of monetary union. As Beddoes puts it, "by 2030 the world will have two major currency zones – one European, the other American. The euro will be used from Brest to Bucharest, and the dollar from Alaska to Argentina – perhaps even Asia. These regional currencies will form the bedrock of the next century's financial stability."[38] But the impact of heightened capital mobility on Canadian exchange rate politics has so far been the opposite: it has bolstered support for a floating exchange rate. The reason is that North American monetary union is hardly attractive in the absence of US support. Unwilling to embrace this option, analysts who might normally favour a fixed exchange rate have thus been prompted, often very reluctantly, to endorse a floating rate.

CONCLUSION

Does Canada's enduring preference for a floating exchange rate provide any lessons for the broader literature on the politics of exchange rate policy-making? At the most general level, it highlights that the task of explaining exchange rate regime choices involves much more than an evaluation of the degree of openness of a country's economy. The Canadian experience suggests instead the usefulness of a multi-level analytical approach that examines the preferences of both domestic economic interests and state policy-makers, as well as the influence of international pressures. At the same time, it highlights a number of limitations in models that have been developed to explain preferences at each level.

These limitations can be briefly summarized. First, although the Canadian case confirms that private sector preferences play a role in determining exchange rate regimes, it highlights how these preferences are highly context-specific, and thus not easily modeled in the kinds of deductive models that many analysts employ. It also suggests that these models often overstate the role of private sector interests in the determination of exchange rate regimes. Second, in circumstances where state policy-makers have autonomy from domestic and external interests, the Canadian experience provides little support for the view that preferences are well explained either by partisan concerns or rationalist models which assume that the primary motivation of politicians is to ensure their own survival. Instead, it points to the usefulness of explanations that examine the kind of structural features of the domestic economy highlighted by OCA theory, as well as explanations that highlight such ideational influences as economic expertise, political-economic ideologies, and even nationalism and national identities (both among state officials and the broader population). The Canadian case also shows that such ideational factors as neoliberalism or nationalism may influence exchange rate regime choices in more complicated ways than is sometimes suggested. Finally, a study of Canada's exchange rate politics reminds us that the significance of international factors in influencing exchange rate regime choices can also be highly context-specific. While heightened capital mobility and the existence of a regional financial leader may have encouraged many European countries to embrace a regional monetary union, they have so far had the opposite effect in the Canadian context because of the content of US monetary policy, sensitivities to the asymmetry of the bilateral Canada-US relationship, and US exchange rate preferences.

The broader relevance of the theoretical points highlighted in this chapter for the study of the political economy of exchange rate regimes is, of course, difficult to discern since they are drawn from only a single-country case study. Indeed, my approach in this book is a rather unfashionable one in the context of the growing literature on the politics of exchange rate regime choices. Prominent in this literature are deductive analytical models which are tested against various statistical indicators drawn from a large group of countries. By contrast, this study uses an in-depth and inductive approach to examine the historical experience of one country. But it is perhaps in this methodological difference that this study's most important broader theoretical importance is revealed. This study of Canada's unusual fixation with floating highlights that many of the deductive models so popular in scholarly literature for studying exchange rate regime politics are unable to provide the kind of detailed and nuanced understanding of the political basis of policy-making that emerges from careful historical and case-study research. This book, in other words, provides an important reminder that abstract model-building must never become too divorced from the specific context in which policy-making actually takes place.

Abbreviations

BCNI	Business Council on National Issues
BIS	Bank for International Settlements
BQ	Bloc Québécois
CBC	Canadian Broadcasting Corporation
CCF	Cooperative Commonwealth Federation
CLC	Canadian Labour Congress
DM	Deutschemark
ECB	European Central Bank
EEC	European Economic Community
EMS	European Monetary System
EMU	Economic and Monetary Union
EU	European Union
FECB	Foreign Exchange Control Board
FOMC	Federal Open Market Committee
FRBNY	Federal Reserve Bank of New York
FTA	Canada–United States Free Trade Agreement (of 1989)
GATT	General Agreement on Tariffs and Trade
IET	Interest Equalization Tax
IMF	International Monetary Fund
LLR	Lender of last resort
LMU	Latin Monetary Union
MNC	Multinational corporation
MP	Member of Parliament

NAFTA	North American Free Trade Agreement
NAMU	North American monetary union
NDP	New Democratic Party
OCA	Optimum currency area
OECD	Organization for Economic Cooperation and Development
PEI	Prince Edward Island
PQ	Parti Québécois
SMU	Scandinavian Monetary Union

Notes

INTRODUCTION

1 A terminological note is required here at the outset of the book. For some, NAMU refers to the creation of a new North American currency that would replace existing national currencies. For others, it refers to the idea that Canada would simply adopt the US dollar. The term is used throughout this book in a general way that includes either of these meanings. But the importance of the distinction is highlighted in chapters 6–8.

2 Sherry Cooper, economist with BMO Nesbitt Burns, quoted in *Financial Post*, 30 January 1999. She predicted NAMU "within five years."

3 Richard Marceau quoted in "Don't Buck Single Currency Trend, Bloc Urges" *Ottawa Citizen*, 14 February 2000. See also Thomas Courchene's argument: "if you look at the way currencies are consolidating around the world, I don't think the Canadian dollar can exist in 10 years" (quoted in Fred Williams, "Imagine a Single U.S.-Canadian Currency," *The Buffalo News*, 12 January 2003).

4 Crow 2002: 125.

5 There are some important exceptions such as Clarkson 2000, Cameron 1986, Cornell 1956, Muirhead 1999, Pauly 2006, Plumptre 1977, and Webb 1992. See also Powell 1999 for a very useful overview of the history of the Canadian dollar.

6 This point was first made by Cornell (1956) in the context of discussing Canadian exchange rate policy in the 1930s to the early 1950s.

7 Pauly 2006.
8 Ted Carmichael quoted in Bowles 2003a: 15.

CHAPTER ONE

1 Canada 1855: 54.
2 McLachlan 1892.
3 Shortt 1986: xviii, 235, 437–40; Powell 1999: 5.
4 Shortt 1986: 885; Longley 1943.
5 Hincks quoted in Masters 1952: 133. See also Shortt 1986: 482.
6 See for example Shortt 1986: 123–5, 383.
7 Shortt 1986: 428–9, 444, 472.
8 Canadian policy-makers were also aware that Canadian banks benefited
   from the fact that their dollar-denominated notes circulated widely in the
   US, providing a good source of profit (Shortt 1986: 428, 515, 553).
9 Shortt 1964: 126.
10 Masters 1952.
11 Quote from Longley 1943: 441.
12 Quote from Masters 1952: 144. See also Longley 1943: 162–76, 242–74,
   373.
13 Shortt 1986: 429, 491.
14 Trevelyan 1851: 1579. See also Grey 1851a.
15 Quoted in Gibbs 1979a: 1239.
16 Masters 1952: 144.
17 Quoted in Masters 1952: 144.
18 Mr J. Smith in Gibbs 1979a: 1240.
19 Shortt 1986: 486; Masters 1952: 138–40.
20 Alexander 1856: 4.
21 Gibbs 1979b: 2782.
22 Gibbs 1979b: 2778.
23 Mr. Gamble in Gibbs 1979b: 2780.
24 Shortt 1986: 488. See also 474–88; Masters 1952: 138–40; McCalla 1969.
25 Although Hincks had said in 1851 that a silver coin issue had primarily symbolic value, two years later he had come to see it as more important in light of
   monetary developments abroad. Because of the rapidly changing gold to silver
   price ratio at this time, he had committed the province to a monometallic gold
   standard in 1851, but he had made the mistake of proposing to leave US silver
   coins with full legal tender status – a move that would leave the province de
   facto on a bimetallic system. British officials pointed out his mistake and advised that the province would need to create a fiduciary silver coinage in

which the quantity of silver coins was closely regulated and the legal tender status of US and other foreign silver coins was ended (from "Minutes of the Board of Treasury, London, On the Coinage and Currency of Canada," 29 June 1852 in Canada 1855). When the US itself transformed its silver coin into a fiduciary currency and moved to a monometallic gold standard in 1853, Canada faced a choice of whether to make US silver coin simply limited legal tender (as British silver coins had become in 1842) or to remove their legal tender status altogether. Hincks chose the latter route, a move that then increased the need for Canada to create its own silver fiduciary coin (Shortt 1986: 483–6, 489–90). In practice, US coins continued to circulate.

26 Masters 1952: 140–1.

27 Canada 1855: 9.

28 See especially Piva 1992.

29 Adam Ainslie's letter of 17 March 1855 in Canada 1855: 54. See also Mackenzie's comments in Gibbs 1979b: 2783–4.

30 Weir 1903: ch16, 161–5.

31 Weir 1903: 137; Shortt 1986: 489–90, 496.

32 Innis and Lower 1933. Like the province of Canada, New Brunswick had its initial effort to transform its monetary standard disallowed in 1850 by British authorities (Grey 1851b).

33 Powell 1999: 8–9. Newfoundland, too, began to issue dollar-based decimal currency in 1865, although it was not until 1877 that a law was passed requiring public accounts to be conducted in dollars. Newfoundland's standard also rated the British pound at the different rate of $4.

34 McLachlan 1892.

35 Acheson 1985.

36 Waite 1972: 110; Canada 1870: 766–7; Canada 1871: 261, 264, 306–7; Canada 1975: 228–30.

37 Innis and Lower 1933: 728.

38 Canada 1870: 819; Canada 1871: 306.

39 Canada 1967: 401. See also 357–8 and Canada 1871: 261. The federal government in fact began early on to collect excise duties in Nova Scotia in Canadian currency (Canada 1967: 411).

40 Powell 1999: 12fn15.

41 Canada 1967: 399; Canada 1871: 522.

42 Canada 1871: 522.

43 Muise 1968.

44 Canada 1967: 401.

45 Canada 1967: 358. See also An Act Respecting Currency, *Statutes of Canada*, 1868: 114–18.

46 Quotes from Canada 1871: 303, 259; Canada 1870: 1350. See also Canada 1967: 358, 397.

47 Canada 1975: 230. For continuing opposition in Nova Scotia, see Canada 1870: 447; Canada 1871: 260.

48 Quotes from Mr Savary and Mr Magill in Canada 1871: 306, 304.

49 Weir 1903.

50 Shortt 1986: 559. See also Weir 1903; Mercator 1867: 28; Canada 1967: 178, 281; Canada 1870: 869; Canada 1975: 465. The experience also led the government to end legal tender status of British and other foreign token silver coins in 1871 (Canada 1871: 259).

51 Thomas Oliver in Canada 1975: 464.

52 Canada 1967: 280–1.

53 Mr Bodwell in Canada 1967: 281.

54 Seigniorage is the sum of money that accrues to an issuer of money due to the difference between the cost of producing money and its nominal value.

55 Shortt 1986: 559; Weir 1903: 160.

56 Longley 1943: 367; Canada 1870: 216, 253–4.

57 Canada 1870: 244, 257–8; Canada 1975; 563, 569; Shortt 1986: 560, 614–16; Robertson 1888; Weir 1903: ch18.

58 Gilbert 1998, 1999.

59 Shortt 1986: 575–9, 612; Canada 1870: 801.

60 Indeed, so limited were the changes in the PEI case that politicians had overlooked the need to extend the Dominion's currency to PEI in a legal sense when it joined Confederation. This was finally done in 1881 (Canada 1881: 1057).

61 Howay et al. 1942: 171–3; Sage 1927: 99; Canada 1881: 1057; Letter from Post Office Official in Victoria, BC, to The Postmaster General, 29 December 1876, NAC, RG3, D-3, vol. 1, file 1876–270.

62 Helleiner 2003a.

63 For a discussion, see Shortt 1986: 554, 708–12; Neill 1991; Goodwin 1961; Palmer 1979: 100–8; Henley 1989.

64 Quotes from Goodwin 1961: 50. While Buchanan's ideas on trade policy were similar to those of Carey, his monetary thinking was closer in spirit to that of Attwood and his Birmingham school of political economy, as Neill accurately notes (1991: 78–82, 102–6).

65 Quoted in Neill 1991: 108. See also Arnold 1862.

66 Henry Carey, letter to Isaac Buchanan, 20 October 1873, NAC, MG24, D16, vol. 20: 17449. Emphasis in original.

67 Quoted in Goodwin 1961: 82.

68 Isaac Buchanan, "The Philosophy and Practice of Currency Reform," 28 October 1879, NAC, MG24, D14, vol. 108: 070979. See also Goodwin 1961: 82.

69 Davis 1867: 11.

70 For example, Canada 1880: 1766.

71 Isaac Buchanan, letter to William Wallace, 7 December 1880, NAC, MG24, D16, vol. 108: 71014.

72 Quoted in Wright 1885: 23.

73 Isaac Buchanan, "Nothing Could Be More Practically Disloyal, Unpatriotic, and UnChristian Than the Hard Money Legislation of England," January 1880, NAC, MG24, D14, vol. 108: 070994.

74 Quoted in O'Hanly 1882: 12.

75 Kealey 1980: 165.

76 For their support of the Conservative Party, see Neill 1968: 10.

77 Shortt 1986: 715; Robertson 1888: 13.

78 For example, Canada 1880: 1762.

79 Canada 1880: 1755.

80 Shortt 1986: 712.

81 For example, Canada 1880: 1754–5.

82 Quote from Laxer 1989: 125. See also Naylor 1975.

83 Jack 1869: 4.

84 Goodwin 1961: 105–6. See also Owram 1985: 367. For the banks' power, see also Naylor 1975: 74; Laxer 1989: 218.

85 See for example Rich 1988: 51.

86 Eichengreen 1992.

87 Shortt 1986: 712. See also Goodwin 1961: 83; Kealey 1980: 165–6.

88 Kealey 1980: 165; Palmer 1979: 102.

89 Kealey 1980: 330, 367–8.

90 Laxer 1989: 125.

CHAPTER TWO

1 Quote from Brecher 1957: 36.

2 Brecher 1957: 36.

3 Laxer 1989: 127; Brodie 1990: 122.

4 Stokes 1939: 53; Brecher 1957.

5 For an interesting discussion of the links to Buchanan's ideas, see Neill 1968.

6 S.H. Drayton, "Our Dollar and Its Exchange Value," 2 September 1925, NAC, MG26, I, vol. 69: 39120–5.

7 Canadian Importers Association, letter to PM Arthur Meighen, 8 November
   1921, NAC, MG26, I, vol. 25: 14977–8.
8 Canada 1949a: 1700. The Canadian government also found that its efforts
   to settle war debts with Britain in this period were complicated by the exchange rate fluctuations; see for example, NAC, MG26, I, vol. 14: 8157ff.
9 R.M. Gidney to Pieree Jay, 4 August 1919, in USNA, RG82, Board of Governors Central Subject Files 334.111. Indeed, even as early as 1917–18, US
   banks in the border areas began urging the US treasury secretary to offer a
   loan to Canada to restore the par value of Canada's currency, and some US
   officials even raised the question of whether Canadian banks should be allowed to join the new US Federal Reserve System; R.C. Leffingwell to
   W. Harding, 3 May 1918, and George Harrison to R.C. Leffingwell, 11 May
   1918, in USNA, RG82, Board of Governors Central Subject File 334.111.
10 Laxer 1989: 14; see also J.C. Elliot, "The Movement of Capital: A Factor in
   Canadian-American Relations," 1935, NAC, RG19, vol. 3990, U-2-10, U.S.
   miscellaneous.
11 G.S. Watts "The Background of Canadian Foreign Exchange and Balance of
   Payments Policy Since the War," 28 April 1952, BCA, LR76-522-22-1: 5;
   Rasminsky 1941: 89fn1; "Trade and Exchange Problems," *Toronto Globe*,
   24 February 1920.
12 Both quotes from J.D. Darling, Memorandum on Anglo-Canadian Exchange, 4 March 1920, p1, NAC, MG26, H1(a), vol. 114: 62813–15. See also
   J.D. Darling, letter to H.H. Stevens, 4 November 1932, NAC, MG27, III, B9,
   vol. 16; L. Amery, letter to Sir George Perley, 17 March 1920, NAC, MG26,
   H1(a), vol. 114. When Empire currency cooperation was discussed at the
   1923 Imperial Economic Conference, the UK treasury made a similar point
   (United Kingdom Treasury, "Currency Co-operation in the British Empire,"
   memorandum prepared by the Treasury, 6 November 1923, RG25, G-1, vol.
   1588, file 159-L-1: 468). During World War One, Prime Minister Bennett
   had shown some interest in a broader proposal to create a currency for the
   whole of the British Empire. But the idea was dropped when British authorities showed no interest. See L. Amery, letter to Colonel Ralston, 25 September 1939, NAC, RG19, vol. 3976, file E1-4; "Hopes Canada to Lead World
   in Rehabilitation of Silver," *Ottawa Citizen*, 18 May 1931; "For British
   Empire Bank," *Ottawa Citizen*, 17 January 1932.
13 Bryce 1986: 34–5.
14 Drayton, "Our Dollar and Its Exchange Value," pp3–4. He advocated
   strengthening the balance of payments with such measures as import tariffs
   and the bolstering of value-added exports.

15 C.A. Curtis, "The Canadian Monetary Situation," address to Canadian Club, Ottawa, 21 November 1931, p8, NAC, RG25, DI, vol. 769, file 332.

16 Bryce 1986: 35.

17 Bordo and Redish 1990; Brecher 1957: 43–4.

18 F. Wile, "Canada Asks U.S. for Money Parity," *Washington Star*, 5 June 1928. This story is well told in "Credit to Jarvis for Dollar Boost," *Ottawa Journal*, 28 April 1930.

19 "An Injustice to Canada," *Courier Journal*, 29 May 1928.

20 Wile, "Canada Asks U.S."

21 Julius Klein to Roy Young, 14 September 1928, USNA, RG82, Board of Governors Central Subject File 334.111; N.A. Robertson to O.D. Skelton, 22 July 1929, NAC, RG25, vol. 1542, file 387.

22 E.L. Smead, W. Cation, and J.E. Crane, "Report of Committee on Redemption of Canadian Currency," 4 September 1929, p2, USNA, RG82, Board of Governors Central Subject File, 334.111.

23 See Mr Smead to Federal Reserve Board, 17 October 1929, and E. Goldenweiser to Minister of Finance, Ottawa, 15 April 1929, USNA, RG82, Board of Governors Central Subject File, 334.111.

24 Federal Reserve Board, "Canadian Currency," Statement for the Press, 15 April 1930, USNA, RG82, Board of Governors Central Subject File, 334.111.

25 Quoted in "Credit to Jarvis."

26 Federal Reserve Board, "Canadian Currency."

27 O.D. Skelton to A.H. Jarvis, 23 April 1930, NAC, RG25, vol. 1542, file 387.

28 Although most Federal Reserve banks continued to accept Canadian currency, they no longer did so at par but rather at the new depreciated market rate. Under prompting from the Federal Reserve's board of governors and the US Chamber of Commerce, all the banks resumed accepting Canadian currency at the market rate in 1934 (Mr Myrick to Mr Smead, 9 March 1934, and President of US Chamber of Commerce to Eugene Black, 3 March 1934, USNA, RG82, Board of Governors Central Subject File, 334.111).

29 Bordo and Redish 1990.

30 Plumptre 1941: 185.

31 Royal Commission on Dominion-Provincial Relations 1940: 154.

32 H. Stevens, memorandum to R.B. Bennett, 12 January 1933, NAC, MG27, III, B9, vol. 16.

33 W.A. Mackintosh, "Confidential" [undated], p3, NAC, RG25, DI, vol. 769, file 332; H. Marshall, "Memorandum from Mr. H. Marshall on the Second Report of the Federation of British Industries," 8 June 1932, pp3–4, NAC,

RG25, G-1, vol. 1588, file 159-L-2; Bryce 1986: 126. Some advocates of a large depreciation argued that it would in fact provide a way of boosting exports to the US in sectors that had been hurt by the US introduction of the Smoot-Hawley tariff of 1930. As one Royal Bank official noted in September 1931, "all kind of food products now debarred by the United States tariff would easily hurdle it" (S.R. Noble, letter to R.B. Bennett, 26 September 1931, p3, NAC, RG25, D1, vol. 769, file 332).

34 US Chamber of Commerce 1932.

35 Royal Commission on Dominion-Provincial Relations 1940: 145. See also G. Robertson, letter to R.B. Bennett, 8 April 1932, NAC, MG26K … UNB:163, vol. 293: 197117.

36 See for example, Royal Commission on Banking and Currency, *Proceedings 1933 v.4*, p2224, NAC, RG33-17, vol. 1; F.E.M. Robinson, letter to H. Stevens, 27 October 1932, NAC, MG27, III, B9, vol. 16; V. Porteous, letter to R.B. Bennett, 5 January 1933, NAC, MG26K … UNB:247, vol. 488: 305689; as well as many letters in NAC, MG27, III, B9, vol. 16; and "Difficulties Experienced by Canadian Firms in Export trade Due to the Exchange Situation," NAC, RG-33-17, vol. 6, file 30-1.

37 T.A. McAuley, letter to H. Stevens, 16 January 1933, p1, NAC, MG27, III, B9, vol. 16.

38 G. Williams 1994.

39 Stevens, memorandum; H.D. Scott 1934: 252; Stokes 1939: 87, 93; Royal Commission, *Proceedings 1933 v.4*: 2224.

40 Robinson, letter to Stevens: 1–2.

41 Some enthusiasts even sent Prime Minister Bennett drawings of the designs that a uniform coinage of the Empire might have (NAC, MG26K … UNB:163, vol. 293: 197150-2).

42 H. Stevens, letter to Sir Josiah Stamp, 8 November 1932, NAC, MG27, III, B9, vol. 16.

43 Stevens, memorandum; Darling, letter to Stevens 1932; "Hopes Canada to Lead."

44 Plumptre 1977: 21.

45 Canada 1933: 190. McPhail was the first woman elected to the federal parliament in 1921 when she represented the United Farmers of Ontario.

46 Canada 1932: 2213–14.

47 Noble, letter to R.B. Bennett: 6.

48 Cornell 1956: 141. See also this case made to Prime Minister Bennett in August 1931 by one writer: "We cannot control the value of American currency, but I can see no reason why Canada should allow the Federal Reserve directors to determine what the value of *our* dollar shall be. Why should

Canadians suffer needlessly because of the incompetence of those in control of the credit basis of the United States, when we have the means of protecting our people from the effects of those mistakes?" (T.B. Macaulay, letter to R.B. Bennett, 14 August 1931, p2, NAC, MG27, III, B9, vol. 16).

49 Noble, letter to R.B. Bennett: 2.

50 S.R. Noble, memo, 23 February 1932, p7, NAC, RG25, D1, vol. 769, file 332. Keynes 1923.

51 Noble, memo: 6–7. S. R. Noble, letter to C.S. Tompkins, 17 March 1932, pp6–7, NAC, RG25, D1, vol. 769, file 332.

52 G. Towers, memorandum, April 1932, p2, NAC, MG26K … UNB:163, vol. 293: 197121–5.

53 Noble, letter to R.B. Bennett; Towers, memorandum: 197124. See also W.C. Clark, "Monetary Reconstruction," July 1932, NAC, RG25, D1, vol. 770, file 333.

54 Macauley, letter to R.B. Bennett.

55 Stevens, memorandum; Brecher 1957: 120. See also Clark, "Monetary Reconstruction": 144–5.

56 Plumptre 1977: 23; J. Stamp, letter to Mr Stevens, 30 November 1932, pp1–2, NAC, MG27, III, B9, vol. 16.

57 R.B. Bennett, letter to C.S. Tompkins, 19 April 1932, NAC, MG26K … UNB:163, vol. 293: 197126.

58 Bryce 1986: 130. See also 78; Bordo and Redish 1990: 373; Mackintosh 1964: 175–6.

59 Royal Commission on Dominion-Provincial Relations 1940: 155. See also Hackett 1935.

60 See also Cornell 1956: 162.

61 Canada 1933: 3208. See also Bryce 1986: 52.

62 C.H. Herbert, "Recent Trends in Currency, Credit Policy and Public Finance in Canada," 23 May 1935, p4, NAC, MG26, I, vol. 158: 97029–41.

63 Bryce 1986: 125. See also Ferguson 1993.

64 Bryce 1986: 82.

65 W.C. Clark, letter to R.B. Bennett, 28 March 1932, NAC, RG25, D1, vol. 769, file 332.

66 Bryce 1986: 80.

67 Clark, "Monetary Reconstruction."

68 W.C. Clark, "Memorandum: Some Comments on an Article by E.S. Bates entitled 'What a Managed Currency Policy Means to Canada,'" 15 November 1933, pp1–2, NAC, MG26K … UNB: 69–70, vol. 297: 200170–6.

69 Clark, "Monetary Reconstruction": 188–9.

70 Clark, letter to R.B. Bennett: 3.

71 Clark, "Monetary Reconstruction": 195.

72 W.C. Clark, memorandum for Mr Dunning, 2 March 1936, QUA, WC, M-I-14-10; A.D. White 1933. See also his rejection of G. White's proposal: "National 'Laissez-Faire': The Control of Foreign Exchange Transactions – Economic Equilibrium Maintained by Controlled Purchasing Power," 1933, and letter to W.C. Clark, 21 December 1933, NAC, RG19, vol. 3982, M-I-10.

73 Stamp, letter to Mr Stevens: 1.

74 Towers, memorandum: 2.

75 Quoted in Brecher 1957: 124.

76 Royal Commission on Dominion-Provincial Relations 1940: 144.

77 Quoted in Brecher 1957: 120.

78 Plumptre 1934: 166.

79 Plumptre 1940.

80 See for example Brecher 1957: 115, 117, 121.

81 McDougal in Knox 1937: 51–2.

82 Clark, "Monetary Reconstruction": 145–7.

83 Clark, "Monetary Reconstruction": 147, 145, 149–50.

84 Clark, "Monetary Reconstruction": 149.

85 Brecher 1957: 120; E.Bates "Canada's Monetary Problems," 24 March 1936, QUA, WC, M-I-I.

86 Curtis 1932: 335–6; Bryce 1986: 128.

87 J.A. McLeod, letter to R.B. Bennett, 19 January 1932, NAC, MG26K ... UNB:163, vol. 293: 196968–71.

88 R.B. Bennett, letter to P. Whitehead, 4 January 1932, NAC, MG26K ... UNB:163, vol. 293: 196939.

89 G. White, letter to W.C. Clark, 21 December 1933.

90 Cornell 1956: 151.

91 Towers, memorandum; Stevens, memorandum.

92 L. Amery, letter to H. Stevens, 28 February 1933, NAC, MG27, III, B9, vol. 16. His colleague Darling continued to press for his ambitious Empire currency scheme backed by a "Super-Bank" which pooled the gold of the empire ("Hopes Canada to Lead"). Amery recommended the creation of a currency board or central bank.

93 Brecher 1957.

94 Mackintosh, "Confidential."

95 Royal Commission, Proceedings, 1933, p2449–50, NAC, RG33-17, vol. 2.

96 Bryce 1986: 82.

97 Stokes 1939: chs3–4; Plumptre 1940: 162.

98 Watts 1933: 9; Stokes 1939: 65, 182; Plumptre 1940: 170.

99 Plumptre 1940.

100 Bryce 1986: 127.

101 Brecher 1957: 130.

102 Quoted in Watts 1993: 16. For Clark's role, see Watts 1993: 14; Brecher 1957: 142.

103 Stokes 1939: 219; Plumptre 1941: 185.

104 Drummond and Hillmer 1989.

105 G. Towers, "General Shareholders Meeting 1936," p9, QUA, JD, box 68, file 482. See also Royal Commission on Dominion-Provincial Relations 1940: 155. For the role of US liquid balances, see also Rasminsky 1941: 90. Most of the optional payment bonds issued before 1914 were payable in either sterling or Canadian dollars. But during the 1920s, a large number of optional payment bonds began to be issued which also allowed payments in US dollars or Canadian dollars (and often all three currencies) (Hackett 1935). For another broader explanation for the stability of the Canadian dollar in this period, see Malach 1955.

106 G. Towers, letter to C.A. Dunning, 14 April 1938, p4, QUA, WC, B-2-10.

107 Stokes 1939: 87, 93; Royal Commission, *Proceedings 1933 v.4*: 2224.

108 Statistics from "Confidential: The External Value of the Canadian Dollar" [no author] 18 September 1935, QUA, JD, box 67, no. 480.

109 G. Towers, letter to W.C. Clark, 20 October 1936, NAC, RG19, vol. 3976.

110 G. Towers, letter to C.A. Dunning, 19 October 1936, pp4–5, NAC, RG19, vol. 3976, file E-1-2.

111 See for example J.A.C. Osborne, "Arguments for Depreciating the Canadian Dollar," 14 May 1935, QUA, JD, box 68, file 484; R. Bryce, "Report on Memorandum Regarding Proposed Adjustment of Exchange Value of Canadian Currency," March 1939, NAC, RG19, vol. 3976; "Confidential: The External."

112 Plumptre 1940: 420.

113 Article X in *Trade Agreement between Canada and the United States of America* (Ottawa: J.O. Patenaude, 1935). The full text is: "In the event that a wide variation occurs in the rate of exchange between the currencies of Canada and the United States of America, the Government of either country, if it considers the variation so substantial as to prejudice the industries or commerce of the country, shall be free to propose negotiations for the modification of this Agreement; and if an agreement with respect thereto is not reached within thirty days following receipt of such proposal, the Government making such proposal shall be free to terminate this Agreement in its entirety on thirty days' written notice" (6). When the agreement was renewed in 1938, this provision remained as article XIII in *Trade Agreement between Canada and the United States of America* (Ottawa: J.O. Patenaude, 1938): 9–10. A similar clause had been inserted in a 1934 trade agreement between the US and France, and the US had begun to insist on

this provision in all the trade agreements it was signing from 1935 onwards (Drummond and Hillmer 1989: 141–7). The Canadian government had also already shown a growing interest in linking trade access to exchange rate movements. Responding to the fact that the US dollar had fallen below the Canadian dollar in value after it had left gold in April 1933, Canada imposed a "dumping duty" on all US exports in November of that year. The duty would vary according to the degree of depreciation of the US currency below the Canadian dollar. The US was not being singled out; Canada had already begun to apply this kind of duty on imports from other countries – including the UK – whose currencies fell below par with the Canadian dollar ("Dumping Duties," *New York Times*, 25 November 1933). The measure provoked a strong US response; in the words of one Canadian official, US policy-makers "violently attacked" it, noting that they had resisted domestic pressure for such duties to be applied against Canada over the previous two years (W.D. Herridge to Secretary of State for External Affairs, "Currency Depreciation," 4 December 1933, NAC, RG25, vol. 2454; see also RG25, G-1, vol. 1581, file 48-X). Fearing retaliation, the Canadian government quickly clarified that the duty would only apply if the depreciation of the US currency was more than 5 per cent below par.

114 "Notes on Currency Adjustment Memorandum," letter from D. Gordon to W.C. Clark, 3 March 1939, NAC, RG19, vol. 3976.

115 A. Skelton, letter to J.A.C. Osborne, 27 March 1935, QUA, JD, box 68, file 484.

116 For example, Skelton, letter to Osborne; Gordon, "Notes on": 2; Bryce, "Report on"; "Confidential: The External": 2.

117 Canada, House of Commons 1939: 47. See also the concerns of Deputy Governor D. Gordon, "Notes on Currency Adjustment Memorandum," 3 March 1939, NAC, RG19, vol. 3976.

118 Fullerton 1986: 100–1; Neill 1991: 141–2; Campbell 1987: 12.

CHAPTER THREE

1 Gordon 1940, "Some Current Problems," address to Toronto Bankers' Educational Association, 10 April 1940, p19, QUA, JD, box 69, no. 475. See also G. Towers, "Address of Mr. Graham Towers," 1 April 1940, p3, Series of Addresses Presented at Study Course April 1 to 12, 1940, NAC, RG19, vol. 3973, B-2-8-10.

2 Towers, "Address of."

3 Fullerton 1986: 96–8; Towers, "Address of": 2; Turk 1956; Muirhead 1999: 59. For an overview of the controls, see Gibbons 1954.

4 Graham F. Towers, "Memorandum re: Exchange Situation, with Special Reference to Memorandum by Beattie and Watts, dated September 28, 1938," p2, BCA, Graham F. Towers Memo #181.

5 Towers, "Address of": 7. See also A. McBain, "Address of Mr. A. MacD. McBain," 10 April 1940, p2, Series of Addresses Presented at Study Course April 1 to 12, 1940, NAC, RG19, vol. 3973, B-2-8-10; Rasminsky 1941: 90.

6 Rasminsky 1941: 90.

7 McBain, "Address of": 1–2.

8 McBain, "Address of": 8; D.L. Dolan, letter to J.L. Ralston, 18 December 1939, p1, NAC, RG19, E-1(c), vol. 2679, file 1-05.

9 Plumptre 1977: 92; Plumptre 1941: 185–9; Rasminsky 1941: 99–101.

10 Towers, "Address of": 3.

11 For example Plumptre 1977: 91.

12 Fullerton 1986: 120–2; Black 1977: 199–204.

13 W.A. Mackintosh, "Memorandum for the Minister: Proposed Steps in the Future Discussion of the Clearing Union and Stabilization Fund Proposals," 2 June 1943, NAC, RG19, vol. 3981, M-1-7-2; see also Muirhead 1999: 97.

14 See for example Plumptre 1977: 28; Muirhead 1999: ch4.

15 J. Williams, letter to Louis Rasminsky, 12 August 1943, p4, QUA, WC, M-1-7-P.

16 J. Williams 1947: 18.

17 J. Williams 1947: xlvii.

18 J. Williams 1947: 207. See also 18, 223.

19 J. Williams 1947: 219–20. Some US government officials involved in the Bretton Woods planning, such as Alvin Hansen, also critiqued White's plan for its insistence that all countries must adopt a fixed exchange rate. In Mikesell's words, Hansen thought that "exchange-rate flexibility was desirable for all but the largest countries" (1994: 11).

20 J. Williams 1947: 18.

21 L. Rasminsky, letter to John Williams, 15 July 1943, QUA, WC, M-1-7-P; W.C. Clark, letter to John Williams, 21 August 1943, and letter to Louis Rasminsky, 19 August 1943, QUA, WC, M-1-7-P. For Rasminsky's lead role in Canadian policy-making towards Bretton Woods, see Granatstein 1981.

22 Muirhead 1999: 106; Rasminsky 1944a.

23 Muirhead 1999: chs1–4.

24 Quoted in Muirhead 1999: 42.

25 Rasminsky 1944a: 10.

26 R. Bryce, "Basic Issues in Post-war International Economic Relations," December 1941, p2, NAC, RG19, vol. 3977, E-3-1. For his influence in bringing Keynesianism to Canada, see Plumptre 1977: 152.

27 Bryce, "Basic Issues": 8. For his role in the Bretton Woods process, see
   Muirhead 1999: 91. See also Royal Commission on Dominion-Provincial
   Relations 1940: 186.
28 G. Towers, "Survey of Canada's Wartime Fiscal and Financial Policy," p5,
   Remarks Delivered to Foreign Exchange Control Board Study Groups,
   11 June 1942, NAC, RG25, vol. 3034, file 4075–40.
29 Quote from Fullerton 1986: 194. Towers was also approached by the US to
   become the first head of the IMF in early 1946, and Keynes approved of this
   idea. Towers, however, refused (Muirhead 1999: 112, 326).
30 Ruggie 1983.
31 Plumptre 1972: 42.
32 Campbell 1987: 22.
33 "Note of a Conversation with Mr.Towers," 2 July 1944, PRO, T247/64.
34 Campbell 1987: 23.
35 Clark, letter to Rasminsky.
36 Rasminsky, letter to Williams.
37 Rasminsky 1944b: 46.
38 Rasminsky 1944a: 13; see also Rasminsky, letter to Williams: 4.
39 Clark, letter to Williams: 2.
40 Williams, letter to Rasminsky, 12 August 1943, p5.
41 R. Bryce, "Report on Memorandum Regarding Proposed Adjustment of
   Exchange Value of Canadian Currency," March 1939, p17, NAC, RG19,
   vol. 3976.
42 Rasminsky 1944a: 14–15.
43 House of Commons, Special Committee on Reconstruction and Re-
   Establishment, Minutes of Proceedings and Evidence, no. 2, 8 March 1944.
   By April 1944, Williams seemed to acknowledge this criticism when he
   noted that exchange rate flexibility for "younger countries" might prove
   disruptive of other countries. He wondered if it would be better for them to
   use exchange controls instead (1947: xlvii).
44 Louis Rasminsky, "Question of Continuing Foreign Exchange Control,"
   12 December 1951, p4, BCA, LR76-115-24.
45 J. Williams 1947: lxxvi.
46 L. Rasminsky, "Proposals for an International Currency Stabilization and
   Clearing Fund," 20 May 1943, p1, NAC, RG19, vol. 3982, M-1-7-4; Clark,
   letter to Rasminsky; Van Dormael 1978: 88.
47 "Unofficial Notes Comparing British, American and Canadian Proposals,"
   [1943], NAC, RG19, E2(g), vol. 3448.
48 Helleiner 1994: ch2. John Williams also endorsed capital controls (e.g.,
   J. Williams 1947d: 47).

49 L. Rasminsky, letter to G.F. Towers, 4 November 1942, QUA, WC, box 10, T-2-9-2- vol. 1.

50 Towers, "Survey of Canada's Wartime Fiscal," p4. See also Bryce, "Basic Issues": 7–8.

51 Horsefield 1969: 106, 118.

52 "Note of a Conversation with Mr. Towers."

53 Horsefield 1969: 118.

54 L. Rasminsky, Meeting of Council of Foreign Relations, 24 January 1942, NAC, RG19, vol. 3976.

55 L. Rasminsky, Outline of Study of Post-war Organization of F.E.C.B.," 11 March 1944, p2, BCA, LR76-179-1.

56 A.O. Gibbons, "Post-War Policy and Organization," 22 March 1944, p2, BCA, FECB, vol. 260.

57 Plumptre 1977: 147–8.

58 "What 'Free' Dollar Means to Business," *Financial Post*, 1–7 October 1950. The government in fact helped them in the end: "In order to assist in the re-establishment of a foreign exchange market in Canada, the FECB, as a temporary measure, undertook to provide the services of two former brokers" (Watts 1993: 83).

59 Quotes from L. Rasminsky, "Notes of Discussions Held with the International Monetary Fund", 2 October 1950, p4, NAC, MG31, E14, vol. 4, file 8a.

60 L. Rasminsky, "Fund Discussion of Fluctuating Exchange Rate for Belgium," 21 September 1949, pp1–2, NAC, MG31, E14, vol. 2, file 7.

61 Muirhead 1999: 140; Fullerton 1986: 242–4.

62 L. Rasminsky, "'Rough Notes': Executive Board Meeting 604," 30 September 1950, p4, NAC, MG31, E14, vol. 2, file 8a.

63 L. Rasminsky, "Report on Washington Discussions Re Floating the Canadian Dollar, Sept. 28–29, 1950," 21 October 1950, p3, BCA, LR76-522-2. See also Fullerston 1986: 243; Rasminsky, "Notes of Discussions": 1; "Draft Minutes, IMF Executive Board Meeting 604," 30 September 1950, p4, NAC, MG31, E14, vol. 2, file 8-IMF.

64 Rasminsky, "Rough Notes": 9.

65 Mackintosh 1951. See also Muirhead 1999: 139; Cornell 1956: 113.

66 Plumptre 1977: 141; Neufeld 1955.

67 See for example Sparks 1986; Wonnacott 1971: 26–7.

68 George Bolton, "The Foreign Exchanges," 30 October 1950, BOE, OV44/6.

69 Canada 1946: 3229–33; Canada 1948: 4397–8; Plumptre 1977: 96.

70 Plumptre 1977: 93.

71 J. Parkinson, "Some Reflections on the Worldwide Devaluations of Sept. 17–19, 1949," NAC, MG31, E14, vol. 2, file 7-IMF; Mundell 1971: 45.

72 Muirhead 1999: 137.

73 "A Method of Combining a Free Exchange Rate with the Present System of Exchange Control in Canada," 31 January 1949, pp1–2, BCA, LR76-115-13-1. The memo is attributed to James Coyne in the Bank of Canada's history of the Canadian dollar (Powell 1999: 38).

74 L. Rasminsky, "Exports of Securities and Present Financial Arrangements with U.S.A.," 17 May 1943, pp8, 10, NAC, RG 19, vol. 3972, B-2-8-9-5.

75 This rationale is reported in George Bolton, "Canadian Post-war Exchange Policy," 30 October 1944, BOE, OV58/35.

76 "The Exchange Upset," St. John's Daily News, 8 July 1946; T. Wayfarer, "Dollars and Dollars," St.John's Daily News, 9 July 1946; Bank of Nova Scotia, "Memorandum on International Exchange Problems with Special Reference to Newfoundland," February 1945, NAC, RG25, vol. 2400, file 2757–40; J.S. MacDonald, letter to Secretary of State for External Affairs, 1 August 1945, and letter to N.A. Robertson, 30 January 1945, in NAC, RG25, vol. 2400, file 2757–40.

77 Muirhead 1999: 133.

78 See also Cornell 1956: 110–11.

79 J. Parkinson, "The High Value of the Canadian Dollar and Its Implications," 24 July 1957, pp9–10, 14–15, BCA, LR76-522-94-1. See also Cornell 1956: 370 for similar views in the early 1950s.

80 "Draft Minutes, IMF Executive Board Meeting 604,": 5–6. IMF managing director Camille Gutt made it clear that this advice was not an *official* IMF suggestion (Rasminsky, "Notes of Discussions": 3). IMF staff also suggested that Canada could offset upward pressure on the exchange rate through more active intervention in the foreign exchange market. They argued that extra foreign exchange reserves could be absorbed with open market operations (and the creation of new government debt, if necessary).

81 "Draft Minutes, IMF Executive Board Meeting 604": 6–7.

82 J. Horsefield, "Canada: The Problem of Capital Imports," pp10–11, IMF Executive Board Special No. 159, 29 September 1950, NAC, MG31, E14, vol. 2, file 8-IMF; "Draft Minutes, IMF Executive Board Meeting 604": 8.

83 Rasminsky, "Rough Notes": 6–7.

84 "Draft Minutes, IMF Executive Board Meeting 604": 6–7.

85 W.C. Clark, "Control of Movement of Funds to Foreign Countries," letter to H. Merle Cochran in U.S. Treasury, 11 December 1940, pp3, 6, NAC, RG19, vol. 3971, B-2-8-9-0. See also W.C. Clark, Canada's Exchange Deficit with the United States, 1941, p4, NAC, RG19, vol. 1941, B-2-8-9-1; Towers 1940: 7; McBain, "Address of": 4; Plumptre 1941: 190; J. Coyne, memo for W.C. Clark, 3 May 1941, p8, NAC, RG19, vol. 3991, file U-3-2-4-1.

86 Rasminsky, "Exports": 5.

87 Rasminsky, "Notes of Discussions": 2.

88 "Draft Minutes, IMF Executive Board Meeting 604": 6–7.

89 See discussion earlier in this chapter, as well as Rasminsky 1943b: 15–16.

90 Canada 1947: 2547.

91 Graham F. Towers, "Statement by Graham F.Towers before Senate Banking and Commerce Committee," 19 August 1946, pp4–5, BCA, FECB, vol. 29-2. See also Towers 1945; Fullerton 1986: 245; Canada 1946: 3044.

92 There was, however, strong support for permanent foreign exchange controls from CCF MPs (see for example Canada 1947: 3039–45, 4420–2, 4545).

93 Parkinson, "Some Reflections": 24.

94 Drew in Canada 1949a: 1616.

95 Canada 1947: 4414. See also Canada 1947: 3039, 4414, 4418, 4428, 4446–7, 4529; Canada 1949a: 1597, 1684.

96 Diefenbaker quoting Hayek in Canada 1948: 407.

97 Irvine in Canada 1947: 4422. See also 4545.

98 McDonnell in Canada 1949a: 1578; see also Canada 1947: 4528; Canada 1949a: 1591, 1712; Canada 1951: 1274. Defenders of exchange controls made the opposite case. Social Credit MP Victor Quelch argued that controls were needed in part to stop US capital inflows, which he saw as inflationary and as encouraging growing indebtedness to the US (Canada 1947: 3040–45, 4420).

99 Jackman in Canada 1947: 3047, 4434. See also 4434, 4446–8, 4511, 4526.

100 Plumptre 1948: 9.

101 Jackman in Canada 1947: 4431. See also 3048.

102 Canada 1947: 4423. See also 4423 and Canada 1949a: 1580, 1685.

103 Canada 1949a: 1685.

104 "A Method": 2. Coyne did, however, argue that the foreign exchange control system should remain in place, at least initially, in a floating system.

105 They preferred a float in which there would be a floor of 90 cents to avoid "wild fluctuation"; Canada 1949a: 1699.

106 Rowe in Canada 1949b: 1018–19. See also Canada 1947: 4417, 4431, 4529; Canada 1948: 422, 546; Canada 1949a: 1696; R. Dehem, "Exchange Rate Policy: Experience, Theory and Application to Canada," 4 September 1951, QUA, JD, box 93, file 961.

107 Canada 1949a: 1696.

108 "A Method": 1.

109 Hackett 1945.

110 C.L. Burton, letter to W.L. Mackenzie King, 7 October 1947, pp2, 3, NAC, RG19, vol. 3976.

111 Muirhead 1999: 139. Cornell notes support for a floating rate in the Canadian financial community since the fall of 1949 (1956: 212–13).

112 P.J. Keogh, "Canada – September–December 1950," pp9–10, BOE, OV58/5. After the Canadian dollar rose above parity with the US dollar in early 1952, a number of Canadian businesses in the tradable sector – such as those in mining and forestry – began to experience economic troubles as a result of the currency movement. With the onset of a recession in 1953–54, many of these business began to petition for the exchange rate to be lowered (Cornell 1956: 369–71, 381–2, 397).

113 Towers, "Memorandum re: Exchange Situation": 2.

114 See also Plumptre 1977: 145.

115 Rasminsky, "Notes of Discussions": 2. See also "Draft Minutes, IMF Executive Board Meeting 604": 8.

116 MacKintosh 1951: 52. See also Plumptre 1977: 145; Dehem, "Exchange Rate Policy."

117 See for example Dehem, "Exchange Rate Policy."

118 Friedman 1953. That article had in fact been written by Friedman in the fall of 1950 as a critique of the European Payments Union.

119 Friedman and Friedman 1998: 189. See also Schembri 2001: 31; Friedman 2001: 413.

120 It may also be worth noting that Donald Gordon left the Bank of Canada in the fall of 1949 before the decision to float was taken.

121 Quoted in Fullerton 1986: 244. See also Canada 1951: 1141.

122 Irvine in Canada 1949a: 1703. See also 1701–2, 1704; Canada 1947: 4421–2, 4545.

123 Canada 1947: 4420. See also 3040–5. Quelch had earlier been a strong opponent of Bretton Woods (Muirhead 1999: 108).

124 Royal Commission on Banking and Finance 1964: 481; De Vries 1969: 161–2; Canada 1962: 2696.

125 G.E. Freeman, "Recent Developments in Canada's Balance of Payments," presented at Meeting of Technicians of Central Banks of the American Continent, May 1954, p6, QUA, JD, box 68, file 488.

126 See for example Royal Commission on Banking and Finance 1964: 482; Wonnacott 1965.

127 Yeagar 1966: 425; Fullerton 1986: 247.

128 Fullerton 1986: 246; Muirhead 1999: 79.

129 Rasminsky, "Question of": 2. For Towers, see Fullerton 1986: 246.

130 Freeman 1954: 7. See also Cornell 1956: ch6.

131 Canada 1949a: 1579–80. At one point, however, McDonnell did seem to suggest the need for unilateral action (Canada 1949a: 1686, 1690].

132 Rasminsky, "Fund Discussion of": 5.

133 Muirhead 1999: 140–1.

134 Rasminsky, "Report on Washington": 5.

135 Horsefield 1969: 273–4. The IMF noted: "the Fund recognizes the exigencies of the situation which have led Canada to the proposed plan and takes note of the intention of the Canadian Government to remain in consultation with the Fund and to re-establish an effective par value as soon as circumstances warrant" (quoted in Horsefield 1969: 274).

136 Rasminsky, "Report on Washington": 5.

137 W. Goforth, "Reactions to the New Canadian 'Floating' Rate," 18 October 1950, p2, QUA, JD, box 93, file 961.

138 L. Rasminsky, "The Following Brief Notes Related to the Meeting of the Board May Be Of Assistance," 2 October 1950, p1, NAC, MG31, E14, vol. 2, file 8a. See also "Draft Minutes, IMF Executive Board Meeting 604": 8; Rasminsky, "Rough Notes": 9–10.

139 Canadian Ambassador to the United States to the Secretary of State for External Affairs, Canada, 3 October 1950, p1, BCA, LR76-522-4. See also Cornell 1956: 106.

140 Rasminsky, "Report on Washington": 4.

141 Cuff and Granatstein 1977.

142 Heilperin 1950: 228.

143 Rasminsky, "Report on Washington": 5.

144 Quoted in Canadian Ambassador to the United States to the Secretary of State for External Affairs, Canada, 3 October 1950, p1, BCA, LR76-522-4.

145 Fullerton 1986: 242–3.

146 See for example Muirhead 1999: 132; Parkinson, "Some Reflections": 23, 29–30; J. Parkinson, "Thoughts on Canadian-American Collaboration on Change in Canadian Dollar," September 1949, p4, NAC, MG31, E14, vol. 2, file 7-IMF.

147 "Draft Minutes, IMF Executive Board Meeting 604": 4. But Towers told a visiting Bank of England official soon after the decision that Canada was very unlikely to return to a fixed exchange rate "in the foreseeable future" (P.J. Keogh, "Canada September–December 1950," p9, BOE, OV58/5).

148 De Vries 1969: 161; Plumptre 1977: 149.

149 "Draft Minutes, IMF Executive Board Meeting 671," 30 April 1951, p5, NAC, MG31, E14, vol. 2, file 9-IMF.

150 De Vries 1969: 161–2.

151 D. Fleming 1985: 490.

152 D.L. McQueen, "A Growth Argument for a Fixed Exchange Rate,"
14 November 1962, p4, BCA, LR76-522-193.

153 Burnham 2003: 65.

154 Burnham 2003: especially 24–9. By 1952, the case for floating included
some broader goals, such as securing sterling's role as an international currency, forcing market-based discipline on the domestic economy, disrupting European integration, and bringing greater balance to Britain's
relationship with the US (Burnham 2003: 69–70). The IMF Executive
Board had also held an informal discussion of the merits of floating on
8–9 May 1951 because of the Canadian case, and the French had even put
forward a proposal to allow floating ("Rough Notes Informal Session 19,"
8 May 1951, and "Rough Notes – Informal Session 20," 9 May 1951, in
NAC, MG31, E14, vol. 2, file 9-IMF).

155 Burnham 2003: 65–6, 131–2.

156 Quoted in Burnham 2003: 66. Other parts of US government were, however, much less supportive of European countries adopting a floating rate,
and their views predominated. Both the State Department and Mutual Security Agency worried that this might undermine their broader strategic efforts to promote European economic and political integration through the
European Payments Union (Burnham 2003: 68). These agencies did not
become involved in determining US policy towards Canada's exchange
rate in this way.

157 Interestingly, British officials argued that British business had the same set
of preferences: "give them a choice between stability of import restrictions
and stability of exchange rates and they'll choose the first every time"
(Otto Clarke, quoted in Burnham 2003: 25).

158 Mundell 1971: 46.

159 L.F. Crick, "Visit to Canada, 17th–28th March 1951," 30 May 1951,
pp1–2, BOE, OV58/5.

CHAPTER FOUR

1 For Coyne's rejection of Keynesianism, see Granatstein 1986: 64. For
Towers, see Fullerton 1986: 256–7.

2 Recall that the bank's initial 1935 rate of 2.5 per cent had not been altered
until 1944 when it was moved to 1.5 per cent. The next change had come
in 1950 when the rate was raised to 2 per cent around the time of the float.

3 See for example Crow 2002: 11.

4 He had an undergraduate degree in history and math, and then studied law
at Oxford.

5 See for example Granatstein 1986: 72; J. Coyne, letter to Donald Fleming, 10 November 1960, NAC, RG19, F1(a), vol. 4099, B-30-1961.

6 A. Plumptre, "Mr. Coyne's Calgary Speech (October 5, 1960)," letter to Mr K.W. Taylor, 14 October 1960, pp7, 1, NAC, RG19, F1(a), vol. 4099. See also Dept of Finance, "Canadian Economic Policy for 1960 and 1961," 18 October 1960, p3, NAC, RG19, F1(a), vol. 4099, B-30-1961; J. Coyne, letter to Donald Fleming, 18 November 1960, pp1–2, NAC, RG19, F1(a), vol. 4099, B-30-1961.

7 D. Fleming 1985: 244.

8 D. Fleming 1985: 290.

9 Muirhead 1999: 194; D. Fleming 1985: 490–1; Canada 1962: 2696.

10 Quoted in Plumptre 1977: 163.

11 "Cabinet Conclusions, May 2, 1962," p2, NAC, RG2, vol. 619.

12 L. Rasminsky, "Fund Executive Board Meeting, May 2," 1962, p2, BCA, LR76-522-177.

13 D. Fleming 1985: 494–5; Granatstein 1986: 86–7.

14 Quoted in Granatstein 1986: 87.

15 Smith 1995: 438; D. Fleming 1985: 495–6.

16 Smith 1995: 438; Nash 1990: 165.

17 Muirhead 1999; Granatstein 1986: 88, 98.

18 Peter Cornell, "More Notes on Canadian Exchange Rate Policy," 16 November 1961, p2, BCA, LR76-522-163.

19 Muirhead 1999: 195–6.

20 Muirhead 1999: 195–6.

21 A. Plumptre, "Exchange Rate Policy," 23 August 1961, p2, BCA, LR76-522-159.

22 For the Bank of Canada, see Muirhead 1999: 195–6.

23 Plumptre, "Exchange Rate": 1–2.

24 De Vries 1969: 162–4; Muirhead 1999: 194–6; Lyon 1968: 331; D. Fleming 1985: 490–1. The British had become upset with the Canadian float even before Canada's announcement of its depreciation in June. See "Draft Letter to Mr. Plumptre," 1 March 1961, PRO, T312/2020.

25 See J. Fleming 1962; Mundell 1961a, 1962, 1963, 1964. For the importance of the Canadian experience to Mundell's thinking, see Thiessen 2000–01: 40; Sparks 1986: 148fn19.

26 Mundell 1961b, 1961a: 516fn8.

27 Louis Rasminsky, "Fund Executive Board Meeting," 2 May 1962, BCA, LR76-522-177.

28 "Cabinet Conclusions": 4.

29 D. Fleming 1985: 495. See also "Cabinet Conclusions": 3.

30 Canada 1962b: 272.

31 Plumptre, "Exchange Rate": 2.

32 Canada 1962: 2695.

33 "Cabinet Conclusions": 4.

34 Published later as McLeod 1965.

35 Canada 1962b: 1295.

36 Kierans 2001: 67, 107.

37 W. Earle McLaughlin, "Excerpt from Address Delivered by W. Earle McLaughlin, President, The Royal Bank of Canada at the 93rd Annual Meeting of Shareholders, January 11, 1962," p4, PRO, T312/2020.

38 D.L. McQueen, "A Growth Argument for a Fixed Exchange Rate," 14 November 1962, BCA, LR76-522-193.

39 Royal Commission on Banking and Finance, vol. 40, 18 September 1962, pp4916–18, NAC, RG33-64, vol. 26.

40 See for example D. Fleming 1985: 174; Plumptre 1977: 165.

41 Kierans 2001: 67; Canada 1962b: 1295; Royal Commission on Banking and Finance, vol. 52, 24 October 1962, pp6546–61, in NAC, RG33-64, vol. 27.

42 See for example Royal Commission on Banking and Finance 1964: 492.

43 Royal Commission on Banking and Finance, vol. 53, 25 October 1962, pp6663, 6668, 6670, 6673, NAC, RG33-64, vol. 27.

44 Some government officials who supported the move to a fixed rate, such as Plumptre ("Exchange Rate": 3, 7), had also acknowledged privately that the peg might have to be defended with capital or trade controls.

45 Quoted in Muirhead 1999: 200.

46 Royal Commission on the Economic Union 1985: 348.

47 The burden of adjustment was softened somewhat through the international loans from the US, Britain, and the IMF, as well as through the use of temporary import surcharges.

48 In addition, as noted below, Canada accepted "pass-through" guidelines that discouraged Canadian firms from relending their US borrowings to third countries. Muirhead 1999: 254–5; Plumptre 1977: 207–9; Wright 1974; Wright and Molot 1974.

49 See for example Wright and Molot 1974: 681. To preserve the currency peg in the face of capital inflows, Canadian authorities had to sell Canadian dollars against foreign currencies, and thus their reserve holdings of foreign currency rose. When the reserves went temporarily above the ceilings on a few occasions (e.g., late 1964 and late 1965), the Canadian government moved to discourage borrowing temporarily in the US, but these initiatives were strongly opposed by the Canadian business community and provinces

(Wright 1974: 149; Muirhead 1999: 266–9, 353fn24; Wright and Molot 1974: 676). Some analysts (e.g., Wonnacott 1971: 52–7) argue that the trajectory of Canadian monetary policy was not in fact altered very much by the reserve ceilings.

50 Wright and Molot 1974: 675; Wright 1974: 147, 153; Muirhead 1999: 259.

51 When these US controls had been introduced in a voluntary fashion in 1965, Canada had been exempt from the controls on US banks after it agreed to lower the reserve ceiling by $100 million (from $2.7 billion to $2.6 billion) and to control the pass-through of funds to third countries. It was not exempt, however, from the voluntary controls on direct investments (although Canadian pressure led the US to announce in 1966 that US subsidiaries in Canada did not need to follow the guidelines so strictly). When the US controls were made mandatory in early 1968, the exemption for bank activity remained, but it was once again not extended to the activities of US transnational companies in Canada (Wright and Molot 1974: 677–9).

52 Smith 1973: 341–1, 345.

53 Plumptre 1977: 216–7.

54 It also again agreed to make more serious efforts to block the pass-through of funds from the US to third countries. Muirhead 1999: 262–4, 271, 279; Wright 1974: 149; Wright and Molot 1974: 679.

55 Canadian officials succeeded after the crisis in gaining greater policy autonomy by securing an agreement in December 1968 that the reserve ceiling rule would be relaxed. Canadian officials pressed for this agreement when the reserve ceiling began to impose a severe constraint on domestic monetary policy in late 1968. The US agreed to this partly because of the earlier Canadian commitment to hold the country's US dollar reserves in US government non-liquid securities; in this context, it was no longer in the US interest to restrict the growth of Canada's reserves. US officials also recognized that the rising Canadian reserve increasingly reflected its borrowings from Europe rather than the US. Indeed, if Canada was forced to restrict these, it could work against the broader US objective of reducing European holdings of dollars (Wonnacott 1971: 45–7).

56 Muirhead 1999: 235.

57 Muirhead 1999: 239; R.W. Lawson, "Notes on Visit to Washington on May 31, 1970 to Explain Canada's Exchange Rate Decision," BCA, LR76-522-250; R.W. Lawson, "Reactions of Dr. Arthur Burns to Canada's Recent Exchange Rate Decision," 11 June 1970, BCA, LR76-522-251.

58 Kierans 2001: 191–6.

59 Lawson, "Reactions of": 1–2.

60 For example, Plumptre 1977: 220–1.
61 "Discussion re Canadian Exchange Rate at BIS, June 6–8, 1970," 19 June 1970, BCA, LR76-522-253.
62 Muirhead 1999: 235–40; De Vries 1976: 478–81; "Discussion re Canadian Exchange Rate."
63 "Discussion re Canadian Exchange Rate": 5.
64 R.W. Lawson, "Summary of Statement by Mr. W. Lawson of the Bank of Canada at the Meeting of the Economic Policy Committee Held 15th June, 1970," annex II of *The Canadian Exchange Rate Action, Working Party no. 3*, Economic Policy Committee, OECD, 30 June 1970, p2, BCA, LR76-522-257-2.
65 Lawson, "Notes on Visit": 3–4.
66 Summarized in "US Press Views of the Floating Dollar," *Globe and Mail*, 4 June 1970.
67 Muirhead 1999: 237–9.
68 Muirhead 1999: 236–7, 349fn25.
69 Department of Finance (Canada), "The International Monetary System," 22 May 1969, PRO, T312/2940. Even once the float had been in place for a year, Canadian officials remained keenly aware of the differing exchange rate preferences of domestic groups. As one Canadian official noted to the IMF, "what was an appropriate rate of exchange for the resource based industries of the far North might not be for the manufacturing sector of Ontario" (Mitchell, "IMF: Canada" no. 146/399/07, PRO, T312/2940).
70 See for example Johnson 1970; Canada 1968: 2738, 6514, 7322; Canada 1969: 4346, 7342–3.
71 Johnson 1970: 9.
72 Johnson 1970: 8.
73 Wolfe 1984.
74 Quoted in Canada 1968: 4469. See also Canada 1969: 4347–50, 5897; Canada 1968: 3226, 3803, 4469, 4537, 5417, 5763, 6803, 7342–3, 7368, 7401.
75 Canada 1970: 7631. See also Levitt 1970: 11–15.
76 Canada 1970: 7631.
77 Swift 1988: 246; Kierans 2001: 191–6.
78 George Post, "Economic Policy Discussion, June 1, 1970," p2, BCA, LR76-657-4; Kierans 2001: 191–6.
79 See nn48, 51, and 54 above.
80 Wright 1974: 157.
81 Levitt 1970: 15. Levitt also quotes a researcher for a Toronto investment house, W.A. Clendenning, arguing that the various balance of payments

agreements had in effect "welded Canada and the U.S. to a form of monetary union" (1970: 14). See also Strange 1976: 268.

82 Johnson 1970: 9.

83 R. Anderson, "Move May Soften Criticism in U.S.," *Globe and Mail*, 1 June 1970.

84 Canada 1970: 7524–7.

85 For the criticism from these sectors, see "Discussion re Canadian Exchange Rate": 2–3.

86 R. Dunn, "Some Aspects of Canada's Recent Experience with a Flexible Exchange Rate," prepared for the Board of Governors of the Federal Reserve System, 6 August 1971, p8, GF Arthur Burns Papers, box 34, "Federal Reserve Board Subject File: Eurodollars (2)," file: Exchange Rates 1971–75.

87 Wonnacott 1971: 64.

88 Quoted in Wonnacott 1971: 72.

89 R. B. McKibbin, letter to the Governor, 7 April 1971, BCA, LR76-522-269; W.C. Hood, "Telephone Call from Mr. Petty, Jan.18, 1971," BCA, LR76-375-34; Wonnacott 1971: 74–8. Government officials were even talking to Canadian and US underwriters about discouraging foreign borrowing. In this same period, the US was also pressing Canada to control capital inflows as a means of helping the US balance of payments situation. In January 1971, for example, one US official suggested that if Canada's federal-provincial relations prevented the government from rationing access to US borrowing then perhaps the US Treasury could take on the role (Hood, "Telephone": 2).

90 Minister of Finance, "Draft Memorandum to the Cabinet: Exchange Policy, March 24, 1971," BCA, LR76-522-265; Minister of Finance, "Draft Memorandum to Cabinet, Policies Affecting the Exchange Rate, May 26, 1971," BCA, LR76-522-270. Regarding the latter, government considered ending the "pass-through" guidelines that Canada had agreed to in the 1960s which limited overseas investment by Canadian firms. It was hoped that move would not only encourage capital outflows but more importantly might prompt the US to end the IET exemption.

91 Muirhead 1999: 291–3; Plumptre 1977: 253. An internal Fed memo from 19 August 1971 calculated the realignment of foreign currencies that were necessary for US to meet its balance of payments targets. It calculated that Canada's dollar needed to rise 12.5 per cent from its mid-1970 level. Only 5 per cent of this had been accomplished at this time; R.G. Bryant, G.Henry, H. Junz, and S. Pizer, "The Magnitude of the U.S. Imbalance and the Changes in Exchange Rates Required," 19 August 1971, GF Arthur Burns Papers, box B54, file: G-10 Ministers Meeting, London, 15–16 September 1971, Briefing Book.

92 A.K. Rowlinson, "Conservation with Mr. Tait," 14 December 1971, PRO, T312/2940; Hayman, "International Monetary Situation" and "International Monetary Situation: Further Canadian Reactions," PRO, T312/2940.

93 De Vries 1985: 40–1.

94 See for example Dunn, "Some Aspects."

95 Fieleke 1971.

96 Chittenden 1971: 198.

97 "Cabinet Conclusions, August 25, 1971," pp2, 5, and "Cabinet Conclusions September 1, 1971," NAC, RG2, vol. 6381; Minister of Finance, "Memorandum to the Cabinet: A Dual Exchange Market, September 7, 1971," BCA, LR76-522-278.

98 G. Williams 1994: 148.

99 "Cabinet Conclusions, October 21, 1971," p15, NAC, RG2, vol. 6381; Minister of Finance, "Draft Memorandum to the Cabinet: The Problem of the Appreciation of the Canadian Dollar, June 9, 1972," BCA, LR76-522-288; "Dual Exchange Markets," 24 April 1972, BCA, LR76-522-282.

100 Turner 1972.

101 "Introduction of Dual Exchange Markets," 7 July 1972, BCA, LR76-522-288; "Dual Exchange Markets."

102 Webb 1992: 167; Crow 2002: 143–4; Courchene 1976.

103 Campbell 1987: 6. See also Drainville 1995; Wolfe 1984.

104 See Donner and Peters 1979; Courchene 1981. Courchene moved to Queen's University in 1988.

105 See for example G. Williams 1994: 149–50; Maslove and Swimmer 1980: 8.

106 See for example Sparks 1986: 135–6.

107 McNamara 1998: 10.

108 G. Williams 1994: 149.

109 Donner and Peters 1979: 24; Campbell 1987: 6; Maslove and Swimmer 1980.

110 Donner and Peters 1979: 23, 29–35, 65.

111 G. Williams 1994: 147–52.

112 For example, Royal Commission on the Economic Union 1985: 307–8.

113 Quoted in Howitt 1986: 94fn6. See also Donner and Peters 1979: 11, 35–7; Howitt 1986: 4; Courchene 1981: 87–90; 1983.

114 Howitt 1986: 92–3, 96–7, 113–17; Courchene 1983: 90.

115 Sparks 1986: 146–7; Crow 2002: 147–58; Laidler and Robson 1993: 84–5; Howitt 1986: 92–3, 96–7; Courchene 1983.

116 See for example McNamara 1998.

117 Clarkson 1985: 164–71; Babad and Mulroney 1995: 185–8; Howitt 1986: 1, 94, 99.

118 Indeed, Howitt notes that, if a trade-weighted index is used, Canada's effective exchange rate appreciated somewhat in real terms in 1981–83 and perhaps even in nominal terms (1986: 69–72, 98, 119–23).

119 Howitt 1986: 1.

120 Quoted in G. Williams 1994: 172.

121 Howitt 1986: 99–105.

122 P. Fortin 2000: 43.

123 Laidler and Robson 1990.

124 Brodie 1990: 28–9.

125 Mackintosh 1964: 177.

126 Innis 1995: 47.

CHAPTER FIVE

1 Howitt 1986: 70.

2 Williamson 1987.

3 Destler and Henning 1989: ch6.

4 Williamson 1987: 172.

5 Destler and Henning 1989: 130; US Congress 1993b: 89–90; Hart 1994: 162; John Valorzi, "Trade Deal Won't Set Dollar, Lobby Says," *Toronto Star*, 18 January 1989; David Crane, "Control of Value of Our Dollar May Be Lost in Free-Trade Pact," *Toronto Star*, 22 March 1986. This suggestion was very similar to the exchange rate clauses in the 1935 and 1938 trade agreements, although I have found no reference to these earlier agreements in the discussions surrounding the FTA.

6 See for example US Congress 1993b: 2–3.

7 Laurie 1993: 297; Crane, "Control of Value."

8 Baucus 1987: 22. Baucus noted that the other three issues concerning Congress were regional effects, agriculture, and contingent protection.

9 Laurie 1993: 296.

10 Laurie 1993: 297; Barlow and Campbell 1991: 17–18. As early as 1984, US Trade Representative William Brock speculated about whether a free trade agreement should be combined with closer macroeconomic policy coordination between the two countries as a way to reduce trade tensions (1984: 72–3). His successor, Clayton Yeutter was more explicit in raising the exchange rate issue in connection with the FTA (Wonnacott 1987: 10).

11 Peter Torday, "U.S. Suggests Ottawa Holds Dollar Down," *Globe and Mail*, 21 May 1986; Hart 1994: 162.

12 Laurie 1993.

13 Putnam and Bayne 1987: 208–9, 217; Funabashi 1987: 137.

14 See for example Doern and Tomlin 1991: 292; Burney 2000: 65–6.

15 Hart 1994: 162. See also Patricia Chisholm, "The Dollar Debates," *MacLean's*, 31 October 1988.

16 Crow 2002: 97–100. Other accounts of the Louvre Accord seem to confirm that this currency agreement was agreed among the G-5, not the G-7; Funabashi 1987: ch8; Volcker and Gyohten 1992: 282.

17 Funabashi 1987: 141.

18 Crow 2002: 102.

19 One further piece of evidence against the idea that the deal was reached might be the fact that the U.S. National Association of Manufacturers did not think the deal had been made. In early 1989, its senior trade official was quoted: "we fought that battle when the deal was being negotiated and we lost it." He argued that his group would raise the issue again if the Canadian dollar fell sharply with the implementation of the free trade agreement (Valorzi, "Trade Deal").

20 Lipsey 1985: 15.

21 Courchene 1990a: 198. See also Wonnacott 1987: 128–9; Hall 1985.

22 Quotes from Royal Commission on the Economic Union 1985: 310, 388. See also pp310–25.

23 Royal Commission on the Economic Union 1985: 310.

24 Royal Commission on the Economic Union 1985: 310, 315, 319.

25 Howitt 1986: 135–6.

26 For an account of Crow's anti-inflationary obsession, see McQuaig (1995: ch3).

27 Harris 1993: 36; Crow 2002: 118, 218. Indeed, in his important January 1988 Eric Hanson Memorial Lecture that set the stage for the monetary tightening, Crow had acknowledged that the precise impact of the monetary policy on the exchange rate was difficult to predict (1988: 9–10). In January 1988, he had also told a House of Commons committee: "I do not think a great deal will happen [to the exchange rate]; we are not talking about the difference between night and day" (quoted in G. Williams 1994: 208fn91).

28 Harris 1993: 36. The situation in fact resembled the US experience in the early 1980s, a point that led some to criticize Crow for not anticipating the problem (e.g., Courchene 1990a). Lipsey had discussed the US experience in the early 1980s but argued it could not happen in Canada because "in the disaster scenario following Canada-United States trade liberalization, capital flees Canada" (1985: 16). Wonnacott had also warned explicitly about the danger of an overly tight monetary policy encouraging excessive capital inflows, and had discussed both the US situation and the earlier Coyne

episode in this respect (1987: 10, 130). He concluded that: "it is important to get macroeconomic policies right" (130).

29 Laidler and Robson 1993: 99; Webb 1992: 180.

30 Crow 2002: 219; see also Crow 1988: 20; Crow 2002: 218; Laidler and Robson 1993: 120–1; Webb 1992: 180.

31 Laidler and Robson 1993: 101–4.

32 Crow 2002: 219.

33 Crow 2002: 122, 163; G. Williams 1994: 171–4; McQuaig 1995: 73–4, 92–3, 101–2, 105; Laidler and Robson 1993: 123.

34 Quotes from Royal Commission on the Economic Union 1985: 310, 360. See also 338–61.

35 See for example G. Williams 1994: 174–6; McQuaig 1995.

36 Courchene 1990a, 1990b, 1992: 172–90; Harris 1993. Courchene stopped short of fully endorsing a fixed exchange rate in his 1990 writings, but he endorsed it as a goal "over the medium term" elsewhere (Courchene 1992: 185).

37 Harris 1993: 41.

38 Lucas and Reid 1991.

39 Grubel 1999: 35, 45fn43.

40 I have not included Grubel's ideas in the following discussion because his work remained unpublished. Grubel noted that his arguments in this earlier period were similar to those that he presented in 1999 (1999: 35). These are described in the next chapter.

41 Harris 1993: 35.

42 Quotes from Courchene 1990a: 195; Courchene 1992: 179.

43 Sparks 1986: 125

44 Lucas and Reid 1991: 430.

45 Fortin (1990) endorsed a fix with a wide 10 per cent band in order to allow the exchange rate to continue to play some role as a shock absorber to external shocks.

46 See also Harris 1993: 44–6.

47 P. Fortin 1990: 139–40; see also Royal Commission on the Economic Union 1985: 343–50.

48 Courchene 1992: 184.

49 Another critic of Canada's floating rate, Mundell, was also highly critical of Crow and previous Bank of Canada policy: "Never since the Federal Reserve let itself get dragged into the Great Depression in the early 1930s has a central bank done so much harm to its people! Had Canada fixed its dollar in the 1970s at parity with the US dollar, it would have had less inflation

than it did in the 1970s and much less unemployment than it had in the 1980s – and it still would have had a viable Conservative Party!" (*Financial Post*, 12 December 2000).

50 Lucas and Reid 1991: 430.

51 Laidler and Robson 1990; Laidler 1990; Laidler and Robson 1991. See also McQuaig 1995: 134–9, 156–64, 246–8.

52 See also Purvis 1990: 57–8.

53 Laidler and Robson 1993: 175. See also Laidler and Robson 1991: appendix B.

54 Laidler and Robson 1991: 49.

55 Purvis 1990: 58.

56 W. White 1994: 23–4.

57 For the view from the bank, see Crow 1993, 1995.

58 Laidler and Robson 1993.

59 G. Williams 1994.

60 Norma Greenaway, "U.S. Trade Chief Rejects Idea of Common Currency," *Montreal Gazette*, 7 February 1991.

61 Quoted in US Congress 1993b: 90.

62 Mancera 1991.

63 Feldstein 1991.

64 Laidler 1991b.

65 See especially Bayoumi and Eichengreen 1994.

66 US Congress 1993b: 40, 2. See also US Congress 1993a: 10–11.

67 US Congress 1993b: 16–17, 89–90.

68 US Congress 1993a: 60–1.

69 US Congress 1993b: 7, 54–55.

70 US Congress 1993a: 49–51, 54. An economist with the American Federation of Labor-Congress of Industrial Organizations (AFL-CIO) also expressed similar fears before Congress at Lafalce's earlier committee hearing (US Congress 1993b: 24–5).

71 An economist with Mexican Action Network on Free Trade, Andres Penaloza, suggested tentative support for the idea in his testimony before Congress: "we must formulate monetary agreements where there is a co-responsibility for the stability of currencies. People must recognize the weakness of our currency as well as its very special condition in the border states" (US Congress 1993a: 202). But he also added that the control of currency was a very key element of a country's sovereignty.

72 Henning 1994: 294.

73 Quote from US Congress 1993b: 22. See also ibid., 2.

74 US Congress 1993b: 20, 35.

75 Kelly McParland, "US$8B Currency Crisis Pact Set," *Financial Post*, 27 April 1994; Douglas Goold, "Credit for Mexico Has Limited Risk," *Globe and Mail*, 20 January 1995.

76 Support came from the IMF, the BIS, and the US Exchange Stabilization Fund. In early January, in the wake of the crisis, the US agreed to raise its swap arrangements with Mexico from $6 billion to $9 billion. Canada also increased its commitment from $1 billion to $1.5 billion at this time (Goold, "Credit for Mexico").

77 Quoted in Graham 1995.

78 Quoted in Gordon Platt, "Let 'Eagle' Fly as Single Currency Economists Urge," *Toronto Star*, 27 August 1995.

79 Platt, "Let 'Eagle' Fly." See also Dorn and Salinas-Leon 1996 for more general discussion of North American monetary integration at this time.

80 Henning 1994: 307.

CHAPTER SIX

1 Grubel 1999.

2 For example, see Ernst 1992.

3 Courchene and Harris 1999.

4 In static terms, Grubel estimated this efficiency gain at about 0.1 per cent of national income, or about $800 million (1999: 9).

5 Justine Hunter, "US Dollar Could Lift our Economy 37%," *National Post*, 19 May 2001. See Rose and Frankel 2002.

6 Courchene 1998: 301. He had developed this thesis in detail in his 1998 book *From Heartland to North American Region State*, co-authored with Colin Telmer.

7 Anne Golden, "In Loonies, We Should Trust." *Globe and Mail*, 29 November 2001.

8 As Courchene and Harris (1999) note, this argument of Grubel was different from their own belief that *misalignments* in exchange rates could delay productivity improvements.

9 Grubel 1999: 43fn13. See also 12–14, 17–18.

10 In Europe, these rules had been seen as necessary to prevent large fiscal deficits in one country from influencing monetary conditions in the entire euro zone.

11 Canada 1999a: 35.

12 Grubel 1999: 15.

13 Courchene and Harris 1999: 15.

14 Zev Singer, "Adopt US Dollar, High-Tech Chief Says," *Ottawa Citizen*, 14 May 2001; Bruce Wallace, "Say It Ain't So," *Maclean's*, 5 July 1999;

Eric Reguly, "Relax, the US dollar Is Already Deeply Rooted," *Globe and Mail*, 26 January 2002.

15 Grubel 1999: 25.

16 The second argument, about the different impacts of exchange rate movements across different regions, was more distinctive to the Canadian case.

17 See for example Carroll and Shaw 2001.

18 See for example Daniel LeBlanc, "Youthful Reform, Bloc MPs Urge United Alternative Currency," *Globe and Mail*, 5 June 1999. A motion from the Bloc Québécois to set up a committee to study monetary union in early 1999 was supported by the Conservative Party and some members of the Canadian Alliance (Marc MacKinnon and Bruce Little, "Canada's Dollar Headed to the Altar?" *Globe and Mail*, 24 June 1999). In June 1999, three Alliance MPs – Jason Kenney, Rahim Jaffer, and Rob Anders – signed a letter with five other Bloc MPs calling for a debate in Parliament on the issue (LeBlanc 1999; Grubel 1999: 46). In October 2000, Kenney also said that the Alliance would be open to exploring the idea of a common currency, although the party's leader at the time, Stockwell Day, said the party did not support it (Tonda MacCharles, "Day Kills Monetary Union Talk," *Toronto Star*, 18 October 2000). In 2001, Day did argue "we need to start discussing dollarization or common currency" (David Crane, "Canadian Monetary Policy Worth Keeping," *Toronto Star*, 4 July 2002).

19 This argument is an updated version of Chant and Acheson's 1972 "public choice" interpretation of the Bank of Canada's behaviour which asserted that many of the bank's actions were driven primarily by concerns of "prestige and self-preservation" (Chant and Acheson 1972: 14). In my view, the importance of this argument is overstated both historically and in the context of the NAMU debate. In Europe, too, few national central banks – the German Bundesbank is an important exception – approached the introduction of the euro with these kinds of considerations at the top of their agenda.

20 Laidler and Poschmann 2000; Robson and Laidler 2002.

21 Although Mundell was very critical of Canada's floating exchange rate for the reasons that supporters of NAMU are, he did not support the creation of a new North American currency or the idea that Canada adopt the US dollar. Instead, he has advocated a hard peg (e.g., Mundell 2000). The debate was reprinted in *Policy Options*, May 2001.

22 Schembri 2001: 33.

23 See for example Robson and Laidler 2002.

24 Mintz and Aba 2002; M. Lévesque 2002.

25 See for example Robson and Laidler 2002; Toronto Dominion Economics 2001: 20; Drummond and Lévesque 2001; McCallum 2000: 239–40.

26 Robson and Laidler 2002: 10–11.

27 Murray 2003: 360.

28 Crow 2002: 125–30.

29 *National Post*, 12 December 2000.

30 See for example Crane, "Canadian Monetary Policy."

31 Thiessen 2000b: 21–2.

32 Even Crow endorsed this policy (2002: 237).

33 Quoted in Les Whittington, "Monetary Union Could Hurt Canada," *Toronto Star*, 5 December 2000.

34 *National Post*, 13 December 2000.

35 Grubel 2000: 249.

36 For example, Robson and Laidler 2002; Laidler and Poschmann 2000: 14.

37 See for example Thiessen 2000b: 21. Primary products were about 35 per cent of total Canadian exports in 1999, down from 60 per cent in 1973 (P. Fortin 2000: 46).

38 For example, Crow 1999: 29. Upward pressure on the US dollar was also reinforced by the fact that many people believed the US dollar to be a relatively safe currency during the international financial crisis.

39 See for example Thiessen 2000b; McCallum 2000: 233–5.

40 Quoted in Drew Fagan, "Governor Carries the Banner for Independent Policy," *Globe and Mail*, 29 December 2001. See also Alan Toulin, "Rift Opens over Dollar's Future," *National Post*, 3 May 2001; Dodge 2002.

41 Quoted in Eric Beauchesne, "Single Currency Not So 'Wacky': Bank," *Ottawa Citizen*, 7 May 2001.

42 Murray 2003.

43 Quoted in MacKinnon and Little, "Canada's Dollar."

44 Laidler and Poschmann 2000: 1; Murray and Powell 2002.

45 For a discussion of the importance of "network externalities" in the use of currencies, see Cohen 1998.

46 Robson and Laidler 2002: 7.

47 See for example Doern and Tomlin 1991; Langille 1987.

48 Theobald 1999. See also Janet McFarland, "Reporting Results the American Way a Growing Trend," *Globe and Mail*, 2 July 1999; Shawn McCarthy, "Liberals Study Closer Ties to US at Cabinet Retreat," *Globe and Mail*, 24 June 1999.

49 Wallace, "Say It." For the BCNI's earlier role in promoting the Canada-US Free Trade Agreement, see Langille 1987.

50 Gordon Pitts, "Time to Scrap the Loonie, Nesbitt Economist Says," *Globe and Mail*, 9 November 2001; Singer, "Adopt."

51 Sandra Rubin, "Drop Loonie, 45% Say in Business Poll," *National Post*, 16 July 2001.

52 Canadian Chamber of Commerce 2002; D'Aquino 2002: 4. But D'Aquino also noted in this speech that the issue of NAMU was high on the agenda of his group's newly formed "North American Committee." In late 2001, D'Aquino also argued that NAMU was likely over the longer term: "Can one assume that the Canadian dollar will be able to function on its own for the fifteen to twenty years, probably not. ... do you think we would have a common currency in less than fifteen years? I would say, yes, it's distinctly possible" (quoted in an interview on *The National*, 1 November 2001, "The National Transcript," <www.tv.cbc.ca/national/trans/T011101.html>, p2.

53 Golden, "In Loonies."

54 P. Fortin 2000: 43.

55 Grubel 1999: 38; Courchene and Harris 1999: 26.

56 Clarkson 2000: 159; Sidney Weintraub and Christopher Sands, "Why Dollarization Is a Canadian Affair," *Globe and Mail*, 21 February 2002. In 1993, 38 per cent of Canadian imports from the US and 45 per cent of exports to the US involved intra-corporate transactions (Clarkson 2002: 190–1).

57 Canada 1999a: 13.

58 Bernard Simon, "Mixed Blessings of Canada's Currency," *New York Times*, 15 January 2002; Michael McCullough, "Debate over Canada Adopting U.S. Greenback Rises to Surface: Western Canada Would Be Stable," *Vancouver Sun*, 26 May 2001; McFarland, "Reporting Results"; Steven Theobald, "Economists Debate Monetary Union," *Toronto Star*, 24 June 1999; Wallace, "Say It."

59 McNamara 1998: 37–41, 98–104.

60 Grubel 1999: 37–8.

61 Jayson Myers quoted in Simon, "Mixed Blessings."

62 See for example Simon, "Mixed Blessings"; Singer, "Adopt"; Peter Kennedy, "Weak Loonie Seen to Offset Lumber Duties," *Globe and Mail*, 29 January 2002.

63 Bowles 2003a: 26fn13.

64 Grubel 1999: 37–8.

65 Toronto Dominion Economics 2004: 12.

66 Toronto Dominion Economics 2004: 12; Hogue 2003.

67 For example, Toronto Dominion Economics 2001; McCallum 1999, 2000. John McCallum, chief economist at the Royal Bank at the time (and subsequently a cabinet minister in the Liberal government), has been a particularly vocal opponent of NAMU.

68 For example, Hunter 1991: 147; Marian Stinson, "Dollar Dealing Peters to a Halt," *Globe and Mail*, 28 October 1995.

69 Jones 1998: 197.

70 As Laxer notes, this was largely because of the existence of a "British sub-ject clause" since the nineteenth century which required that the directors of a bank – or at least a majority of them, after the law was altered in 1890 – be British subjects (1989: 216–18).

71 Laidler and Poschmann 2000: 17; Robson and Laidler 2002: 18; Courchene and Harris 1999: 21. The importance of the issue of access to clearing sys-tems has been apparent in the European context. In the lead-up to the cre-ation of the euro in Europe, private bankers from countries such as Switzerland and the UK expressed deep concerns about the threat to their business if the new payments and settlements system for the euro – called TARGET – discriminated against banks from countries that did not join the euro (e.g., Gillian Tett, "Euro Hopes Left out in Cold," *Financial Times,* 2 August 1996; Gillian Tett, "EU 'Risks Financial War' over Target," *Financial Times,* 23 October 1996; Andrew Gowers and Gillian Tett, "Bank of England Chief Warns of EMU Rift," *Financial Times,* 16 Septem-ber 1996.

72 See for example Nystrom 2002; Jackson 2000; Blacklock 2000; Seccareccia 2002, 2003; Stanford 2003; Wallace, "Say It." For the FTA debate, see for example Doern and Tomlin 1991.

73 See for example Vaiou 1995; Young 2000; Green Party 1994.

74 Notermans 2001: 4. See also Rhodes 2002; Josselin 2001.

75 Notermans 2001.

76 Rhodes 2002: 310.

77 Veiden 2001.

78 Notermans 2001: 270.

79 McNamara 1998.

80 Aylott 2001: 159.

81 Notermans 2001.

82 Pekkarinen 2001.

83 Gamble and Kelly 2001; Josselin 2001.

84 Nystrom 2002; Jackson 2000. Blacklock highlights how these pressures would be particularly negative for many women who "form the core of the non-unionized flexible labour force in Canada" (2000: 2). She also notes that if NAMU were accompanied by fiscal constraints women would be more negatively affected by welfare state cutbacks because they "underpin the care economy." These concerns are also raised by European feminists in their analyses of EMU (Vaiou 1995; Young 2000).

85 Jackson 2000: 6.

86 Ken Georgetti, "It Would Be Folly to Adopt the US Dollar," *Globe and Mail,* 2 July 1999.

87 Ken Georgetti, "It Would Be Folly."
88 Jackson 2000: 3.
89 Nystrom 2002.
90 Nystrom 2002: 2.
91 Stanford 2003: 62.
92 "In Defence of Canada's Independent Dollar," *Globe and Mail*. 14 August
   2001.
93 Quoted in Stueck 2002.
94 McCallum 1999: 6.
95 Courchene and Harris 1999: 24.
96 Courchene and Harris 1999: 14.
97 For example, Jackson 2000: 2, 5.
98 Robson and Laidler 2002: 12.
99 Sandra Rubin, "Loonie Gone within Five Years, Says CIBC's Rubin," *Financial Post*, 28 July 2001. See also Wallace, "Say It." The BCNI also highlighted in 1999 that one reason it opposed NAMU was its conclusion "that
   the debate itself was not worth the traumatic clash it would provoke with
   economic nationalists" (Wallace, "Say It").
100 See for example Jonung 2004.
101 Haxby 1983: ch12.
102 J.A.C. Osborne, "Bank of Canada Notes," 4 Febrary 1936, p7, QUA, WC.
103 Another nationalist issue concerning the Bank of Canada notes related to
   their bilingual wording. For this issue, see chapter 8.
104 Nystrom 2002: 1.
105 Martin Goldfarb, "A Country Is Not a Business," *Globe and Mail*, 2 January 2002.
106 Golden, "In Loonies."
107 Quoted in Wallace, "Say It." See also P. Fortin 2000: 43.
108 Courchene and Harris 1999: 22; Grubel 1999: 5.
109 Canada 1999a: 6.
110 Helleiner 2003a.
111 P. Fortin 2000; for Mundell, see "Dollars, Taxes, and the State," *Financial
   Post*, 13 April 2000. See also Buiter 1999.

CHAPTER SEVEN

1 Grubel argues that the board of his North American Central Bank would have
  representation from all three countries, with the specific level of representation
  being determined "according to their economic importance" (2000: 245).
2 Harris 2000: 95. See also Courchene 1998: 324; Courchene and Harris
  2000: 15. For a similar argument, see Marceau 1999.

3 For example, Courchene and Harris 1999: 25.

4 For a more detailed discussion of this history, see Helleiner 2003b.

5 In its colony of Puerto Rico, the US made the US dollar the exclusive currency.

6 See Kemmerer 1916.

7 For the meaning of "seigniorage," see ch1 n54.

8 Robert Barro, "Let the Dollar Range from Seattle to Santiago," *The Wall Street Journal*, 8 March 1999.

9 Quoted in "Resistance to Argentine 'Dollar,'" *New York Times*, 24 January 1999.

10 Courchene and Harris 1999.

11 William Walker, "Currency Issue May Reach Cabinet," *Toronto Star*, 24 June 1999; Carlsen 2003. In 1999, however, Fox's party, the National Action Party, had proposed a Congressional bill to rule out dollarization (Julia Preston, "Mexico Measures Identity in Dollars," *New York Times*, 19 May 1999).

12 Formal dollarization might also have the advantage of ending a kind of currency mismatch between assets and liabilities which exacerbated financial crises. For these various arguments in favour of dollarization, see for example Schuler and Stein 2000; Schuler 2000; Hausmann 1999; Jameson 2001; Starr 2001.

13 For example, McTeer 2000; Chriszt 2000; Velde and Veracierto 2000.

14 Mack 2000: 2.

15 Mack 2000: 3.

16 Schuler and Stein 2000: 6.

17 Quoted in Schuldt 2003: 241.

18 Schuler and Stein 2000: 8. In a broader sense, the political economist Benjamin Cohen (2002) – himself not a supporter of dollarization diplomacy – has also noted that full dollarization could give the US extra leverage over foreign governments. He recalls the way in which the Panamanian government was vulnerable to US monetary pressures during the Noriega years because of its dependence on the dollar for its currency. See also Kirshner 1995.

19 Quoted in Ines Capdevila, "The Benefits of Dollarization." *National Post*, 19 February 2000. See also Schuler and Stein 2000: 5.

20 Michael Gavin in US Senate 1999b. See also the comments of David Malpass in US Senate 1999b.

21 Judy Shelton in US Senate 1999a. See also Schuler and Stein 2000: 7.

22 Summers 1999: 3.

23 Bogetic 2000; Rochon and Seccareccia 2003: 6.

24 Schuler and Stein 2000: 8.

25 Cohen 2002; D'Arista 2000: 5; Rochon and Seccareccia 2003: 5.

26 For the supporters, see the testimony of David Malpass (of Bear, Stearns and Co.) and Michael Gavin (of Warburg Dillon Read) in US Senate (1999b).

27 Summers 1993: 32.

28 Cohen 2002.

29 Mack 2000: 3.

30 Mack 2000: 3. See also Schuler and Stein 2000: 7.

31 Quote from D'Arista 2000:3.

32 Summers 1999: 3.

33 For example, Altig 2002; Beddoes 1999.

34 Bergsten 1999: 5. In response to these arguments, some supporters of dollarization diplomacy have argued that there is a simple way to guarantee that the Fed is not influenced by foreign pressure. This could be accomplished by changing the Federal Reserve Act to make its purpose that of pursuing price stability (Schuler 2000: 11). This change might also increase the attractiveness of full dollarization abroad since the dollar's value would be more trustworthy (US Senate 1999a).

35 US Senate 1999a.

36 Quoted in Jonathan Peterson, "Latin America Ponders Dollar as Currency of the Realm," *The Detroit News*, 3 April 1999.

37 Schuler and Stein 2000: 7.

38 Chriszt 2000: 35. Although Chriszt opposed dollarization, he supported the idea of North American monetary union based on a more ambitious European-style model.

39 Sidney Weintraub and Christopher Sands, "Why Dollarization Is a Canadian Affair," *Globe and Mail*, 21 February 2002.

40 Bergsten 1999: 5.

41 Bergsten 1999: 6.

42 Spiegel 1999: 2.

43 Chriszt 2000: 34–5.

44 Grubel 1999: 30–2; Courchene and Harris 1999: 22.

45 Helleiner 2003b.

46 Cohen 2002: 73.

47 Summers 1999: 4.

48 Quoted in Spiegel 1999: 2.

49 The one minor concession has been the suggestion in some US quarters that the US might be willing to produce US dollar notes with different designs for each foreign country that dollarized. See for example Schuler and Stein 2000: 11.

50 Chriszt 2000: 37.

51 NFO CFgroup 2002.

52 Laidler and Poschmann 2000: 18. See also Robson and Laidler 2002; "A Single Currency? The US Won't Buy It," *Globe and Mail*, 4 July 2002.

53 Robson and Laidler 2002: 12.
54 Quoted in Alan Toulin, "Dollar Dip 'Deviation' Says Report," *National Post*, 4 April 2001.
55 Anne Golden, "In Loonies, We Should Trust," *Globe and Mail*, 29 November 2001.
56 In their 1999 publication, Courchene and Harris argued that it was "presumably a non-starter, except as a last resort" (21). In his 1999 Senate testimony, Courchene was also ambivalent: "Unlike an average economist, there is a bit of nationalism in me that suggests 'NAMU, yes; dollarization, not sure'" (Canada 1999a: 34). See also Grubel 1999: 27. Perhaps chastened by the outcome of the US debate, Courchene and Harris two years later suggested that they were in fact willing to argue that unilateral dollarization was still superior to Canada's existing floating exchange rate (Eric Beauchesne, "Canada Needs US Dollar: Report," *Ottawa Citizen*, 7 May 2001).
57 Mundell 2000.
58 Courchene and Harris 1999: 17. This point is also applicable to the NAMU proposal since advocates envision a transition phase to NAMU in which Canada first establishes a fixed exchange rate (Courchene and Harris 1999: 20–3; Grubel 1999: 29). See also McCallum 2000: 235–6.
59 P. Fortin 2000. See also McCallum 2000: 229–31, 241.
60 Weintraub and Sands, "Why Dollarization."
61 William Daley quoted in Walker, "Currency Issue."
62 Cohen 2002. US labour groups have also not been actively engaged in the issue (Cohen 2002).
63 Molano 2000: 5.
64 The only reference I have seen to the Canadian exchange rate in US Congressional debates during the time of dollarization debates came in January 2001 when some members of Congress expressed concerns about how the depreciation of Canada's currency was contributing to the widening US trade deficit with Canada. But the point was not even made in the context of the dollarization debate. It referred to a study that argued that the Canadian depreciation only had a major impact on the trade deficit in agricultural products; for trade in industrial products, the impact was much less substantial (Kim et al 2001; US Congress 2001).
65 Weintraub and Sands, "Why Dollarization."
66 See for example Kaltenthaler 1998.
67 Grubel 1999; Courchene and Harris 1999: 23. See also Cohen's analysis (2002).
68 Under their proposal, Canada would also keep seigniorage revenue, as well as maintain its existing clearing system and its own national financial regulatory

system. They also suggest Canada's currency could retain distinctive national symbols while bearing the mark of the North American central bank.

69 For these two suggestions, see Roy Culpepper, "A Common Currency for the Americas?" *Globe and Mail*, 23 March 2001; Pastor 2001: 114, respectively. These suggestions raise the question of whether different regions in Canada would be represented in some way. Nystrom, for example, predicts that Canada might be divided into four reserve districts: "one reserve bank for Central Canada, another one each for western and eastern Canada and one bank for Québec" (2002: 1). This scenario would, however, raise an obvious constitutional complication; the federal government retains exclusive power over issues relating to currency. Since it would also complicate the voting structure on the FOMC, the US might resist this strongly. An alternative decision-making model might be to retain a single reserve bank for Canada but create a number of regional branches within it. Most of the existing US reserve banks have such branches, each with their own boards of directors. These directors, however, are selected in a centralized manner by both the respective reserve bank directors and the federal board of governors (Havrilesky 1995: 2). This method of representation would obviously not be very attractive to regional voices in Canada.

70 Former bankers are also prominent (Woolley 1984: 78). For the election process, private banks are divided into three groups according to the size of their capital. Each group elects (on a one bank, one vote principle) one of the "Class A" directors (the three that represent the banks) and one of the "Class B" directors (the three that represent the public).

71 Morris 2000: 83–4; Havrilesky 1995: ch9; Woolley 1984: 64; von Hagen 2000: 221.

72 Woolley 1984: 49–50. See also Havrilesky 1995: 294.

73 In the early 1990s, for example, the chair of the House Banking Committee, Henry Gonzales, sponsored a bill to have the US president (confirmed by Senate) appoint all reserve bank presidents and to have six of the nine directors (instead of three presently) of each reserve bank be chosen to represent a cross-section of the population inclusive of small business, labour, consumer and community organizations, and women and minorities. His bill also called for a study of the appropriateness of the boundaries of existing reserve districts and of the requirement that private banks purchase the stock of, and receive dividends from, the reserve banks (e.g., Havrilesky et al. 1993).

74 See for example Woolley 1984: 36.

75 His one concession to the New York banks was the creation of a banker-controlled Federal Advisory Council that could make recommendations to the Fed Board. This council still exists.

76 See for example Woolley 1984: 41–4; Havrilesky 1995: 86–105; Wheelock 2000.

77 Gruben et al. suggest that Mexico and Canada should push for the following representation on the FOMC: (1) one representative for each country on the board of governors and (2) the heads of the Bank of Canada and Bank of Mexico as voting members on the FOMC (2003: 297).

78 Board members must be chosen with due regard to "a fair representation of the different commercial, industrial, and geographical divisions of the country" (Amtenbrink 1999: 141–2). There is also a requirement that seven governors must come from different reserve districts, although this requirement does not guarantee that all districts will be represented. It is simply designed to prevent one region of the country from being overrepresented (Havrilesky 1995: 4).

79 With respect to discount rate changes, the boards of directors of each of the twelve reserve banks make a recommendation to the federal board of governors about discount rate changes every two weeks. The board is not, however, bound by these recommendations.

80 Havrilesky 1995: 4, 290.

81 But the significance of this should not be overstated, as two recent authors recently noted: "in these [FOMC] meetings, regional information is studied more as an aid to filling out the national picture, as opposed to being a concern, per se, for the FOMC. In addition, the FOMC's historically strong leadership, as exemplified by Paul Volcker in the past and Alan Greenspan currently, favors a national approach to policy making. Tilting the FOMC even more toward the national perspective are the financial and political systems shared by all regions. In the end, the FOMC mainly focuses on aggregate economic conditions" (Carlino and DeFina 2000: 64).

82 Dyson 2000.

83 Laidler 1999; Buiter 1999; and even Courchene 1999: 313.

84 See for example Chriszt 2000: 37; Buiter 1999; P. Fortin 2000.

85 Pringle and Turner 1999; Dyson 2000: 239.

86 Dyson 2000: 33.

87 See for example Verdun and Christiansen 2000.

88 The one area where the Council of Ministers has a little more influence is exchange rate policy. The Council can provide guidelines to the ECB about the "general orientations" of exchange rate policy as long as these do not interfere with the goal of maintaining price stability.

89 Pringle and Turner 1999: 240–1.

90 These lines of authority were endorsed once again in a 1992 report accepted by all the major federal political parties at the time and justified in the

following way: "in the democratic society, a public policy instrument as powerful as monetary policy cannot be entirely removed from the political process ... the elected government must remain ultimately accountable for the monetary policy followed" (quoted in Laidler and Robson 1993: 127).

91 For example, Morris 2000.

92 For example, Laidler and Poschmann 2000.

93 Dyson 2000: 216–19.

94 Courchene and Harris 1999: 22. See also Courchene and Harris 2000: 15; Harris 2000: 95.

95 For example, Courchene 1999.

96 Quoted in Alan Toulin and Joel-Denis Bellavance, "Bank Aims to Cosy Up to Quebec: Crow Hurt Image," *Financial Post*, 27 March 2001, emphasis added.

97 Dyson 2000: 244.

98 Ross Laver, "The Need to Take Risks," *Maclean's*, 20 December 1999.

99 NFO CFgroup 2002. The results were similar to an Environics survey in 2002 which found 53 per cent of respondents saying a common currency for the US and Canada was a good idea, while 45 per cent thought it was not. In 1999, the same survey gave the results of 46 per cent and 39 per cent, respectively (Center for Research and Information on Canada 2003).

100 Laver, "The Need."

101 Crow 2002: 121.

102 Sandra Rubin, "Loonie Gone within Five Years, Says CIBC's Rubin," *Financial Post*, 28 July 2001.

CHAPTER EIGHT

1 The point supports Brodie's more general argument about the significance of regionalism in Canadian politics (1990: 3).

2 "Bloc Wants Talks on US Dollar," *Globe and Mail*, 10 December 1998.

3 Canada 1999b: 1400.

4 R. Lévesque 1968: 45.

5 Lisée 1994: 145; Fraser 1984: 41.

6 Parti Québécois 1972: 135; Pentland 1977: 225; McRoberts 1988: 259.

7 See for example Canadian Press 1978; McRoberts 1988: 304; Richard Daignault, "Common Money Unlikely," *Montreal Star*, 19 May 1978; Peter Hadekel, "A Dollar for Quebec?" *Winnipeg Free Press*, 27 May 1978; "Customs Union Only Need for Quebec, Parizeau Says," *Globe and Mail*, 17 July 1978; R.Gibbens, "Bourassa Attacks PQ Dollar Plan," *Montreal Star*, 17 May 1978.

8 Quoted in the "Separate Currency Eyed," *Vancouver Sun*, 25 July 1977. See also McRoberts 1988: 308; Gibbens, "Bourassa Attacks"; Leslie 1979: 23.

9 McRoberts 1988: 308.

10 Lemco 1994: 137.

11 Quoted in "The White Paper on Quebec's Referendum," *Globe and Mail*, 2 November 1979.

12 Leslie 1979: 17.

13 Leslie 1979: 17–18.

14 Quoted in Andrew Phillips, "Economists Scoff at PQ Energy, Monetary Proposals," *Montreal Gazette*, 22 April 1980. See also Fraser 1980; Bourassa 1980.

15 Fraser 1980.

16 Commission on the Political and Constitutional Future of Quebec, 1991: 58.

17 Parti Québécois 1994: 57; Freeman and Grady 1995: 124–6; Don Mac-Donald, "Parizeau Keen on Canadian Dollar," *Vancouver Sun*, 28 May 1991; "Quebec's Currency Might Be Pegged to U.S. Dollar," *The Chronicle-Herald*, 4 April 1991.

18 Lemco 1994: 139.

19 Quebec could, however, compensate by demanding to pay a smaller share of the federal debt, as the Bélanger-Campeau commission suggested (Laidler and Robson 1991: 25–6; Robson 1995: 12–13).

20 Cornellier 1995: 129–30. The Bloc, for example, discussed a common monetary authority whose board of directors would be made up of four members appointed by Quebec and eight by Canada, as well as (in a non-voting capacity) the deputy finance ministers of the two countries and the heads of the Bank of Canada and Bank of Quebec. Decisions would be made when nine votes were cast in favour, and the governor and deputy governor would be appointed by a committee of ministers from both countries, which would also have ultimate authority over the board in the event of a conflict.

21 For example, Sarah Scott, "Quebec Would Keep Dollar for Role in Central Bank: Landry," *Montreal Gazette*, 15 January 1991; Parti Québécois 1994: 60.

22 Quoted in Richard Mackie, "Use of Canadian Dollar Wouldn't Make Sense, Leader Says," *Globe and Mail*, 3 August 1995.

23 Canada 1995: 14927.

24 Quoted in Montreal Gazette, "To Use U.S. Dollar," *Montreal Gazette*, 16 March 1999.

25 For example Nystrom 1999; 309.

26 Helleiner 2003a.

27 For a picture, see *Globe and Mail*, 2 November 1979, 12.

28 McRoberts 1988: 309.

29 Hugh Anderson, "Dollar Tailspins on Quebec Talk of Own Currency,"
   Globe and Mail, 18 May 1978; Bloomberg Business News, "Quebec Residents Stash Cash in Ontario," *Globe and Mail*, 27 October 1995.
30 R. Lévesque 1979: 85. See also R. Lévesque 1968: 40.
31 Quoted in "Parizeau Scoffs at the Idea of Losing Dual Citizenship," *Calgary
   Herald*, 12 December 1991.
32 Parti Québécois 1994: 85.
33 Quoted in Barrie McKenna and Alan Freeman, "Parizeau Admits to War
   Chest," *Globe and Mail*, 3 November 1995. The PQ had developed a
   "Plan O" before the vote which made available $37 billion of liquid funds
   that could be used in the event of a yes vote for activities such as defending
   the Canadian dollar or purchasing all Quebec and Hydro-Québec bonds in
   circulation in case of a panic. Quebec's finance minister had access to
   $17 billion of this total, while the rest was held by three Quebec-based
   banks (the National Bank, Laurentian Bank, and Mouvement Desjardins)
   ("PQ Stashed away $37-billion as Panic Fund," *Globe and Mail*, 18 May
   1996; McKenna and Freeman, "Parizeau").
34 Robson 1995.
35 This raises the question of why the idea of an independent Quebec adopting
   the US dollar unilaterally had not been raised earlier. It was in fact raised in
   the 1990s by some people. Landry mentioned it in 1991, but rejected the
   idea then since it "would give the Americans a bigger influence over the
   Quebec economy, which would not be desirable" (quoted in Scott, "Quebec
   Would"). When running for the PQ in 1994, Richard Le Hir (former head of
   the Quebec Manufacturers Association) had also raised the idea, but
   Parizeau apparently told him to drop it (Robert Gibbens, "Quebec Dollar
   Uproar," *Financial Post*, 30 July 1994; Jennifer Ditchburn, "Bloc Mulls
   Over Possibility of US Dollar as Common Currency," Canadian Press
   Newswire, 9 December 1998. Parizeau himself briefly mentioned it in 1995
   (Andre Picard, "P.Q. Plans Own Currency, Johnson Says," *Globe and Mail*,
   16 February 1995).
36 One more negative effect, however, would be that Quebec might bear more
   of the financial cost of political uncertainty in the province. Without NAMU
   in place, Quebec's separation would undoubtedly produce downward pressure on the Canadian dollar, thereby ensuring that all Canadians assume
   some of the cost of this political uncertainty. If NAMU were in place, however, financial markets would likely simply charge higher interest rates on
   Quebec government borrowing. The rest of the country would thus be more
   insulated from the financial effects of separation (Courchene and Laberge
   2000: 315).

37 Parizeau 1999: 8.

38 D. Bueckert, "Quebec Could Acquire Terrific Negotiating Leverage with Ottawa over Sovereignty by Threatening to Adopt the U.S. Dollar As Its Currency, Says Former Premier Jacques Parizeau," Canadian Press Newswire, 29 January 2000.

39 R. Lévesque 1968: 42.

40 Quoted in John Saunders, "Sharing the Dollar: Who Calls the Tune?" *Montreal Gazette*, 12 April 1980.

41 Marceau 1999; Alan Toulin and Joel Denis Bellavance, "Bank Aims to Cosy Up to Quebec: Crow Hurt Image," *Financial Post*, 27 March 2001.

42 R. Lévesque 1968: 43. See also Pentland 1977: 225; R. Lévesque 1979: 86.

43 B. Fortin 1978.

44 Picard, "P.Q. Plans."

45 Marceau 1999. See also Bloc 2002.

46 Canada 1999b: 1350.

47 Lemco 1994: 140–2.

48 Marceau 1999.

49 Marceau 1999.

50 Shulman 2000.

51 Beine and Coulombe 2003.

52 Courchene and Laberge 2000: 296.

53 R. Lévesque 1968: 44.

54 Fraser 1984: 41.

55 R. Lévesque 1979: 85–6.

56 Graham Fraser, "PQ Skirts Currency Reality," *Montreal Gazette*, 12 February 1980.

57 Quotes from Shortt 1964: 127; Shortt 1986: 220, 387.

58 For example, Black 1977: 95; NAC, MG26K ... UNB: 413, vol. 832: e.g., pp516894, 516911–12. The demand for bilingual money had been long-standing. Prime Minister Wilfrid Laurier had, for example, been pressed on the issue in 1907 and he had rejected it: "For my part I never yet saw an occasion where a bank note printed in English was not properly understood by the French people; and I am quite sure that a bank note printed in French would be understood by the English people to be exactly what it means" (quoted in memo in NAC, MG26K ... UNB:413, vol. 832: 516943).

59 Deputy Governor Osborne told New Zealand central bankers that he wanted this result not just because it was desired by the French speaking population but also because producing separate English and French notes "gives a lot of extra trouble to the Bank of Canada"; J.A.C. Osborne, letter to L. Lefeaux (Reserve Bank of New Zealand), 15 June 1936, P1, QUA, JD, box 67, file 481.

60 Quote from J.A. Robinson, president of the "New Brunswick English Speaking League Limited, Moncton Branch No.1," to Bennett, 12 June, NAC, MG26K ... UNB:413, vol. 832: 516896. The text is from a resolution passed by this branch.

61 Quoted in Scott, "Quebec Would."

62 Marceau 1999.

63 For example, Marceau 1999.

64 Parti Québécois 1994: 57–8; "Ottawa 'Can't Prevent' Use of Canadian Dollar," Vancouver Sun, 19 September 1995.

65 Quoted in "Sovereign Quebec Would Use Canadian Dollar, Parizeau Insists," Globe and Mail, 22 February 1992. See also Parti Québécois 1994: 57–8.

66 Even this arrangement was not a product of a formal political arrangement. Instead, it was devised by the Canadian Chamber of Commerce in 1935 when it presented the first slate of candidates for election by what were then the private shareholders of the bank. The initial Bank of Canada act required that the elected directors represent varied occupations in the following manner: two from primary industries, two from commerce and manufacturing, and three from other occupations (Stokes 1939: 194). But as 12,000 people became shareholders of the bank in 1934, it quickly became apparent that the election of these directors would be very complicated. The government initially encouraged trade and vocational associations to sponsor candidates, but the Canadian Chamber of Commerce soon submitted a slate of nominees that were all elected during the first vote in January 1935. In creating this slate, the Chamber devised guidelines that mixed occupational and regional criteria in the following ways: the two people representing primary industry would come from the Maritimes and the Prairies; Ontario and Quebec would be represented by one commercial and one miscellaneous occupation each; and British Columbia would receive the last miscellaneous occupation slot. This set of guidelines was adopted, although it produced a controversy within the business community because it excluded mining and forestry interests in Ontario from representation (Stokes 1939: 205–6; Watts 1993: 24; Babad and Mulroney 1995: 19–20). When the government created additional directors upon assuming majority ownership of the bank in 1936, it assigned these to those provinces not yet represented. The model of every province being represented by at least one director – and Quebec and Ontario receiving two – has remained since this time.

67 Laidler 1991a; Coleman 1991b.

68 When the bank was first created as a privately-owned institution, a veto power was granted to the cabinet-appointed governor over the decisions of

the privately-elected board of directors. This measure was included as a concession to the Parliamentary opposition that wanted the bank to be more accountable to the public. When the bank became publicly-controlled in 1936, the government gave itself the power to disallow the governor's veto and the veto power was then withdrawn in 1967 (Watts 1993: 21).

69 Coleman 1991a.

70 The Government of Quebec opposed the creation of the bank partly on the grounds that the existing monetary system of the country was not in need of reform. But it also worried that the bank would be politically controlled. More specifically, it suggested that the bank might give special favours to provinces which supported the federal government. (Royal Commission on Banking and Currency 1933b: 2254–60).

71 Royal Commission on Banking and Currency 1933a: 95–6.

72 For example Coleman 1991a: 732.

73 See for example Royal Commission on Banking and Currency 1933b: 2270–1.

74 Stokes 1939: 159. The bank was initially created as a privately-owned institution whose governor was appointed by cabinet but whose board of directors was elected by the private shareholders. When a new Liberal government came to power, it bought out a majority of the shares in 1936 and then nationalized the bank entirely in 1938 (Stokes 1939: 222–37).

75 Livingston 1986: chs7–8.

76 Royal Commission on Banking and Finance, *Hearings of Royal Commission on Banking and Finance*, vol. 56, 30 October 1962, pp7120–5, 7140, NAC, RG33-64, vol. 27. The commission also interviewed an official from the US Fed about its decision-making processes and that official made the case that the reserve banks help to provide regional input and to legitimate the Fed across the country (Royal Commission on Banking and Finance, *Hearings of Royal Commission on Banking and Finance*, vol. 33, 20 July 1962, p3909, NAC, RG33-64, vol. 25.

77 Laidler 1991a; Crow 2002: 16–22; Howitt 1991.

78 Lemco 1994: 35.

79 The government also proposed some reforms unrelated to the issue of regional representation, such as changing the bank's charter to make price stability its primary goal, and replacing ad hoc appearances of bank officials before Parliament with semi-annual ones. Proposals put forward by other observers at the time included measures to make board member positions full-time and with longer terms; to give provincial governments direct representation on the board; to allow provincial legislatures a role in questioning bank directors; and to create "regional" deputy governors.

80 Thiessen 2000a: 2.
81 Toulin and Bellavance, "Bank Aims."
82 Michael McCullough, "Debate over Canada Adopting U.S. Greenback Rises to Surface: Western Canada Would Be Stable," *Vancouver Sun*, 26 May 2001. See also Senator Pat Carney's comment: "Who pays the cost of adjustment [under NAMU]? ... I have a horrible feeling that it will not be central Ontario, and it will not be Quebec" (Canada 1999a: 17). Neoliberal analysts in the West have tried to portray these adjustment costs in a positive light. In BC, for example, Grubel argues that Canada's floating exchange rate has artificially bolstered the resource-exporting sector, and directed labour and capital away from high-technology, "sunrise" industries.
83 Sandra Rubin, "Drop Loonie, 45% Say in Business Poll," *National Post*, 16 July 2001.
84 Toulin and Bellavance, "Bank Aims."
85 Quoted in Montreal Gazette, "To Use U.S. Dollar."
86 Alesina and Barro 2001.
87 Gibson in Grubel 1999: 3.
88 See for example Beine and Coulombe 2003; Atkinson 1991: 55; Courchene and Laberge 2000: 294. A 1997 report commissioned by the British Columbian government suggested that BC might want to adopt the US dollar if Quebec separation prompted British Columbia to consider the same divorce from the rest of Canada (Weatherbe 1997).

CONCLUSION

1 See for example McNamara 1998: 14.
2 For a recent survey, see Broz and Frieden 2001.
3 Frieden 1991, 1996a, 1996b, 2002, 2003.
4 Frieden 1996b: 111.
5 McNamara 1998: 35. Frieden briefly acknowledges this possibility (2002: 840).
6 Frieden acknowledges that some firms may regard the benefits of reduced currency volatility as unimportant (2002: 840).
7 The relative stability of the exchange rate during the 1930s and the 1950–62 and post-1970 periods might encourage questions about whether the Canadian exchange rate regime is in fact best characterized as a floating exchange rate regime. In recent years, the question of the correct classification of exchange rate regimes has been hotly debated. While the IMF has traditionally relied on the official statements of national governments, Reinhart and Rogoff (2002) have developed an alternative classification system based on the *actual behaviour* of exchange rates. On this basis, they classify

the Canadian dollar as "de facto peg" in the 1950–62 period and a "de facto moving band" vis-à-vis the US dollar after 1970. But this measurement system tells us little about the policy intentions and actions of national governments, the very things which are the focus of this and any other effort to study the political economy of exchange rate regimes. Indeed, according to the Reinhart-Rogoff system, variations in the degree of economic shocks alone could account for differences in the classification of countries' exchange rate regimes. As we have seen, the relatively stability of the floating Canadian dollar vis-à-vis the US dollar in these periods – as well as in the 1930s – often had little to do with government policy. (And this stability is also exaggerated by the label "de facto peg" in the 1950–62 period, given that the Canadian dollar's value ranged from US$0.91 to US$1.06 in these years). An alternative methodology for measuring de facto exchange rate regimes developed by Levy-Yeyati and Sturzenegger (2002) attempts to bring in policy actions more directly by including changes in international reserves. Focusing only on the 1974–2000 period, they classify Canada's exchange rate regime in most years as a "float" (and some years as a "dirty float/crawling peg" regime, notably 1974, 1975, 1981, 1983, 1986, 1989, 1991). Their approach – which itself has some problems – would also have generated a "float" result for the 1930s and the 1950–62 period.

8 For example, Harris 1993.

9 Even in the early 1930s when these groups did push for the abandonment of the gold standard, most advocates of currency depreciation favoured a re-pegging of the currency to sterling rather than a floating exchange rate.

10 Plumptre 1977: 226.

11 There have been business lobby groups, such as the BCNI, which have strongly influenced government policy, but they are not representative of the entire Canadian business community.

12 Henning 1994. But it is not clear that this would explain the position taken by the banks because, as we have seen, even the manufacturing sector was rarely pushing for a float. For the nature of Canada's financial system, see Stanford 1999.

13 Frieden briefly acknowledges this possibility (2003: 310).

14 The Canadian experience thus reinforces Willett's argument that "the more such [exchange rate] adjustments are seen as being the direct result of government policies, the greater the political effects are likely to be. Thus the greater is the influence of market forces in the short run determination of exchange rates, the less politicized are exchange rate adjustments likely to be. This logic presents a strong case for flexible exchange rates" (2004: 23).

15 Frieden 2002: 839fn20, 840.

16 Henning 1994: 26.

17 McNamara 1998: 35. See also 7–8, 32–41. A similar critique is advanced by Giovannini 1995.
18 McNamara 1998; Gowa 1988; Broz and Frieden 2001: 328.
19 Coleman 1991b: 214.
20 Broz and Frieden 2001: 328.
21 Bernhard and Leblang 1999.
22 Quote from Clark 2002: 743.
23 Bernhard and Leblang 2002.
24 Bernhard and Leblang 1999.
25 Hallerberg 2002.
26 For a discussion of this approach, see Freeman 2002: 902; McNamara 1998; Odell 1982; Andrews and Willett 1997: 489; Kirshner 2000; Kirshner 2003.
27 Frieden 2003: 308. For a more detailed analysis of the enduring relevance of OCA theory for exchange rate regime choices, see Willett 2003.
28 When this basis of support for a floating rate has come from Bank of Canada officials themselves, some analysts have argued that it may also have reflected these officials' desire to increase the bank's prestige and autonomy – as I noted in chapter 6. This "rationalist" line of argument is reminiscent of the public-choice interpretation of the bank's behaviour of Chant and Acheson (1972), but I have not found much evidence to support it in the context of the Bank of Canada's interest in a floating exchange rate regime.
29 See for example McNamara 1998; Bernhard et al. 2003.
30 Freeman 2002: 896.
31 Bowles 2003b.
32 Abdelal 2003; Risse et al. 1999; Kaelberer 2004; Jonung 2004.
33 See also Wang 2003; Helleiner 2003a.
34 See for example Goldstein and Keohane 1993.
35 Blyth 2002: 34.
36 Henning 1994.
37 Andrews 1994.
38 Beddoes 1999: 8.

Bibliography

ARCHIVES

Bank of Canada Archives, Ottawa, Canada (BAC)
    Foreign Exchange Control Board Files (FECB)
    Louis Rasminsky Files (LR)
Bank of England Archives, London, UK (BOE)
Gerald Ford Presidential Library, Ann Arbor, Michigan, USA (GF)
National Archives of Canada, Ottawa, Canada (NAC)
Public Record Office, London, UK (PRO)
    Colonial Files (CO)
    Treasury Files (T)
Queen's University Archives, Kingston, Ontario, Canada (QUA)
    John J. Deutsch Papers (JD)
    W.C. Clark Files (WC)
United States National Archives (USNA)

CITED WORKS

Abdelal, Rawi. 2003. "National Strategy and National Money: Politics and the End of the Ruble Zone, 1991–94." In *Monetary Orders*, ed. J. Kirshner. Ithaca: Cornell University Press.

Acheson, T. 1985. "The National Policy and the Industrialization of the Maritimes 1880–1910." In *Industrialization and Underdevelopment in the Maritimes 1880–1930*, ed. T. Acheson. Toronto: Garamond Press.

Alesina, A. and R. Barro. 2001. "One Country, One Currency?" In *Currency Unions*, ed. A. Alesina and R. Barro. Stanford: Hoover Institution.

Alexander, J. 1856. *A Few Hints on Decimalizing the Currency*. Toronto: Maclear and Co.

Altig, David. 2002. "Dollarization: What's in It for US?" *Economic Commentary* (Federal Reserve Bank of Cleveland). 15 October.

Amtenbrink, Fabian. 1999. *The Democratic Accountability of Central Banks*. Oxford: Hathethert Publishing.

Andrews, David. 1994. "Capital Mobility and State Autonomy." *International Studies Quarterly* 38: 193–218.

Andrews, David and Tom Willett. 1997. "Financial Interdependence and the State: International Monetary Relations at Century's End." *International Organization* 51 (3): 479–511.

Arnold, W. 1862. *Money and Banking*. Toronto: Blackburn's City Hall Steam Press.

Atkinson, Lloyd. 1991. "A Comment." In *Two Nations, One Money*, ed. D. Laidler and W. Robson. Toronto: C.D. Howe Institute.

Aylott, Nicholas. 2001. "The Swedish Social Democratic Party." In *Social Democracy and Monetary Union*, ed. T. Notermans. New York: Berghahn.

Babad, Michael and Catherine Mulroney. 1995. *Where the Buck Stops: The Dollar, Democracy and the Bank of Canada*. Toronto: Stoddard.

Barlow, Maude and Bruce Campbell. 1991. *Take Back the Nation*. Toronto: Key Porter Books.

Baucus, M. 1987. "A Congressional Perspective." In *Building a Canadian-American Free Trade Area*, ed. F.S. Edward Fried and Philip Trezise. Washington: Brookings Institution.

Bayoumi, T. and Barry Eichengreen. 1994. "Monetary and Exchange Rate Arrangement for NAFTA." *Journal of Development Economics* 43: 125–65.

Beddoes, Zanny M. 1999. "From EMU to AMU? The Case for Regional Currencies." *Foreign Affairs*. July/Aug: 8–13.

Beine, Michael and Serge Coulombe. 2003. "Regional Perspectives on Dollarization in Canada." *Journal of Regional Science* 43 (3): 541–70.

Bergsten, Fred. 1999. "Dollarization in Emerging-Market Economies and Its Policy Implications for the United States." *Statement before the Joint Hearing of the Subcommittee on Economic Policy and the Subcommittee on International Trade and Finance: Committee on Banking, Housing and Urban Affairs*. United States Senate. 22 April.

Bernhard, W. and D. Leblang. 1999. "Democratic Institutions and Exchange-Rate Commitments." *International Organization* 53 (1): 71–97.

– 2002. "Political Parties and Monetary Commitments." *International Organization* 56 (4): 803–30.

Bernhard, W., J. Lawrence Broz, and William Clark. 2002. "The Political Economy of Monetary Institutions." *International Organization* 56 (4): 693–723.

Black, C. 1977. *Duplessis.* Toronto: McClelland and Stewart.

Blacklock, Cathy. 2000. "Dollarization in the Western Hemisphere." Speaking notes for roundtable on socio-political ramifications of alternate currency arrangements, Ottawa, North-South Institute, 4–5 October.

Blyth, Mark. 2002. *Great Transformations: Economic Ideas and Institutional Change in the Twentieth Century.* Cambridge: Cambridge University Press.

Bogetic, Zeljko. 2000. "Full Dollarization: Fad or Future?" *Challenge* 43 (2): 1–14.

Bordo, M. and A. Redish. 1990. "Credible Commitment and Exchange Rate Stability: Canada's Interwar Experience." *Canadian Journal of Economics* 23 (2): 357–80.

Bowles, Paul. 2003a. "Money on the (Continental) Margins: Dollarization Pressures in Canada and Mexico." Mimeo.

– 2003b. "Explaining the Differences between Monetary Union Debates in Australia and Canada: The 'Tyrannies of Distance and Proximity' or 'Contingent Neoliberalism'?" Paper prepared for workshop on "Britain and Canada and their Large Neighbouring Monetary Unions," University of Victoria, BC, 17–18 October.

Bourassa, R. 1980. *L'unité monétaire et l'unité politique sont indissociables.* Montreal: Parti Libéral du Québec.

Brecher, I. 1957. *Monetary and Fiscal Thought and Policy in Canada 1919–1939.* Toronto: University of Toronto Press.

Brock, W. 1984. "Canadian-U.S.Trade Negotiations: A Status Report." In *U.S.-Canadian Economic Relations: Next Steps?,* ed. Edward Fried and Philip Trezise. Washington: Brookings Institution.

Brodie, J. 1990. *The Political Economy of Canadian Regionalism.* Toronto: Harcourt Brace Jovanovich.

Broz, Lawrence and Jeffry Frieden. 2001. "The Political Economy of International Monetary Relations" *Annual Review of Political Science* 4: 317–43.

Bryce, R. 1986. *Maturing in Hard Times: Canada's Department of Finance through the Great Depression.* Montreal: McGill-Queen's University Press.

Buiter, Willem. 1999. "The EMU and the NAMU: What Is the Case for North American Monetary Union?" Douglas Purvis Memorial Lecture, 29 May. Toronto: Canadian Economic Association.

Burney, D. 2000. "Where There's the Will. ..." In *Free Trade: Risks and Rewards,* ed. L.I. MacDonald. Montreal: McGill-Queen's University Press.

Burnham, Peter. 2003. *Remaking the Postwar World Economy: Robot and British Policy in the 1950s.* London: Palgrave MacMillan.

Cameron, Duncan. 1986. "Monetary Relations in North America" *International Journal* 42: 170–98.

Campbell, Robert. 1987. *Grand Illusions: The Politics of the Keynesian Experience in Canada, 1945–1975*. Peterborough: Broadview.

Canada, Dominion of. 1870. *Debates of the House of Commons*. 3rd session, 1st Parliament. Ottawa: Ottawa Times.

– 1871. *Parliamentary Debates*. 4th session, 1st Parliament. Ottawa: Ottawa Times.

– 1880. *Parliamentary Debates*. 3rd session, 4th Parliament, vol. 1. Ottawa: Maclean, Roger and Co.

– 1881. *Parliamentary Debates*. 3rd session, 4th Parliament, vol. 2. Ottawa: Maclean, Roger and Co.

– 1932. *House of Commons Debates*. 3rd session, 17th Parliament. Ottawa: F.A. Acland.

– 1933. *House of Commons Debates*. 4th session, 17th Parliament. Ottawa: J.O. Patenaude.

– 1946. *Debates, House of Commons*. 1st session, 20th Parliament. Ottawa, Edmond Cloutier.

– 1947. *Debates, House of Commons*. 2nd session, 20th Parliament, vol. 3. Ottawa: Edmond Cloutier.

– 1948. *Debates, House of Commons*. 4th session, 20th Parliament. Ottawa: Edmond Cloutier.

– 1949a. *Debates, House of Commons*. 5th session, 20th Parliament. Ottawa: Edmond Cloutier.

– 1949b. *Debates, House of Commons*. 1st session, 21st Parliament. Ottawa: Edmond Cloutier.

– 1951. *Debates, House of Commons*. 4th session, 21st Parliament. Ottawa: Edmond Cloutier.

Canada, Government of. 1962a. *House of Commons Debates*. 5th session, 24th Parliament. Ottawa: Roger Duhamel.

– 1962b. *House of Commons Debates*. 1st session, 25th parliament. Ottawa: Roger Duhamel.

– 1967. *House of Commons Debates*. 1st session, 1st Parliament. Ottawa: Government of Canada.

– 1968. *House of Commons Debates*. 2nd session, 27th Parliament. Ottawa: Roger Duhamel.

– 1969. *House of Commons Debates*. 1st Session, 28th Parliament. Ottawa: The Queen's Printer.

– 1970. *House of Commons Debates*. 2nd session, 28th Parliament. Ottawa: The Queen's Printer.

– 1975. *House of Commons Debates.* 2nd session, 1st Parliament. Ottawa: Information Canada.

– 1995. *House of Commons Debates.* 1st session, 32nd Parliament. Ottawa: The Queen's Printer.

– 1999a. *Proceedings of the Standing Senate Committee on Banking, Trade, and Commerce.* Issue 48, 25 March.

– 1999b. *House of Commons Debates.* 1st session, 36th Parliament. Ottawa: Government of Canada.

Canada, House of Commons. 1939. *Memoranda and Tables Respecting the Bank of Canada.* Ottawa: Government of Canada.

Canada, Province of, Legislative Assembly. 1855. *A Decimal Currency – Weight and Measures.* 3rd and 4th reports of the Standing Committee on Public Accounts. Quebec: Lovell and Lamoureux.

Canadian Chamber of Commerce. 2002. "Canada-US Integration: Directions for the Future." *Submission to the Standing Committee on Foreign Affairs and International Trade, House of Commons.* June.

Carlino, Gerald and Robert DeFina. 2000. "Monetary Policy and the U.S. States and Regions: Some Implications for European Monetary Union." In *Regional Aspects of Monetary Policy in Europe,* ed J. von Hagen and C. Waller. Boston: Kluwer Academic Publishers.

Carlsen, Laura. 2003. *NAFTA Minus.* Silver City, NM: Interhemispheric Resource Center.

Carroll, William and Murray Shaw. 2001. "Consolidating a Neoliberal Policy Bloc in Canada, 1976 to 1996." *Canadian Public Policy* 27 (2): 195–217.

Center for Research and Information on Canada. 2003. *Canada and the United States: An Evolving Partnership.* Montreal: Center for Research and Information on Canada.

Chant, John and Keith Acheson. 1972. "The Choice of Monetary Instruments and the Theory of Bureaucracy." *Public Choice* (Spring): 13–32.

Chittenden, G. 1971. "Discussion." In *Canadian-United States Financial Relationships,* ed. Federal Reserve Bank of Boston. Boston: Federal Reserve Bank of Boston.

Chriszt, Michael. 2000. "Perspectives on a Potential North American Monetary Union." *Economic Review* (Federal Reserve Bank of Atlanta) 85 (4): 29–38.

Clark, W.R. 2002. "Partisan and Electoral Motivations and the Choice of Monetary Institutions under Fully Mobile Capital." *International Organization* 56 (4): 725–49.

Clarkson, Stephen. 1985. *Canada and the Reagan Challenge.* 2d ed. Toronto: James Lorimer and Co.

– 2000. "The Joy of Flux: What Europe May Learn from North America's Preference for National Currency Sovereignty." In *After the Euro*, ed. C. Crouch. Oxford: Oxford University Press.

– 2002. *Uncle Sam and Us*. Toronto: University of Toronto Press.

Cohen, B.J. 1998. *The Geography of Money*. Ithaca: Cornell University Press.

– 2002. "US Policy on Dollarization: A Political Analysis." *Geopolitics* 7 (1): 63–84.

Coleman, William. 1991a. "Monetary Policy, Accountability and Legitimacy: A Review of the Issues in Canada." *Canadian Journal of Political Science* 24 (4): 711–34.

– 1991b. "Fencing Off: Central Banks and Networks in Canada and the United States." In *Policy Networks: Empirical Evidence and Theoretical Considerations*, ed. Bernd Marin and Renate Mayntz. Frankfurt/Boulder: Campus/Westview.

Commission on the Political and Constitutional Future of Quebec, 1991. *The Report of the Commission on the Political and Constitutional Future of Quebec*. Quebec: Government of Quebec.

Cornell, Peter McCaul. 1956. *Flexible Exchange Rates: The Canadian Case*. Ph.D. thesis, Department of Economics, Harvard University, Cambridge Massachusetts. HU 90.6930. Courtesy of the Harvard University Archives.

Cornellier, Manon. 1995. *The Bloc*. Trans. R. Chodos, S.Warren, and W. Taylor. Toronto: James Lorimer and Co.

Courchene, Thomas. 1976. *Money, Inflation, and the Bank Of Canada: An Analysis of Canadian Monetary Policy from 1972 to Early 1975*. Montreal: C.D. Howe Institute.

– 1981. *Money, Inflation, and the Bank of Canada, Volume II: An Analysis of Monetary Gradualism, 1975–80*. Montreal: C.D. Howe Institute.

– 1983. *No Place to Stand? Abandoning Monetary Targets – An Evaluation*. Toronto: C.D. Howe Institute.

– 1990a. "Rethinking the Macro Mix: The Case for Provincial Stabilization Policy." In *Taking Aim: The Debate on Zero Inflation*, ed. R. York. Toronto: C.D. Howe Institute.

– 1990b. "Zero Means Almost Nothing: Towards a Preferable Inflation and Macroeconomic Policy." *Queen's Quarterly* 97 (4): 543–61.

– 1992. *Rearrangements: The Courchene Papers*. Oakville: Mosaic Press.

– 1998. "Towards a North American Common Currency: An Optimal Currency Area Analysis." In *Room to Manoeuvre? Globalization and Policy Convergence*, ed. T. Courchene. Kingston: John Deutsch Institute for the Study of Economic Policy.

– 1999. "Alternative North American Currency Arrangements: A Research Agenda." *Canadian Public Policy* 25 (3): 308–14.

Courchene, Thomas and Colin Telmer. 1998. *From Heartland to North American Region State: The Social, Fiscal and Federal Evolution of Ontario.* Toronto: Faculty of Management, University of Toronto.

Courchene, Thomas and Marc-Antoine Laberge. 2000. "The Future of the Canadian Currency Union: NAFTA and Quebec Independence." In *Regional Aspects of Monetary Policy in Europe*, ed. J. von Hagen and C. Waller. Boston: Kluwer Academic Publishers.

Courchene, Thomas and Richard Harris. 1999. *From Fixing to Monetary Union: Options for North American Currency Integration.* C.D. Howe Institute Commentary No.127. Toronto: C.D. Howe Institute.

– 2000. "North American Monetary Union: Analytical Principles and Operational Guidelines." *North American Journal of Economics and Finance* 11: 3–18.

Crow, John. 1988. *The Work of Canadian Monetary Policy.* Edmonton: University of Alberta, Department of Economics.

– 1993. "Monetary Policy under a Floating Exchange Rate Regime: The Canadian Experience." Mimeo. Lecture at the Stockholm School of Economics, Stockholm, Sweden, 22 April.

– 1995. *Two and a Half Cheers for Canadian Monetary Sovereignty.* C.D. Howe Institute Commentary No. 73. Toronto: C.D. Howe Institute.

– 1999. "Any Sense in a Canadian Dollar?" *Policy Options* (March): 29–34.

– 2002. *Making Money.* Etobicoke: John Wiley and Sons.

Cuff, Robert and J.L.Granatstein. 1977. "The Rise and Fall of Canadian-American Free Trade, 1947–8." *Canadian Historical Review* 58 (4): 459–82.

Curtis, C.A. 1932. "The Canadian Monetary Situation." *Journal of Political Economy* 40 (3 June): 314–37.

D'Aquino, Thomas. 2002. "Enterprise and the Public Policy Challenge: From Priorities to Action in 2002." Notes for address to the Annual General Meeting of the Canadian Council of Chief Executives, 15 January. Niagara-on-the-Lake: Canadian Council of Chief Executives.

D'Arista, Jane. 2000. "Dollarization: Critical US Views." Notes for a presentation to the North-South Institute Conference "Dollarization in the Western Hemisphere," 4–5 October. Ottawa: North-South Institute.

Davis, Robert. 1867. *The Currency: What It Is and What It Should Be.* Ottawa: Hunter, Rose and Co.

De Vries, Margaret. 1969. "Fluctuating Exchange Rates." In *The International Monetary Fund 1945–1965.* Vol. 2, *Analysis*, ed. M. De Vries and J.K. Horsefield. Washington: International Monetary Fund.

– 1985. *The International Monetary Fund 1972–78.* Vol. 1. Washington: International Monetary Fund.

Destler, I.M. and C.R. Henning. 1989. *Dollar Politics: Exchange Rate Policy-making in the United States.* Washington: Institute for International Economics.

Dodge, D. 2002. "Dollarization and North American Integration." *Bank of Canada Review* (Autumn): 41–4.

Doern, Bruce and Brian Tomlin. 1991. *Faith and Fear: The Free Trade Story.* Toronto: Stoddart.

Donner, Arthur and Douglas Peters. 1979. *The Monetarist Counter-Revolution: A Critique of Canadian Monetary Policy 1975–1979.* Toronto: James Lorimer and Co.

Dorn, James and Roberto Salinas-Leon. 1996. *Money and Markets in the Americas.* Vancouver: The Fraser Institute.

Drainville, Andre. 1995. "Monetarism in Canada and the World Economy." *Studies in Political Economy* 46: 7–42.

Drummond, Don and Marc Lévesque. 2001. "Plus ça change ..." *Globe and Mail.* 12 December.

Drummond, I. and N. Hillmer. 1989. *Negotiating Freer Trade: The United Kingdom, the United States, Canada and the Trade Agreement of 1938.* Waterloo: Wilfrid Laurier University Press.

Dyson, Kenneth. 2000. *The Politics of the Euro-Zone.* Oxford: Oxford University Press.

Eichengreen, Barry. 1992. *Golden Fetters.* Oxford: Oxford University Press.

Ernst, Alan. 1992. "From Liberal Continentalism to Neoconservatism: North American Free Trade and the Politics of the C.D.Howe Institute" *Studies in Political Economy* 39: 109–40.

Feldstein, M. 1991. "Does One Market Require One Money?" In *Policy Implications of Trade and Currency Zones,* ed. Federal Reserve Bank of Kansas City. Kansas City: Federal Reserve Bank of Kansas City.

Ferguson, Barry. 1993. *Remaking Liberalism: The Intellectual Legacy of Adam Shortt, O.D. Skelton, W.C. Clark and W.A. Mackintosh, 1890–1925.* Montreal: McGill-Queen's University Press.

Fieleke, N. 1971. "The Hedging of Commercial Transactions between the U.S. and Canadian Residents: A View from the United States." In *Canadian-United States Financial Relationships,* ed. Federal Reserve Bank of Boston. Boston: Federal Reserve Bank of Boston.

Fleming, J. 1962. "Domestic Financial Policies under Fixed and Under Floating Exchange Rates." *International Monetary Fund Staff Papers* 9 (3): 369–80.

Fleming, Donald. 1985. *So Very Near: The Political Memoirs of the Honourable Donald M. Fleming*. Vol. 2, *The Summit Years*. Toronto: McClelland and Stewart.

Fortin, Bernard. 1978. *Les Avantages et les coûts des différentes options monétaires d'une petite économie ouverte: un cadre analytique*. Montreal: Official du Québec.

Fortin, Pierre. 1990. "Can the Costs of an Anti-Inflation Policy Be Reduced?" In *Taking Aim: The Debate on Zero Inflation*, ed. R. York. Toronto: C.D. Howe Institute.

– 2000. "Should Canada Dump its Floating Regime?" *World Economic Affairs* 13 (2): 43–7.

Fraser, Graham. 1984. *P.Q.: René Lévesque and the Parti Québécois in Power*. Toronto: Macmillan.

Freeman, Alan and Patrick Grady. 1995. *Dividing the House: Planning for the Canada without Quebec*. Toronto: HarperCollins Publishers.

Freeman, J. 2002. "Competing Commitments: Technocracy and Democracy in the Design of Monetary Institutions." *International Organization* 56 (4): 889–910.

Frieden, J. 1991. "Invested Interests." *International Organization* 45: 425–51.

– 1996a. "The Impact of Goods and Capital Market Integration on European Monetary Politics." *Comparative Political Studies* 29 (2): 193–222.

– 1996b. "Economic Integration and the Politics of Monetary Policy in the United States." In *Internationalization and Domestic Politics?*, ed. Robert Keohane and Helen Milner. Cambridge: Cambridge University Press.

– 2002. "The Real Sources of European Currency Policy." *International Organization* 56 (4): 831–60.

– 2003. "The Political Economy of Dollarization: Domestic and International Factors." In *Dollarization*, ed. E. Levy-Yeyati and F. Sturzenegger. Cambridge: MIT Press.

Friedman, M. 1953. "The Case for Flexible Exchange Rates." In his *Essays in Positive Economics*. Chicago: University of Chicago Press.

– 2001. "Canada and Flexible Exchange Rates." *Bank of Canada Review* (Autumn): 413–16.

Friedman, M. and R. Friedman. 1998. *Two Lucky People*. Chicago: University of Chicago.

Fullerton, Douglas. 1986. *Graham Towers and His Times*. Toronto: McClelland and Stewart.

Funabashi, Yoichi. 1987. *Managing the Dollar*. Washington: Institute for International Economics.

Gamble, Andrew and Gavin Kelly. 2001. "The British Labour Party and Monetary Union." In *Social Democracy and Monetary Union*, ed. T. Notermans. New York: Berghahn.

Gibbons, Alan. 1954. "Foreign Exchange Control in Canada, 1939–51." *Canadian Journal of Economics and Political Science* 19: 35–54.

Gibbs, E., ed. 1979a. *Debates of the Legislative Assembly of United Canada 1841–1867*. Vol. 10, part 2, *1851*. Montreal: Centre de Récherche en Histoire Économique du Canada Français.

–, ed. 1979b. *Debates of the Legislative Assembly of United Canada 1841–1867*. Vol. 11, part 4, *1852–53*. Montreal: Centre de Récherche en Histoire Économique du Canada Français.

Gilbert, Emily. 1998. "'Ornamenting the Façade of Hell': Iconographies of Nineteenth-Century Canadian Paper Money." *Environment and Planning D: Society and Space* 16: 57–80.

– 1999. "Forging a National Currency: Money, State Building and Nation Building in Canada." In *Nation-States and Money*, ed. E. Gilbert and E. Helleiner. London: Routledge.

Giovannini, Alberto. 1995. "Economic and Monetary Union: What Happened? Exploring the Political Dimension of Optimum Currency Areas." In *The Debate on Money in Europe*, ed. A. Giovannini. Cambridge: MIT Press.

Goldstein, Judith and Robert Keohane, eds. 1993. *Ideas and Foreign Policy: Beliefs, Institutions and Political Change*. Ithaca: Cornell University Press.

Goodwin, C. 1961. *Canadian Economic Thought: The Political Economy of a Developing Nation 1814–1914*. London: Cambridge University Press.

Gowa, Joanne. 1988. "Public Goods and Political Institutions: Trade and Monetary Policy Processes in the United States." *International Organization* 42: 15–32.

Graham, George. 1995. "Freshmen Fire at Clinton's Mexican Package." *Financial Times*. 20 January.

Granatstein, J.L. 1986. *Canada 1957–1967*. Toronto: McClelland and Stewart.

– 1981. "The Road to Bretton Woods: International Monetary Policy and the Public Servant." *Journal of Canadian Studies* 16: 174–87.

Green Party, The. 1994. *European Election Manifesto*. London: The Green Party.

Grey, E. 1851a. "Canadian Currency." 21 January. Reprinted in *The Elgin-Grey Papers 1846–1852*, ed. S.A. Doughty. Ottawa: J.O. Patenaude, 1937.

– 1851b. "Earl Grey to Earl of Elgin." 9 April. Reprinted in *The Elgin-Grey Papers 1846–1852*, ed. S.A. Doughty. Ottawa: J.O. Patenaude, 1937.

Grubel, Herbert. 1999. *The Case for the Amero: The Economics and Politics of a North American Monetary Union*. Vancouver: The Fraser Institute.

– 2000. "Toward North American Monetary Union." In *Money, Markets and Mobility*, ed. T. Courchene. Montreal: McGill-Queen's University Press.

Gruben, W., M. Wynne, and C. Zavazaga. 2003. "Implementation Guidelines for Dollarization and Monetary Unions." In *Dollarization*, ed. Eduardo Levy Yeyati and Federico Sturzenegger. Cambridge: MIT Press.

Hackett, W.T. 1935. "Canada's Optional Payment Bonds." *Canadian Journal of Economics and Political Science* 1 (2): 161–70.

– 1945. *Bretton Woods*. Toronto: Canadian Institute of International Affairs.

Hall, R. 1985. "Exchange Rates, Financial Markets and Trade Liberalization: Summary of the Proceedings of a Research Symposium." In *Domestic Policies in the International Economic Environment*. Vol. 12 of *Studies for Royal Commission on the Economic Union and Development Prospects for Canada*. Toronto: University of Toronto Press.

Hallerberg, M. 2002. "Veto Players and the Choice of Monetary Institutions." *International Organization* 56 (4): 775–802.

Harris, Richard 1993. *Trade, Money, and Wealth in the Canadian Economy*. Benefactor's Lecture. Toronto: C.D. Howe Institute.

– 2000. "The Case for North American Monetary Union." *Isuma: Canadian Journal of Policy Research* (Spring): 93–6.

Hart, M. 1994. *Decision at Midnight: Inside the Canada-US Free-Trade Negotiations*. Vancouver: University of British Columbia Press.

Hausmann, Ricardo. 1999. "Should There Be Five Currencies or One Hundred and Five." *Foreign Policy* 116 (Fall): 65–79.

Havrilesky, Thomas. 1995. *The Pressures on American Monetary Policy*. 2d ed. Dordrecht: Kluwer.

Havrilesky, Thomas, Henry Chappell, John Gildea, and Rob McGregor. 1993. "Congress Threatens the Fed." *Challenge* (March–April): 50–7.

Haxby, James. 1983. *Striking Impressions: The Royal Canadian Mint and Canadian Coinage*. Ottawa: The Royal Canadian Mint.

Heilperin, Michael. 1950. "United States-Canadian Partnership for the Revival of Multilateral Trade." *International Journal* (Summer): 217–29.

Helleiner, Eric. 1994. *States and the Reemergence of Global Finance*. Ithaca: Cornell University Press.

– 2003a. *The Making of National Money: Territorial Currencies in Historical Perspective*. Ithaca: Cornell University Press.

– 2003b. "Dollarization Diplomacy: US Policy towards Latin America Coming Full Circle?" *Review of International Political Economy* 10 (3): 406–29.

Henley, Kevin. 1989. "The International Roots of Economic Nationalist Ideology in Canada, 1846–1885." *Journal of Canadian Studies* 24 (4): 107–21.

Henning, C. Randall. 1994. *Currencies and Politics in the United States, Germany and Japan*. Washington: Institute for International Economics.

Hunter, W.T. 1991. *Canadian Financial Markets*. Peterborough: Broadview Press.

Hogue, Robert. 2003. "Rapid Rise in C$ Raises Warning Flags." *Economic Analysis* (Bank of Montreal Financial Group, Economics Department). 6 June.

Horsefield, J.K. 1969. *The International Monetary Fund.* Vol.1, *Chronicle.* Washington: IMF.

Howay, F.W., W. Sage, and H. Angus. 1942. *British Columbia and the United States.* New York: Russell and Russell.

Howitt, Peter. 1986. *Monetary Policy in Transition: A Study of Bank of Canada Policy, 1982-85.* C.D. Howe Institute Policy Study No.1. Toronto: C.D. Howe Institute.

– 1991. "Constitutional Reform and the Bank of Canada." In *Economic Dimensions of Constitutional Change.* Vol. 2, ed. Robin Boadway, Thomas Courchene, and Douglas Purvis. Kingston: John Deutsch Institute for the Study of Economic Policy.

Innis, H. 1995. *Staples, Markets and Cultural Change: Selected Essays.* Ed. Daniel Drache. Montreal: McGill-Queen's University Press.

Innis, H. and A. Lower, eds. 1933. *Select Documents in Canadian Economic History 1783-1885.* Philadelphia: Porcupine Press.

Jack, Peter. 1869. *Letters on Banking and Currency.* Halifax: A. and W. Mackinlay.

Jackson, Andrew. 2000. "Social Impacts of 'Dollarization.'" Notes for a presentation to the North-South Institute Conference "Dollarization in the Western Hemisphere," 4–5 October. Ottawa: North-South Institute.

Jameson, Kenneth. 2001. "Latin America and the Dollar Bloc in the 21st Century: To Dollarize or No?" *Latin American Politics and Society* 43: 1–35.

Johnson, H. 1970. "Canada's Floating Dollar in Historical Perspective." *International Currency Review* (July/August): 4–9.

Jones, Erik. 1998. "Portugal towards EMU." In *Joining Europe's Monetary Club,* ed. E. Jones, J. Frieden, and F. Torres. New York: St Martin's Press.

Jonung, Lars. 2004. "The Political Economy of Monetary Unification: The Swedish Euro Referendum of 2003." *Cato Journal* 24 (1–2): 123–49.

Josselin, Daphne. 2001. "Trade Unions for EMU: Sectorial Preferences and Political Opportunities." *West European Politics* 24 (1): 55–74.

Kaelberer, Mathias. 2004. "The Euro and European Identity." *Review of International Studies* 30: 161–78.

Kaltenthaler, Karl. 1998. *Germany and the Politics of Europe's Money.* Durham: Duke University Press.

Kealey, Greg. 1980. *Toronto Workers Respond to Industrial Capitalism, 1867–1892.* Toronto: University of Toronto Press.

Kemmerer, Edwin. 1916. "A Proposal for Pan-American Monetary Unity." *Political Science Quarterly* 31: 66–80.

Keynes, John Maynard. 1923. *Tract on Monetary Reform*. London: Macmillan.

Kierans, Eric. 2001. *Remembering*. Toronto: Stoddart.

Kim, M., William Nganje, and Won Koo. 2001. "Exchange Rates and Bilateral Trade: Examples from CUSTA." *Review of the Financial Report of the 21st Century Commission on Productive Agriculture: Hearing Before the Committee on Agriculture, Nutrition and Forestry*. United States Senate, 107th Congress, 1st session. 30 January 2001. Washington: US Government Printing Office.

Kirshner, Jonathan. 1995. *Currency and Coercion*. Princeton: Princeton University Press.

– 2000. "The Study of Money." *World Politics* 52: 407–36.

–, ed. 2003. *Monetary Orders*. Ithaca: Cornell University Press.

Knox, F. 1937. "Financial Interrelationships: Roundtable Discussion." In *Canadian-American Affairs*, ed. Albert Corey, Walter McLaren, and Reginald Trotter. New York: Ginn and Co.

Laidler, David. 1990. "Rapporteur's Comments." In *Taking Aim: The Debate on Zero Inflation*, ed. R. York. Toronto: C.D. Howe Institute.

– 1991a. *How Shall We Govern the Governor?* Toronto: C.D. Howe Institute.

– 1991b. "One Market, One Money? Well, Maybe ... Sometimes ..." In *Policy Implications of Trade and Currency Zones*, ed. Federal Reserve Bank of Kansas City. Kansas City: Federal Reserve Bank of Kansas City.

– 1999. "Canada's Exchange Rate Options." *Canadian Public Policy* 25 (3): 324–32.

Laidler, David and Finn Poschmann. 2000. *Leaving Well Enough Alone: Canada's Monetary Order in a Changing International Environment*. C.D. Howe Institute Commentary No. 142. Toronto: C.D. Howe Institute.

Laidler, David and William Robson. 1990. *The Fix Is Out: A Defense of the Floating Canadian Dollar*. C.D. Howe Institute Policy Study No. 18. Toronto: C.D. Howe Institute.

– 1991. *Two Nations, One Money?* Toronto: C.D. Howe Institute.

– 1993. *The Great Canadian Disinflation: The Economics and Politics of Monetary Policy in Canada, 1988–1993*. C.D. Howe Institute Policy Study No. 19. Toronto: C.D. Howe Institute.

Langille, David. 1987. "The Business Council on National Issues and the Canadian State." *Studies in Political Economy* 24: 41–85.

Laurie, N. 1993. "The Exchange Rate: 1988–91." In *Canada under Free Trade*, ed. Duncan Cameron and Mel Watkins. Toronto: James Lorimer and Co.

Laxer, Gordon. 1989. *Open for Business: The Roots of Foreign Ownership in Canada*. Toronto: Oxford University Press.

Lemco, Jonathan. 1994. *Turmoil in the Peaceable Kingdom.* Toronto: University of Toronto Press.

Leslie, Peter. 1979. "Equal to Equal: Economic Association and the Canadian Common Market." Institute of Intergovernmental Relations. Kingston: Queen's University.

Lévesque, Marc. 2002. "Has Canada's Burn-Out Dollar Sparked a Fire-Sale of Canadian Companies?" *Topic Paper: TD Economics.* 3 July.

Lévesque, René. 1968. *An Option for Quebec.* Toronto: McClelland and Stewart.

– 1979. *My Quebec.* Trans. Gaynor Fitzpatrick. Toronto: Methuen.

Levitt, Kari. 1970. *Silent Surrender.* Toronto: Macmillan.

Levy-Yeyati, Eduardo and Federico Sturzenegger. 2002. "A *De Facto* Classification of Exchange Rate Regimes: A Methodological Note." Mimeo. Buenos Aires: Universidad Torcuato Di Tella.

Lipsey, R. 1985. "Which Way for Canada at the Crossroads?" Rapporteur's Comments prepared for the proceedings of the Ontario Economic Council Conference "Canadian Trade at a Crossroads," 14 August.

Lisée, Jean-François. 1994. *The Trickster: Robert Bourassa and Quebecers 1990–1992.* Abr. and trans. R. Chodos, S. Horn, and W. Tayor. Toronto: James Lorimer and Co.

Livingston, James. 1986. *Origins of the Federal Reserve System.* Ithaca: Cornell University Press.

Longley, Ronald Stewart. 1943. *Sir Francis Hincks.* Toronto: University of Toronto Press.

Lucas, R.F. and B. Reid. 1991. "The Choice of Efficient Monetary Arrangements in the Post Meech Lake Era." *Canadian Public Policy* 17 (4): 417–33.

Lyon, Peyton. 1968. *Canada in World Affairs 1961–63.* Toronto: Oxford University Press.

Mack, Connie. 2000. "Dollarization and Cooperation to Achieve Sound Money." Presentation at conference "Dollarization: A Common Currency for the Americas?" 6 March, Federal Reserve Bank of Dallas. Available at <http://www.dallasfed.org/htm/dallas/events/mack.html>.

Mackintosh, W.A. 1951. "A Note on the Canadian Dollar." *International Journal* 6 (3): 50–3.

Mackintosh, W.A. 1964. Reprint. *The Economic Background of Dominion-Provincial Relations.* Toronto: McClelland and Stewart. Originally published as appendix 3 of the *Royal Commission Report on Dominion-Provincial Relations.* Ottawa: Government of Canada, 1940.

Malach, V. 1955. "The International Business Cycle and Canada, 1927–1939." *Canadian Journal of Economics and Political Science* 21: 88–100.

Mancera, M. 1991. "Characteristics and Implications of Different Types of Currency Areas." In *Policy Implications of Trade and Currency Zones*, ed. Federal Reserve Bank of Kansas City. Kansas City: Federal Reserve Bank of Kansas City.

Marceau, Richard. 1999. "A Quebec Perspective on a North American Currency." *Canadian Parlimentary Review* 22 (2): 2–4.

Maslove, Allan and Gene Swimmer. 1980. *Wage Controls in Canada: 1975–78.* Montreal: The Institute for Research on Public Policy.

Masters, D.C. 1952. "The Establishment of the Decimal Currency in Canada." *Canadian Historical Review* 33 (2): 129–47.

McCalla, D. 1969. "The Commercial Politics of the Toronto Board of Trade, 1850–1860." *Canadian Historical Review* 50 (1): 51–67.

McCallum, John. 1999. "Seven Issues in the Choice of Exchange Rate Regime for Canada." *Current Analysis* (Royal Bank of Canada). February.

– 2000. "Engaging the Debate: Costs and Benefits of a North American Common Currency." In *Money, Markets and Mobility*, ed. T. Courchene. Montreal: McGill-Queen's University Press.

McLachlan, R.W. 1892. "Annals of the Nova Scotian Currency." *Proceedings and Transactions of the Royal Society of Canada* 10 (2): 33–68.

McLeod, A.N. 1965. "A Critique of the Fluctuating-Exchange-Rate Policy in Canada." *The Bulletin* (C.J. Devine Institute of Finance, Graduate School of Business Administration, New York University) 34–5 (April-June).

McNamara, Kathleen. 1998. *The Currency of Ideas.* Ithaca: Cornell University Press.

McQuaig, Linda. 1995. *Shooting the Hippo: Death by Deficit and Other Canadian Myths.* Toronto: Viking.

McRoberts, Kenneth. 1988. *Quebec: Social Change and Political Crisis.* 3d ed. Toronto: McClelland and Stewart.

McTeer, Bob. 2000. "Concluding Comments at the Dallas Fed's Dollarization Conference." Presentation at conference "Dollarization: A Common Currency for the Americas?" 6–7 March, Federal Reserve Bank of Dallas.

Mercator. 1867. *A Letter to the President of the Montreal Board of Trade on the Silver Question.* Montreal: John Lovell.

Mikesell, Raymond. 1994. *The Bretton Woods Debates: A Memoir.* Essays in International Finance No.142. Princeton: International Finance Section, Department of Economics.

Mintz, Jack and Shay Aba. 2002. *Preserving Control.* Toronto: C.D. Howe Institute.

Molano, Walter. 2000. "Addressing the Symptoms and Ignoring the Causes: A View from Wall Street on Dollarization." Presentation at conference "Dollarization: A Common Currency for the Americas?" 6–7 March, Federal Reserve Bank of Dallas.

Morris, Irwin. 2000. *Congress, the President and the Federal Reserve*. Ann Arbor: University of Michigan Press.

Muirhead, Bruce. 1999. *Against the Odds: The Public Life and Times of Louis Rasminsky*. Toronto: University of Toronto Press.

Muise, D. 1968. "The Federal Election of 1867 in Nova Scotia: An Economic Interpretation." *Collections of the Nova Scotia Historical Society* 36: 327–51.

Mundell, Robert. 1961a. "Flexible Exchange Rates and Employment Policy." *Canadian Journal of Economics and Political Science* 27 (4): 509–17.

– 1961b. "A Theory of Optimum Currency Areas." *American Economic Review* 51: 657–64.

– 1962. "On the Appropriate Use of Monetary and Fiscal Policy for Internal and External Balance." *IMF Staff Papers* 9: 70–9.

– 1963. "Capital Mobility and Stabilization Policy under Fixed and Flexible Exchange Rates." *Canadian Journal of Economics and Political Science* 29 (4): 475–85.

– 1964. "Problems of Monetary and Exchange Rate Management in Canada." *National Bank Review* 2 (September): 77–86.

– 1971. "Discussion." In *Canadian-United States Financial Relationships*, ed. Federal Reserve Bank of Boston. Boston: Federal Reserve Bank of Boston.

– 2000. "Fixed against Flexible Exchange Rates: Interview with Robert Mundell." *World Economic Affairs* 3 (2): 57–61.

Murray, John. 2003. "Why Canada Needs a Flexible Exchange Rate." In *The Dollarization Debate,* ed. D. Salvatore, J. Dean, and T. Willett. Oxford: Oxford University Press.

Murray, John and James Powell. 2002. "Is Canada Dollarized?" *Bank of Canada Review* (Autumn): 3–11.

Nash, Knowlton. 1990. *Kennedy and Diefenbaker*. Toronto: McClelland and Stewart.

Naylor, R.T. 1975. *The History of Canadian Business 1867–1914*. Vol. 1, *The Banks and Financial Capital*. Toronto: James Lorimer and Co.

Neill, R. 1968. "Social Credit and National Policy in Canada." *Journal of Canadian Studies* 3 (1): 3–12.

– 1991. *A History of Canadian Economic Thought*. London: Routledge.

Neufeld, E. 1955. *Bank of Canada Operations, 1935–54*. Toronto: University of Toronto press.

NFO CFgroup. 2002. *Currency Options for Canada: What Canadians and Americans Think*. Toronto: NFO CFgroup.

Notermans, Tom. 2001. "Introduction." In *Social Democracy and Monetary Union*, ed. Tom Notermans. New York: Berghahn.

Nystrom, Lorne. 1999. "Common Currency." Available at <http://lornenystrom.ca/pfdollarization.htm>.

– 2002. "Dollarization." Available at <http://lornenystrom.ca/pfdollarization.htm>.

Odell, John. 1982. *U.S. International Monetary Policy*. Princeton: Princeton University Press.

O'Hanly, John. 1882. *On Money and Other Trade Questions, Being a Review of Mr. Wallace's Speech on an Inconvertible Currency*. Ottawa: C.W. Mitchell.

Owram, Doug. 1985. "Economic Thought in the 1930s: The Prelude to Keynesianism." *Canadian Historical Review* 66 (3): 344–77.

Palmer, Brian. 1979. *A Culture in Conflict: Skilled Workers in Industrial Capitalism in Hamilton, Ontario, 1860–1914*. Montreal: McGill-Queen's University Press.

Parizeau, Jacques. 1999. "Globalization and the National Interests: The Adventure of Liberalization." In *Out of Control: Canada in an Unstable Financial World*, ed. B. MacLean. Ottawa: Canadian Centre for Policy Alternatives.

Parti Québécois. 1972. *Quand nous serons vraiment chez nous*. Montreal: Parti Québécois.

– 1994. *Quebec in a New World*. Trans. Robert Chodos. Toronto: James Lorimer and Co. French ed. 1993.

Pastor, Manuel. 2001. *Towards a North American Community*. Washington: Institute for International Economics.

Pauly, Louis. 2006. "Leaders, Followers and Buffers in the International Monetary Arena: A Comparative Study of Exchange Rate Policymaking in Austria and Canada." In *International Monetary Power*, ed. David Andrews. Ithaca: Cornell University Press.

Pekkarinen, Jukka. 2001. "Finnish Social Democracy and EMU." In *Social Democracy and Monetary Union*, ed. Tom Notermans. New York: Berghahn.

Pentland, Charles. 1977. "Association after Sovereignty?" In *Must Canada Fail?*, ed. R. Simeon. Montreal: McGill-Queens University Press.

Piva, Michael. 1992. "Government Finance and the Development of the Canadian State." In *Colonial Leviathan: State Formation in Mid-19th-Century Canada*, ed. Allan Greer and Ian Radforth. Toronto: University of Toronto Press.

Plumptre, A. 1934. "Canadian Monetary Policy." In *The Canadian Economy and Its Problems*, ed. H. Innis and A. Plumptre. Toronto: Canadian Institute of International Affairs.

– 1940. *Central Banking in the British Dominions*. Toronto: University of Toronto Press.

- 1941. *Mobilizing Canada's Resources for War.* Toronto: MacMillan.
- 1948. *What Shall We Do with Our Dollar?* Toronto: Canadian Institute of International Affairs.
- 1972. "Canadian Views." In *Bretton Woods Revisited*, ed. A. Acheson, J. Chant, and M. Prachowny. Toronto: University of Toronto Press.
- 1977. *Three Decades of Decision: Canada and the World Monetary System, 1944–75.* Toronto: McClelland and Stewart.

Powell, James. 1999. *A History of the Canadian Dollar.* Ottawa: Bank of Canada.

Pringle, Robert and Matthew Turner. 1999. "The Relations between the European Central Bank and the National Central Banks within the Eurosystem." In *From EMS to EMU: 1979 to 1999 and Beyond*, ed D. Cobham and G. Zis. New York: St Martin's Press.

Purvis, D. 1990. "The Bank of Canada and the Pursuit of Price Stability." In *Zero Inflation*, ed. R. Lipsey. Toronto: C.D. Howe Institute.

Putnam, R. and N. Bayne. 1987. *Hanging Together: Cooperation and Conflict in the Seven-Power Summits.* London: Sage.

Rasminsky, Louis. 1941. "Foreign Exchange Control: Purposes and Methods." In *Canadian War Economics*, ed. J.F. Parkinson. Toronto: University of Toronto Press.

- 1944a. "International Credit and Currency Plans." *Foreign Affairs* 23 (July): 3–17.
- 1944b. "Plans for Post-War Currency Stabilization." *The Canadian Banker* 51: 31–47.

Reinhart, Carmen and Kenneth Rogoff. 2002. "The Modern History of Exchange Rate Arrangements: A Reinterpretation." NBER Working Paper 963. Washington: National Bureau of Economic Research.

Rhodes, Martin 2002. "Why EMU Is – or May Be – Good for European Welfare States." In *European States and the Euro*, ed. K. Dyson. Oxford: Oxford University Press.

Rich, G. 1988. *The Cross of Gold: Money and the Canadian Business Cycle 1867–1913.* Ottawa: Carleton University Press.

Risse, Thomas, Daniela Engelmann-Martin, Hans-Joachim Knopf, and Klaus Roscher. 1999. "To Euro or Not to Euro." *European Journal of International Relations* 5: 147–87.

Robertson, W.J. 1888. *A Brief Historical Sketch of Canadian Banking and Currency.* Toronto: William Briggs.

Robson, William. 1995. *Change For a Buck? The Canadian Dollar after Quebec Secession.* C.D. Howe Institute Commentary No. 68. Toronto: C.D. Howe Institute.

Robson, William and David Laidler, 2002. *No Small Change: The Awkward Economics and Politics of North American Monetary Integration.* Toronto: C.D. Howe Institute.

Rochon, Louis-Philippe and Mario Seccareccia. 2003. "Introduction." In *Dollarization,* ed. L.P. Rochon and M.Seccareccia. New York: Routledge.

Rose, Andrew and Jeffrey Frankel. 2002. "Estimating the Effect of Currency Unions on Trade and Output." *Quarterly Journal of Economics* 117 (2): 437–67.

Royal Commission on Banking and Currency. 1933a. *Report of the Royal Commission on Banking and Finance.* Ottawa: J.O. Patenaude.

– 1933b. *Proceedings of the Royal Commission on Banking and Finance.* Ottawa: J.O. Patenaude.

Royal Commission on Banking and Finance. 1964. *Report.* Ottawa: Government of Canada.

Royal Commission on Dominion-Provincial Relations. 1940. *Report of the Royal Commission on Dominion-Provincial Relations Book 1: Canada 1867–1935.* Ottawa: Government of Canada.

Royal Commission on the Economic Union and Development Prospects for Canada. 1985. *Report.* Vol. 2. Ottawa: Government of Canada.

Ruggie, John. 1983. "International Regimes, Transactions and Change." *International Organization* 36 (2): 379–405.

Sage, W. 1927. "The Annexation Movement in British Columbia." *Transactions of the Royal Society of Canada* 21 (2): 97–110.

Schembri, L. 2001. "Conference Summary: Revisiting the Case for Flexible Exchange Rates." *Bank of Canada Review* (Autumn): 31–7.

Schuldt, Jürgen. 2003. "Latin American Official Dollarization: Political Economy Aspects." In *The Dollarization Debate,* ed. D.Salvatore, J. Dean, and T. Willett. Oxford: Oxford University Press.

Schuler, Kurt. 2000. *Basics of Dollarization.* Washington: United States Senate, Joint Economic Committee.

Schuler, Kurt and Robert Stein. 2000. "The Mack Dollarization Plan: An Analysis." Presentation at conference "Dollarization: A Common Currency for the Americas?" 6 March, Federal Reserve Bank of Dallas.

Scott, H.D. 1934. "Control of Foreign Exchange Rates." In *The Canadian Economy and Its Problems,* ed. H. Innis and A. Plumptre. Toronto: Canadian Institute of International Affairs.

Seccareccia, Mario. 2002. *North American Monetary Integration: Should Canada Join the Dollarization Bandwagon?* Ottawa: Canadian Centre for Policy Alternatives.

– 2003. "Is Dollarization a Desirable Alternative to the Monetary Status Quo?" *Studies in Political Economy* 71/72: 91–108.

Shortt, Adam. 1964. "History of Canadian Metallic Currency." In *Money and Banking in Canada,* ed. E.P. Neufeld. Toronto: McClelland and Stewart.

– 1986. *History of Canadian Currency and Banking, 1600–1880.* Toronto: Canadian Bankers Association.

Shulman, Stephen. 2000. "Nationalist Sources of International Economic Integration." *International Studies Quarterly* 44: 365–90.

Smith, Denis. 1973. *Gentle Patriot: A Political Biography of Walter Gordon.* Edmonton: Hurtig Publishers.

– 1995. *Rogue Tory: The Life and Legend of John G. Diefenbaker.* Toronto: MacFarlane, Walker and Ross.

Sparks, Gordon. 1986. "The Theory and Practice of Monetary Policy in Canada: 1945–83." In *Fiscal and Monetary Policy,* ed. J. Sargent. Toronto: University of Toronto Press.

Spiegel, Mark. 1999. "Dollarization in Argentina." *Economic Letter* (Federal Reserve Bank of San Francisco) 99 (29): 1–3.

Stanford, Jim. 1999. *Paper Boom.* Ottawa: Canadian Centre for Policy Alternatives.

– 2003. "What Future for the Loonie?" *Studies in Political Economy* 71/72: 59–66.

Starr, Pamela. 2001. "Pesos for Dollars? The Political Economy of Dollarization in Latin America." *The Brazilian Journal of Political Economy* 21: 62–77.

Stokes, M. 1939. *The Bank of Canada.* Toronto: MacMillan.

Strange, Susan. 1976. *International Monetary Relations.* Oxford: Oxford University Press.

Stueck, Wendy. 2002. "Central Bank Urged to Speak on Dollar." *Globe and Mail.* 28 June.

Summers, Larry. 1993. "Rules, Real Exchange Rates and Monetary Discipline: World Bank Discussion Paper No. 207." In *Proceedings of a Conference on Currency Substitution and Currency Boards,* ed. Nissan Liviatan. Washington: World Bank.

– 1999. "Press Release: Deputy Treasury Secretary Lawrence H. Summers Senate Banking Committee Subcommittee on Economic Policy and Subcommittee on International Trade and Finance." 22 April. Available at <http://www.ustreas.gov/press/releases/pr3098.htm>.

Swift, Jamie. 1988. *Odd Man Out: The Life and Times of Eric Kierans.* Toronto: Douglas and McIntyre.

Thiessen, Gordon. 2000a. "Accountability and Transparency in Canada's Monetary Policy: Remarks by Gordon Thiessen to the Metropolitan Halifax

Chamber of Commerce." 27 January. Available at <http://www.bankofcanada.
ca/en/speeches/sp-1.htm>.

– 2000b. "The Conduct of Monetary Policy When You Live next Door to a
Large Neighbour." *World Economic Affairs* 3 (2): 19–23.

– 2000–01. "Can a Bank Change? The Evolution of Monetary Policy at the
Bank of Canada 1935–2000" *Bank of Canada Review* (Winter): 35–46.

Toronto Dominion Economics. 2001. *The Penny Drops.* 24 April. Toronto: TD
Economics.

– 2004. *Loonie Tunes – Understanding the Rally in the Canadian Dollar and
Its Consequences.* 10 February. Toronto: TD Bank Financial Group.

Trevelyan, C.E. 1851. Letter to H. Merivale. 30 February. In *The Elgin-Grey
Papers 1846–1852*, ed. S.A. Doughty. Ottawa: J.O. Patenaude, 1937.

Turk, Sidney. 1956. "The Canadian Foreign Exchange Control Board: Its Gen-
esis and Exodus." *The Canadian Banker* 63 (2): 95–111.

Turner, John. 1972. "Notes for an Address by Finance Minister John N. Turner
to the International Monetary Conference at Le Château Champlain, Montreal, May 9, 1972." Ottawa: Information Services, Department of Finance.

United States Chamber of Commerce. 1932. *Protection against Depreciated Currency Competition.* Washington: Chamber of Commerce of the United States.

United States Congress. 1993a. "The North American Free Trade Agreement."
Hearing before the Committee on Banking, Finance and Urban Affairs,
House of Representatives, 103rd Congress, 1st session. 8 September 1993.
Washington: United States Government Printing Office.

– 1993b. *NAFTA and Peso Devaluation: A Problem for US Exporters?* Washington: United States Government Printing House.

– 2001. "Review of the Final Report of the 21st Century Commission on Productive Agriculture." Hearing before the Committee on Agriculture, Nutrition and Forestry, US Senate, 107th Congress, 1st session. 30 January 2001.
Washington: United States Government Printing Office.

United States Senate. 1999a. Senate Committee on Banking, Housing and Urban
Affairs, Subcommittee on Economic Affairs and Subcommittee on Interna-
tional Trade and Finance. *Hearing on Official Dollarization in Emerging-
Market Countries.* 22 April.

– 1999b. Senate Committee on Banking, Housing and Urban Affairs, Subcommittee on Economic Affairs and Subcommittee on International Trade and
Finance. *Hearing on Official Dollarization in Emerging-Market Countries.*
15 July.

Vaiou, Dina. 1995. "Women of the South after, Like before, Maastricht." In
Europe at the Margins, ed. C. Hadjimichalis and D. Sadler. New York: John
Wiley and Sons.

Van Dormael, Arnand. 1978. *Bretton Woods: Birth of a Monetary System*. London: MacMillan.

Veiden, Pal. 2001. "The Austrian Social Democratic Party." In *Social Democracy and Monetary Union*, ed. T. Notermans. New York: Berghahn.

Velde, François and Marcelo Veracierto. 2000. "Dollarization in Argentina." *Economic Perspectives* (Federal Reserve Bank of Chicago) 1st quarter: 24–38.

Verdun, Amy and Thomas Christiansen. 2000. "Policies, Institutions and the Euro: Dilemmas of Legitimacy." In *After the Euro*, ed. Colin Crouch. Oxford: Oxford University Press.

Volcker, P. and T. Gyohten. 1992. *Changing Fortunes*. New York: Times Books.

von Hagen, Jurgen. 2000. "The Composition of Bank Councils for Monetary Unions." In *Regional Aspects of Monetary Policy in Europe*, ed. Jurgen von Hagen and Christopher Waller. Boston: Kluwer Academic Publishers.

Waite, P.B. 1972. *Confederation, 1854–1867*. Toronto: Holt, Rinehart and Winston of Canada.

Wang, Hongying. 2003. "China's Exchange Rate Policy in the Aftermath of the Asian Financial Crisis." In *Monetary Orders*, ed. J. Kirshner. Ithaca: Cornell University Press.

Watts, G. 1993. *The Bank of Canada: Origins and Early History*. Ottawa: Carleton University Press.

Weatherbe, Steve. 1997. "Thinking the Unthinkable: Gordon Wilson and Gibson Pondered the Separation of Quebec and BC." *British Columbia Report* 8 (51): 8.

Webb, M. 1992. "Canada and the International Monetary Regime." In *Canadian Foreign Policy and International Economic Regimes*, ed. A.C. Cutler. and M. Zacher. Vancouver: University of British Columbia Press.

Weir, William. 1903. *Sixty Years in Canada*. Montreal: John Lovell and Son.

Wheelock, David. 2000. "National Monetary Policy by Regional Design: The Evolving Role of the Federal Reserve Banks in Federal Reserve System Policy." In *Regional Aspects of Monetary Policy in Europe*, ed. Jurgen von Hagen and Christopher Waller. Boston: Kluwer Academic Publishers.

White, Andrew D. 1933. *Fiat Money Inflation in France*. New York: D. Appleton-Century.

White, William. 1994. *The Implications of the FTA and NAFTA for Canada and Mexico*. Technical Report No. 70. Bank of Canada.

Willett, Thomas. 2003. "Optimum Currency Area and Political Economy Approaches to Exchange Rate Regimes." Paper presented at the workshop "Britain and Canada and their Large Neighbouring Monetary Unions," University of Victoria, 17–18 October.

– 2004. "The Political Economy of Exchange Rate Regimes and Currency Crises." Background paper for the workshop "Political Economy of Exchange Rates," Claremont College, 1–2 April.

Williams, Glen. 1994. *Not for Export*. 3d ed. Oxford: Oxford University Press.

Williams, John. 1947. *Postwar Monetary Plans and Other Essays*. 3d ed. New York: Alfred Knopf.

Williamson, J. 1987. "Appendix: A FEER for the Canadian Dollar." In *The United States and Canada: The Quest for Free Trade*, ed. P. Wonnacott. Washington: Institute for International Economics.

Wolfe, David. 1984. "The Rise and Demise of the Keynesian Era in Canada, 1930–1982." In *Readings in Canadian Social History*, vol. 5, ed. M.Cross and G. Kealey Toronto: McClelland and Stewart.

Wonnacott, P. 1965. *The Canadian Dollar, 1948–62*. Toronto: University of Toronto Press.

– 1971. *The Floating Canadian Dollar*. Washington: American Enterprise Institute for Public Policy Research.

– 1987. *The United States and Canada: The Quest for Free Trade*. Washington: Institute for International Economics.

Woolley, John. 1984. *Monetary Politics: The Federal Reserve and the Politics of Monetary Policy*. Cambridge: Cambridge University Press.

Wright, Gerald. 1974. "Pervasive Influence: The Case of the Interest Equalization Tax." In *Continental Community?*, ed. W. Axline, J. Hyndman, P. Lyon, and M. Molot. Toronto: McClelland and Stewart.

Wright, G. and M. Molot. 1974. "Capital Movements and Government Control." *International Organization* 28 (4): 671–88.

Wright, M. 1885. *The "Torpedo," or Ten Minutes on the National Currency Question, "Beaverbacks."* St Catherines: E.J. Leavenworth.

Yeagar, Leland. 1966. *International Monetary Relations*. New York: Harper and Row.

Young, Brigitte. 2000. "Disciplinary Neoliberalism in the European Union and Gender Politics." *New Political Economy* 5 (1): 77–98.

Index

Abbott, Douglas, 84, 87
Addis, Charles, 63
adjustment, exchange rate as
    tool for balance of pay-
    ments, 7, 244–6; in 1930s,
    57–60, 68; in 1940s and
    50s, 70, 80, 85, 92, 101–
    2, 104; in 1962–85 pe-
    riod, 106, 111–12, 123–
    33; in FTA/NAFTA debates,
    142–4, 147, 150, 153,
    157; in NAMU debate, 9,
    161, 168–9, 179, 183,
    192–4, 222, 244–6
Alberta, 63, 147
Amery, Leo, 50, 61, 264n92
Argentina, 187–8, 192, 195,
    198, 214
Attwood, T., 33, 258n64
autonomy, monetary policy,
    6–8, 240, 244–7; in
    1870s, 37; in interwar, 40,
    51, 55–7; in 1940s and
    1950s, 67–70, 74, 79–80,
    85, 89, 103; in 1962–85
    period, 106, 115–22, 127,
    129–33; in FTA/NAFTA de-
    bate, 143–4, 157; in
    NAMU debate, 10, 167–8,
    183

Baker, James, 140–1
balance of payments. *See* ad-
    justment
Baldridge, Malcolm, 140
Bank of Canada: bilingual
    notes of, 225–6; creation
    of, 60–3; decision-making
    within, 12, 202, 208,
    226–30, 294n69, 300n66,
    300n68, 301n79. For
    bank's monetary policy,
    see autonomy
banks. *See* financial institu-
    tions; United States, banks
Baucus, Max, 139, 152–3
Beddoes, Zanny, 250
Beine, Michael, 224, 231
Bélanger-Campeau Commis-
    sion, 217, 297n19
Bennett, Richard, 51–2, 54–
    5, 61–2, 225, 260n12
Benson, Edgar, 124
Bergsten, Fred, 192–4
Bernhard, William, 243
Bernstein, Edward, 83–4,
    88, 101
Blacklock, Cathy, 289n84
Blyth, Mark, 248
Bolton, George, 85
Bouchard, Lucien, 214, 218

Bouey, Gerald, 145
Bourassa, Robert, 215–17,
    220, 225, 229
Bowles, Paul, 173, 247
Bretton Woods, 64–5, 69,
    72–84, 91–7, 102, 104,
    111, 118, 246, 248,
    267n19
Britain: in nineteenth cen-
    tury, 20, 22–3; in interwar
    years, 43–4, 49; in 1940s
    and 50s, 70, 72, 78, 82,
    98, 101; in EMU debate,
    175, 177, 185
British Columbia, 25, 31,
    50, 147, 302n88
Brock, William, 281n10
Brodie, Janine, 296n1
Brownlee, John, 63
Bryce, Robert, 52, 62, 76,
    80, 93, 103, 178–9
Buchanan, Isaac, 32–8, 40,
    67, 181, 245, 258n64
Buiter, William, 206
Bundesbank. *See* Germany
Burns, Arthur, 118–19
business. *See* private eco-
    nomic actors

Campbell, Robert, 127